Indian Economy and Society

in the Era of Globalisation and Liberalisation

ESSAYS IN HONOUR OF PROF. AM KHUSRO

Indian Economy and Society

in the Era of Globalisation and Liberalisation

ESSAYS IN HONOUR OF PROF. A M KHUSRO

Editors : C H Hanumantha Rao
B B Bhattacharya
N S Siddharthan

Academic Foundation
NEW DELHI

First published in 2005 by

Academic Foundation
4772-73 / 23 Bharat Ram Road, (23 Ansari Road), Darya Ganj, New Delhi - 110 002 (India).
Phones : 23245001 / 02 / 03 / 04. Fax : +91-11-23245005. E-mail : academic@vsnl.com
www : academicfoundation.com

Indian Economy and Society in the Era of Globalisation and Liberalisation
Editors : C.H. Hanumantha Rao, B.B. Bhattacharya, N.S. Siddharthan
ISBN 81-7188-420-2

Designed and typeset by Italics India, New Delhi.
Printed and bound in India.

Contents

Section I

Agriculture, Land Reform and Anti-poverty Programmes

...CONTD. ...

Section II

Environment

Section III

Globalisation, Liberalisation and Trade

...CONTD. ...

Section V
Population

...CONTD. ...

Section VI
Secularism and Religion

List of Figures and Tables

FIGURES

...CONTD. ...

TABLES

...CONTD. ...

Appendix Tables

Preface

Professor A.M. Khusro was a professor at the Institute of Economic Growth (IEG) right from its inception, and his association with the IEG continued till the end. During his long association with the IEG, spanning about four and a half decades, he enriched IEG's academic and campus life in several capacities – as Professor, Director, Member of the Board of Governors and Chairman of the Board of Governors. In all these he made distinct contributions – guided a record number of students for Ph.D., inducted into the IEG new and young talent and, equally significant, made campus life enjoyable. As a token of gratitude, the members of the IEG family decided to pay an affectionate tribute to the departed colleague and teacher by bringing out a volume containing research papers pertaining to several themes that were cherished and valued by him.

All the contributors to this volume have been members of IEG's faculty/alumnus and have made important contributions in the respective field during their affiliation to the IEG. The themes covered in this volume include topics on which Professor Khusro had worked and also emerging research areas where he wished to see the involvement of IEG's faculty. He was very particular that IEG, in addition to undertaking studies in traditional research themes, should venture into new and inter-disciplinary fields that are likely to gain prominence. The themes included in this volume cover both – established as well as new areas of research.

We considered it appropriate to begin the volume with the theme *Agriculture, Land Reforms and Anti-Poverty Programmes*, as Professor Khusro began his career at IEG investigating these problems. He retained his interest in these areas, in particular, on issues relating to poverty. The next theme on *Environment* is closely related to the broad theme, e.g., Agriculture and Poverty and, in some respect, takes off from this theme. The papers included under this relate to newly emerging interdisciplinary research focusing on ecology, economics and environment, gender and community forestry, and the cleaning of our rivers. Environment is one of the two themes in which Professor Khusro wanted the IEG to expand its research activities. The other theme is *Globalisation, Liberalisation and Trade*. Professor Khusro actively worked for the creation of a Centre at the IEG to work on this latter theme. The papers included in this section deal with the impact of liberalisation and the World Trade Organisation regime on the quantity and quality of foreign direct investments, exports, productivity, and growth of firms.

The next three themes viz., *Macro Models and Growth, Population* and *Secularism and Religion* are areas where IEG has a tradition of undertaking several important research studies with distinction since its very inception. However, over the years the focus on these themes has changed and papers included in this volume reflect that change. Thus issues relating to macroeconomic imbalances, female education and fertility, reproductive and child health care and fertility are new that have emerged in recent years. Studies on secularism and religion were always close to Professor Khusro's heart and he published and delivered lectures on these issues till the very last. This volume aptly concludes with two important contributions in this area.

We do hope that the essays in this volume would stimulate interest in research which Professor Khusro would have liked to encourage and strengthen.

Most of the papers included in this volume have appeared in reputed journals and we wish to acknowledge with thanks the journals/copyright holders for kindly permitting us to reproduce them either in their original form or in an abridged form.

Institute of Economic Growth
University of Delhi
October 20, 2004.

C.H. Hanumantha Rao
B.B. Bhattacharya
N.S. Siddharthan

Contributors to the Volume

C.H. Hanumantha Rao

B.B. Bhattacharya

N.S. Siddharthan

Ashok Gulati

S.N. Mishra

S.K. Ray

Kanchan Chopra

Bina Agarwal

Anil Markandya

M.N. Murty

Nagesh Kumar

Ramesh Chand

Aradhna Aggarwal

Bishwanath Goldar

Anita Kumari

K. Lal

K. Subbarao

K. Krishnamurty

Sabyasachi Kar

Ashish Bose

P.N. Mari Bhat

S.C. Gulati

P.C Joshi

T.N. Madan

Brief profile of the contributors follows....

C.H. Hanumantha Rao is, at present, Honorary Professor and Chairman, Institute of Economic Growth, University of Delhi, and Centre for Economic and Social Studies, Hyderabad; and member of the National Advisory Council. Prof. Rao did his Ph.D. from the University of Delhi in 1962 and was a Post-Doctoral Fellow, at the Department of Economics, University of Chicago, during 1966-67. He worked at the Institute of Economic Growth, University of Delhi (1961-92). He published over 100 research papers in professional journals, and several books including *Technological Change and Distribution of Gains in Indian Agriculture* (1975) and *Agricultural Growth, Rural Poverty and Environmental Degradation in India* (1994). Prof. Rao was awarded Rafi Ahmed Kidwai Memorial Prize for 1974-75, by the Indian Council of Agricultural Research, for Outstanding Contribution in the field of Agricultural Economics; received H.K. Batheja Award for the Best Book published in Economics in India during 1993-94; and received the Financial Express Award in 1995 for Lifetime Work in Economics. Prof. Rao was a member, Seventh and Eighth Finance Commission; member, Planning Commission, 1982-86; and member, Economic Advisory Council to the Prime Minister, 1982-84. He also served on several other expert committees appointed by the Government of India, including as Chairman, National Commission on Rural Labour, 1990-91; Chairman, Technical Committee on DPAP & DDP, 1993-94; Chairman High Powered Fertilisers Pricing Policy Review Committee, 1997-98; and Member, Board of Directors, Reserve Bank of India, 1994-2000. He also served as member, Technical Advisory Committee (TAC) of the Consultative Group on International Agricultural Research (CGIAR), 1997-98. He was President, the Indian Society of Agricultural Economics, 1989; The Indian Society of Labour Economics, 1995; and the Indian Society of Ecological Economics, 2000-2001. He was awarded 'Padma Bhushan' by the President of India in 2004.

B.B. Bhattacharya is currently Director of the Institute of Economic Growth (IEG), Delhi, a premier social science research and training institute in India. Ph.D. in Economics (1971) from Delhi School of Economics, University of Delhi and Ford Foundation Post-Doctoral Scholar of University of California, Berkeley (1980-81), Prof. Bhattacharya specialises in econometric modelling and forecasting, macroeconomics, monetary economics, development economics, public finance and international finance. A leading expert in econometric modelling and forecasting, his forecasts and analysis are frequently quoted by both print and electronic media and are used by the Central and the State Governments and national and international agencies, such as the Reserve Bank of India and the World Bank. He has published seven books and more than 50 technical papers in national and international journals. Prof. Bhattacharya has, over the years, held several distinguished positions in many learned societies and institutions. He was President of the Indian Econometric Society (2003-04); served as member of many important committees and commissions of the Government of India, Planning Commission and the Reserve Bank of India; was the Chairman of the Government of India (Ministry of Agriculture) Committee to review Capital Formation in Agriculture and member of the National Statistical Commission, Planning Commission Working Group for Estimation of Resources for the Tenth Five Year Plan and Steel Ministry Core Task Group for Steel Policy 2020. Currently, he is the President of the Indian Association of Research in National Income and Wealth and member of the Editorial Board of the *Indian Economic Journal, Indian Journal of Economics* and the *Journal of Income and Wealth*. He is Chairman of the Government of India Expert Committee on the International Comparison Programme, and member of the Central Statistical Organisation Advisory Committee for National Accounts and Ministry of Employment Working Group on Employment Monitoring.

N.S. Siddharthan, Ph.D., is Head, V.K.R.V. Rao Centre for Studies in Globalisation, Institute of Economic Growth, Delhi. He works in the areas of technology, multinationals, and globalisation. His research studies have appeared in journals such as, *The Economic Journal, Oxford Bulletin of Economics and Statistics, The Journal of Development Studies, Economics of Innovation and New Technology, Applied Economics, Development and Change, Journal of Economic Behavior and Organization, Journal of Business Venturing, Japan and the World Economy, International Business Review, Developing Economies, Weltwirtschaftliches Archiv, Transnational Corporations, The Indian Economic Review,* and *Economic and Political Weekly.* He also has to his credit a number of books published by reputed publishing houses in India and abroad. Dr. Siddharthan has ongoing and past collaborations in research with several Institutions that include Hitotsubashi University, Tokyo; Institute of Developing Economies, Tokyo; Erasmus University, Rotterdam; United Nations University INTECH, Maastricht, The Netherlands; University of Toronto, Canada; Georgetown University, Washington DC, USA; University of Oxford, UK; and University of Antwerp, Belgium.

Ashok Gulati, earlier Head of the NABARD Chair Unit at the Institute of Economic Growth, is presently the Director of International Food Policy Research Institute (IFPRI) in Washington, D.C., U.S.A. Prof. Gulati's research has been on agriculture and rural development, and he has published several books and a large number of papers in professional journals. He has served a number of international organisations and has worked as a member for several committees of the Government of India.

S.N. Mishra graduated in science from Benaras Hindu University, did his M.A. in economics from Gorakhpur University, and Ph.D. from Delhi University in 1966. In early 1970s he did his post-doctoral work at the Centre for Development Planning, Erasmus University, Rotterdam. Much of his professional career was spent at the Institute of Economic Growth, where he was appointed Professor of Economics in 1976, and later served as Director (1990-95). In the late 1980s and 1990s he had teaching professorship at the University of Tokyo and Hosei University respectively. Apart from scores of research papers Dr. Mishra has ten books to his credit, of which one is edited for the ICSSR. Currently as Chairman of the Society for Economic and Social Research (SESR), he is actively working in the field of environment and livestock.

S.K. Ray was former NABARD Chair Professor and Head, Agricultural Economics Research Unit at Institute of Economic Growth, Delhi. His area of research has been agriculture and rural development. He has published several books and a large number of papers in professional journals. Prof. Ray has served a number of international organisations and has worked as a member for several committees of the Government of India, the Reserve Bank of India and the NABARD.

Kanchan Chopra is Professor at the Institute of Economic Growth, Delhi and heads the Environmental and Resource Unit. In the last two decades, she has published extensively on issues at the interface of environment and development, in particular water and forest resource management and common property resources. She is Associate Editor, *Environment and Development Economics*, and member, Editorial Advisory Board, *Ecological Economics*. Prof. Chopra is an Associate of the lately initiated Ecological and Environmental Economics Programme of the Beijer Institute of Ecological Economics hosted by the ICTP, Trieste. She was one of the Founder members of the Indian Society for Ecological Economics and its First President. Currently she is also Member, Assessment Panel of the Millennium Ecosystem Assessment, an assessment supported internationally by UNEP, World Bank and other international bodies 2001-2005 and Member, Advisory and Management Committee, South Asian Network on Development and Environmental Economics. She is President for the 64th Conference of the Indian Society of Agricultural Economics (December 2004).

Bina Agarwal is Professor of Economics at the Institute of Economic Growth, Delhi. She is also Vice-President of the International Economic Association and President of the International Association for Feminist Economics. She has held distinguished positions at Harvard, Columbia, Michigan and Minnesota. She has authored three books and edited five. Her book *A Field of One's Own: Gender and Land Rights in South Asia* (Cambridge University Press, 1994) won the A.K. Coomaraswamy Book Prize 1996; the Edgar Graham Book Prize 1996; and the K.H. Batheja Award 1995-96. She was the first Asian to win the first two awards. In

2002, she received the Malcolm Adhiseshiah award for distinguished contributions to Development Studies. She is currently working on some theoretical and empirical aspects of gender, environment and collective action.

Anil Markandya is an economist who has worked in the environmental field for over twenty five years. He obtained his doctorate from the London School of Economics in 1974 with a thesis on the Economics of Pollution. Since then he has taught at University College, London, at universities in Australia, France, Italy and United States. From 1992 to 1996 he was Research Associate at the Harvard Institute of International Development and a Faculty Associate from 1996-1998. In April 1996, he took up the Chair of Economics at Bath University in the UK. Professor Markandya has been an advisor to several governments on environmental, health and related issues, as well as to international bodies such as OECD, the World Bank, the European Commission and the regional development banks. On climate change he has been advising UNEP, as well as the Asian Development Bank and the European Commission. His consultancy work is carried out through Metroeconomica Ltd., a company, which he founded in 1983 and of which he is director. He is author of around two hundred books, monographs, articles and reports on environmental economics, including the landmark "Blueprint for a Green Economy" (1989) and contributions to the United Nations Agenda 21 proceedings on "Financing Sustainable Development".

M.N. Murty is currently Professor of Economics at Institute of Economic Growth, Delhi. He is author of seven books and has published a number of research papers in the reputed international and national journals in the areas of Environmental Economics and Public Economics. He has teaching experience at University of Birmingham, U.K., Jawharlal Nehru University, and Delhi University.

Nagesh Kumar is Director-General of Research and Information System for the Non-aligned and Other Developing Countries (RIS), New Delhi. Ph.D. in Economics from Delhi School of Economics, Dr. Kumar has previously served the United Nations University-Institute for New Technologies, Maastricht, the Netherlands, directing its research programme on Globalisation, FDI and technology transfers. He has also been a consultant to the World Bank, ADB, UNCTAD, UNIDO, UN-ESCAP, ILO, among others. Recipient of the Exim Bank's first Trade Research Award and a GDN Research Medal, Dr. Kumar has written extensively on developmental impact of FDI, regional economic integration in Asia, WTO and development, new technologies and development, among other themes and is a co-editor of *South Asia Economic Journal.*

Ramesh Chand is currently Professor and Head – Agricultural Economics Unit at Institute of Economic Growth, Delhi. He was Principal Economist at

National Centre for Agricultural Economics and Policy Research (Indian Council of Agricultural Research) from 1996 to 2002 and before that he has worked as Professor of Marketing at Punjab Agricultural University, Ludhiana. He was Visiting Professor at University of Wollongong, NSW Australia (2000) and Visiting Fellow at Institute of Developing Economies, Chiba Shi, Japan (2003). Ph.D. in Agricultural Economics from Indian Agricultural Research Institute, New Delhi, Prof. Ramesh Chand's thesis was selected for Jawaharlal Nehru Award of Indian Council of Agricultural Research in recognition of its outstanding Research contributions. He worked as consultant for FAO, ESCAP, World Bank, Indian Institute of Foreign Trade, Delhi and Government of Punjab. He is presently engaged in research on Trade Liberalisation, WTO and Asian Agriculture, Food Policy and Development Economics. He has authored five books and 55 research papers.

Aradhna Aggarwal is Reader in Economics at Kirori Mal College, University of Delhi. She has also been working as Senior Fellow, Consultant for the Indian Council for Research on International Economic Relations (ICRIER) since 2001. She earned her Ph.D. in Economics from Delhi School of Economics, University of Delhi. Her thesis was awarded the prestigious Professor Chhablani prize in recognition of its research contributions. She is also a recipient of the 'Global Development Network' (GDN) award for her research paper on technology. Her research interests include international trade, FDI, technology transfer, R&D, WTO-related issues and economic reforms. She has made presentations at several international conferences. Her work has appeared in *World Development, Journal of Development Studies, Research Policy, Transnational Corporation* and *Technology in Society*.

Bishwanath Goldar (M.A. and Ph.D. from Delhi School of Economics) is a Professor of Economics at the Institute of Economic Growth, Delhi. He specialises in industrial economics, international trade and environmental economics. He has written a book, several reports and a large number of papers, including some published in international professional journals, on productivity, employment and wages in Indian industries, protection of Indian industries, trade reforms, water pollution, contingent valuation, arsenic contamination of groundwater, and trade in health services.

Anita Kumari, Ph.D. in Economics from University of Delhi, has been a researcher at the Institute of Economic Growth (IEG), Delhi. She is currently a SRT fellow at the IEG. She has published several papers in academic journals and books.

K. Lal, earlier a Reader at the Institute of Economic Growth, is presently working as Researcher at the United Nations University, Institute for New Technologies (UNU/INTECH), Maastricht, The Netherlands. His area of specialisation is information technology and development. He has published several papers in Journals like World Development,

Research Policy, Information Economics and Policy, Information Society, and Science Technology and Development.

K. Subbarao, until 1988, was on the faculty of the Institute of Economic Growth. During 1981-83, he was a visiting fellow at the University of California at Berkeley. He joined the World Bank Group in December 1988. He recently retired from the Bank as its Lead Economist for the Africa Region, responsible for analytical work on poverty and social protection. Dr. Subbarao's extensive research work included equity and efficiency implications of government interventions in grain markets, income distributional implications of agricultural price policy interventions in India, and on anti-poverty programmes. At the Bank, Dr. Subbarao has played a major role in both analytical and policy work on poverty, particularly in the domain of safety nets and anti-poverty programmes in many countries of Asia and Africa.

K. Krishnamurty had a long tenure as Professor, and for some years as Director, at the Institute of Economic Growth. He is currently Honorary Professor at the Administrative Staff College of India, Hyderabad. Earlier, he has been on the research staff of the World Bank and the IMF. He was President of the Indian Econometric Society and also of the Andhra Pradesh Economic Association. Krishnamurty's research is largely focussed on India. His contributions lie in the areas of macro econometric modelling, consumption, savings, investment and external trade behaviour; and international trade in primary commodities. He has several research publications to his credit and has served on the editorial committees of Indian and international academic journals beside having supervised M.Phil. and Ph.D. dissertations. He has been associated with several committees of government and academic institutions.

Sabyasachi Kar is a faculty at the Institute of Economic Growth, Delhi. His interests are in macroeconomics and development economics with particular focus on the Indian economy. In the last few years, he has been working on the Indian macro-economy and presented forecasts and policy analysis of the economy on a regular basis. He also studies regional issues within the Indian economy and has a number of publications from his research. Dr. Kar teaches growth economics, regional economics and macro-modelling techniques at the institute. He is a consultant to the Global Development Network (GDN) and a member of the advisory committee to the ASSOCHAM.

Ashish Bose is Honorary Professor at the Institute of Economic Growth, Delhi. He is also Distinguished Professor at the Institute for Integrated Learning in Management (IILM), New Delhi. Currently, he is Chairman of the Expert Committee on "Census Data on Religion", appointed by the National Commission on Minorities. He is also a member of the Independent Commission on Development and Health in India. He was formerly Jawaharlal Nehru National Fellow.

P.N. Mari Bhat is a Professor at the Population Research Centre, Institute of Economic Growth Delhi. Earlier, he was Director, Population Research Centre, Dharwad and Associate Fellow at the Centre for Development Studies, Thiruvananathapuram. Educated in the Universities at Mysore, Andhra and Pennsylvania, he is an internationally known expert in Indian demography. He has served as consultant to several UN Organisations and been visiting faculty at Harvard, Minnesota and Manitoba. He has authored over fifty articles in reputed national and international journals and co-authored a book on Indian Vital Rates published by the National Academy of Sciences, USA.

S.C. Gulati is Professor at the Population Research Centre, Institute of Economic Growth, Delhi. He specialises in econometrics and population-development-environment studies. He has authored and co-authored several books including 'Fertility in India: An Econometric Analysis of a Metropolis'; 'Women's Status and Reproductive Health Rights'; 'Contraceptive Use in India'; 'Migration, Common Property Resources and Environmental Degradation'; and 'Reproductive Health in Delhi Slums'. He has published several articles in national and international journals on population, development and environmental issues.

P.C Joshi is a leading social scientist widely known for his contributions to studies on development and social change in India from a radical perspective. He was Professor and Director, Institute of Economic Growth; and also President of the Society for Labour Economics; President of the Indian Sociological Society; Chairman, Software Committee for Doordarshan; Member, National Commission for Rural Labour and Jawaharlal Nehru National Fellow. He is the author of numerous works in English and Hindi, including *Land Reforms in India* (1975); *Culture, Communication and Social Change* (1989); *Secularism and Development: The Indian Experiment* (1995); *Mahatma Gandhi: The New Economic Agenda* (1996); *Social Science and Development: Quest for Relevance* (1996); *Communication and National Development* (2002); Prominent among his work in Hindi are: *Bhartiya Gram* (1966); *Parivartan Aur Vikas Ke Sanskritic Ayam* (1995); *Swapna Aur Yathartha* (2000).

T.N. Madan, Ph.D. in Social Anthropology from Australian National University, is presently Honorary Treasurer, Institute of Economic Growth, Delhi and Chairman, Centre for Study of Developing Societies, Delhi. Dr. Madan has been a visiting Professor at several foreign universities. He has contributed significantly as an author as well as in senior editorial capacities to various reputed national and international journals. Recipient of innumerable awards and honours for his academic contributions, Dr. Madan has also authored, co-authored and edited a large number of books and he continues to write actively as an expert on various socio anthropological issues. His forthcoming books include *Marriage, Family and the Household : Select Essays* (OUP), and *Religion in the Modern World and Other Essays.*

Acknowledgements

Most of the papers included in this volume have appeared in reputed journals and books and we wish to acknowledge the following journals/ books that hold the copyrights, for kindly permitting us to reproduce them either in their original form or in an abridged/updated form.

Journals

American Journal of Agricultural Economics

K. Subbarao, "Public Works as an Anti-Poverty Programme: An Overview of Cross Country Experience", *American Journal of Agricultural Economics*, May 1997.

Cambridge University Press

A. Markandya and M.N. Murty, "Cost-Benefit Analysis of Cleaning Ganges: Some Emerging Environment and Development Issues", *Environmental and Development Economics*, February 2004, Volume 9.

Developing Economies

Bishwanath Goldar and Anita Kumari, "Import Liberalisation and Productivity Growth in Indian Manufacturing Industries in the 1990s", *Developing Economies*, December 2003.

Economic and Political Weekly

N.S. Siddharthan, "Professor A.M. Khusro: A Tribute", *Economic and Political Weekly*, September 13, 2003.

C.H. Hanumantha Rao and Ashok Gulati, "Indian Agriculture: Emerging Prespectives and Major Policy Issues", *Economic and Political Weekly*, December 31, 1994. (The paper published in this volume is an abridged and updated version).

Nagesh Kumar, "Host Country Policies, WTO Regime and the Global Patterns of FDI Inflows: Recent Quantitative Studies and India's Strategic Response", *Economic and Political Weekly*, January 6, 2001.

N.S. Siddharthan, K. Lal, "Liberalisation and Growth of Firms in India", *Economic and Political Weekly*, May 17, 2003.

K. Krishnamurty, "Five Decades of Macroeconometric Modelling Research for India: A Synoptic Veiw", *Economic and Political Weekly*, October 19, 2002.

T.N. Madan, "Freedom of Religion", *Economic and Political Weekly*, March 15, 2003.

Indian Journal of Agricultural Economics

S.K. Ray, "Land System and its Reforms in India", *Indian Journal of Agricultural Economics*, Vol. 51, Nos. 1 and 2 January – June 1996. (The paper published in this volume is a revised and condensed version).

Journal of Development Studies

www.tandf.co.uk/journals

Aradhna Aggarwal, "Liberalisation, Multinational Enterprises and Export Performance: Evidence from Indian Manufacturing", *Journal of Development Studies*, February 2002.

World Development (Elsevier)

P.N. Mari Bhat, "Reciprocity between Female Education and Fertility in India", *World Development* (Elsevier), 2002, Vol. 30(10).

Books

Allied Publishers Private Limited

B.B. Bhattacharya and Sabyasachi Kar, "Growth and Macroeconomic Imbalances in India", published as a chapter in a book, published by Allied Publishers Private Limited, 2004.

United Nations University World Institute for Development Economic Research (UNU-WIDER)

Bina Agarwal, "Hidden Dimensions of Community Forestry in South Asia: A Gender Analysis", published as a chapter in a book published by UNU/WIDER and Clarendon Press, Oxford, 2002.

Vikas Publishing House Pvt Ltd.

P.C. Joshi, "Whither Indian Secularism? Some Reflections", an earlier version of the paper was published by Vikas Publishing House Pvt. Ltd., 1995.

PROF. A.M. KHUSRO
(1925 -2003)

Professor A.M. Khusro: A Tribute

N.S. SIDDHARTHAN

Introduction

Professor A.M. Khusro passed away in New Delhi on August 24, 2003. He was 78. His was a multi-faceted personality: an outstanding teacher, he was extremely popular with students; an exceptionally good research guide, he produced a record number of Ph.D. scholars in economics from Delhi University; a well-liked Vice-Chancellor, a successful diplomat, Member, Planning Commission, Chairman, Finance Commission and head of charitable institutions. Above all, he was a good human being who respected human dignity and showed exemplary courtesy to all irrespective of their status in society and hierarchy in institutions. I have known him since 1967, first as his student, later as a co-author and a colleague. In all these years never have I heard him raise his voice even under provocation or resort to harsh language and slander. These noble qualities made him a role model for his students and associates.

Above and beyond teaching and research, Professor Khusro advised the Government of India on economic policy in his various capacities: as Professor; Director, and Chairman, Institute of Economic Growth (IEG); Member, Planning Commission; Member, Economic Advisory Council of the Prime Minister; Chairman, Agricultural Credit Review of the RBI; Director, RBI; Editor, Financial Express; and Chairman, Finance Commission. His advice to government was based on sound economic theory and research findings. He was of the firm view that "theoretical underpinnings are important. Not everything that is theoretically sound can be put into practice but nothing should ever be put into practice if it is not theoretically sound, as it is doomed to failure from the beginning. Much of what is seen as failure and non-implementation of laws, plans and policies is actually the result not of *malafide* omissions of the politicians and administrators but of the fact that the original proposition was not theoretically valid and feasible in the first place" (Khusro 1994, Preface, pp iii-iv).

Contributions to Monetary Economics

Professor Khusro began his research career in monetary economics. His Ph.D. thesis at the University of Leeds in the early 1950s was *"An Investigation of Liquidity Preference"*, where he tested some of the basic propositions of macroeconomics. He carried out tests for the UK for two periods: 1919-1948 and 1885-1919, and for the USA for the period 1921-1948. The study for the UK was published in *Yorkshire Bulletin of Economics and Social Research* in 1952. This study has been quoted extensively by Nobel Laureates like Paul Samuelson, Milton Friedman, James Tobin and Franco Modigliani. Later he conducted a similar investigation for India for the period 1937-52 and published it in *Indian Economic Review*. In these studies he mainly analysed the factors that explain the level of the rate of interest in a given economy. In particular two factors were investigated, first, the role of the public's demand to hold money and, second, the nature and role of the elasticity of the liquidity preference schedule. His results did not fully support the Keynesian relationships. The stock of idle money did not determine the interest rates while other variables like the volume of monetary assets and the marginal rates of tax explained interest rates better. His study revealed that interest rate, net of taxes, was explained fairly well by the ratio of idle money to liquid assets.

The study, *"An Econometric Model of Banking in India"* (Khusro and Siddharthan 1972), sought to answer two questions, namely, first, how best should commercial banking service improve both on the side of providing credit (mainly advances) and on the side of mobilising and managing deposits, and, second, how should commercial banks – apart from being controlled by the Reserve Bank – control themselves in money creation? In seeking an answer to these questions, the model analysed the determinants of the various assets and liabilities in the balance sheets of Indian Scheduled Banks. On the liability side the model analysed the determinants of the demand for and the supply of deposits, and, on the side of assets, the determinants of the demand for and the supply of bank loans and advances, investment in government securities and bank reserves. However, it was argued that the assets and liabilities of banks are not mutually independent and tend to influence each other. Hence, it would be a very limited and partial view, if the analysis were confined to the determinants of a single item in the balance sheet. Thus the study argued in favour of portfolio determination as a whole, and showed that banks tended to optimise their whole portfolio and not the return on one asset in that portfolio.

Contributions to Agricultural Economics

Another major area of Professor Khusro's contribution has been agricultural economics and food security. In this field, he has published more than five books. In addition his paper (1967), "The pricing of foodgrains in India" published in *Quarterly Journal of Economics*, has been acknowledged as a major contribution to literature. His interest in agricultural economics dated back to his pre-Delhi University days. During his short stay as a lecturer in Hyderabad in the early and the mid-1950s he undertook a study that was published by Osmania University Press (1958), titled *"Economic and Social Effects of Jagirdari Abolition and Land Reforms in Hyderabad"*. Later after joining IEG he published several research papers and a book on the theme "land reforms and returns to scale in Indian agriculture" (Khusro 1964, 1969a, 1969b, and 1973a). These studies aimed at examining in some detail disincentive of tenure and the disabilities of size. He argued that in fixing land ration, considerations of equity and considerations of productivity must combine. His main conclusion was that, with the then existing technology, dominated by bullock-use, farms ought not to be below a five acre size. However, beyond that size constant returns to scale prevailed and therefore land ceiling was size neutral. Furthermore, his studies showed that redistributive considerations would not be in conflict with productivity considerations.

With regard to the pricing of foodgrains in India, the prevailing view in the 1960s was that in economies with a low degree of monetisation, where neither much of output is destined for nor much of input purchased from the market, price mechanisms would not be relevant. Farmers will not respond to prices. Professor Khusro's (1967) study contested this widespread view on people's rigidities to prices. His study showed that price mechanism was as compelling a force in the Indian economy as in any other. Using appropriate theoretical tools, he tried to understand the working of prices and concluded, "It might well be that the harm done to Indian agriculture, in terms of destroying the incentive to produce more with better techniques and a more efficient combination of new and old inputs, emanates in a large measure from a lack of understanding of the price mechanism and the consequent adoption of false pricing policies" (Khusro 1967: Page 272). This observation is as much relevant today as it was in the 1960s. False pricing policies with regard to both inputs like water, electricity, pesticides and fertilisers, and, outputs of agricultural products have resulted in the misuse of resources and the persistence of wrong cropping patterns.

His studies on buffer stocks (Khusro 1973b) were mainly concerned with (1) the principles of efficient operation of foodgrain stocks, (2) the most efficient technique and the most economical size of foodgrains storage, (3) the optimal distance between storages, and (4) the required amount of grain stock and storage to be provided in each State of India. In dealing with these issues he was concerned with the public sector stocks and storage only. The study also covered certain other aspects like financing of stocks, cheapest techniques of storage, least cost size of storage and alternative concepts of stocks.

Contributions to Poverty and Developmental Studies

Towards the second half of the 1990s Professor Khusro's interests moved on to analysing the nature and causes of the poverty of nations resulting in a major book (Khusro 1999). This book, "*The Poverty of Nations*", is mainly devoted to an analysis of the simultaneous existence of poverty and affluence everywhere. The motive for the study came from his observation that despite the growth of affluence everywhere no area of the globe is free from poverty, including some of the most affluent countries and regions. In analysing poverty, he did not merely take into account the number of people below the defined poverty norm but also considered other indicators like literacy, education, health care and life expectancy. His study covered 24 countries grouped in five different categories. These countries represent 67 per cent of the world's population. He recommended a poverty reduction strategy based on a combination of reliance on market forces (for efficiency) with public expenditures on health, education and unemployment benefits. It was important to consider the whole set of measures as a package and not rely exclusively on any one item.

Successful Institution Builder and Administrator

Professor Khusro demonstrated that it was possible to combine courtesy, civility and a caring attitude with hard administrative decisions and succeed as an administrator. He often remarked that most institutions, after a couple of decades of existence, started deteriorating. His formula for arresting the deterioration was based on the well known economic principle, namely, the margin should be higher than the average. In particular, he emphasised that the marginal addition to the faculty should be higher than the current average level of the faculty; if not, the average will decline and with that the decline of the institution will begin. He introduced fresh talent in the institutions he headed. He was the most popular and successful director of the Institute of Economic Growth. He inducted several new scholars and enlivened the campus atmosphere by encouraging social gatherings. He entertained people around him with anecdotes and *Sufi* verses – always with a twinkle in his eye. He was the favourite tennis coach for the children of the campus. His tenure as Vice-Chancellor of Aligarh Muslim University was marked by academic expansion and campus peace. He was one of those who completed the full term. Later he was elected Chancellor of the University. As president of the Agha Khan Foundation he introduced several innovative schemes to benefit society.

"If you can talk to the crowds and keep your virtue,
Or walk with Kings – nor lose the common touch"

These words of Rudyard Kipling aptly sum up Professor Khusro, the man.

References

Khusro, A.M. (1952): "An Investigation of Liquidity Preference", *Yorkshire Bulletin of Economic and Social Research*, 4(1).

————. (1957). "Liquidity Preference in India", *Indian Economic Review*, Vol. 3. pp. 24-40.

————. (1958). *Economic and Social Effects of Jagirdari Abolition and Land Reforms in Hyderabad*, Osmania University Press, Hyderabad.

————. (1964). "Returns to Scale in Indian Agriculture", *Indian Journal of Agricultural Economics*, 19(3&4), 51-80.

————. (1967). "Pricing of Food in India", *Quarterly Journal of Economics*, 81(2), pp. 271-285.

————. (1969a). "Agricultural Revolution and the Price Mechanism", *Indian Journal of Agricultural Economics*, 24(1), pp. 1-13.

————. (1969b). "Farm Size and Land Tenure in India", *Indian Economic Review*, 4(2), pp. 123-146.

————. (1973a). *The Economics of Land Reform and Farm Size in India*, Macmillan, Delhi.

————. (1973b). *Buffer Stocks and Storage of Foodgrains in India*, Tata McGraw-Hill, New Delhi.

————. (1994). *Unfinished Agenda: India in the World Economy*, Wiley Eastern Limited, New Delhi.

————. (1999). *The Poverty of Nations*, Macmillan, London and St. Martin Press, New York.

Khusro, A.M. and N.S. Siddharthan (1972). *An Econometric Model of Banking in India*, Banking Commission, Technical Studies, Reserve Bank of India, Bombay, pp. 1-77.

List of Professor Khusro's Publications

Articles

1. 1952, An Investigation of Liquidity Preference, *Yorkshire Bulletin of Economic and Social Research*, 4(1).
2. 1953, The Incidence of Taxation in India: The Marginal Rate of Tax, *Indian Journal of Economics*, 33(131).
3. 1957, Liquidity Preference in India, *Indian Economic Review*, 3(3), pp. 24-40.
4. 1958, Pruning the Plant: An Enquiry, *Economic Weekly*, 10 (4-6), pp. 205-211.
5. 1961, Income Redistribution in India, *Yojana*, 5(1), pp. 45-48.
6. 1961, Inter-Sectoral Terms of Trade and Private Policy, *Economic Weekly*, 13 (4-6), pp. 289-300.
7. 1963, Taxation of Agricultural Land: A Proposal, *Economic Weekly*, 15 (4-6), pp. 275-282.
8. 1964, A Correct Understanding, *Seminar*, 60(60), pp. 36-39.
9. 1964, Agriculture Requires Integrated Approach, *Yojana*, 8(24), pp. 16-17.
10. 1964, Returns to Scale in Indian Agriculture, *Indian Journal of Agricultural Economics*, 19(3-4), pp. 51-80.
11. 1967, Postponing Investment, *Yojana*, Vol. 11; Dec., p. 5.
12. 1967, Pricing of Food in India, *Quarterly Journal of Economics*, 81(2), pp. 271-285.
13. 1967, Prescription for Agriculture, *Seminar*, Vol. 91, pp. 14-18.
14. 1967, Recession Inflation and Economic Policy, *Economic and Political Weekly*, 2(41), pp. 1857-1862.
15. 1967, Rural Development, *Voluntary Action*, Nov.-Dec., pp. 11-16.
16. 1968, Public Sector Neglected, *Seminar*, Vol. 105, pp. 13-16.
17. 1969, Agricultural Revolution and the Price Mechanism, *Indian Journal of Agricultural Economics*, 24(1), pp. 1-13.
18. 1969, Farm Size and Land Tenure in India, *Indian Economic Review*, 4(2), pp. 123-146.
19. 1971, Banking Efficiency and Banking Growth, *Economic and Political Weekly*, 6(23), pp. 1150-1152.

20. 1972, India-Bangladesh Trade and Investment Prospects, *United Asia*, 24(1), pp. 29-32.

21. 1973, Khusro, A.M., *Analysis of Agriculture Land in India by Size of Holding and Tenure,* (mimeo), Institute of Economic Growth, Delhi.

22. 1973, Rural India Call for More Land Reforms. *Yojana*, 17(22), pp. 847-848.

23. 1973, Rural Scene, *Yojana*, p. 847.

24. 1974, Irreversible Improvements have Occured but the Inflationary Context Hits Me in the Eye, in Raj Kapila (ed.), *India at Cross: After 25 Years of Independence*, Free Press Syndicate, Delhi.

25. 1974, Economic Development and Inter-Sectoral Labour Supply: The Indian Case, *International Social Science Journal*, Vol. 26, pp. 284-301.

26. 1974, India's Economic Policy: Critique and an Approach, *Productivity*, 15(1), pp. 17-36.

27. 1975, Import Policy for 1975-76, *Indian Management*, 14(11).

28. 1978, Wages Prices and Productivity, *Lokudyog*, 12(3).

29. 1980, Transnational Corporations and Comparative Advantage, *Eastern Economist*, Mar. 14, pp. 542-544.

30. 1983, His thought Permeates our Planning Process, *Yojana*, 27(19) pp. 4-6.

31. 1983, Industrialisation is the Basis of Planned Economy, *Yojana*, 27(6) pp. 18-21.

32. 1984, Economic Planning and National Development, *Lokudyog*, 18(6) pp. 3-8.

33. 1984, Economists and Indian Development, *Indian Economic Journal*, 32(1) pp. 1-36.

34. 1984, Shaping India through Planning, *Yojana*, 28(11) pp. 4-7.

35. 1988, Quality of Indian Growth, *Economic and Political Weekly*, 23(36) pp. 1857-1862.

36. 1991, Old Order Changeth Yielding Place to New, *Indian Economic Journal*, 39(2) pp. 1-13.

37. 1993, Khusro, A.M., *International Economic Disorder: Presidential Address*, IEA.

38. 1993, International Economic Disorder, *Indian Economic Journal*, 40(4) pp. 1-12.

39. 1995, Reforms Sans Employment, *Indian Journal of Labour Economics*, 38(1) pp. 35-40.

40. 1995, "Effect and Future Direction of Economic Policy Reform", *Understanding India's Economic Reforms*, Vol. 4, Academic Foundation.

Books

1. 1958. Khusro, A.M., *Economic and Social Effects of Jagirdari Abolition and Land Reforms in Hyderabad,* Hyderabad: Osmania University Press.
2. 1961. Khusro, A.M. and Agarwal, A.N., *Problem of Co-operative Farming in India,* Asia Publishing House.
3. 1962. Khusro, A.M., "Study in Demand and Supply of Labour in the Non-Agriculture Section of the Indian Economy", *Economic Development with No Population Transfers,* Asia Publishing House.
4. 1965. Khusro, A.M. *et al., Study in the Working of the Intensive Area Scheme – Khadi and Village Industries Commission,* Khadi and Village Industries Commission.
5. 1967. Khusro, A.M., *Survey of Living and Working Conditions of Students of the University of Delhi,* Asia Publishing House.
6. 1968. Khusro, A.M, ed., *Readings in Agricultural Development,* Allied Publishers.
7. 1969. Khusro, A.M., *Agricultural Transformation in India,* Allied Publishers.
8. 1969. Khusro, A.M., *Report of the Expert Group on the Monetary Impact of PL480 Transactions,* Government of India.
9. 1971. Khusro, A.M. and N.S. Siddharthan, *An Econometric Model of Banking in India,* IEG, Mimeograph papers.
10. 1973. Khusro, A.M., *Buffer Stocks and Storage of Foodgrains in India,* New Delhi: Tata McGraw-Hill.
11. 1973. Khusro, A.M., *The Economics of Land Reform and Farm Size in India,* Delhi: Macmillan.
12. 1973. Khusro, A.M. *et al., Indian Foodgrain Marketing,* Prentice-Hall of India.
13. 1973. Khusro, A.M. *et al., Inflation and India's Economic Crisis,* Vikas Publishing House.
14. 1979. Khusro, A.M., *Indian Economy: Stability and Growth,* Prachi Prakashan.
15. 1980. Khusro, A.M., *Future of Developing Economics,* ICCR.
16. 1984. Khusro, A.M., *Economic Planning and National Development,* Deptt. of Personnel and Administrative Reform.
17. 1990. Khusro, A.M. *et al., Industrial Policy,* Vikas Publishing House.
18. 1990. Khusro, A.M., *Review of the Agriculture Credit Systems in India,* RBI.
19. 1993. Khusro, A.M., *Managing the Indian Economy,* Har-Anand Publications.
20. 1994. Khusro, A.M., *Unfinished Agenda: India in the World Economy,* New Delhi: Wiley Eastern Ltd.
21. 1996. Khusro, A.M., *Monetary and Banking Econometrics,* New Age International.
22. 1999. Khusro, A.M., *The Poverty of Nations,* London: Macmillan/New York: St. Martin Press.

Ph.D. Theses Awarded Under the Supervision of Prof. A.M. Khusro

Sr. No.	*Name of the Scholar*	*Title of the Thesis*	*Supervision*
		1960	
01.	K.N. Sinha	Levels of Living in Rural Bihar	A.M. Khusro
		1961	
02.	A.N. Rajamani	Land Reforms in the Madras State: 1947-1957	A.M. Khusro
		1962	
03.	P.V. John	Some Aspects of the Structure of Indian Agricultural Economy: 1947-48 and 1957-58	A.M. Khusro
		1963	
04.	R. Thamarajakshi	Agriculture-Industry Relationship in India: 1948-49 to 1958-59	A.M. Khusro
		1966	
05.	S.N. Mishra	A Study in the Economics of Livestock in India	A.M. Khusro
		1967	
06.	Sushil Kumar	Price Behaviour in India: 1900-1960	A.M. Khusro
07.	M. Yadava Reddy	India's Basic Industries: A Study in Growth and Inter-Industry Relationships: 1946-60	A.M. Khusro
		1971	
08.	B.B. Bhattacharya	The Role of Real and Monetary Factors in the Short-term Determination of Incomes in India	A.M. Khusro K.L. Krishna
		1972	
09.	N.S. Siddharthan	International Liquidity: Determinants of Foreign Assets Holding	A.M. Khusro
		1973	
10.	H.L. Bhatia	Liquidity of Public Debt in India	A.M. Khusro
11.	S.K. Ray	Stabilising Foodgrains Availability and Prices through Buffer Stocks Operation: An Econometric Approach	A.M. Khusro

Contd. ...

...Contd. ...

Sr. No.	*Name of the Scholar*	*Title of the Thesis*	*Supervision*
12.	G.R. Saini	Economics of Farm Management with Special Reference to Some Selected Holdings in Uttar Pradesh	A.M. Khusro
		1975	
13.	P.S. Vashishtha	Issues in Technological Adaptations and Agricultural Development—An Analysis of Production Functions in Punjab Farms	A.M. Khusro A.L. Nagar
		1978	
14.	S.A.H. Zaidi	Costs and Returns in Banking in India, 1962-71	A.M. Khusro
		1980	
15.	N. Ramamurthy	Economic of Storage and Conservation of Water in Nazamsagar Project in A.P.	A.M. Khusro

Section I

Agriculture, Land Reform and Anti-poverty Programmes

1

Indian Agriculture: Emerging Perspectives and Major Policy Issues[1]

C.H.HANUMANTHA RAO
ASHOK GULATI

1. Backdrop and the Winds of Change

1.1 The Backdrop

Two major economic changes have occurred during early-1990s, which are likely to have far reaching implications on India's economic development in general and agriculture in particular. Any strategy for agricultural sector, if it is to be realistic, must pay due recognition to these economic changes.

First, India launched a process of economic reforms since July 1991. Besides macro-stabilisation and structural reforms, this is designed to integrate the domestic economy with global economy. The process was initiated first in the industrial sector during early-1990s, and thereafter inched towards agricultural sector, with occasional hiccups and reversals in the later years of the reform process. What impact reforms in the industrial sector would have on agriculture, and what is likely to happen when Indian agriculture is fully exposed to world agriculture, are pertinent issues to keep in mind before one thinks of delineating the broad contours of an agricultural strategy.

Second, the Uruguay round of GATT was concluded with India as one of the signatories. Agriculture has been brought in its fold for the first time, and its trading rules are being rewritten. The Doha Development round was launched in November 2001 with a view to further liberalise the world agricultural markets. Although the Doha Development Round ran into rough weather during the fifth

---

1. This is an abridged and updated version of the paper originally prepared by the authors at the International Food Policy Research Institute, Washington, D.C. in September–October 1994.

ministerial conference of the World Trade Organisation (WTO) in September 2003 at Cancun in Mexico, yet it would be naïve to presume that Indian agriculture will remain insulated from the world agriculture for long. It would be only appropriate for India to assess the likely implications of emerging global changes, and accordingly re-chalk her agricultural strategy with a view to maximise gains from the new opportunities opened by trade under WTO, and to guard from any possible adverse impact from trade liberalisation.

It is against this backdrop that a modest attempt is made in this paper to spell out the basic ingredients of such an agricultural strategy. Obviously, a desirable strategy would be the one that can make Indian agriculture a vibrant and cost effective sector boosting production of food and fibre, raising consumption levels through domestic production and exchange (exports/imports), generating productive employment and thereby acting as the most effective 'safety net' and poverty alleviating programme, while duly protecting the environment. It is this type of a strategy that can put Indian agriculture, and also overall growth of the economy, on a sustainable path.

1.2 Changes and their Likely Impact on Agriculture

It is widely known that Indian industry has enjoyed a high degree of protection (very high by world standards), and for quite a long period, especially during the 1970s and 1980s, past the stage of infancy, through trade policy. What is, however, less known is that during the same period Indian agriculture has been disprotected. Recent research relating to protection accorded to industry and agriculture, particularly during the post-green revolution period, reveals that trade policies have favoured industry and discriminated against agriculture. The process of economic reforms ushered in July 1991 is expected to correct this 'bias' by gradually globalising the two sectors. In essence, what this would imply is that the industrial prices in real terms would come down and agricultural prices would go up from their existing levels, leading to favourable terms of trade for agriculture.

Further, the overvalued exchange rate was corrected first by devaluing rupee by more than 20 per cent in July 1991, and then making it fully convertible on current account. This made much of agriculture as export competitive sector in the years immediately following these changes. Opening up of Indian agriculture under WTO, and the expected changes in world agriculture, would most likely accelerate this process of correction in terms of trade. The major implication of these twin phenomena would be a change in the relative incentive structures in the economy, with agriculture likely to attract more resources from the private sector in the years to come than has been the case so far.

The macro-economic stabilisation process launched in July 1991 also led to a fiscal squeeze in public sector investment in almost all sectors, including agriculture. This is somewhat discomforting because it would act as a constraining factor even to private investment, to the extent two are complementary to each other. Thus, reduction in public sector investment can curtail the potential of growth in Indian agriculture quite significantly.

Another important point to be noted at this juncture is that for the trade policies to work their way fully through incentive environment, domestic marketing reforms would have to be carried out. It would involve freer movement of agricultural commodities, gradual phasing out of purchase levies (e.g. in case of rice and sugar), abolition of monopsonistic procurements (as in case of cotton in Maharashtra), introduction of futures markets, amendment/abolition of Essential Commodities Act to the extent it imposes restrictions on movement, stocking, and pricing of goods.[2] This is essential to complete the pull of demand side factors; otherwise the incentive environment for investments in agriculture related activities will remain only partial.

With this macro scenario in the background, and the likely changes on the horizon, agricultural strategy must see how best and how fast to benefit from the opportunities, as also to provide protetive cover against any threat of unemployment following structural adjustment and inflation. It is here that the research done under ICAR-IFPRI collaborative Research Programme is most timely and useful. This helps us to understand the various complexities ingrained in the supply side factors, be it research and technology, irrigation, fertilisers, or infrastructure. The nation must ensure that these supply factors are well in place so that maximum mileage can be attained from the demand pull that would be thrown up by the macro changes. It is reforms in these supply side factors, which are critical for raising

2. Some of these restrictions have been relaxed in 2002 and 2003 in the wake of unprecedented accumulation of foodgrain stocks with the government that peaked at 63 million tonnes in July 2002 (see Economic Survey, GoI, 2002 and 2003).

the aggregate supply response, which would ensure sustainable growth of agriculture and also provide a momentum to the overall growth of the economy. In fact, the desired impact of structural reforms would largely depend upon the degree of preparedness of supply side factors, which ultimately may condition the very pace of reforms in the economy.

2. Emerging Perspectives and Goals of Agricultural Policy

2.1 Emerging Perspectives

An interesting feature of the recent experience is the deceleration in the demand growth rate for foodgrains, despite the rise in per capita income and the decline in the relative prices of foodgrains.[3] This downward shift in the demand for foodgrains is basically attributable to the changing consumer tastes and preferences on account of the increasing availability of a wide variety of food items other than foodgrains as well as a wide range of non-agricultural goods and services in rural areas, within an institutional framework where there has not been any improvement in the distribution of income over a long period.

This is dramatically illustrated by the trend of a significant decline in the per capita consumption of foodgrains in rural Punjab and Haryana, despite a high per capita income growth. In these states, the energy requirements on account of manual labour would have declined due to the increasing mechanisation of agriculture, and the demand for, as well as the availability of, a wide variety of non-foodgrain and non-agricultural consumption goods would have increased both on account of the rise in per capita incomes and the rising levels of development in general. This emerging scenario in respect of food balance opens up the prospects for, and indeed necessitates, the export of foodgrains, especially in view of the comparative advantage that the country enjoys in respect of the production of rice and wheat in most of the years. This export potential of foodgrains would help further strengthen the food security at home.

3. The relative prices of foodgrains had been falling since early 1970s and continued through 1980s mainly as a result of the green revolution. But during the 1990s, especially in the second half, the relative prices of grains have seen some improvement due to first opening up of exports and then due to large increases in their procurement prices.

Achieving food security has so far been the overriding goal of agricultural policy in India. Opening up agricultural trade should now be seen as a major opportunity for raising overall economic growth rate by exploiting the comparative advantage that India possesses in agriculture, improving the efficiency of resource-use in agriculture, technological upgradation of the rural sector, and for providing the much needed safety net in the process of structural adjustment by way of greater employment and income generation for the poor as well as softening the rigour of inflation.

Opening up trade will improve the incentives by raising producer prices, even after the subsidies are cut down substantially. However, non-price factors such as public investment in infrastructure, technological changes, human development and institutional reforms are at least as important as incentive prices, in inducing effective supply response even after the effect of price-induced innovations are accounted for. Therefore, a big push in public effort on the former set of measures is called for, particularly in areas where there is strong complementarity with private investment. Indeed, the pace for freeing trade should bear some rational relationship to the domestic supply augmentation, so that there is no undue rise in the domestic prices of essential food items. Such a sequencing is necessary for ensuring equity even with the proper targeting of the public distribution of foodgrains, as the consumer expenditure on food as a proportion to the total expenditure is sizeable in a low income country like India. Further, such a policy is necessary for sustaining the process of economic reform itself in a populous democratic polity where the incidence of absolute poverty is still quite high.

3. Agricultural Performance: Investment, Growth and Productivity

3.1 Investment

As expected, liberalisation of trade and industry in India have had a beneficial impact on agriculture by turning the terms of trade in its favour which, in turn, has attracted greater private investments into this sector. The agriculture price index as per cent of manufacturing with 1993-94 as base (100) improved to 117.5 in 2001-2002 (Rao 2005). Private sector capital formation in agriculture rose by nearly 40 per cent betwen 1993-94 and 2000-2001 raising its share to 76.5 per cent in total capital formation in agriculture. On the other hand, public sector capital formation in agriculture, which showed a decline in the 1980s, continued to decline in the post-reform period of 1990s, recording the lowest ever share (23.5 per cent) in total agriculture capital formation in 2000-2001.[4] However, thanks to the significant rise in private sector capital formation in agriculture in the 1990s, the total gross capital formation in agriculture in the late-1990s recovered to the level obtaining in the late-1970s (Gulati and Bathla 2002; Rao 2005).

The rising subsidies for agriculture during this period have made considerable inroads into the surpluses available for public investment in agriculture. These subsidies, open as well as hidden, on agricultural inputs *e.g.* fertilisers, irrigation, electricity and credit rose from about 44 per cent of the combined plan expenditure by the central and state governments on agriculture, irrigation, and Special Area Programmes in the early eighties [Triennium Ending (TE) 1983-84] to about 83 per cent towards the close of the eighties (TE 1989-90).

Ironically, the level of input subsidies in the post-reform period of 1990s was much higher than in the 1980s. Whereas in 1989-90, the total of farm subsidies on power, fertiliser and irrigation at 1981-82 prices reached the level of Rs.53 billion, they nearly doubled reaching Rs.104 billion in 1999-2000. At 1993-94 prices, they crossed Rs.250 billion in the same year (Gulati and Narayanan 2003). As against this, Gross Fixed Capital Formation by Public Sector in Agriculture at 1993-94 prices stood at less than Rs.50 billion in 1999-2000 (Gulati and Narayanan 2003, Figure 1.1). It is clear from this that even a modest reduction of subsidies, say, to the extent of 20 per cent could enable the government to double its investment in agriculture.

Agriculture in India is essentially a state subject. The recent reforms aimed at macro-economic stabilisation, desirable in themselves, have, nevertheless, had a short-term adverse effect on capital expenditures on agriculture both by the central and state governments. The reduction in central tax revenues led to a significant decline in the revenues of the states, particularly of the less developed ones, as the statutory transfers to states, which have a significant in-

---

4. Although in the initial years of the reform process, there was some improvement in the public sector capital formation in agriculture (see Figure 1.1), it could not be sustained and that may have been one of the reasons why growth rate in agriculture after 1997-98 slowed down drastically.

Figure 1.1

Subsidies and Investments in Indian Agriculture

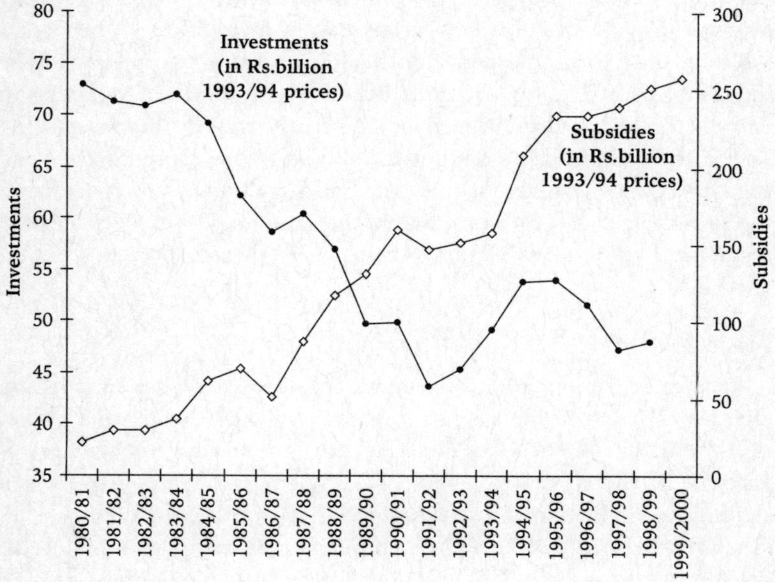

built progressivity, account for a substantial proportion of these revenues. Besides, the central transfers to states—both grants and loans—as a proportion to GDP have also gone down significantly.

The observed decline in investment, unless reversed, has potential to slow down the future growth of output and jeopardise food security at national as well as at household level. It is pertinent to note in this context that a big spurt in agricultural output over a fairly long period following the opening up of the economy in China is attributable basically to the very high rate of investment in agriculture, realised in part by using surplus labour, over a period of at least three decades, and the extreme misallocation of available capital and other resources under the communes and the collectives. In India, on the other hand, the rate of investment in agriculture went up for only about a decade following the green revolution and the development of human capital has been slow with few inefficiencies in the allocation of resources at the farm level.

3.2 Growth

The trend growth rate of total crop production declined from 3.2 per cent per annum in the 1980s (1980-81 to 1989-90) to 2.3 per cent per annum in the 1990s (1990-91 to 1999-2000). The growth rate of average yield per hectare from crops halved from 2.6 per cent to 1.3 per cent over the same period (RBI 2003*a*). However, owing to the increasing diversification of agriculture away from crop production to dairying, meat, poultry, vegetables and fruits, *etc.*, in response to the rise in their demand on account of the rise in per capita income and the consequent changes in the tastes and preferences of consumers, the growth rate of GDP from agriculture and allied activities showed a smaller decline from 3.1 per cent to 2.76 per cent over this period (Rao 2005).[5]

3.3 Productivity

The area under foodgrains has declined somewhat during the eighties. The entire increase in foodgrains output during this period is, therefore, the result of the rise in productivity per hectare on account of the increase in yield raising inputs. There has been a significant increase in the productivity of all inputs combined or total factor productivity (TFP). As the empirical studies under IFPRI-ICAR Programme show, the TFP accounts for one-third of output growth during 1957-85. The contribution of total factor productivity rose to over 50 per cent of output growth in the post-green revolution period. Public research and extension and private research have been the major sources of increase in total factor productivity, public research and extension accounting for over two-thirds of increase in total factor productivity after 1975. Foreign and domestic inventions together account for over 30 per cent of TFP growth, indicating the large impact of inventions in fertiliser, machinery, and chemicals, which have a high complementarity with public research. Apart from the market infrastructure, the effect of irrigation on TFP is strongly positive, indicating that irrigation had an impact on productivity over

5. It may be worth noting that in the immediate years following economic reforms, say from 1992-93 to 1996-97, the growth rate in agricultural GDP had significantly improved to almost 3.8 per cent per annum. But it could not be sustained due to various reasons that range from slowing down of public sector investments in agriculture to emerging demand constraints resulting from steeply falling world prices of agricultural products, especially grains and cotton, in the wake of south-east Asian crisis and rising subsidies by the OECD countries.

and above its contribution as an input. As expected, the effects of literacy are positive, showing the importance of human capital development in productivity growth.

It appears that the deceleration in foodgrains output in the 1990s is explained not only by the slow growth of inputs like irrigation and fertilisers but also by the declining contribution of total factor productivity (TFP). According to a recent study, the contribution of TFP to the growth rate in output already declined to around 30 per cent in the late-1980s (Desai and Namboodiri 1997). This declining trend in TFP has continued in the 1990s basically on account of the stagnation in the expenditure on Agricultural Research and Extension as a proportion to GDP from agriculture (Kumar 2002).

Government expenditure on agricultural research and extension being the most important determinant of TFP, its level in relation to the value of agricultural output and its distribution over different commodities and regions would hold the key to the growth of output, efficiency in resource allocation and the distribution of gains from the growth in productivity.

The rate of return to investment in public research and extension has been as high as over 60 per cent in respect of public research and over 50 per cent in respect of extension. These high rates of return on investments in research and extension are attributable, in no small measure, to the spread of new technology to the new regions and crops in the 1980s.

4. Prime Movers of Growth

4.1 Development and Diffusion of Technology

Adequate funding of public research, appropriate economic signals for setting right priorities in research, whether public or private, and favourable institutional framework and the resulting incentives for the absorption of new technology are the three basic prerequisites for the proper development and diffusion of new technology. These are best ensured when the demarcation of the relative roles of the state and markets or the public and private sectors in agriculture is rational. A number of studies have shown that favourable macro-economic environment including openness in trade have been conducive to the adequate development and diffusion of new cost-reducing technologies in agriculture. This has happened on account of favourable terms of trade for agriculture, inducement to improve quality and reduce costs for becoming internationally competitive, prices reflecting truly the scarcities of resources so that research is directed to save on the scarce factors and the adequate allocation of resources—public as well as private—for research and extension.

Heavy subsidies on inputs like chemical fertilisers, surface irrigation, electricity for pumping water and on farm credit, apart from causing macro-economic imbalances and shortage of resources for public investment in research and other infrastructure, discourage research in new areas like biotechnology which saves on chemical inputs and is environment-friendly, discourage the development and adoption of innovations for the conservation of water and energy, and, in general, encourage capital-intensive techniques.

The achievement of the Indian agricultural system so far in respect of raising yields in the unirrigated and the unfavourable agro-climatic regions are not comparable with those realised for the irrigated areas in the early years of green revolution. Even in irrigated areas, the yields under the seed-fertiliser technology have been hovering around their peak for some time. The tools of emerging biotechnology like genetic engineering, tissue culture and so on seem to offer significant possibilities for breaking these barriers. Although some advanced centres of research in biotechnology have been established in the country, it is not clear how such priorities find their place in the existing agricultural research system in India. It is necessary to have a fresh look at the priorities of the Indian agricultural research system in the light of these emerging prospects and for adequately taking into account the socio-economic factors relevant in the evolution of new technologies. India is currently investing only about 0.3 per cent of its agricultural gross domestic product in agricultural research as against 0.7 per cent in the developing countries, as a whole, and as much as 2-3 per cent in the developed countries. Therefore, there is considerable scope for diverting incremental outlays for the priority areas in research.

4.2 Irrigation

Irrigation has been the cradle where HYV seeds and fertiliser consumption thrived to bring about a green revolution in Indian agriculture during late-1960s and early-1970s. In the course of 50 years of planning, India has exploited nearly 60 per cent of its available irrigation potential of 58.5 million hectares from the major and medium irrigation projects. Over 400 such projects were in the pipeline at various stages for completion during the Ninth Five Year Plan. When these projects are completed, bulk of the available irrigation potential will have been exploited.

Thanks to the availability of power in large parts of the country for pumping water for irrigation, as much as 78 per cent of the available potential of 81.4 million hectares from minor irrigation sources, consisting predominantly of ground water resources, has already been exploited. Further progress towards the exploitation of the remaining potential hinges on the availability of power for pumping water in the eastern states where as much as 75 per cent of their ground water potential still remains to be exploited (Government of India, Ninth Five Year Plan).

In the irrigation sector, highest priority may be given first to maintain the existing irrigation facilities, and then to develop rest of the irrigation potential in the country. And this can not be done without significantly stepping up the rate of investment in this sector. The manner of spending, however, should be such as to devote the largest chunk of this investment on O&M of the existing facilities and completing the projects already at hand. There are estimates that at the current levels of investment, the projects in hand will take about 28 years for completion. This needs to be brought down to about 10 to 15 years. For this the rate of investment will have to be almost doubled.

In order to generate resources for accomplishing the above task, it is essential that pricing of canal waters, as also institutional reforms in its management and ownership be given due importance. Financial autonomy of irrigation departments with a condition that they have to recover at least all the O&M expenses from the beneficiaries can be one of the ways to proceed with reforms in this sector. Also, a two part tariff system for pricing, and involvement of water users associations (WUAs) in management and ownership of canal networks (starting with distributories) through 'water bonds' should be placed high on the agenda for reforming the irrigation sector. An Expert Committee of Government of India has highlighted the problem, and suggested a two part tariff system for pricing of canal waters. First, there should be a fixed charge to the farmers who happen to be in the command area of the canal; and two, have a volumetric price (in the long-run) for the quantities of water used by the farmers. If one were to recover all O&M charges and 1 per cent of the capital cost, the charge to the farmers is not more than 6 per cent of the gross output on their irrigated lands. This is very much within the charge of 5 to 12 per cent recommended by the Irrigation Commission of 1972.

In the case of groundwater, the prime concern remains that of overdrafting, which is not a healthy sign as the economy's capacity to depend upon this "buffer" during years of drought is adversely affected. One of the important steps to check this problem of overdrawal would be to introduce volumetric pricing of electricity, while involving farmers' organisations in the collection of electricity dues on commission basis. In case collection of electricity dues through farmers' organisations fails, it would be desirable to give it to the private corporate bodies. While the power sector reforms envisage a significantly larger role for private sector in generation, we feel it will remain partial without privatising the distribution.[6] In fact, privatisation of power distribution should have preceded privatisation of power generation. The other would be to evolve a proper institutional framework whereby surface and groundwater could be monitored, and overdrafting of groundwater can be avoided/minimised.

Water conservation schemes with the help of farmers (preferably under their ownership) in dry land areas need to be undertaken at a much larger scale than has been the case so far, attracting financial resources from the farmers wherever feasible.

Salinity and waterlogging problems in the commands of major irrigation schemes can be minimised by recognising them explicitly at the designing stage itself, and corrective measures contained in the scheme. Conjunctive use of surface and groundwater can go a long way in addressing this problem, and appropriate steps be taken for its promotion. Appropriate pricing of water and electricity will also help in this direction. Further, proper drainage facilities, involving farmers' groups, need to be created where this problem has become very acute.

4.3 Fertilisers

In the case of fertilisers, there seems to be an overriding concern for removal of subsidies. This concern emanates primarily from its

6. Lately, some states have started privatising the distribution of power. But it has remained largely restricted to urban areas. The challenge of privatising power distribution in rural areas is much more daunting, given that much of power consumption in agriculture is not even metered currently.

burden in the Central budgets rather than from the desire to reform the fertiliser sector as such. To find a way out of the present day concerns without harming the long term objectives of this sector, it would be worth noting the major findings of research in this area.

An interesting finding of the empirical studies is that the rate of adoption of fertiliser use is somewhat lower amongst small farmers compared to large farmers, owing mainly to credit constraints, but those who adopt use higher doses of fertilisers than the big farmers. This relationship is more pronounced on unirrigated and partially irrigated plots, but breaks down on irrigated ones. In fact on irrigated plots larger farmers use higher doses of fertilisers than small and marginal. It is possible that small farmers improve the quality of their unirrigated plots through the use of surplus labour whereas the quality of irrigation is better on large farms on account of higher investment in minor (controlled) irrigation.

The use of N, P and K is quite unbalanced not only in low consumption areas but even in high consuming and advanced pockets. The responses (average and marginal) of wheat and rice to fertiliser consumption (NPK) are highest in Central (Madhya Pradesh and Rajasthan) and Eastern (Bihar, Orissa, West Bengal, Assam and other NE states) regions, and Uttar Pradesh. This indicates that there is sizeable scope of raising wheat and rice production simply by inducing a redistribution in the consumption of fertilisers in favour of high response regions, and by promoting balanced use of N, P and K through appropriate policy measures.

Research elsewhere also shows that fertiliser consumption has lately become more sensitive to its real price than was the case about two decades ago, presumably because of lower fertiliser response at higher levels of consumption. This is particularly true of those pockets that use fertiliser consumption very intensively and account for substantial share in all India consumption of fertiliser. But the elasticity of fertiliser consumption to its real price still remains much below its elasticity with respect to non-price variables.

The domestic production of fertilisers has gone up substantially, leading to a high degree of self-sufficiency. The growth has been very rapid especially during 1980s primarily because of two reasons. One, the Retention Price Scheme launched in 1977 provided good incentive environment for the industry, and two, the discovery of oil and gas fields at Bombay High helped the growth of gas based fertiliser plants.

However, by late-1980s, it was increasingly being realised that the fertiliser production is becoming high cost at the margin, and that RPS was inducing over capitalisation of plants. This has been leading to a very rapid growth in fertiliser subsidy, almost making it financially unsustainable in the Central budget.

Whereas the consumption of all fertilisers (NPK) more than doubled during the 1980s from 5.5 million tonnes in 1980-81 to 12.5 million tonnes in 1990-91, their consumption stood at 16.7 million tonnes in 2000-2001, representing a rise of only about 33 per cent over the 1990s (Government of India, Economic Survey, 2002-2003). What is worse, subsidy on Urea has resulted in unbalanced use of Nitrogen, Phosphorus and Potassium fertilisers which was in the ratio of 8.5:3.1:1 in 1998-99 as against the desirable ratio of 4:2:1(R.B.I. 2003*a*). This has led to a decline in the productivity of fertilisers apart from depleting soil nutrients.

Implications of these research findings for policy are amply clear:

First, wider distribution of fertilisers needs to be promoted by covering the regions which have hitherto used very low doses of fertilisers (for example, Central and Eastern regions and Uttar Pradesh in case of wheat and rice). This is a challenging task as a pre-condition of its success would be to launch a massive drive towards water conservation schemes on the one hand and drainage on the other. This is because quite a sizeable chunk of this area suffers from water logging in irrigated tracts. Harvesting water in water scarce regions and proper drainage in water logged areas can set the ground for adoption of HYVs and the demand for fertilisers. Besides, an extensive network of rural infrastructure needs to be created (including roads and credit) in these regions, which will facilitate timely and adequate supplies of fertilisers, particularly in the Eastern states. Such a network of rural infrastructure will also help in establishing an appropriate interface of input markets with output markets in these regions.

Second, a boost to soil testing facilities and extension effort to educate the farmers regarding the benefits of balanced use of fertilisers would go a long way. This needs to be reinforced by transmitting right pricing signals (relative prices of N, P and K), which are historically at most distorted levels. There is a large scope to increase production simply by promoting balanced use of N, P and K, and by removing micro-nutrient deficiencies.

Third, subsidies are no longer required to promote this "new" input; if they have to be given they should be targetted to low consumption areas where response is highest (for example, Eastern and Central regions, and UP, especially for wheat and rice).

Fourth, production of fertilisers has to be made efficient by withdrawing Retention Price Scheme and exposing the domestic production to foreign competition by decanalising imports of fertilisers along with a provision of reasonable import duty to safeguard against any dumping or abrupt drop in international prices.

Fifth, the farm gate price of nitrogenous fertilisers needs to be gradually raised and then decontrolled, especially when P and K have been decontrolled. It would give correct pricing signals for balanced use of N, P and K, and thereby help in raising agricultural production with the same amount of total fertiliser consumption.

Sixth, to minimise the possible adverse impact of this rise in farmgate price of fertiliser, the savings in fertiliser subsidy be ploughed back into basic agricultural infrastructure such as watershed programmes in moisture stress areas, which in turn will raise the fertiliser demand in those high response regions. Further, organic manure may be accorded a high priority for its eco-friendly characteristics compared to chemical fertilisers, and also because it may be more attractive economically once subsidies are phased out from chemical fertilisers.

5. Institutional Reforms

5.1 Credit Reform

Credit for agriculture has to expand at a faster rate than before because of the need to step up agricultural growth for generating surpluses for exports, and also because of the changing product mix towards animal husbandry, fisheries, horticulture *etc.*, which will necessitate larger investments.

In view of the scarcity of credit and the very high rates of interest charged in the informal credit markets in rural areas, the small and marginal farmers stand to benefit immensely from the easy and timely *availability* of credit from the institutional sources rather than from the low rates of interest charged. It would, therefore, be essential to ensure the *availability* of institutional credit to the farmers, particularly the small and marginal farmers, by ensuring a stipulated share for agriculture, as is being done at present. In the absence of such a stipulation, the well-known tendency on the part of the bankers to reduce unit costs by serving a small number of big borrowers rather than a large number of small borrowers would result in squeezing credit to the needy sections.

Although there is a marginal improvement in the growth rate of direct institutional credit to agriculture and allied activities in the 1990s, the growth of credit to the small and marginal farmers and for investment slowed down considerably in this period. According to the Reserve Bank of India Report on Currency and Finance, 2001-2002, "...there is a deceleration in the scheduled commercial banks' disbursements of direct finance to small farmers from 15.1 per cent in the 1980s to 11.0 per cent in the 1990s. Similarly, the annual compound growth rate of direct finance (disbursements) to marginal farmers, decelerated to 13.0 per cent from 18.1 per cent during the same period. The annual compound growth rates of medium/long term loans disbursed to agriculture and allied activities (direct advances), which are important for private sector capital formation in agriculture, have shown deceleration to 9.7 per cent in the 1990s from 11.5 per cent in the preceding decade."(RBI 2003*b*)

Credit institutions need to be accorded greater autonomy by doing away with administrative and political interference in their day-to-day functioning. The managerial cadre and other staff have to be made more professional through proper recruitment and appropriate training. The loan advances should be based on the professional appraisal of projects instead of being based on the targets for the disbursement of credit, as is often the practice now. Loan sanctions should be accompanied by professional follow-up to ensure the profitability of investment by reducing the rate of mortality and sickness in these ventures.

The follow-up services for enhancing the productive utilisation of credit, and the repayment performance could be improved through group-lending schemes. Participation of voluntary agencies, women activists, thrift societies *etc.*, especially in the backward regions, would contribute to reducing transaction costs to the banks as well as clients. All this would call for the reorientation of the outlook of banks, posting of competent personnel in rural areas, and a system of incentives and rewards related to the performance of the specific tasks having a bearing on long-term development as well as meeting the needs of the weaker sections.

5.2 Agrarian Reforms

The ceiling on the ownership of land holdings served to arrest the concentration of land ownership and, indeed, there is evidence of some decline in the concentration of land ownership. However, owing to population growth and sub-division of land holdings, the average size of both ownership and operational holdings has come down, even though the proportion of area held by the small and the marginal farmers has increased. The proportion of area held under tenancy, especially pure tenancy, has declined on account of the resumption of land by the owners for self-cultivation induced by technological change as well as impelled by the tenancy legislation. This explains the rise in the concentration of operational holdings, although this concentration is still lower than that in ownership holdings because small and marginal holdings still lease-in more area than they lease-out and large holdings lease-out more area than they lease-in.

According to the empirical studies conducted under IFPRI-ICAR Research Programme, where seed-fertiliser or land-augmenting technology has been adopted widely, the improved viability of small holdings has contributed to slowing down the incidence of landlessness. Also, in areas of technological dynamism, medium and large holdings have expanded their operated area significantly by leasing-in land from the small and marginal holdings. The rural non-farm employment opportunities as well as wages have increased in such high-growth areas thus reducing rural poverty and relieving pressure on agricultural land.

What are the implications of this experience for policies on land tenure? With population pressure on agricultural land still persisting and there being, as yet, not enough evidence of economies of scale in Indian agriculture on account of scale neutrality of seed-fertiliser technology and few indivisibilities arising out of mechanisation, there appears little justification for doing away with the ceiling on the ownership of land at this stage, especially because the farmers are able to augment their operational holdings in response to the changing technological and economic factors.

However, this experience also suggests that freeing lease market for land may contribute to equity as well as efficiency of resource-use. The pure tenants as well as the small and marginal farmers would be able to augment their operational holdings by leasing-in area in situations where there is pressure on land and where wages are low and poverty is high. This may also contribute to the more efficient use of land, labour and other resources. On the other hand, in areas experiencing technological change and high growth where population pressure on land is low and wages are high, the marginal farmers may gain by leasing-out their area and taking up non-farm employment. In such situations of high wages and high rate of mechanisation, the medium and large farmers leasing-in area would be able to make a fuller use of their fixed equipment.

Experience also shows that consolidation of land holdings and improving land records will give a fillip to investment in irrigation by raising the profitability of such investment and by improving credit-worthiness of farmers.

Besides, freeing up lease markets for land, there is also need for introducing some innovative institutions that facilitate vertical integration between farms, firms and forks (retail chains). This is particularly needed to fully exploit the potential of high value agriculture, the demand for which is rising at much faster pace than cereals. This high value agriculture comprising of fruits and vegetables, dairy, fishery, poultry, *etc.* is perishable in nature and has high post-harvest losses emanating from lack of infrastructure, processing facilities and assured markets. Retail chains and processing facilities need to be encouraged at large scale, with backward integration with farmers, be they under private or cooperative sector, with domestic or foreign investments. The next revolution in Indian agriculture has to come from value addition, but the policy environment is still embedded in commodity production rather than upstream value addition. It would require different kind of institutional environment and infrastructure investments, if this revolution has to succeed.

5.3 Participation of Women

There has been an increase in the participation rate of female labour in agriculture. This is due to the rise in the seasonal demand for labour for operations traditionally performed by female labour following the spread of new seed-fertiliser technology, the rise in the demand for female labour in activities like dairying and to the increase in the employment of male labour in non-agricultural activities. As a result, there has been a rise in the real wages of female labour relative to those for male labour. However, the levels of labour input as well as wages are still lower in the case of female labour when compared to male labour.

Apart from improving agricultural practices and protecting environment, strengthening the position of women farmers and female labour, in general, contributes significantly to the well-being of the household, as women allocate a greater part of their income for household expenditure than men, thus improving the nutrition and care of children, particularly girls. Changes in property rights in favour of women, evolution of technologies to suit women farmers, increasing the number of women extension workers, education and training of women farmers, strengthening the thrift societies run by women, and other such measures may help them to better exploit the emerging opportunities.

6. Concluding Remarks

The process of economic reforms, as also the gradual opening up of Indian agriculture, has helped turn the terms of trade in favour of agriculture. It has created a better incentive environment for agriculture than had been the case during preceding decades. To fully exploit this opportunity, a major reform in supply side factors and institutional structures is needed besides a clean sweep to dismantle all export controls on agricultural commodities as well as domestic controls in terms of stocking limits, movement restrictions, levies, and so on. It is these supply side factors—technology, fertilisers, irrigation, infrastructure, and credit—and institutional innovations that can create ennabling environment for participation of small holders, which raise aggregate supply response, and can be the prime movers behind accelerated and sustainable growth of Indian agriculture. Further, as demand shifts from cereals to high value agriculture products such as fruits and vegetables, milk and milk products, meat and fish, *etc.* it would require major investments in fast moving infrastructure as well as innovative institutions that facilitate vertical integration of farms with firms and retail chains. It is such institutional innovations that would cut down transaction costs, reduce market risk and post-harvest losses, introduce proper grades and standards, food safety norms, and make Indian agriculture not only globally competitive but also put it on a higher growth trajectory with participation from small holders as well.

References

Desai, Bhupat M. and N.V. Namboodiri (1997). *Determinants of Total Factor Productivity in Indian Agriculture* (mimeo), Indian Institute of Management, Ahmedabad.

Government of India (2003). *Economic Survey* 2002-2003.

Government of India, Planning Commission, *Ninth Five Year Plan*.

Gulati, Ashok and Seema Bathla (2002). *Capital Formation in Indian Agriculture: Trends, Composition and Implications for Growth*, National Bank for Agriculture and Rural Development (NABARD), Mumbai.

Gulati, Ashok and Sudha Narayanan (2003). *The Subsidy Syndrome in Indian Agriculture*, Oxford University Press, New Delhi.

Reserve Bank of India (2003a). *Annual Report 2002-03*.

————. (2003b). *Report on Currency and Finance 2001-2002*.

Rao, C.H.H. (2005). *Agriculture, Food Security, Poverty and Environment: Essays in Post-Reform India*, Oxford University Press, New Delhi.

2

Sustainable Livestock Development in India[1]

S.N. MISHRA

1. Introduction

In the present paper our main concern is to articulate a long-term strategy for sustainable livestock development in India. Sustainability problem of development in general had arisen from environmental concerns, about development's impact on the local (national) and global environment, and about the manner and mode of utilisation of natural resources, renewable and non-renewable. Livestock anywhere are a renewable natural resource. A given livestock population is sustainable in the sense that it can be replaced (renewed) by breeding. But livestock production, viewed as flow of livestock products from the population need not be sustainable, since production requires additional natural resources like land, feed and water, which may not be available in required quantity and quality. It is, therefore, necessary to explore and set the conditions for sustainable livestock production.

However, these conditions can't be the same for all types of livestock production systems and resource endowments. In the world today there are many livestock production systems. These are classified into three broad groups (1) pasturage (grazing) systems, (2) mixed farming systems in which livestock production is integrated with agriculture, and (3) industrial systems in which livestock production is organised along industrial business lines. The characteristic differences among these broad groups are touched upon in the following section.

---

1. Professor A.M. Khusro had the great gift of supervising a doctoral thesis almost on any subject in economics. In mid-1960s he supervised my thesis, "A Study in the Economics of Livestock in India". Neither the student nor the teacher had a choice in this as it was decided by the Director of the Institute, Dr. V.K.R.V. Rao. Now that I am back as a student of livestock and environment in India, this paper is submitted as a token of my tribute to the teacher, Dr. A.M. Khusro.

In India mixed livestock farming system predominates. And, there again large ruminants have predominant position. A general framework of the mixed farming system as practiced in India, depicting the linkages between agriculture, ruminant livestock population and production system and environment is presented in Section 3. Section 4 is devoted to a brief description of the state of livestock economy. Both these sections are preparatory to articulation of the strategy for sustainable development of the system. The strategy and the public policy implications of the strategy are discussed in Section 5. In Section 6, I have pointed out to inadequacy of livestock related information base and lack of public support for socio-economic research in livestock. The last section has my concluding observations.

2. Livestock Production Systems

As mentioned earlier, livestock farming currently in practice around the world falls into three broad groups: pasturage, mixed farming, and industrial production systems. The systems are distinguished, one from the other, according to the mode of sourcing feed for the livestock. In the pasturage system, as the name suggests, animals directly feed themselves by grazing and browsing on pastures or open range lands. In the temperate regions of North and South America, pasturage is practiced in the form of ranching in which vast tracts of pasture lands are privately owned or held on lease. The forage availability on such pastures is maintained by periodic seeding and fertiliser applications. In contrast to this, in the arid, semi-arid and mountainous regions of Asia and Africa, pasturage is traditionally practiced by pastoral communities on open, public range lands. Since forage availability on the rangelands varies with climatic conditions and seasons of the year, these communities usually follow a transhumance cycle, moving herds from one to the other rangeland. In Western Himalayas, for example, pastoral communities like *Gujar* and *Gaddies* move their herds from high to low altitudes and back during the summer-winter cycles. Irrespective of it's form, pasturage is an extensive system of livestock production, requiring considerable area of land per head of livestock.

The mixed farming system, in which animal husbandry is integrated with crop production, is an intensive system of production. Animal feed — dry fodder (crop residues) and green fodder — is produced and fed to animals at the level of the farming unit.

Concentrates as by-products of grain processing such as husk, bran, broken foodgrain residues (*chunni, khuddi*) were earlier also produced at the farm household level using traditional labour intensive technology. Oilcake too was produced not beyond the village level using bullock-drawn rotary press. With industrial development, grain processing has increasingly moved away to power driven milling industry. As a result, concentrate by-products now flow back to farms either directly from the mills or in the form of compounded feed through marketing channels. This development has reduced the self-reliance of the mixed farming system at the farm level, but not at the macro, national level.

Unlike pasturage and mixed farming system, industrial livestock production system at the enterprise level is free from land constraint for sourcing feed. All of it's feed requirements is met from external supplies through the market. Typical examples are feed-lot system in the advanced industrial countries and dairy production enterprises in the urban and peri-urban areas of the developing countries. In the first case meat animals (cattle or pigs) are subjected to close door intensive feeding for fattening before being sent out for slaughter. In the second case too animals in-milk (cow or buffalo) are kept on high rations, while dry animals and calves, as far as possible, are removed from the production enterprise. The industrial system at the enterprise level or even at the national economy level may appear to be free from land constraint, but as animal feed at the primary stage comes from land, this system as well makes a demand on land within or outside of the country concerned. If a Dutch swine is fattened on cassava feed imported from Thailand, Thailand must allocate land for cassava production to that extent.

The livestock production systems also differ in their economic motivations. The industrial livestock production system is driven by profit motive, and is subject to market forces of supply and demand for inputs and outputs. The motive of production under pasturage and mixed farming vary across countries and regions depending upon the general level of the economic development and relative resource endowment, in particular as between land and labour. Ranchers in North and South America are driven by profit motive, and produce for the market. For the pastoral communities in Asia and Africa pasturage, on the other hand, is simply a source of livelihood. Similar differences exist in the developed and developing world in respect of mixed farming. In the European Community dairy farmers, who produce forage crop for feeding their dairy herd on the farm, are profit maximisers. Quite in contrast, in the densely populated South Asian region, where foodgrains production is the primary goal, farmers maximise milk output from the few dairy animals they are able to maintain on their farms, in addition to plough bullocks. They look to livestock as a secondary source of income and employment of family labour.

Just as livestock production systems differ in their economic motives, so they do in respect of their interactions with the environment. Interaction is mostly situation (site) specific with the natural resource base, land, water, plant, micro flora, biodiversity and air. There is, however, one common global atmospheric impact from all types of ruminant production systems, namely, emission of methane (CH_4) which contributes to global warming, hence climate change. As regards situation specific interaction of different livestock production system a good account can be found in Cees de Haan, *et al.* (1997). From the environmental angle, the authors conclude that the mixed farming systems are most benign.

3. Mixed Farming System in India

In the present section we provide a general framework of livestock production under mixed farming system as practiced in India. It relates to bovine stock, cattle and buffaloes, with which agriculture is integrated. Small ruminant (sheep and goat) production takes place on the side lines of this system. The framework, as can be seen from the accompanying chart, demonstrates the relationships or linkages that exist between livestock, agriculture and environment. It is meant to guide us in articulating the strategy for sustainable development later on.

Livestock production under mixed farming system in India has certain socially desired output goals. Cattle traditionally have been (are) reared primarily to provide animal draught power (animal energy) required for agricultural operations. Milk output from the cattle system is a second priority. In fact, one might say milk is produced anyway since certain number of cows have to be maintained for replacing the required stock of working bullocks. Quite in contrast, milk output is the first priority goal of the buffalo system. Since buffalo bullocks are rarely used in agricultural operations, animal draught power is hardly a goal of the buffalo production system. As regards meat output, it is not a system goal either of cattle or buffaloes. Cow is sacred to Hindus. In most Indian states there is either prohibition or restriction on slaughter of 'cow and its progeny'. Buffalo is neither sacred, nor is there restriction on slaughter of buffaloes. However, despite religious taboo and preferences some beef and buffalo meat is produced in the country, which supplies to the needs of non-Hindus, Muslims and Christians in particular. In addition to socially desired outputs, the system produces outputs of joint products and by-products. The joint products are: (1) dung and urine excreted by the animals, and (2) methane, a greenhouse gas, formed in the digestive tracts of the animals in the process of feed fermentation (enteric fermentation) and released by them largely through eructation. The joint products have important environmental implications, as we will see later. There are many by-products of the system such as hides, hoof, horn, hair, bone, offals and casings from slaughted and dead animals. The outputs of these go as raw materials to various crafts and industries in which leather industry is the most prominent.

Let us now look at the systems linkages with agriculture. Feed input to the system comes from agriculture, at the micro farm level, as well as at the macro level. Much of it consists of agricultural by-products — dry fodder and concentrates. To provide for green fodder, some land is allocated to production of fodder crops. At the farm level people also collect green fodder from standing crops of foodgrains and oilseeds during weeding and thinning operations. Livestock system provides animal energy to agriculture. Animal energy is a flow from the stock of working animals. It is embodied in the work performed by the latter in various agricultural operations. Thus, there is an interdependence between livestock and agriculture through energy exchange between the two. Energy (and nutrients) in the form of feed flows to livestock from agriculture and a part of that is returned to agriculture in the form of animal energy. Another part of that energy and nutrients is returned to agriculture in the form of dung (urine) used as manure. The interdependence just noted is at first weekend and then finally eliminated by agricultural mechanisation. Animal energy which was internally generated in the mixed farming system is now replaced by externally supplied fossil fuel. The self-reliance characteristics of the system is thereby lost. In a situation of mechanised agriculture, mixed livestock farming simply means that the farmer produces forage crops and feed grains for feeding the livestock on the farm. It is in this sense that livestock production is integrated with agriculture. This is the form of mixed farming currently practiced in the developed world.

The environmental impact of the mode of livestock farming is depicted in the accompanying chart. The environmental impact occurs both on its input as well as output side. On the input side the impact is largely on the natural resource base, land in particular. To the extent agricultural by-products — dry fodder and concentrates — are utilised as animal feed, the system saves land, in other words, does not make a claim on additional land for feed production. From another perspective the livestock work as a recycling machine for agricultural 'waste' (crop residues and concentrates), which are inedible for human consumption.

On the output side, environmental impacts are due to animal energy used in agriculture, management and utilisation of dung output, and methane production from enteric fermentation of feed. The stock of working animals from which energy is derived is a renewable source of energy. Secondly, animal energy use saves fossil-fuel, a non-renewable source of energy. And, finally it prevents emission of greenhouse gases, CO_2 in particular from burning of fossil-fuel, if the animal energy were to be replaced by fossil-fuel. As mentioned in the preceding section dung used as manure replaces chemical fertilisers. As against the latter, it is renewable organic source of soil fertilisation. To the extent it replaces chemical fertilisers, it prevents greenhouse gases emission that would otherwise occur in their manufacture, and saves non-renewable mineral resources required for manufacture. In India part of the dung output is used as domestic fuel in the form of dry dung-cake, specially by farm households for cooking purposes. In this form dung is a renewable bio-energy source. It saves fossil-fuel (coal) or alternative bio-fuel like firewood. There is no net emission of CO_2 from its burning as the carbon emitted is sequestered by the surrounding plant biomass, in other words, utilised to form carbohydrates through photosynthesis.

We, thus, see that most environmental impacts of the mixed farming system are of beneficial nature. Methane output from enteric fermentation of feed is the only one that has negative environmental impact. Its emission contributes to global warming and climate change. Against the backdrop of mixed farming framework presented in this section we give a brief account of the current state of livestock economy of India in the following section.

Figure 2.1

Chart Showing Linkages Between Livestock Population (Bovines), Production System and Environment

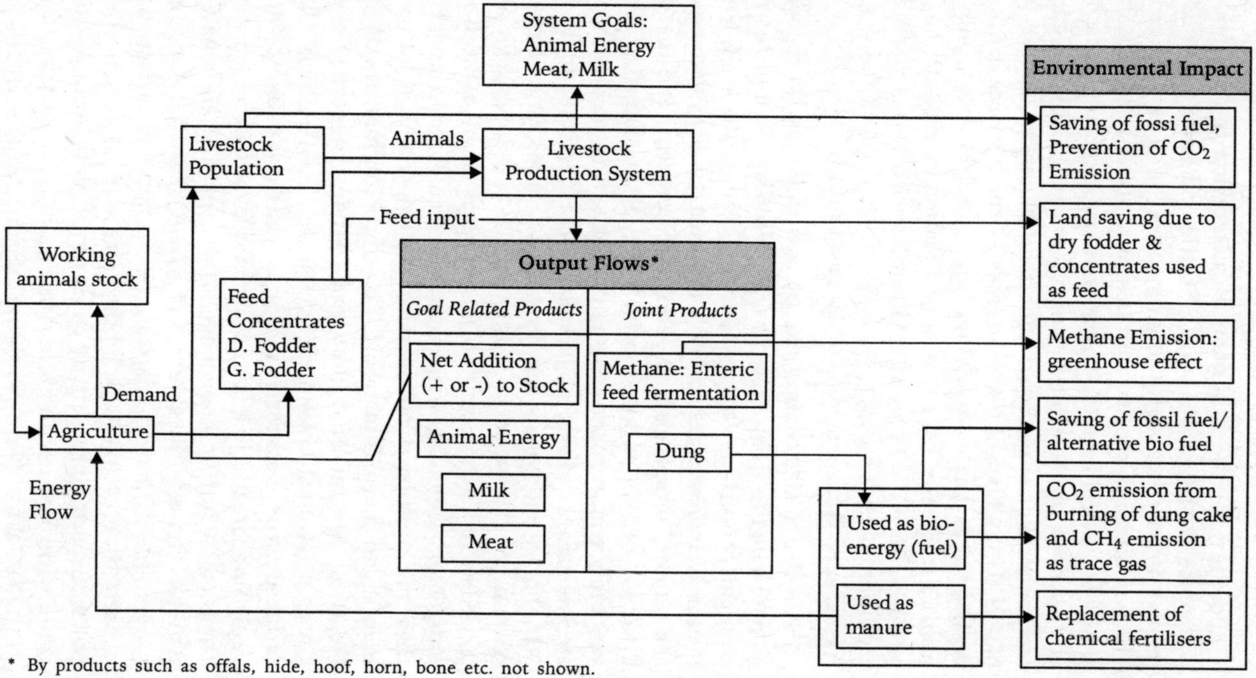

* By products such as offals, hide, hoof, horn, bone etc. not shown.

D = Dry, G = Green

4. Livestock Biodiversity

Bovines are the backbone of mixed farming system in India. Difference in the growth rates of cattle and buffaloes indicates their relative importance and changing composition of the bovine stock. The sex and age specific composition of cattle and buffaloes has slowly but surely been moving in favour of increasing milk production and against production of animal energy. Growing agricultural mechanisation has played an important role in this. Indeed, as a result of this the number of cattle bullocks — the livestock census category designated as 'males over three years used for work only' declined from 71 million in 1972 to about 53 million in 1992. During the same period, the number of agricultural tractors increased from 142 thousand in 1972 to 1.22 million in 1992 (Govt. of India, Ministry of Agriculture, Indian Livestock Census 1992).

For a large size country like India with her varied topography and climate ranging from snow covered Himalaya in the North to sub-tropical conditions in the Southern Peninsula, a high degree of livestock biodiversity is naturally expected. Biodiversity is indicated by the number of species and sub-species present, and the number of different breeds within species. The latter also indicates genetic variability within species. As enumerated in livestock censuses, there are ten species of livestock in India. These are; cattle, buffaloes, sheep, goat, horses and ponies, donkey, camel, yak, mithun and pigs. Yak and mithun are sub-species of cattle. On the basis of current knowledge, cattle, excluding yak and mithun have as many as 26 well defined indigenous breeds. Buffaloes have no less than 15 breeds; some of these are considered as best milk-breeds in the world. Goats have 20 breeds, and sheep as many as 40 breeds, (GoI, Ministry of Agriculture, Deptt. of Animal Husbandry and Dairying, Report of the Steering Group a National Livestock Development Policy, 1996). The number of breeds within a species indicates genetic variability. The numbers regarding breeds just given are not based upon up-to-date and complete scientific knowledge. Only now the National Bureau of Animal Genetic Resources (NBAGR), Karnal has initiated a programme of genetic mapping. As a matter of a fact, till recently conservation of livestock biodiversity was not a concern of public policy. Expected productivity gains (milk, meat, wool per animal) nor could withstand environmental stress, and, therefore, yielded to high mortality rates (GoI, Ministry. of Agriculture, Deptt. of Animal Husbandry and Dairying, 1996).

4.1 Feed Availability, Requirement and Consumption

Since feed is critical to livestock production and its environmental impact, a few observations relating to feed are in order. Major sources of animal feed in the country are: (1) agricultural by-products (dry) fodder and concentrates, and (2) cultivated green fodder. The output of both the by-products depends upon the volume of agricultural output, which in turn depends upon yields of crops and cropped area. The output of cultivated green fodder too depends upon the yield and area allocated for fodder crop production. A notable point is that there is an actual and potential trade-off between output of feed as agricultural by-product and feed from fodder crop production. With negligible scope for increasing land area under cultivation as is presently the case in India, a shift of area to fodder crops will add to fodder output but there will be a corresponding fall in the by-product feed from other crops.

Whereas output of green fodder in any year ought to be equal to its availability as animal feed, that may not be true in the case of by-products. International trade in concentrates affects their domestic availability. India has for long been an exporter of oil-cake and meal largely to European Community (EC) countries. To the extent of such exports, net domestic availability of concentrates is reduced. Feed compounds manufactured out of domestic supplies of concentrates, if noted as animal feed within the country, make no difference to concentrates availability. If exported, it reduces the availability. Availability is also affected by non-feed uses of agricultural by-products. There are reports that a good portion of soyabean oil-cake output in India finds its way to human consumption. Similarly, in agriculturally advanced regions of the country such as Punjab rice straw is burned after harvest, not to mention its increasing use as a packaging material in the country.

The nutritional requirement of the livestock population in any year may be more, equal to or less than the net availability of feed. On the other hand, actual consumption i.e. feed intake in any year cannot exceed net availability. In short, considered *ex-post* consumption must equal availability. The condition also provides a check on the validity of consumption and availability estimates. If *post-facto*, the two are not equal to each other then the estimate of either of the two or both are incorrect. Estimate of consumption has acquired an importance it never had before. All the direct and indirect environmental effects of a livestock production system, as we will see in the following sub-section, are related to feed consumption rather than to feed availability or requirement.

It is rare to find studies on feed consumption (intake) of different categories of livestock. The exceptions are those by Amble *et al.* (1965) and Jain and Shivtar Singh (1990). In both of these *consumption* of different types of feed per day per animal of the different categories of bovines are available. The primary source for arriving at the all India feed consumption rates in both these studies are sample surveys, including repeat surveys conducted by the Indian Agricultural Statistics Research Institute (IASRI) since the second half of 1950s to early 1980. The surveys were conducted in the typical livestock tracts of the country. Both sets of estimates of all India consumption rates of bovines involve wide assumptions. However, in comparison to Amble's rates, in every item Jain and Shivtar Singh's rates are higher as expected, since agricultural production by-product feed output had been growing while bovine stock had been growing at a slower rate (Mishra and Sharma, 1990).

4.2 Environmental Impact

Utilising the food consumption rates provided by Jain and Shivtar Singh (1990) we have made a study of the environmental impact of the country's livestock production system with reference to bovine population as of 1992 (Mishra and Dikshit, 2004). The effects fall into two broad groups: global and local (national). Emission of green house gases or their emission prevented has global warming effect. Local effects are in the nature of resource saving. According to our estimate, in 1992 total methane (CH_4) emission from the bovine production system was of the order of 9.767 million metric tonnes (MT). Most of it is from enteric fermentation of feed fed to animals, or emission from 'manure management' (0.202 MT) and from burning of dung cake (0.21 MT) are negligible. At the same time, 6.0 MT of CO_2 emission was prevented due to animal energy used in agriculture in place of fossil-fuel (diesel). This much of emission would occur if over 70 million working animals in 1992 were replaced by tractors. At the replacement rate of 12 bullocks to a tractor, replacement of the stock would require 6.0 million tractors and about 20 MT of diesel oil to run them annually, burning of which would cause CO_2 emission. Thus, use of animal energy yields double environment benefit; saves fossil-fuel and prevents CO_2 emission. Furthermore, it contributes to

India's self-reliance as the country imports 70 per cent of it's petroleum requirement.

Local impacts are all environmentally beneficial. Our estimates show that if agricultural by-products (dry fodder and concentrates) used as animal feed were to be replaced by cultivated green fodder, as much as 46 million hectare of land would be required to produce it. Currently India devotes about 5 per cent of the total cropped area i.e. not more than eight million hectare for green fodder production. Dry dung cake is a renewable bio-energy source. If it was to be replaced by another bio-energy source, fuel wood, production of latter would require 2.0 million hectare of land to be kept continuously under fuel wood plantation. Besides considerable land saving due to the system, dung used as manure in terms of nutrients saves 2.5 million tonnes of ammonium sulphate, about 0.5 million tonnes of superphosphate and 0.8 million tonnes of muriate of potash. And, being an organic fertiliser it sustains natural fertility of the soil. We also attempted, under certain assumptions, to estimate the value of these benefits. We found that the total value of the environmental benefits (about Rs.120000 crore) was larger than the value of output of the livestock sector (Rs. 79,000 crore) in 1997-98. One obvious conclusion is that any sustainable development strategy of the livestock economy should be able to retain, indeed try to enhance, its environmental benefits.

5. Sustainable Development Strategy

5.1 General Observations

A production system is sustainable in the sense that output flow from the system can be maintained indefinitely in future, if the materials and energy inputs to the system are derived from renewable resources. If input level remains constant, the output flow will remain constant, and, thus, the system will remain stationary, just replacing itself as time passes. But human effort always is to increase the flow of output either by increasing the level of inputs or by changing the technology of production. However, irrespective of technology, there is an upper limit to the flow of materials and energy inputs from the renewable resources, if the latter are not depleted, damaged or endangered in the process of pushing up the flow of inputs. Therefore, development can be sustainable only if the renewable resources, from which the production system receives its materials and energy inputs, are maintained in future, in quantity and quality.

A livestock production system is sustainable since the animals engaged in the production process receive nutrients and energy from feed, and feed is a renewable resource. However, feed production depends upon land, which is an all time limitational resource. This is true whether feed is obtained from grazing on rangeland, produced using land or as by-products of agriculture. For a given growth rate of feed availability, growth in output flow can take place either by increasing the size of livestock population, or increasing yield rates of animals or both. If, the initial or actually realised yield rates are lower than the potential rates, the latter course of development is more efficient.

The sustainability conditions discussed above relate to renewable and limitational resource base of the livestock production system. There are two more conditions system's sustainable development ought to satisfy. Firstly, it should not reduce livestock biodiversity and genetic variability. These are now considered as genetic wealth of the country concerned, inherited from the past. The present generation, therefore, has no right to tamper with it, and should leave it as such for future generations. Secondly, harmful environmental effects of the production system like emission of greenhouse gases should not increase, rather be reduced in the course of development.

5.2 Sustainable Livestock Development Strategy

We take it for granted that in India mixed farming mode will continue to be in practice in future. We also assume that, following the past trend, the bovine population which is at the core of the mixed farming system, will not be growing at a rate higher than 1.0 per cent a year. Indeed it may come to stabilise at a certain level, since growth rates of cattle and buffaloes have been decelerating (Birthal and Parthasarthy Rao, 2002). A development strategy, in general consists of three sets of elements, (1) goals, (2) means to achieve the goals, and (3) policies to put the means into action. The strategy of development in our specific context is discussed below.

5.2.1 Development Goals

At present livestock production system is geared to production of milk, meat and animal energy. The social preference ordering among these products was discussed in Section 3. This preference ordering is not likely to change in the near future. In the long run, however, if agricultural mechanisation is not contained, the demand for animal energy will decline. This will have two consequential effects — one environmental, and the other economic. The environmental effect would be increasing use of non-renewable fossil-fuel sources of energy in agriculture, and corresponding rise in emission of green house gases, CO_2 in particular. The second effect would be declining rate of replacement of working animals' stock, particularly of cattle bullocks, the predominant part of the stock. This will pose the increasing problem of disposal of male cattle calfs, more so if the reproduction rate of the cattle population were to increase as it ought to increase, since the breeding efficiency of the population (ratio of cows in-milk to total number of breedable cows) is presently quite low, less than 50 per cent. The traditional mode of male calf disposal, as in the case of buffaloes, of letting it die of starvation, besides being cruel, is economically inefficient, since a certain cost has been incurred from its embryo stage to birth and on to suckling age. Even if the replacement rate of cattle bullock stocks is restrained from falling as a matter of sustainable development strategy, improvement in the breeding efficiency of the cattle population will continue to pose this problem. Since the scope for culling by slaughter is extremely limited, male calfs (including of buffaloes) should be reared up to a certain age, before being exported for meat to other countries. This will enlarge the opportunity to produce milk for domestic demand and bovine meat animals for world demand. Thus, the goals of sustainable livestock development in India ought to be:

(1) To increase flow of outputs of milk and meat animals;

(2) To continue using animal energy in agriculture;

(3) To conserve livestock biodiversity and genetic variability within species, and

(4) To minimise greenhouse gases emission from the production system.

It may be noted that there is no conflict among these goals. Conservation of biodiversity and genetic variability is an ethical goal. So it stands on its own. And, goal number (1), (2) and (4) are simultaneously achievable without affecting each other adversely.

5.2.2 Means to Achieve the Goals

The essential means to achieve the goals is a well fed, healthy animal, irrespective of its age, sex and function. That every member of the livestock population acquires such a status, the enabling means are availability of feed and fodder sufficient to meet the nutritional requirement of the population and health care facilities. Availability of dry fodder and concentrates has been growing *pari-pasu* with growth in agricultural production. Green fodder availability has also been growing with increase in area under irrigation, even though the share of fodder area to cropped area has remained constant. In fact, because agriculture's growth rate has been substantially higher compared to the growth rate of livestock population, per animal availability has been increasing (Mishra and Sharma, 1990). During 1990s agricultural growth had slackened, but it was still higher than the growth rate of the bovine population. The prospect for increasing per animal feed availability in future appears promising, also because of current policy emphasis on agricultural diversification which favours livestock production. The real problem is how to enhance nutritive value of available feed, specially of dry roughages at the field level.

As regards health care facilities, these fall into two groups: (1) facilities for surveillance, prevention and control of epidemic diseases like rinder pest, foot and mouth disease, and (2) veterinary facilities, including artificial insemination centres which cater to livestock with individual farmers. There is already a vast public infrastructure in the country of the second type of facilities. With increasing market orientation in all sorts of services, it is likely that veterinary facilities will increase under private initiative. The first type of facilities by their very nature belong to public sector. Provision of these facilities is found to be very inadequate (Deptt. of AH&D, Steering Group, Report, 1996).

As nutrition and health of the livestock population improves with time, its reproductive and productive characteristics are bound to improve. Better nutritive feeding alone will lead to increase in the breeding efficiency of cattle and buffaloes, will reduce the age at first calving, prolong the productive age, and will reduce age and sex-specific mortality rates. It will increase the milk yield per milch animal, as also yield per animal in-milk.

Besides nutrition and health related means, purposive intervention in the breeding processes is another means to improve the productive traits of animals. Crossbreeding of indigenous cows with exotic breeds started in early 1960s and pursued till date. India is a classic example of such intervention with single purpose of increasing milk production in the country, completely ignoring the other goal of the cattle system, namely animal energy required for agriculture. Originally crossbreeding was supposed to cover only so called 'non-descript' indigenous cows. But latter it was extended to cover even well defined indigenous cattle breeds like Haryana, Gir, Rathi, Tharparker and Sahiwal. Along the same line, the 'non-descript' buffaloes across the country began to be crossed with well-known breeds like Murrah for the same purpose. Admittedly, behind all this effort at crossbreeding, there was no consciousness regarding conservation of genetic variability within the cattle and buffalo population in the country. Man has been doing selective breeding, choosing best bulls to sire the females in his stock from the time livestock were domesticated. This route to improve productive traits does not interfere with the genetic variability of a population composed of several breeds, provided selection is within breeds. The point is that selective breeding is the suitable means for increasing productive traits as well as for serving the third goal of sustainable development, namely conservation of livestock biodiversity and genetic variability.

5.3 Policy Implications

The means to achieve goals of sustainable livestock development require a package of state policies to set them in action. It must be recognised, however, that the role of the state is limited since livestock production is in private hands. Wherever private agents are involved, policies can be only promotional, and can be implemented through a set of incentives and disincentives. There are, however, areas of social interest in which private behaviour needs to be regulated or direct state action is necessary, as for instance health related areas. Let us now consider policy options that exist in respect of feeding, breeding and animal health.

Feeding of animals is in private hands. Better digestibility of feed, specially of roughages, is known to contribute to better nutrition and productivity as well as reduce methane emission from enteric fermentation of feed. Considerable research on feed digestibility has been done in the country. But adoption of techniques and method for improving digestibility at the farmers' level is poor (Khub Singh and C.S. Prasad, 2002). Perhaps involvement of farmers in generation and adoption of technology may yield better result. Production of concentrate-by-products has been moving to milling industries. This has led to fast growth of compound feed manufacturing. Here it is necessary for the state to set quality standards and monitor its implementation.

As regards breeding policy, we have already commented upon indiscriminate crossbreeding followed so far. The focus should now shift to selective breeding, keeping in view the agro-climatic conditions in which well known breeds have evolved. As regards the unknown category bracketed as 'non-descript', the urgent task is to do their genetic mapping in different livestock tracts of the country. Conservation of threatened species like donkey, camel, horses and ponies and yak should also form part of the breeding policy. Here again the success of breeding and conservation policy will depend upon cooperation and involvement of concerned people such as farmers, their associations, and breeders' organisations.

In the course of half a century of development planning a vast network of health related infrastructure has already been built in the country. All that is needed is to improve the quality of the services provided to livestock holders. It has been suggested that charging a fee for the service provided may help in toning up the system. However, infrastructure for surveillance and disease control and so also quarantine facilities at ports are quite inadequate. These need to be strengthened. A health inspection system would become necessary before quarantine stage when export of bovine male calfs for meat production in other countries becomes a feasible proposition.

Research and Development (R&D) in animal sciences and technologies relating to feeding, breeding and health is a necessary complement of any livestock development strategy. Under the aegis of the Indian Council of Agricultural Research (ICAR) a pretty large establishment in terms of the number of scientists, labs and research stations is already there in place. A review of technologies generated in various areas shows impressive performance. But their extension, rather adoption at field level appears to be woefully inadequate. How to achieve this end should be the major question before policymakers. For the animal scientists and technologists it is now necessary to integrate environmental aspects of livestock production system into their work.

Finally, mechanisation of agriculture based on fossil-fuel needs to be contained in the interest of sustainable development of the mixed farming system. State governments have been providing subsidy and soft loan to farmers, mostly large farmers for purchase of tractors. Then there are instances of free power supply to farmers for political considerations. All these incentives must be removed. From environmental angle alternative to animal energy are other renewable source of energy such as solar and wind based energy.

6. Information Base and Socio-Economic Research

In a recent lecture I have reviewed the status of livestock statistics in India (Mishra, 1999). You look at any aspect, be it livestock numbers, feed fed to animals, output quantities, estimates of output values or of value added, available statistics suffer from lack of quality, reliability and timeliness. Then, there are aspects on which statistics are simply not available. A good and updated information base is as much necessary for policymaking as for economic and social research relating to livestock. And, for the success or failure of policies at the ground level, research of the latter type is equally necessary.

But economic and social research relating to livestock has not received the attention it deserves (Mishra, 1995). Indeed, it has been the last priority of academic professionals and government research institutions. There are in the country umpteen number of Agricultural Economics Research Centres maintained by the Ministry of Agriculture, Government of India. But livestock is assiduously kept out of their research purview. It should come as no surprise that there is not even one centre in this large country devoted to economic and social research on livestock, or for that matter, on environment aspects of the livestock production systems. One palpable reason for poor research interest in this area has been lack of promotion and financial support from government agencies, including those that are directly concerned with agricultural or livestock development in the country.

7. Concluding Observations

In this paper, we have made an attempt to distinguish between different livestock farming systems and then have tried to show that the mixed farming system, in which livestock and agriculture are integrated or interdependent, is environmentally most benign. Based on the experience of mixed farming system in India, we have delineated its characteristics, the linkages between livestock and agriculture, between the livestock population and livestock production system, and the impact of the latter on environment, both on it's input as well as output side. We have then given a brief quantitative account of India's livestock economy in order to prepare the ground for examining the conditions of it's sustainable development. A system based upon renewable sources of material inputs and energy is by definition sustainable. So, we have concluded that India's mixed farming system is open for sustainable development in future, provided appropriate state policies are adopted. In the past policies have been formulated and implemented from top down. Success, however, depends upon reversing the direction of policy formulation and implementation. Finally, we have pointed out that information base and socio-economic research relating to livestock in India, so crucial for formulation of right policies and their implementation, is woefully inadequate.

References

Amble, V.N. *et al.*, (1965a) "Feed Requirement of Bovines and Possibilities of Meeting Them", *Indian Journal of Agricultural Economics*, Vol. 20, No. 1, January-March.

Birthal, P. and Parthasarathy Rao, P. (eds), (2002). "Technology Options for Sustainable Livestock Production in India", *Proceedings of the Workshop on Documentation, Adoption, and Impact of Livestock Technologies in India*, 18-19 Jan 2001, ICRISAT, Patancheru, India.

Cees de Haan *et al.*, (1997), "Livestock and the Environment: Finding A Balance", *Report of Study Coordinated by the FAO, the United States Agency for International Development and the World Bank*, FAO, Rome.

Government of India, *15th Indian Livestock Census, 1992*, Directorate of Economics and Statistics, Department of Agriculture & Cooperation, Ministry of Agriculture, New Delhi.

Government of India, Ministry of Agriculture, Deptt. of Animal Husbandry and Dairying (1996). *Report of the Steering Group on National Livestock Development Policy*, New Delhi.

Jain, J.P. and Shivtar Singh (1990). "Qualitative and Quantitative Insufficiency of Livestock Feeds by 2001 AD, and Possibilities of Bridging the Gap", *Indian Journal of Animal Sciences*, 60(10), 1224-1229, ICAR, New Delhi.

Mishra, S.N. and R.K. Sharma (1990). *Livestock Development in India: An Appraisal*, Institute of Economic Growth (IEG), Vikas Publishing House, Delhi.

Mishra, S.N. (1995). "India's Livestock Economy: A Perspective on Research", *Indian Journal of Agricultural Economics*, Vol. 50, No.3.

————. (1999). "Dr. V.G. Panse Memorial Lecture: The Status of Livestock Statistics in India", *Journal of the Indian Society of Agricultural Statistics*, Vol. 52(3), pp. 273-289.

Mishra, S.N. and A.K. Dikshit (2004). *Environment and Livestock in India*, Manohar Publishers & Distributors, Delhi.

Singh, Khub and C.S. Prasad (2002). "Potential of Nutritional Technologies in Improving Livestock Productivity" in Birthal and Parthasarthy Rao (ed.), *op.cit.*

3

Land System and its Reforms in India[1]

S.K. RAY

Even with a dismal if not pathetic record of performance, land reforms programme in India enjoys such a high respectability and popular support, that an adverse criticism of it is viewed almost as a sacrilege. This love and faith on the programme, however, was shaken by the economic crisis that surfaced in 1991. Several scholars are now acknowledging the futility of its further continuation, and urging the governments to make changes in land policy (Dandekar, 1994; Vyas, 1994; Rao and Gulati, 1994; Appu, 1995). Persons passionately involved with the programme too agree that it needs a more dispassionate re-examination.

To appreciate the context in which the need to recast the land policy is now felt, this study makes an attempt to review the land system and its reforms in India. A summary account of the land reforms programme in post-independent India is presented first. This is followed by presenting an appraisal of the last five decades experience of implementing land reforms programme. It is against this background the emerging perspectives and policy issues are discussed in the last section. To provide a flavour of the comments and criticisms made on the subject, the study borrows liberally from the writings of some keen observers of Indian rural scene.

1. Land Reforms Programme in Post-independent India

At the time of Independence, India inherited a semi-feudal agrarian structure with onerous tenure arrangements over substantial areas. The ownership and control of land was highly concentrated in a relatively few landlords and intermediaries. The principal interest of

1 Revised and condensed version of a paper published in *Indian Journal of Agricultural Economics*, Vol.51, Nos.1 and 2, Jan.-June 1996.

this controlling group in agriculture was to extract maximum rental from tenants, either in cash or in kind. Often tenants of land under intermediary and landlord control sublet their lands in smaller plots to working cultivators, thus smaller holdings increased. Under this arrangement, economic motivation to develop farm land for increased production or to improve the economic conditions of cultivators was lacking. At the same time, working cultivators after paying high rent had no surplus to invest in farm improvement. They had neither resources nor knowledge for increasing agricultural production. Thus the agricultural land resource of India, along with its operators was gradually impoverished because economic motivation tended toward exploitation rather than toward investment and improvement.

With increasing pressure on land the operating land base of many working cultivators was further reduced. Land occupancy rights became increasingly insecure. Often cultivators were continuously shifted from one plot to another according to the whims of superior holders. Land was divided into small fragments, each owned or leased by cultivators whose objective was subsistence. Together then, the size and distribution of land holding, cultivation practices and product sharing, operated concertedly to hold down farm income. Over time, a large number of farms became disincentive-ridden due to size disability. A substantial portion of such cultivators sought to supplement their farm income by working as hired labourers competitive with even poorer landless workers. Independent India thus emerged with serious imbalances in man-land relationship among the three principal groups in the agricultural sector, *viz.*, proprietors, working cultivators and labourers.

1.1 Policy Objectives for Structural Reorganisation

Following Independence, land reform as well as the abolition of intermediaries was considered an essential prerequisite for increasing agricultural production and for establishing an egalitarian society. Each of India's Five Year Plans since 1951 had set forth a policy for land reform. The land reform programmes were built around three major types of land reform measures: abolition of intermediary tenures, regulation of size of holding and, settlement and regulation of tenancy. As a result of these programmes, it was hoped that a different set of rights and duties would emerge in which the freedom of each interest would be regulated and some interests considered harmful for progress in agriculture would be eliminated.

Land policy as laid down in the First Five Year Plan can be viewed from two angles: (i) conception of different interests in land, and (ii) the effect of man-land relationship on agricultural production. It was conceived that the freedom with which intermediaries transacted their business had an adverse effect on agricultural production. The First Plan, therefore, set out to regulate the interests of intermediaries, large owners, small and middle owners, tenants-at-will, and landless workers. The Plan recognised the pattern of land occupancy and cultivation as a fundamental issue of national development.

The Second Five Year Plan stated: "the abolition of intermediaries and the protection given to tenants are intended to give the tiller of the soil his rightful place in the agrarian system and by reducing or eliminating the burden he has borne in the past, to provide him with fuller incentives for increasing agricultural production. Similarly, to bring the tenant into direct relation with the State and to put an end to the tenant-landlord nexus are essential steps in the establishment of a stable rural economy" (Government of India, 1956, p. 178). Complementary to these objectives were the policies of land ceilings, consolidation of holdings and encouragement of co-operative joint farming.

The central thesis behind the abolition of intermediaries was that ownership of land be clearly identified with management and operation of land. The owner himself should operate and manage the farm business.

Ceiling on land holdings were designed to offset the extremely uneven distribution of agricultural land. The policy implications of this measure were (i) to meet the land hunger of working cultivators, (ii) to reduce disparity in agricultural incomes, in ownership and in the use of land, and (iii) to increase employment opportunity in the rural sector. At the same time, consolidation of holdings was advocated to consolidate the scattered holdings of individual cultivators to form a single tract susceptible to more efficient management.

While ceiling on holdings and consolidation of plots were planned to increase the land base of the working cultivators, it was argued that reforms through structural changes could be secured only when the actual tillers of the soil were given a fair share of the fruits of their labour. This called for an overall change in the tenurial conditions of cultivators. Tenancy reforms were launched to confirm the rights of occupancy of tenants, secure their possession of tenanted land and also regulate rents on leased land.

But there existed a very large number of very small holdings. This group of minuscule holdings constituted one of the most difficult problems in agricultural reorganisation. The possibility of co-operative farming as a means of overcoming the difficulties presented by tiny holdings was discussed. It was pointed out that if these smaller holdings were grouped into larger units and farmed co-operatively then the advantage of large-scale organisation would become available. Larger financial resources for agricultural development could be provided and the volume of employment increased.

The rationale for co-operative farming grew out of an examination of the man-land ratio and the supposed economies of scale achievable on large-size units, even though there is little evidence to support the contention that greater per capita production will be forthcoming if holdings are pooled and cultivated jointly. Studies of farm management have indicated that the size of the holding and the yield under traditional agriculture are inversely correlated. The statistical basis of this generalisation has been challenged and it is now accepted that it is difficult to generalise from aggregate data that have not been subjected to careful scrutiny. However, it appears that if adjustment is made for differences in soil fertility, and proper yield and income variables are chosen, then there will be a strong general tendency towards constant returns to scale in Indian agriculture. This, along with the natural reluctance of cultivators to give up their newly won rights to land, seriously hindered co-operative farming. The failure of co-operative farming as a policy was tacitly admitted in the Fourth Five Year Plan when no additional programmes were proposed.

The net effect of all these reforms was presumed to loosen the rigidly stratified rural society so that each cultivator in accordance with his capability could find an opportunity to advance. The owner was envisaged to become the manager as well as the operator of his holdings.

1.2 The Reform Controversy

From the very beginning, legislative measures for overall agrarian reorganisation faced resistance from several quarters. The subject was widely discussed and debated. Many argued that ceiling and tenancy legislation would in effect infringe upon constitutional guarantees.

Others opined that the proposed legislation was an 'eye wash' and did not go far enough.

The adequacy of the underlying economic analysis on which the programmes were based was challenged by several economists.[1] They expressed fear that agricultural production of the country would be seriously affected if larger holdings were reduced to smaller size by the imposition of ceilings. They argued that the smaller the size of holding, the lower the standards of efficiency and manoeuvrability in management. Distribution of land to a large number of cultivators in small holdings would increase the number of small holders and reduce agricultural production. The economic use of machinery and the adoption of modern methods of agriculture would not be easy to obtain for smaller farms; ceilings on holdings could not bring out enough land to meet the land hunger of the working cultivators and agricultural labourers. Further, it was argued that land is property; imposition of a capital levy in the form of ceiling on agricultural holding would be an injustice when similar measures were not simultaneously adopted for other sectors.

For several years both the Union and State Governments remained prisoners of indecision on this issue. Hesitancy on the ceiling issue was reflected in the original draft outline of the First Five Year Plan.

> "On the larger farms, production will fall and, for a period at any rate, on the other farms also, and it may well be that the decline in production may have a serious effect on the well-being and stability of rural society as whole" (quoted by Thorner, 1955, pp. 62-63).

The final version of the First Five Year Plan took a firmer position:

> "From the social aspect, which is not less important than the economic, a policy for land may be considered adequate in the measure in which, now and in the coming years, it reduces disparities in wealth and income, eliminates exploitation, provides security for tenant and worker and, finally promises equality of status and opportunity to different sections of the rural population (Government of India, 1953b, p. 184).

In formulating the land policy towards substantial owners of land, the First Five Year Plan remarked:

1. For an excellent commentary on the debate and discussion on the subject that followed, see (Dandekar, 1994, pp. 41-88).

> "If it were the sole object of policy to reduce the holdings of the larger owners with a view to providing for the landless or for increasing the farms of those who now have uneconomic fragments, the facts at present available suggest that these aims are not likely to be achieved in any substantial measure. The question whether some limit should not be placed on the amount of land that an individual may hold has, therefore, to be answered in terms of general principles rather than in relation to the possible use that could be made of land in excess of any limit that may be set.... It appears to us that, in relation to land (as also in other sectors of the economy) individual property in excess of any norm that may be proposed has to be justified in terms of public interest, and not merely on grounds of individual rights or claims. We are, therefore, in favour of the principle that there should be an upper limit to the amount of land that an individual may hold" (Government of India, 1953b, pp. 187-188).

As a first step towards reorganisation of the land holding system, the Planning Commission suggested a census on land holdings during 1953. The proposal, however, was coldly received by the State Governments. In explaining this, Thorner commented:

> "In many cases this was taken to mean that the imposition of ceilings might be deferred until after the census of land-holding had been completed. It became clear both to opponents and proponents of ceiling limits that the information collected could be used to buttress the arguments of one or the other side. It was also appreciated that the data obtained would depend in larger part on the way the questionnaires were framed" (Thorner, 1955, pp. 62-63).

The Planning Commission schedules of January 1954 for the proposed census of land holdings failed to impress the State Governments until it was diluted further and made acceptable to all the states in November 1954. But even this weakened form of the proposed census of land holdings did not materialise. Only Hyderabad conducted a well designed survey. Uttar Pradesh refused to conduct a census while Kashmir did not participate on the ground that the question of redistribution of land had already been settled. Some states copied the *patwari* records, some confined the census for holdings of size ten acre and above and some conducted a nominal sample survey only (see Thorner, 1955, pp. 62-63). In his review of the entire episode, Thorner wrote:

> "Based upon the faulty village records and the seriously defective January, 1954 schedules, they may well prove inaccurate and misleading. In retrospect the tussle over the census can be seen as yet another phase in the broader controversy over limitations.
>
> While the officials wrangled over schedules and categories, the landlords hastened their steps to forestall the possible effects of ceilings.... The past few years have witnessed a nation-wide wave of displacement of tenants by landlords. There have also been innumerable partitions of family properties, with the aim of making units of ownership appear smaller than they really are so that the landlords will be able to slip under the proposed ceilings. For the same purpose there have been many transfers to relatives outside the immediate family, to caste fellows, and to 'friends' (e.g., the *Benami* transactions reported, for example, from Travancore). In view of the special consideration urged for efficiently managed farms (the breaking up of which would presumably lead to a fall in output), some large owners have thought it wise to purchase tractors. Since the land reforms typically place the holdings of co-operatives and joint-stock companies outside their purview, more than a few families have transformed themselves into cooperatives; some affluent landlords have organised themselves into corporations for the production and refining sugarcane" (Thorner, 1955, pp. 68-69).

2. Impact of Structural Reorganisation

Land policy in the First Five Year Plan was thus formulated without sufficient knowledge about the size and distribution of land holdings in the rural sector. A considerable volume of data was collected for the first time in the Eighth Round (1954) of the National Sample Survey (NSS) for size and distribution of land holdings. However, the draft report of the NSS Eighth Round was only submitted to the Union Government in January 1960, nearly six years later. It, therefore, did not serve the purpose of planners to assess the magnitude of the problem involved in structural reorganisation.

Defects in policy planning became conspicuous in the implementation stage of the land reform programme. Legal, administrative and other factors became principal bottlenecks. In the process, the error of doing the right things too slowly became increasingly costly. Policymakers failed to take into account the importance of the time dimension for the success of these reforms. A go-slow programme of implementation failed to make effective impact upon many working cultivators.

Under the Indian Constitution, land reform is a state subject. Apart from the broad principles directly bearing on the distribution of land resources, tenancy relations are under the control of the several states. Consequently, while the main features of the reform legislation in different states are practically identical, there is a wide difference in the scope of the work actually undertaken. The result is that tenancy problems are concentrated in certain states and are not as important in other states.

As a result of a series of investigations and personal observations, it is generally conceded that the reforms are not complete. For example, while rents may be limited by law to one-fourth of the crop in a given state, this law is not enforced in many cases. Furthermore, land ownership can be divided among the members of a joint family so that each member can own his legal share of the land with the result that the total family holding is several times above the legal limit. The large number of evictions, many justified on the grounds of a reform provision which encouraged the right of land resumption for self-cultivation, and the so-called 'voluntary' surrender of land which were especially prevalent during the 1950s give visible evidence that security of tenure is not an accepted fact of life in India.

Under the conditions prevailing before the introduction of the seed-fertiliser technology some observers have argued that the weaknesses in tenancy, rent control, *etc.*, have not been important constraints on production. However, the problems of land tenancy and ownership have acquired special significance with the technological advances in agriculture. Land cultivated on tenancy or rented arrangements can enable the cultivator to enlarge the scale of his operations to economically justify mechanisation and his own water supply. However, the increased productivity of the high-yielding varieties (HYVs) has also led to a trend of rising rents, or in the absence of income from this source, the reclaiming of land for owner cultivation. As a result, both the returns from, and the security of, rented and leased lands are apparently decreasing.

A cultivator who does not have security of tenure or who must pay a high proportion of output in rents is less likely to invest in land improvements, adopt HYVs or use inputs up to the optimal economic amounts. Therefore, tenants are likely to suffer a relative decline in income compared to owners, as the modern technology becomes more widely spread.

In order to safeguard the interests of the tenants, the Chief Ministers' conference in July 1967 recommended the following measures:

1. Tenants in cultivating possession of land should not be disturbed and should be given complete security of tenancy by: (i) staying all evictions, (ii) suspending the right of resumption where such right has been given to landowners, and (iii) regulating voluntary surrenders in such a way that landowners do not get an advantage by persuading tenants to surrender their tenancy.
2. The rate of rent should be reduced to the level of one-fourth or one-fifth of the gross produce so that the tenant is in a position to improve his land.
3. Record of tenancy should be prepared as a special operation and maintained up-to-date.
4. Special attention should be given to ensure credit and other facilities to tenants and small holders for increasing agricultural production.

Since the 1967 Chief Ministers' Conference, many more meetings have followed, each pledging faithful implementation of reform measures. But, as the 1978-83 Draft Five Year Plan (Government of India, 1978) observed, the will to implement the policy has been sadly lacking all along.

In a painstakingly completed study, Appu has made a critical appraisal of policy, legislation and implementation of land reforms in India since Independence. He observed that "the significant features of all those laws were the slow pace of legislation, inadequacies in the content of the legislation, the time-consuming procedures laid down and the role of the judiciary in frustrating the implementation of the enacted laws" (Appu, 1995, p. 210). Notwithstanding these serious limitations, Appu was of the opinion that "the implementation of the laws for the Abolition of Intermediary Interests was far more satisfactory than the implementation of the laws enacted in later years for the Reform of Tenancy and the imposition of Ceilings on Agricultural Holdings" (Appu, 1995, p. 210). He wrote:

> "The most important beneficial result of the reform was that it put an end to the system of parasitic intermediaries and brought some 25 million erstwhile tenants into direct relationship with the state.... With the abolition of intermediary interests the principal tenants became owners of the land. The erstwhile principal tenants acquired a higher social and political status leading to a shift in the rural power structure. The more visible demonstration of this shift is the emergence of persons belonging to the upper layers of the so-called backward castes in the leadership of political parties.." (Appu, 1995, pp. 210-211).

On tenancy reform Appu found that it "...has not put an end to absentee ownership of land nor has it led to the disappearance of tenancies. It has only resulted in tenancies being pushed underground..." (Appu, 1995, p. 214). Summing up the performance on this front he wrote:

> "....Taking country as a whole, by 1992 ownership rights had been conferred on (or tenancy rights had been protected of) some 11 million tenants on 14.4 million acre of land. That constituted no more than 4 per cent of the operated area. It is interesting to note that the seven states of Assam, Gujarat, Himachal Pradesh, Karnataka, Kerala, Maharashtra and West Bengal account for 97 per cent of the beneficiaries. Practically no benefits accrued to the tenants in the other states. Even in these seven states tenancy reform led to the large scale eviction of tenants. Except in West Bengal, share-cropper by and large remained beyond the pale of tenancy reform everywhere. Only in West Bengal and Kerala did those in the lowest rungs of the peasant society receive solid benefits on the implementation of tenancy reform. The rights of some 14 lakh share-croppers were protected in West Bengal and in Kerala some 2.84 lakh rural poor, mostly agricultural labourers, became owners of tiny homesteads. As a result of tenancy reform there has been a sharp fall in the area of land under tenancy. From over one-half of the operated area on the eve of the reform, the area under tenancy has come down to about 15 per cent of the operated area now. The tenants acquired ownership rights or were made secure in only about 4 per cent of the operated area. Thus the

> reform led to the rural poor losing access to some 30 per cent of the operated area" (Appu, 1995, pp. 213-214).

The performance regarding the implementation of ceiling on agricultural holdings has turned out to be more disappointing. Appu observed:

> "....As a result of the implementation of the old and the new laws, by 1992 only about two million hectare of surplus land could be distributed to some 4.76 million beneficiaries. Thus the efforts spread over a period of three and a half decades to enforce ceilings and take over surplus land led to the redistribution of less than 2 per cent of the operated area. If we look into the performance of individual states, we find that the area distributed as a percentage of the total area operated is 17.4 for Jammu and Kashmir, 6.36 in West Bengal and five in Assam. In all the other states only less than one per cent of the operated area could be distributed. Obviously, the imposition of ceilings and the redistribution of surplus land made no impact on the agrarian structure in most states" (Appu, 1995, p. 216).

On balance, there seems to be some reasons to conclude that agrarian reorganisation in India has failed to make any considerable impact on the socio-economic conditions of the working cultivators. Indeed, the record so far is so depressing and frustrating that even an able administrator like Appu, who championed and spent a considerable part of his career in administering land reform programmes noted:

> "Thus the programmes of land reform implemented since Independence did not lead to any significant re-distribution of land, or, the removal of all the obstacles to increasing agricultural production. Of the three programmes considered in this study, the laws for the abolition of intermediary interests were implemented fairly well. But in the case of tenancy reform and ceilings on holdings, the policies adopted were ambivalent and there were large gaps between policy and legislation and between legislation and implementation. We have seen that as a result of the implementation of the tenancy laws, tenants became owners of or acquired rights in only about 4 per cent of the operated area. The enforcement of ceilings led to the redistribution of less than 2 per cent of the operated area. Thus these two measures taken together led to the

redistribution of only about 6 per cent of the operated area" (Appu, 1995, p. 217).

3. Emerging Perspectives and Policy Issues

It is against the background of the last five decades experience that the need to reformulate the land policy of India should be considered. Even persons emotionally attached with land reform programmes agree that the scope for improving implementation through legislative measures is now very limited. They point out, the socio-economic and political environment in which these programmes were introduced have changed so dramatically, that it would be almost impossible to carry out the reforms. Appu described the changed environment as follows:

> "....If the political will in favour of meaningful land reform was weak at independence and weaker still later on, it is non-existent today. Land reform has practically disappeared from the agenda of most political parties. This, in my view, is the inevitable consequence of the great changes that have taken place in the social and economic fields. With the abolition of intermediary interests the erstwhile superior tenants belonging mostly to upper and middle castes acquired a higher social status. Rise in agricultural productivity, rising land values and higher incomes from cultivation have added to their economic strength. Substantial landowners who wield great authority in rural India are bitterly opposed to ceilings on agricultural holdings. They are able to have their way because no serious efforts have been made to organise the landless and the land poor and enlist their support in favour of reforms. As for tenancy reform is concerned, there is a certain commonality of interest between all landowners - large, medium, small and even marginal. They are all passionately attached to their land and all of them are opposed to conferring benefits on insecure tenants. In the first round of land reform only the intermediaries were adversely affected. They were few in number and were weak politically. They had also made themselves obnoxious by aligning themselves with the colonial power. So it was easy enough to abolish intermediary interests. And it was done without hurting them much. But injuring the interests of the present class of landowners is an entirely different proposition. No political party that wishes to win

> elections and come to power can afford to do that. At the time of independence this class of landowners did not wield much political and economic power, and with a modicum of political will the reforms could have been implemented. But now it has become almost impossible to carry out the reforms" (Appu, 1995, pp. 232-233).

Dramatic changes have also taken place in agriculture. A fundamental and dynamic process of change with far-reaching consequences was introduced in Indian agriculture in 1965. This significant development was the introduction of modern scientific inputs of high-yielding seed varieties, controlled irrigation, chemical fertilisers, plant protection and mechanised power in tested management 'packages'.

The deeper significance of a technologically dynamic agriculture is that it provides opportunity to move from subsistence to viable economic farming and creates new potential for accelerated economic growth well beyond the agricultural sector. To exploit fully the potential created by this new environment in Indian agriculture, Dandekar argued that the structure of production should be changed (Dandekar, 1994). He observed with concern:

> "....that the policymakers did not see that a concomitant change in the relations of production was needed, was deplorable. In fact, they thought that the new technology had made even a small farmer viable so that the ceilings on land holdings could be further lowered. They missed two points. First, even with improved productivity, there is a limit to the population a given land can support at a minimum subsistence, the expectation about which itself changes over time, as it should, and leave behind a surplus for investment. Second, a new technology by itself does not change a static agriculture into a dynamic agriculture. It requires that the dynamism be passed on to the farmer, the essence of which is an opportunity to grow as a farmer. A ceiling on his landholding denies him such an opportunity. The same is true of the present tenancy laws which have practically abolished lease market in land" (Dandekar, 1994, p. 372).

Dandekar was forthright in making the policy prescription: "Hence, the first (emphasis added) item on the agenda of future agricultural policy should be the existing ceilings on landholdings and tenancy laws;

they should be removed altogether or should be relaxed in stages" (Dandekar, 1994, p. 373). Dandekar was aware of the criticisms which his policy recommendations might invite but, he dismissed them as ideological hangover bordering on hypocrisy. He wrote:

> "If this is done, enterprising farmers will enlarge their holdings by buying or leasing-in lands of small and marginal farmers, for whom it is not worth staying in agriculture. Consequently, landlessness will increase, as will employment of hired labour in agriculture. There is a strong aversion to this development and it is argued that it be avoided at all cost; that the population presently subsisting on agriculture should be held in agriculture and, as far as possible, kept self-employed even if on small and marginal farms. The view is held on two different ideological grounds. One is that self-employment is a value in itself and, whatever be the level of subsistence it may provide, it should be preferred to wage employment whatever be the wage. One would respect this, as one should respect all moral values, were it not for the fact that the exponents of it are almost all salaried and not self-employed persons.
>
> The other ideological ground is that this will lead to 'capitalist' farming, and to inevitable exploitation of labour. The prerequisite condition of capitalist agriculture is that it brings in capital into agriculture which is essential for adoption and exploitation of new technology. If the capital is generated within agriculture, that is, 'surplus value' in Marxian terminology which is at the bottom of what Marx called 'exploitation' of hired labour. But, if the workers would not leave any 'surplus value' behind for ploughing back into production, the economy would stagnate...." (Dandekar, 1994, pp. 373-374).

The strength of Dandekar's argument also contains its weakness. It fails to recognise fully the ground realities of the environment in which the proposed policy changes have to seek acceptance and a fair chance for implementation. True, the crisis that surfaced in the early 1990s from the acute domestic and international economic pressure and threatened to destroy the credibility of the country in international financial markets provided a necessary environment for initiating economic reforms. But, economic compulsion alone is not enough. Social and political compulsions are also important conditioning factors in making the policy environment receptive for change. Unfortunately, those have not yet become conducive to make Dandekar's policy prescription the first item on the agenda of future agricultural policy.

Modern technology, be it for agriculture or for industry, is in general labour saving and capital intensive. Indeed, available empirical evidence shows that the employment elasticity of output in agriculture has fallen sharply in the post-new technology period (Bhalla, 1987; Bhalla *et al.*, 1991; Ray, 1992). Consequently, any unrestrained opportunity to grow through modernisation of agriculture can only be at the cost of aggravating further the problem of unemployment. Dandekar's policy prescription is a deliberate attempt to create this situation for promoting growth in agriculture. He was in favour of building up pressure so that those who are not in a position to leave behind any surplus value for ploughing back in agriculture are forced to leave agriculture. But, where would they go? Obviously, not to industry, as it is also supposed to grow with labour saving modern technology. To resolve the dilemma, Dandekar made two suggestions: (i) to implement a minimum support price for labour, that is, "a minimum wage which, if the capitalist farmer would not pay, the government shall pay and employ the labour on worthwhile work"; and (ii) to the extent possible, employ the unemployed "in the creation of the social and physical infrastructure necessary for agricultural development rather in the operation of cultivation" (Dandekar, 1994, p. 374). These are laudable suggestions but, since the governments in India are presently going through acute financial difficulties, it is very difficult to implement them unless efforts are made to open up new avenues for mobilisation of resources.

It would be of interest to visualise the situation if the existing ceiling and tenancy laws were repealed. As agricultural income is not taxed, there would virtually be a beeline to make investments in land. Not only enterprising farmers would start enlarging their holdings by buying or leasing-in land; businessmen and moneyed people from other walks of life would also enter agriculture to make smashing profits. A convenient route to convert black money into white would thus be firmly established. Luxury farm houses would come up to which rich people would retreat to spend holidays and breathe fresh air. Land prices would soar and speculators would have a field day. The problem of uneconomic holdings would no longer remain. Millions of small and marginal farmers would be squeezed out from their small and tiny plots. However, in the absence of employment opportunities elsewhere, they would remain in agriculture and work in the estates of big landowners as tenants or wage labourers. In short, rural India would acquire a modern look closely resembling the U.S. and other developed countries, though it would continue to carry a huge labour force desperately struggling to eke out living directly or indirectly from agriculture.

The social and political costs of giving rural India such a modern look at this juncture need to be examined, especially when the incidence of poverty has still remained very high. Repealing the existing ceiling and tenancy laws would no doubt provide opportunities to enterprising farmers and moneyed people to grow; modernisation of agriculture might progress rapidly; the trickle down effect too might provide a minimum level of subsistence to all to survive. But the distribution of income would become more skewed, the gap between the rich and the poor would further widen, and the social friction would sharply intensify.

Moreover, the intense love of the intellectuals to study the poverty in India has not only emboldened them to speak with moral overtones but it has also in the process encouraged the politicians to make increasingly tall promises. The politics of competitive populism has now spread its tentacles to all political parties. It has made hypocrisy an accepted way of political life in India. Therefore, if the lack of political will has made implementation of land reforms legislation difficult, the politics of competitive populism, at least for some time to come, would also not allow withdrawal of these legislations.

It thus appears that the present policy environment is unlikely to permit drastic changes in the existing land reform legislations. Several measures need to be taken before considering such changes. An appropriate first step in this direction would be the imposition of agricultural income tax and agricultural holding tax. These measures fit well in the newly advocated philosophy for market-friendly approach. They can also help to mobilise the much needed resources for employing the unemployed in the creation of social and physical infrastructure for agricultural development. Moreover, a progressive agricultural holding tax may act as a deterrent against formation of large holdings in the future - while at the same time, it may encourage greater efficiency of farmers who insist on retaining their large holdings.

At the same time, several measures should be taken to discourage farming on uneconomic holdings. Innovative schemes, such as the free boring of wells provided in eastern Uttar Pradesh, should be used to encourage small and marginal farmers to consolidate their holdings. However, consolidation of holdings cannot considerably improve the areal extent of uneconomic holdings. Therefore, a floor limit should be imposed on the size of holding. Simultaneously, small and marginal farmers should be allowed to lease-in or lease-out land with adequate safeguards, so that they could adjust the sizes of their holdings and maintain them above the floor levels.

A plea is being made to relax the ceiling laws in order to encourage corporate sector to enter agriculture for commercial production of high-value and processed agricultural products, and earn thereby valuable foreign exchange for the country. Rather than relaxing the existing ceiling laws it would be better to consider the command area approach followed by the sugar industry and the area-based contract farming approach adopted by some corporate sector farms. Both provide an opportunity to earn foreign exchange without any direct involvement of the corporate sector in the production of required agricultural raw materials. The corporate sector should be welcomed as partners in the task for social and economic upliftment of rural India. They should set up agro-processing units in the rural areas and help in diversifying agriculture, encourage contract farming especially among small and marginal farmers by extending extension and marketing facilities, and also develop the required physical infrastructure support in their areas of operation. But their direct involvement in agricultural production should be firmly resisted till the workforce dependent on agriculture declines significantly to a low level.

The nitty-gritty of future agricultural policy should be worked out only after fully recognising the social, political and cultural milieu in which it has to operate. Increasingly sophisticated technologies are now available which can dramatically push up the growth rate of agriculture. However, not all of them are acceptable and desirable in the present Indian situation.

References

Appu, P.S. (1995). *Land Reforms in India: A Survey of Policy, Legislation and Implementation*, Land Reforms Unit, Lal Bahadur Shastri National Academy of Administration, Mussoorie, U.P. (mimeo).

Bhalla, Sheila (1987). "Trends in Employment in Indian Agriculture, Land and Asset Distribution", *Indian Journal of Agricultural Economics*, Vol. 42, No.4, October-December.

Bhalla, Sheila; Abhijit Sen, Rohini Nayyar and M.D. Sathe (1991). "Study Group on Employment Generation", in Government of India (1991), *Report of the National Commission on Rural Labour*, Vol. II Ministry of Labour, New Delhi.

Dandekar, V.M. (1994). *The Indian Economy: 1947-92, Volume 1, Agriculture*, Sage Publications India Pvt. Ltd., New Delhi.

Government of India (1953a). *Agriculture Legislation in India, Vol. IV - Land Reforms (Abolition of Intermediaries)*, Economic and Statistical Advisor, Ministry of Food and Agriculture, New Delhi.

————. (1953b). *The First Five Year Plan, 1951-56*, Planning Commission, New Delhi.

————. (1956). *Second Five Year Plan*, Planning Commission, New Delhi.

————. (1963). *Progress of Land Reforms*, Planning Commission, New Delhi.

————. (1978). *Draft Five Year Plan, 1978-1983*, Planning Commission, New Delhi.

Rao, C.H. Hanumantha and Ashok Gulati (1994). "Indian Agriculture: Emerging Perspectives and Policy Issues", *Economic and Political Weekly*, Vol. 29, No. 53, December 31.

Ray, S.K. (1992). "Development of Irrigation and Its Impact on Pattern of Land Use, Output Growth and Employment Generation", *Journal of Indian School of Political Economy*, Vol. 4, No. 4, October-December.

Thorner, Daniel (1955). *The Agrarian Prospect of India*, Delhi University Press, Delhi.

Vyas, V.S. (1994). "Agricultural Policies for the Nineties - Issues and Approaches", *Economic and Political Weekly*, Vol. 29, No. 26, June 25.

4

Public Works as an Anti-Poverty Programme

An Overview of Cross-Country Experience

K. SUBBARAO

Public works programmes have been important counter-cyclical interventions in developed and developing countries. These programmes were used in some Western countries during the depression years of the 1930s. More recently, several developing countries in Asia, Africa, and Latin America have adopted such programmes in some form or another. In terms of person-days of employment created, the programmes in Bangladesh and India are perhaps the largest in the world. Employment in India's nationwide programme (known as *Jawahar Rojgar Yojna,* or JRY) reached a billion workdays by 1995.

I begin here with a brief discussion of the role of public works as a safety net and then present the available cross-country experience on various aspects of the programme. The conclusions are then summarised.

1. Public Works: An Overview of Conceptual Issues

The argument for public works in nineteenth century England centred around the ethic of work — often long and nasty work. The programme is playing a different role in low-income developing countries. Its role is that of a safety net — conferring transfer and/ or stabilisation benefits to the poor, while at the same time using the poor's labour to build infrastructure for development. The programme's effectiveness depends on the benefits (transfer as well as stabilisation benefits), costs, and the way resources are raised to finance the programme. What guidance can theory provide us on these aspects?

The transfer benefit to a worker from a day's employment in public works amounts to the wage he gets from the scheme, net of any costs incurred — both the costs of participation (such as the cost of transport) and the earnings lost from alternative employment (Ravallion, Datt and Ravallion 1992). If the costs of participation and income from alternative sources are negligible, and the programme has no effect on the labour market and the structure of wages, the transfer benefit approximates to the programme wage times the duration of employment. Quite plausibly, the assumptions are unlikely to hold in reality. Unless the scale of the programme is very limited, the programme is likely to put an upward pressure on the wage rate, thereby reducing the demand for labour. Moreover, the costs of participation and foregone earnings are only rarely zero. Depending upon the impact of the scheme on the wage rate, the foregone earnings, and the costs of participation, the transfer benefit may be higher or lower than the programme wage.[1] Apart from the wage rate, the share of wages in total cost and the duration of employment determine the total transfer benefits going to workers.

One argument advanced is to keep the programme wage low so that the poor are self-selected into the programme. A low wage rate is most likely to keep the non-poor out of the programme. However, a low wage will also result in lower transfer earnings per (poor) participant. It keeps the overall participation rate low while at the same time ensuring a disproportionate number of poor participants than would be the case if the wage rate is most likely to lead to rationing of jobs under the scheme, apart from attracting non-poor workers to the programme.

The potential income gains from a works programme can be exaggerated if the source of financing is ignored. If employment is expanded entirely through an aid-financed public works programme, the advantage (transfer benefits) to workers is straightforward. However, if the programme is financed out of general tax revenues, it would be important to examine (a) the counterfactual situation, namely, would the participants of the programme have benefited more (less) from alternative ways of spending the same budgetary resources, and (b) if a works programme has expanded at the expense of other activities conferring non-labour income for the poor (*i.e.*, educational or hospital services). Rarely does one find empirical evidence on either issue. Yet, a discussion of how a works programme is financed is important for an understanding of the true benefits of the programme.

1. For an analytical model that clarifies the issue further, see Ravallion.

The stabilisation benefit of the programme depends on its timing. For example, if the programme's timing synchronises with the agricultural slack seasons when the demand for labour is low, workers are most likely to gain from the resulting income stabilisation and consumption smoothing. Stabilisation benefits from unanticipated declines in farm activity in bad agricultural years may be even higher than from anticipated declines in slack seasons. Even if the transfer benefits are small, income stabilisation can pre-empt acute distress and prevent poor households from onerous adjustments such as distress-selling of productive assets in bad agricultural years. In other words, the risk benefits conferred by a works programme *via* its insurance function can be as important as the transfer benefits to the poor *via* its distribution function.

Finally, the particular design features, the institutional framework, and the type of implementing agencies (*e.g.*, line ministries of the government, private contractors, non-governmental agencies, or a combination of the above) also influence how much benefits the programme is in fact transferring to the poor. If the implementing agencies and the institutional framework are strongly attuned to leakages, the poor who participate in the programme may have to pay a part of wages either to officials or contractors or politicians, or incur other transaction costs that may reduce the transfer benefits of the programme. But the design of the programme can also be rendered beneficial for certain vulnerable groups. For example, the mode of payment of wages – cash or in-kind (food) – is an important design feature that influences participation decisions. Payment of wages in-kind or piece-wage payments may attract more women than men to worksites.

The programme features (especially the level of the wage rate and the timing of the programme) and the design features (implementing agencies and the institutional framework) together determine the programme's efficacy as an anti-poverty intervention and its cost effectiveness. The cost effectiveness of the programme can be gleaned from the cost per job created, and the cost per one dollar of transfer to the poor.

The next section discusses cross-country experience with respect to financing, wage rate and targeting, duration, and timing of employment, share of wages in total cost, cost per job created, and the impact on poverty and incomes.

2. Public Works: Cross-Country Experience

Not all aspects of a programme's experience are available for every country. For example, data on mean consumption per person are available only for a few countries. I now review the available empirical evidence on each aspect of the programme.

2.1 Financing and Scale of Operations

Sources of financing influenced both the duration and character of programmes. Thus in the 1950s and 1960s, bilateral food aid (mostly wheat under US PL 480) financed food-for-works programmes in India and Bangladesh. As food-aid diminished, food-for-works was replaced by cash-for-work. The programme began to be funded entirely from domestic sources in India, accounting for its sustainability. By contrast, in most countries of Africa, bilateral donors funded many public works programmes. Donor funding meant a net (additional) transfer of income to the poor. But the programmes were shortlived, lasting only as long as donor support lasted. Depending upon historical circumstances and source of financing, scale of operations varied across countries (Table 4.2).

2.2 Wage Rate and Targeting

The wage rate is a key element determining the distributional outcomes of the programme. One important way to ensure that the programme reaches the poor is to maintain the programme wage at a level no higher than the ruling market wage rate for unskilled labour. This practice also helps keep overall costs down. In most countries, governments set the levels for minimum wage for unskilled labour. Though minimum wages are legally binding, their enforcement varies, especially within large countries. Whether the minimum wage is higher or lower than the ruling market wage and whether or not it is enforced are empirical questions; even in the same country the relationship between the two might vary over time and, in large countries, across regions. In countries where the market wage is less than the minimum wage, the poor may be self-selected to the programme if the programme wage is set at a level no higher than the ruling market wage, even if it were lower than the statutory minimum wage. However, political and legal constraints may make it difficult to maintain the programme wage at levels less than the minimum wage. Not surprisingly, there is much cross-country variation (Table 4.1).

The wage rate was set at 70 per cent of the minimum wage in Chile; it was about 25 per cent higher than agricultural market wages in the Philippines; it was equal to the statutory minimum wage in Kenya. In India, the nationwide programme of JRY maintained its wages at the statutory minimum wage, though market wages were much lower than the minimum wage in many regions. In the Maharashtra Employment Guarantee Scheme (MEGS) also, the programme wage was equal to the minimum wage. But the minimum wage remained lower than the ruling market wage until 1988. In 1988, the minimum wage as well as the programme wage were doubled. This upward revision of the wage rate in 1988 contributed to job rationing, thereby eroding the "guarantee" of employment expected of the programme (Datt and Ravallion 1994). In Tanzania and Botswana, because the programme wage rate was maintained at a level higher than it was in comparable unskilled activities, jobs had to be rationed — particularly during droughts when the poor's need for participation in public works was the greatest (Teklu 1994a). The programme wage in Kenya and the Philippines was also found to be higher than the market wage for unskilled labour; as a result, substantial numbers of the non-poor

Table 4.1

Public Works: Programme Wage (PW), Minimum Wage (MNW), and Market Wage (MW) in Selected Countries

Country	*Programme*	*PW in Relation to MNW and/or MW*
Bangladesh	Cash For Work, 1991-92	PW<MW
India	(a) Cash For Work, JRY, 1991-92	PW=MNW>MW
	(b$_1$) MEGS: upto 1988	PW=MNW<MW
	(b$_2$) After 1988	PW=MNW>MW
Pakistan	IGPRA* III, 1992	PW<MW
Philippines	Cash For Work 1990	PW>MW
	Food For Work 1987	PW**>MW
Botswana	Cash For Work	PW<MNW, but >MW
Kenya	Cash For Work, 1992-93	PW=MNW>MW
Chile	Cash For Work 1987	PW<MNW=MW

Source: Compiled from Subbarao, *et al.*, (1996).

Note: * = IGPRA: Income Generation Programme for Refugee Areas, funded by UN Agencies:

** = programme wage includes cash wages plus the monetary value of food supplied by the programme.

were attracted to the programme (Teklu 1994a; Subbarao, Ahmed, and Teklu). But in some countries (Burkina Faso, Senegal, and Sri Lanka), the programme wages were lower than market wages. The lesson: A relatively high wage rate is most likely to result in job rationing.

2.3 Duration and Timing of Employment

While a lower programme wage is most likely to render the programme self-targeted, its careful timing (so as to synchronise it with the agricultural slack season) might also help in enhancing stabilisation benefits. India's JRY, though generating over 800-850 million person-days of employment annually, conferred relatively small transfer benefits inasmuch as the person-days of employment per person as well as per household remained modest — often no more than five per family per month (Dev). This small level of job creation is clearly insufficient to raise the incomes of poor families. Nevertheless, the programme operated intensively during the agricultural off-peak season: as many as 55 million persons gained employment in the agricultural off-peak seasons. Because of the timing of the programme, "consumption-smoothing" (stabilisation) benefits were considerable, despite its other disadvantages. In MEGS also, Walker and Ryan show that the risk benefits conferred by the scheme are considerable. Although jobs were rationed and the total number of person-days of employment sharply declined after the wage rate doubled in 1988, stabilisation benefits of the scheme continued as the MEGS operated intensively in off-seasons in both 1980-81 and 1990-91 (Figure 4.1). In Kenya and Tanzania, not only were programme wage rates higher but the timing of public works was synchronised with the busy agricultural season, thereby significantly diminishing both the transfer and stabilisation benefits to the poor (Teklu 1994a, 1994b). In Bangladesh, too, the food-for-work programme was poorly synchronised with seasonal patterns of need for work and food.

2.4 Share of Wage Cost in Total Cost

In most programmes, the share of wages to total cost of programmes varied between 0.3 to 0.6 (Table 4.2). While a higher share is desirable for higher transfer benefits to be conferred on the poor, many factors determine this ratio, including the nature of the asset to be created, the duration and timing of the works, and, most of all, the availability of technically and economically feasible labour-

Figure 4.1

Labour Attendance Under the EGS

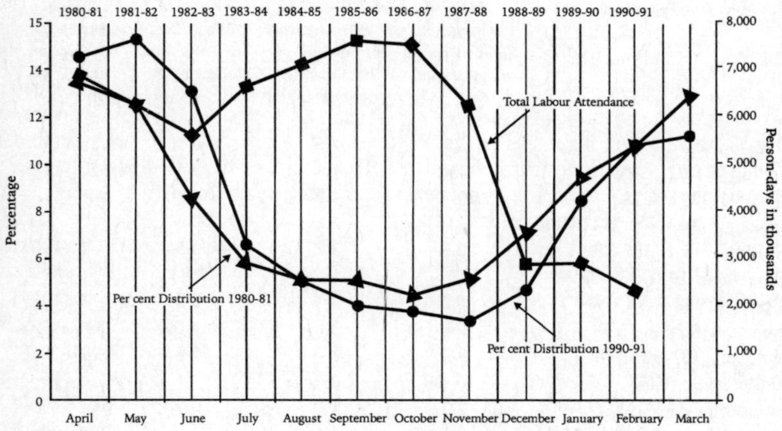

based methods of production. In most road construction activities, the share of wages to total cost ranged between 0.4 per cent to 0.5 per cent. Where the work has been entrusted to private contractors, the outcome with respect to the share of wage cost to total cost is unpredictable. Evidence from Ghana suggests that timely availability of project funds is important for the adoption of labour-based methods (Stock and de Veen).

2.5 Cost Per Job Created

Various factors influence the cost per job created including the mix of locals and expatriates involved in the implementation of sub-projects; the delivery mechanism selected, particularly the modalities of hiring private contractors, the wage rate; the capital-intensity of operations; and administrative capacity. Disaggregated information on the above factors is hard to come by, so it is difficult to disentangle the various factors underlying the variations in cost per job created.

Available data on cost per job created, which belong to late-1980s or early-1990s, are shown in Table 4.2. There is much cross-country variation — from as low as $1 per person day of employment created in Bangladesh to $8 in Bolivia. To place cross-country comparisons in

Table 4.2

Public Works: Scale of Operations and Costs for Selected Countries

Country/Year/Programme	*Scale of Operation (million person-days annual)*	*Total Cost (Wage & nonwage) per person-day of Employment Created US$*	*Ratio of Wage Cost to Total Cost (Per cent)*	*Mean Consumption per person per month (year) US$*
Bangladesh: 1991-92, FFW	15	1.6	0.5	46.85 (1990)
India:1991-92, CFW (JRY)	850	1.3	0.6	28.40 (1990)
1991-92, MEGS	100-180	1.2	0.51	
Pakistan: 1992, CFW (IGPRA)	5.15	2.8	0.6	
Philippines: 1990, CFW	0.3	3.2	0.5	61 (1988)
Botswana: 1992-93, CFW	7	1.7	0.63	
Ghana: 1988-91, CFW	0.5	3.4	0.2	73 (1988)
Kenya: 1992-93, CFW	0.6	3.0	0.3-0.4	58.6 (1992)
Bolivia: 1982-90 CFW	8-9	8.0	0.4	86.2 (1990)
Chile: 1987, CFW	40-45	0.5	—	131.4 (1990)
Honduras: 1990-91, CFW	2.5	1.0	0.4	42.8 (1990)
Costa Rica: 1991-94, CFW	8.9	4.0	—	99.7 (1990)

Source: Compiled from K. Subbarao *et al.*, (1996).

Note: FFW: Food For Work; CFW: Cash For Work; JRY: Jawahar Rojgar Yojna, a nationwide programme of public works; MEGS: Maharashtra Employment Guarantee Scheme; IGPRA: Income Generation Programme for Refugee Areas, funded by UN agencies.

perspective, mean consumption per person per month are also shown. The main finding is that not all countries managed to create jobs at low cost. Low-income developing countries in Asia and Africa — Bangladesh, India, Botswana, Tanzania — have incurred a cost person-day in the (modest) range of \$1-\$2. Honduras and Chile in Latin America have incurred a lower cost per job created than other countries in the region. The variations in the cost of job created seem to widen when evaluated in PPP exchange rates. Table 4.3 shows data on annual cost per job created in public works, evaluated at PPP exchange rates in seven countries. The cost appears to be much too high for Senegal and Ghana.

Few studies have examined the cost per dollar of income transferred through public works programmes. The data released by Concurrent Evaluation Report, Ministry of Rural Development, suggest that India's nationwide programme of JRY transferred one rupee of income to participants at a cost of Rs. 1.9 (including the amount of transfer) in 1991. It is well-known that JRY participants included the poor as well as the non-poor, largely because the programme wage was higher than the market wage. Taking into account the extent of mistargeting, the programme required an expenditure of Rs. 4.35 (including the amount of transfer) to transfer one rupee of income to a poor participant.

Table 4.3

Annual Cost of Job Creation in Public Works Under Different Social Funds (in US$/Job)

	Egypt	*Honduras*	*Nicaragua*	*Madagascar*	*Bolivia*	*Senegal*	*Ghana*
Cost per job at market exchange rates	1,401	2,120	2,580	786	2,700	5,445	2,122
Cost per job at PPP exchange rates	7,212	9,759	14,302	3,620	9,388	12,100	10,610

Source: Bank staff estimates, as cited in K. Subbarao *et al.*, (1996).

2.6 Impact on Incomes, Poverty, and Social Life

Evaluations of works programmes in general, and Maharashtra Employment Guarantee Scheme in particular, suggest significant transfer and stabilisation benefits. Numerous micro studies have shown that 60 per cent to 70 per cent of the participants of India's nationwide programme (JRY) and the MEGS belonged to poor households. The immediate net income gain from works programmes as a percentage of total gross earnings is high. For example, the severity of poverty has fallen from 5.0 per cent to 3.2 per cent owing to participation in the EGS (Datt and Ravallion 1992). Dev notes significant social gains: "The EGS also discourages sexual barriers and inequality... Women now dress better and their economic power has given them a better status in their families." (p. 54).

Datt and Ravallion (1992) show that workers in EGS did forego earnings from alternative sources, but the foregone earnings are not substantial. Nevertheless, their findings suggest that the opportunity cost of a participant's time needs to be factored in while designing the programme. Foregone income can be lowered by more flexible timing, by adoption of piece-rates and task-based mode of payment, providing work closest to homes, and by expanding the programme in agricultural slack seasons. Women's participation seem to be particularly sensitive to the flexibility in timing and location of work.

3. Conclusions

Three general conclusions can be drawn from the reviewed experience.

First, the level of the wage rate is critical in determining the distribution of benefits from the programme, as well as how much of the programme is targeted toward the poor. Maintaining the programme wage at the level no higher than the ruling market wage for unskilled labour can enable the poor to self-select themselves into the programme.

Second, the timing and duration of employment determine the nature of benefits offered by the programme; in general, the more narrowly the programme is restricted to operate only during agricultural slack seasons, the lower the transfer benefits and the higher the stabilisation benefits. Even if transfer benefits are small, the programme's stabilisation (risk) benefits can be substantial. However, a public works programme entirely for consumption-smoothing purposes is more appropriate where poverty is transient — the numbers of the vulnerable rising during bad agricultural years and in slack seasons and falling in good years and peak agricultural seasons — than in countries with chronic and severe poverty. In countries subject to serious interyear fluctuations (*e.g.*, Ethiopia) and in countries where poverty gap ratios are high, the need for rendering the programme year-round (thus raising the transfer benefits to the poor) assumes greater importance.

Third, the programme can be designed so as to encourage greater participation of women, a higher degree of involvement of the private sector, and lower transaction costs for the poor to participate in the programme.

References

Datt, G., and M. Ravallion, (1992). "Behavioral Responses to Workforce: Evidence for Rural India", LSMS Working Paper, World Bank, Washington DC.

———. "Transfer Benefits from Public Works Employment: Evidence for Rural India." *Economic Journal,* 104(1994): 1346-69.

Dev, S.M. (1996). "India's MEGS: Lessons from Long Experience", mimeo., Indira Gandhi Institute of Development Research, Bombay.

Ravallion, M. (1987). "Market Responses to Anti-Hunger Policies: Effect on Wages, Prices and Employment", WIDER Working Paper No. 28.

Stock, E., and J. de Veen, (1996). "Expanding Labour-Based Methods in Road Programmes", Mimeo., World Bank, Africa Technical Department, Washington DC.

Subbarao, K., A. Ahmed and T. Teklu, (1995). "Philippines: Social Safety Net Programmes: Targeting, Cost Effectiveness and Options for Reform", Discussion Paper No. 317. World Bank, Washington DC.

Subbarao, K., A. Bonnerjee, J. Braithwaite, S. Carvalho, K. Ezemenari, C. Graham, and A. Thompson (1997). "Safety Net Programmes and Poverty Reduction: Lessons from Cross-Country Experience", *Directions in Development Series,* The World Bank, Washington DC.

Teklu, T. (1994a). "Minor Road Programme in Kenya: Potential for Short-term Poverty Reduction through Asset Creation", mimeo., International Food Policy Research Institute, Washington DC.

———. (1994b). "Labour-Intensive Rural Roads in Kenya, Tanzania and Botswana: Some Evidence on Design and Practice", mimeo., International Food Policy Research Institute, Washington DC.

Walker, T., and J. Ryan, (1990). *Village and Household Economies in India's Semi-Arid Tropics,* Johns Hopkins, Baltimore.

Section II

Environment

5

Economics, Ecology and the Environment

A Developing Country Perspective[1]

KANCHAN CHOPRA

"...... Creating new forms of dialogue between science and society is the challenge of the year 2000. Researchers often underline the limits of knowledge and place research among the different factors influencing public authorities action.

...... Such a new contract between research and society should be elaborated, and the environmental question seems to be a good field of application"[2]

1. Introduction

The last two hundred years after the Industrial Revolution witnessed a rise in the scale of economic activity. The rapid advancement of technology and better modes of social organisation extended the frontiers of this activity at hitherto unprecedented rates. However, the last quarter century of this millennium has seen an increasing recognition of the many ways in which the limits to the earth's tolerance of expanded human activity are being stretched. At the global level, this shall count as one of the major extensions of the frontiers of human knowledge and understanding during this period. An offshoot of such an understanding is the need

- to determine what constitutes uncompensated anthropogenic environmental risk to the life support systems of the earth,
- to determine the impact of avoiding such risks on the nature and scale of economic activity and

---

1. This paper is a revised version of the Presidential Address delivered at the First Biennial Conference of the Indian Society for Ecological Economics held at Bangalore in 1999. It was subsequently published in a volume entitled "Ecological Economics for Sustainable Development" (Academic Foundation 2001).
2. Adapted from Faucheux (1999).

- to suggest modes of evolution of societal and individual behaviour which enable the above to be taken into account in the decision-making of individuals, communities and governments.

Clearly, no one science can provide the answers to the questions raised in the above context. Not all answers are even available or possible given the present level of evolution of human understanding. Among other disciplines, Economics has attempted to reorganise itself to provide answers. It has used insights from sociology and political science in doing so. Ecological economics has tried to provide some of the answers. The process is a continually evolving one. One principle is however clear. A large part of the answer to the problems listed above lies at the interface between different traditionally defined disciplines. This paper intends to:

- Examine how economics has developed to deal with the problems of environmental degradation.
- Focus on the gaps in its evolution and to examine whether the manner in which ecological economics has developed globally in the last ten years or more helps to fill in these gaps. Or is it that it provides a workable alternative paradigm?
- Review some developments on the interface of economics and other social sciences and to see whether there exist any lessons to be learnt there.

The above issues shall be viewed primarily from a developing country perspective. In a world marked by economic, social and political cleavages, the extent to which economic activity impacts natural environments differs between nations. So does the manner in which civil society reacts to the realisation that an irreversible impact exists at times. In developed countries, the policy sometimes centres round the attempt to export degradation beyond the frontiers of individual nation states. In other situations, alternative technologies are adopted in the process of production. Simultaneously attempts are made to put more accountable social systems in place. The problem becomes more acute in developing countries with low levels of income struggling for "development". The imperative of harnessing a larger part of all resources, human, natural and economic for use in the present is very dominant. The call for conservation seems somewhat misplaced. However, if one moves into the broader social and cultural context which prevails in most of the developing world, it is interesting to observe that an understanding of the human interaction with nature has always been built into it.

It appears then that the essence of the situation in developing countries is marked by a dilemma. The macro picture relegates resource and environment linked issues to the background, often to be brought into the forefront only at the behest of international agencies or in the course of political negotiations centred around the management of the global commons such as the climate change. At the local levels, natural resources constitute a significant issue, both from the consumption and livelihood viewpoints and the emergence of non-governmental organisations has drawn the attention of civil society to this fact. It is in the background of this complex mosaic that interdisciplinary issues affecting the environment shall be placed and studied in this paper.

2. Economics and the Environment

Of late the study of economy-ecology interactions has gone far even within the limits imposed by the discipline of Economics. Firstly, it is understood that economic activity uses natural resources and also returns waste to nature and more importantly, the scale of that activity is determined independently of the rate of replacement of resources or the waste absorption capacity of the environment. At low levels of economic activity, the asymmetry goes unnoticed because the inputs required to be extracted are small. Traditional microeconomics treats environmental effects as externalities of production or consumption (Pigou 1932 and Ayres and Kneese 1969). As long as the uncompensated technological externalities of the production and consumption processes are small, the environment, principally watercourses and the air absorb the residuals of these activities. Beyond certain scales of economic activity, the pervasive nature of these externalities and limits on the waste assimilative capacity of environmental sinks results in the need for such residues to be treated as a part of the materials balancing problem in the economy. The problem of externality management thus moves from the realm of microeconomics to that of macroeconomic management of the flow of materials in an input-output framework. The presence of waste generating externalities imposes a constraint on production levels in such a framework.[3] In principle, a new level of activity and corresponding prices can be defined for an economy, a level of activity

3. This happens primarily when one realises that "nature does not permit the destruction of matter except by annihilation with anti-matter" (Ayres and Kneese 1969).

that takes account of constraints of the new kind. For a number of reasons, explained at length in the literature, however, it may be an exercise of considerable complication and somewhat little practical return to do this. For, the institutional structure to convert the prices of "environmental capabilities" needs to be envisioned and moved towards simultaneously. Such a complete exercise in material balancing may at best be better attempted at the regional level. However, models of the mass balance-general equilibrium genre of Ayres and Kneese (1969) Maler (1974) and Perrings (1987) yielded important results linking with later developments in ecological economics.[4]

The constraints imposed on growth of consumption by the nature and rates of regeneration of environmental resources have been analysed using optimal control methods. In the earlier contributions starting from the early-seventies and even earlier, issues of decision making with respect to resource use for development or conservation have been studied using optimal control theory (Krutilla and Fisher 1975, Fisher, Krutilla and Cicchetti, 1972). It is worth recalling that a number of these early writings, with roots in conventional cost-benefit analysis, conclude that in the presence of irreversibility and mutual dependence between projects (even by the criterion of net present value), the net present value of utility accruing from them is maximised by conservation or refraining from development in the present.[5]

More recent developments within the framework of control theory have extended the analysis to take account of the multiple functions that environmental resources perform in relation to human survival and economic activity. Seibert (1981 and 1987) for instance develops models where the constraints on welfare maximisation in an inter-temporal context include rates of regeneration and levels of extraction of resources as also levels of pollution accumulation. The conditions for sustainable economic development (defined as maintaining a certain level of consumption or welfare per capita for future generations) are derived in this framework. While results vary typically, it is important to note that two important parameters that

4. Note for instance the result that since the waste generated in the process of production is seldom inert, higher rates of physical growth imply higher rates of change in the processes of the environment (Perrings 1987).

5. See Fisher and Peterson (1976) for a review of the earlier literature.

determine the attainability or otherwise of sustainable development are the rate of time preference and the rate of regeneration of the resource. If the first is higher than the second, the stock of resources is driven to zero in a finite time and the situation is unsustainable.[6]

Further, if the resource stock has an amenity value and provides utility,[7] the rate of extraction is more gradual and imposes limits on economic growth. Barbier (1989) and Barbier and Markandya (1989) suggest that an essential criterion for sustainable development is: maximising the net benefits of economic development subject to maintaining the services and the quality of natural resources over time. A minimum viable level of the stock of environmental assets is built in as a constraint in addition to restrictions on rates of degradation, use of assets and levels of regeneration. Some of the results obtained in this specification are of interest. A low initial level of environmental quality results in environmentally unsustainable development. The discount rate makes the strategy of increased present consumption optimal. This implies that an economy with a high discount rate requires a higher initial level of environmental quality to avoid a growth path that is environmentally unsustainable. The above is indeed a significant result, in particular from the viewpoint of low income developing countries. It is perhaps important also to remember that it is obtained using standard tools of economics.

3. Outstanding Issues, Ecological Economics and the Study of Natural Systems

Certain basic principles of ecology and physical characteristics of the functioning of natural systems are not taken into account in the above manner of viewing economy-environment interactions. This is the main thrust of ecological economics. At the macro level, it has resulted in several alternative developments. One school maintains that economists should pay more attention to the flow of energy in an economic system. This led to the so called "energy theory of value" and to a discussion of "economics as social physics".[8] The second

6. For an analysis of the different models and their implications, refer to Klaassen and Opschoor (1991).

7. Such a condition formalises the requirement that environmental preservation adds to utility i.e. note for instance the utility derived from scenic beauty.

8. See Martinez-Alier (1991) who also discusses why these developments remained on the periphery of the social and natural science disciplines for a number of decades.

school, perceived by some to be the mainstream of ecological economics argues that the economy should be viewed as the one-way entropic throughput of energy and materials and not as a circular or spiral flow of exchange value between producers and consumers. Arguing that economic growth is a thermodynamic process, dependent for its continuation on the supply of environmental low entropy, this second macro view leads on to issues of the sustainability of the scale of economic activity.

The above constitutes a point of departure for the theory of ecological economics at a macro and somewhat abstract level. It suggests a constraint on economic activity that is not reflected in market prices as they function. However, suggesting limits to the functioning of markets is not new in economics. Welfare economics and its applications are full of discussions of the divergence of social and private cost and the alternative notions of value. And a large number of social contracts are based on institutions other than the market. The working of markets in all societies is overruled and limited by notions of justice dispensed through the existence of laws. This happens when society perceives these aspects to be important enough to be enshrined in laws and conventions that govern and limit the working of economic institutions. The universal principle of entropy underlying economic activity has not yet found such a translation partly because the nature of the constraints that it imposes are either not understood or are not equally binding at all times and places.

An understanding of the working of specific ecosystems and the impact of an increased volume of economic activity on their functioning is central to the development of environmental and ecological economics. While the general-equilibrium and mass balance models conclude that higher rates of growth imply higher rates of change in the processes of the environment, the threshold values where such rates of change undermine crucial life support systems are not always known. These are indeed space and time dependent in addition to being determined by rates of use emerging from biotic interference. For individual ecosystems such as lakes, wetlands, forests and indeed types of forests, the dynamics of their functioning needs to be interpreted in the context of the above mentioned constraints. Further, this needs to be done in a language common to different disciplines and at a level of aggregation that makes sense both from the ecological and the socio-economic viewpoint. Mathematical modeling perhaps provides such a common language.[9] One could also think of other possibilities. The results of such an exercise are sure to lead to an extension of the frontiers of all sciences with questions being asked about:

- the role of resilience in measuring eco-system health and the consequent relevance of stochastic rather than deterministic models in their context (Ives 1995)
- the wisdom of using smooth and continuous damage functions as is often done in environmental economics
- the presence or otherwise of substitutability between human made and natural capital and between different kinds of natural capital (Turner, Perrings and Folke 1996)
- the possibility of "ecologically bounded use of natural resources as the normative starting point of economic theory"(Pandit 1997).

There evidently exist unresolved issues at the frontiers of ecology and economics which offer interesting vistas for theoreticians to delve into. The answer to these questions must be sought at desegregated eco-system levels to carry conviction in particular in a developing country scenario where competing demands on resources are persistent and often of a compelling kind.

4. Valuation of Environmental Resources and Institutions: Economics, Sociology and Anthropology

Valuation of environmental resources is another area of debate in environmental and ecological economics. It is clear that the market cannot fully value environmental resources. In economic theory, this is another instance of the incompleteness of markets and values expressed in market prices. Environmental economics has thrown up methodologies of valuation outside the market. The development of techniques for valuation based on stated preferences expressed through the use of contingent markets is one example.[10] These alternative approaches to the valuation of environmental resources serve the purpose of highlighting the many dimensional nature of "value". In certain situations, they may be of use to policymakers in decision making.

9. Example of such exercises being carried out exist in different parts of the world. See Maler (1999) for a study of the implications of a modeling of the ecology of shallow lakes for the nature of functions governing external impacts of fertiliser use in the catchment.

10. See Mitchell and Carson (1989) for an introduction to and analysis of these methods.

It is important to interpret these attempts in the spirit in which they are meant: as attempts to capture significant aspects of value. The non-additivity of value arrived at using alternative approaches to the concept remains.[11] The use of multi-criteria analysis in analysis of policy problems that have environmental impacts makes explicit this non-commensurable nature of alternative approaches to value.[12]

A more significant case of incomplete markets impacting the diverse kinds of value accruing from environmental resources is that of future markets. The interests of future generations are not taken into account in present day decision making with respect to the environment. It is important to note that even if environmental values are incorporated into decision making, "sustainability will not come about unless each generation is committed to transferring to the next sufficient natural resources and capital assets to make development sustainable" (Howarth and Norgaard 1992). Evidence with respect to private rates of discount does not seem to suggest such a commitment.[13] The somewhat limited development of futures markets in environmental resources is partly due to this. The other factor contributing to it is incomplete information: hence the emphasis on the "precautionary principle" in the context of policy with respect to preservation of life supporting natural systems.

The above discussion highlights an important lacuna in the development of this area of research. Behavioural sciences are not integrated into the calculus of ecological thinking. Shogren (1998) makes a strong case for such an integration if science is to define environmental policy. The ecological critique of economics has a considerably long lineage but has not so far been able to impact mainstream economics due partly to "the separation of the natural and the social sciences" (Martinez-Alier 1991). An important component in any integration shall have to be *via* the factors determining human behaviour.[14]

Such an integration is also perhaps attempted more effectively with reference to specific issues. In the context of climate change, for

---

11. See in this context, the discussion in Chapter 9 of Chopra and Kadekodi (1997).
12. See the discussions in Munda, Nijkamp and Reitveld (1994). Applications including to the siting of nuclear power plants [Reitveld and Jannsen (1989)] have also been made.
13. See for instance the evidence with respect to individual discount rates as reflected in the purchase of energy saving durables in Haussman (1979).
14. The unwillingness of ecological economics to consider explicitly social and natural power relations has also been commented on by others. See for example Gale (1998).

instance it is often wondered why energy-efficient technologies are not adopted by firms even when they do not seem to imply higher cost (Shogren 1998). While a part of the answer may be in imperfect knowledge, a part of it is in the notion of "transaction cost" of any change, a notion which reflects behavioural patterns of people in real world situations. This behaviour pattern and the possibility of evolution to a new pattern is often "path-dependent". How fast people adapt to new situations and the manner in which new institutions evolve is then a function of where they begin from which determines the "transaction cost" of such a change.[15]

The concept of "value" which finds reflection in a society's values reflects also the manner in which it is structured, in other words the prevailing institutions governing people's behaviour. It is now well established that rates of discount of the future and norms of valuation of environmental and social resources are determined by prevailing institutional structures.[16] If prevailing institutional structures ensure that future uncertainty is guaranteed against, the future need not be discounted heavily by individuals. Such an assurance almost always requires cooperation between stakeholders in specific situations. In other words, "getting institutions right" is an essential complement to the policy of "getting the prices right" in the search for policy instruments for environmental management.

At another level of analysis, game theory attempts to answer the question: "When and why do people cooperate ?" The insights it offers are important in understanding how alternative institutions emerge. Natural resource management problems have been modeled as prisoners' dilemma games, repeated prisoners' dilemmas, assurance games, dove/hawk games and so on. By and large however, game theory concentrates on conditions under which stable solutions can exist. It is preoccupied with conditions determining stable equilibrium rather than processes of change. Even though attempts are being made to model changing norms of players into game theoretic approaches and they offer useful insights,[17] it is often more fruitful,

15. North (1990) discusses these issues at length.

16. See Bromley (1991) for an in depth discussion of the interdependence of notions of value and institutional structures.

17. Schotter (1981) sees norms as determining a chance distribution on the strategies of players. Okuno-Fujiwara and Postlewaite (1990) provide a framework for modeling social norms into random matching games. Field (1984) however, challenges the possibility of modeling changing norms using game theory. Bardhan (1993) also seems to agree that in depth studies of change processes may yield more insight into how institutions evolve.

in a policy context to look at details of the process of change in the creation and evolution of institutions.

The literature in this area is again substantiated by the insights provided by concerns and studies conducted at the more desegregated local levels. A large part of the understanding of the links between economic activity, livelihood generation and incentives for and against conservation oriented management of natural resources comes from these studies with origins in economics, anthropology and sociology.[18] This understanding is essentially inter-disciplinary in nature and it shall be useful to examine it in some depth, in the particular context of India.

The dependence of the rural poor on environmental common property resources for livelihood generation and consumption has been highlighted in a large number of studies on the basis of empirical evidence.[19] Why then would the rural poor contribute to environmental degradation by overextraction as has been maintained implicitly in policy circles? A number of explanations were offered for the apparent contradiction:

- the poor have a high rate of discount for the future due to low levels of income
- population pressure constitutes the major reason for degradation of natural resources
- a large part of the degradation of the environment is the consequence of the failure of the market and the state to provide appropriate modes of management of natural resources.

The emergence and efficacy of alternative institutional forms of environmental management in countries of South Asia during the eighties were found to counter each of these factors, *albeit* to different degrees.[20] The evolution of these owed a great deal to individual commitment, largely in the non-governmental sector, but sometimes with critical inputs from individuals within government. Documentation of the manner of evolution of these alternative

---

18. See for instance Ostrom (1990), Wade (1987), Chopra, Kadekodi and Murty (1990). For a succint interpretation of these studies and their implication see Bardhan (1993).
19. See for instance Jodha's pioneering inquiry (1986) into the relationship between the rural poor and common property resources.
20. This paper focuses more on India, basically due to the author's familiarity with the country.

experiments exists.[21] In initial studies on these grassroots movements, there did exist a tendency to treat "local level institutions" as a kind of romantic closed system which could correct all ills existing in alternative institutional structures. Moreover, early efforts at the creation of alternative local level institutions of natural resource management though few and far between, tended to be focused and effort-intensive. Note, for instance the heavy capital and labour investment in the much discussed Sukhomajri experiment.[22] Similar analysis of other early interventions came up with optimistic pictures of their impact on management of natural resources and its impact on local livelihoods and resource regeneration. It seemed that a kind of complementarity existed between income generation and resource conservation when the institutional structure was properly specified.

The early literature then presented a somewhat rosy picture of grassroots initiatives. Gradually, the number of these initiatives increased over time and their nature diversified. A large part of this expansion took place constituting a kind of reaction to the excessive centralisation of decision making that had marked the phase of natural resource management. Expansion, however also threw up indifferent kinds of intervention by urban based and not so participatory organisations. With expansion came conflict with existing structures of power, both political and economic. At times, internal dissension within local level communities also came to the fore. The question then came to be asked: what are the set of conditions that lead to cooperative behaviour in the management of natural resources at the local level?

The answer to such a question has been sought through an application of theory and econometric techniques to the interpretation of links between factors affecting the emergence of alternative paradigms of management of natural resources in local situation. Such studies, though few and far between gave content to

21. See for instance, Panagare and Panagare (1992) for a documentation of the experiment of watershed management in Ralegan Sidhi, Maheshwari *et al.* (1990) for Tejpura in Jhansi, Bahuguna (1992) for Harda in Madhya Pradesh, Saint (1993) for Udaipur in Rajasthan, Chopra *et al.* (1990) for villages in Haryana. Also see the series of studies by the Society for Wasteland Development, Development Alternatives and the Centre for Science and Environment.

22. Total investment on a per hectare basis came to about Rs. 22,000 compared to an average expenditure of Rs. 10,000 per hectare on similar programmes for the country as a whole. Even so, a cost-benefit analysis revealed that rates of return were in the range of 14 to 19 per cent for this project. Chopra (1996) reviews some of these studies in the context of watershed management.

the black box of "institutional change at local levels", expanding simultaneously on the association of this change with other macro level changes in and around these communities. Agarwal and Yadama (1997) studied for example, the impact of population and market pressures on forest resources in the presence of alternative institutional forms of management of these resources in the Kumaon region of Uttar Pradesh.[23] Indices used for assessing institutional strength include the age of the *panchayat*, the frequency of elections and the level of monitoring and enforcement of rules of behaviour. The last factor was found to impact resource conditions more closely than others, leading to the conclusion that co-management of forests by communities and forest department was perhaps viable. In another study Chopra and Gulati (1998) find that the number of years that a local level intervention has been operating is crucial in determining its impact on economic and demographic variables. This study posits that stress migration from rural areas in Udaipur district of Rajasthan decreased and was possibly reversed due to the introduction of better management of common property resources in these areas.

Limits to local level participatory management of natural resources are also indicated by some recent studies. When such management takes the form of pooling and management of private land, the process could take a considerable period of time before reaching a stable solution. Even when rules with respect to sharing of output and returns to owners of resources are well defined, the process is slow and uncertain. Kadekodi (1998) for instance, shows that depending on conditions governing the process of change, it may take from thirty to sixty years for a stable new institution to be established. Using data from an experiment in Palamau district of Bihar, he also illustrates that certain values of the parameters may imply the absence of convergence to a stable solution. Sethi and Somanathan (1996) using a model of evolutionary game dynamics integrated with resource stock dynamics, show that certain threshold values of relevant parameters need to be adhered to for social norms to be followed and to result in resource conservation through the functioning of local level institutions. When these values are crossed, it may lead to a lowering of the stock of resources, possibly its eventual extinction. One such

23. The institutional forms in existence included management by the forest department, by the revenue department and by the community. Three districts in the region are studied.

operational parameter is the efficacy of social sanctions. A decline in their efficacy due to the incursion of outsiders or of outside interest through the operation of market forces is expected to lead to a breakdown of the cooperative norm. Lise (1997) has studied common pool resource management in three states of India using an econometric-cum game theoretic approach. The game theoretic formulation throws light on the characteristics of the equilibrium in each of the three situations. It is interesting to note that more details with respect to the determinants of the social and economic participation are provided by the related econometric analysis.

Notwithstanding the existence of limits to local level participatory management of resources, evidence from studies of farmer managed irrigation systems in Nepal, the Philippines and other developing countries shows that such management is marked by a degree of innovative adjustment in dealing with variations in physical systems and participants' endowments. Ostrom and Gardner (1993) show that farmer managed systems lead to skillfully crafted rules which result in enhanced agricultural yield and efficiency. The design of such institutions needs hard bargaining between stakeholders over extended periods of time resulting in an acknowledgement of mutual interdependency. The outcome in terms of the forging of longer term relationships makes for stability of the systems that survive. It is to be noted however that "getting the institutions right is a difficult, time-consuming and conflict invoking process. It is a process that requires reliable information about time and place variables as well as a broad repertoire of culturally acceptable rules" Ostrom (1990).

All this has in it a lesson for the management of the global commons as well. In the management of climate change and CO_2 emissions, a considerable amount of attention is centred around tradable permits and the use of market instruments. Developed countries, on whom the onus for limiting emissions to predetermined levels falls, are so to say able to buy the right to a greater share in the use of the atmosphere, a global common. As Bardhan (1993) points out, tradability often undermines the reliability of a long term relationship between beneficiaries. It may be more useful to have nation states work out innovative bargaining solutions to the problem.

5. Future Directions

The focus of this paper has been on two issues:

- The first related to the significance of thermodynamic principles in determining production processes, more specifically the dynamics of natural systems and the reasons for the inability of social sciences and even societal decision making to account for them on a large enough scale.
- The second related to the evolution of institutions other than the market in the management of the environment and the light that a perspective from different social sciences can throw on this process.

Both issues need to be viewed from the developing country perspective in which, for the foreseeable future at least, development shall be a critical preoccupation. Underlying both is the commonality that issues relating to the linkages between the working of natural, economic and social systems are space and time determined. A fruitful direction of work for the evolution of environmental and ecological economics in the developing country perspective would be to operationalise the nature of such linkages in diverse economic and social situations and for different eco-systems. This shall help to provide answers to questions relating to the impact of economic activity on natural systems and on the waste assimilative capacity of the earth.

References

Agarwal, Arun and Gautam N. Yadama (1997). "How Do Local Institutions Mediate Market and Population Pressures on Resources? Forest Panchayats in Kumaon, India", *Development and Change* 28 (3), pp. 435-466.

Ayres, R.U and A.V. Kneese (1969). "Production, Consumption and Externalities", *American Economic Review,* 59. pp. 282-297.

Bahuguna, V.K. (1992). *Collective Resource Management: An Experience in Harda Forest Division,* Regional Centre for Wasteland Development, Indian Institute of Forest Management, Bhopal, India.

Barbier, E.B. (1989). *Economics, Natural Resources Scarcity and Development: Conventional and Alternative Views,* Earthscan, London.

Barbier, E.B. and Anil Markandya (1989). "The Conditions for Achieving Environmentally Sustainable Economic Development", mimeo, London Environmental Economics Centre, pp. 89-01, London.

Bardhan, Pranab (1993a). "Symposium on Management of Local Commons", *Journal of Economic Perspectives,* 7 (4), pp. 87-92.

————. (1993b). "Analytics of the Institutions of Informal Cooperation in Rural Development", *World Development,* 21 (4), pp. 633-639.

Bromley, D (1991). *Environment and Economy: Property Rights and Public Policy,* Basil Blackwell, Oxford, U.K.

Burness, S., R. Cummings., G. Morris and I. Paik (1980). "Thermodynamic and Economic Concepts as Related to Resource-use Policies", *Land Economics,* 56, pp. 1-9.

Chopra, Kanchan, Gopal K. Kadekodi and M.N. Murty (1990). *Participatory Development: People and Common Property Resources,* Sage Publications, New Delhi.

Chopra, Kanchan (1996). "The Management of Degraded Land: Issues and an Analysis of Technological and Institutional Solutions", *Indian Journal of Agricultural Economics,* 51 (1 & 2), pp. 238-248.

Chopra, Kanchan and Gopal K. Kadekodi (1997). "Natural Resource Accounting in the Yamuna Basin: Accounting for Forest Resources", mimeo, Institute of Economic Growth, Delhi.

Chopra, Kanchan and S.C. Gulati (1998). "Environmental Degradation, Property Rights and Population Movements: Hypotheses and Evidence from Rajasthan", *Environment and Development Economics* 3, pp. 35-57.

Daly, H.E. (1986). "Thermodynamic and Economic Concepts as Related to Resource-use Policies: Comment", *Land Economics,* 62, pp. 319-34.

————. (1991). "Steady State Economics", Second Edition with New Essays, Island Press, Washington DC/Covelo.

Faucheux, S. (1999). "Towards a System of 'Vigilant Foresight' based on Complementarity of Actors", *ESSE Newsletter,* p. 1.

Field, A.J. (1984). "Micro-economics, Norms and Rationality", *Economic Development and Cultural Change,* 32, pp. 683-711.

Fisher, A.C., J.V. Krutilla and C.J. Cicchetti (1972). "The Economics of Environmental Preservation: A Theoretical and Empirical Analysis", *American Economic Review* 62 (4), pp. 605-19.

Fisher, A.C. and F.M. Peterson (1976). "The Environment in Economics: A Survey", *Journal of Economic Literature,* 14, pp. 1-33.

Gale, F.P. (1998). "Theorising 'Power' in Ecological Economics", *Ecological Economics,* pp. 131-138.

Haussman, J. (1979). "Individual Discount Rates and the Purchase and Utilisation of Energy Using Durables", *Bell Journal of Economics* (10), pp. 33-54.

Howarth, R.B. and R.B. Norgaard (1992). "Environmental Valuation under Sustainable Development", *American Economic Review,* Papers and Proceedings, pp. 473-477.

Ives, A.R. (1995). "Measuring Resilience in Stochastic Systems", *Ecological Monographs*, 65 pp. 217-233.

Jodha, N.S. (1986). "Common Property Resources and Rural Poor in Dry Regions of India", *Economic and Political Weekly*, XXX (27), July 5, pp. 1169-181

Kadekodi, G.K. (1998). "Common Pool Resources: An Institutional Movement From Open Access to Common Property Resources", *Energy Sources*, 20 pp. 317-332.

Klaassen, Ger. A.J. and Johannes B, Opschoor (1991). "Economics of Sustainability or the Sustainability of Economics: Different Paradigms", *Ecological Economics*, Vol. 4, pp. 93-115.

Krutilla, J.V. and A.C. Fisher (1975). *The Economics of Natural Environments: Studies in the Valuation of Commodity and Amenity Resources*, Johns Hopkins Press, Baltimore.

Lise, W. (1997). "An Econometric and Game Theoretic Approach to Common Pool Resource Management: Case Studies in Rural India", Ph.D Dissertation, University of Delhi, Delhi.

Maheshwari, R.C., D.P. Singh and V.M. Ambekar (1990). "A Case Study of Irrigated Watershed Management", Tejpura, Jhansi, Third IWRS National Symposium on Water Shed Development and Management, Kanpur.

Maler, K.G. (1974). *Environmental Economic: A Theoretical Enquiry*, Johns Hopkins University Press, Baltimore, Maryland.

Maler, K.G. (1999). "Deep Economics of Shallow Lakes: Economic-Ecological Modelling", mimeo lecture delivered at Institute of Economic Growth, Delhi.

Martinez-Alier, J. (1991). "Ecological Perception and Distributional Conflicts: A Historical View" in F. Dietz, F. vander Ploeg and J. vander Streaten. (ed) *Environmental Policy and The Economy*, Elsevier Science Publishers, Netherlands.

Mitchell, R.C. and R.T. Carson (1989). *Using Surveys to Value Public Goods: The Contingent Valuation Method*, The Johns Hopkins University Press for Resources for the Future, Washington D.C.

Munda, G., P. Nijkamp and P. Reitueld (1994). "Qualitative Multicriteria Evaluation for Environmental Management", *Ecological Economics*, 10, pp. 97-112.

North, D.C. (1990) *Institutions, Institutional Change and Economic Performance: Political Economy of Institutions and Decisions*, Cambridge University Press, Cambridge.

Okuno-Fujwara and A. Postlewaite (1990). *Social Norms in Random Matching Garnes*, mimeo, University of Tokyo, Tokyo.

Ostrom, E. (1990). *Governing the Commons: The Evolution of Institutional for Collective Action*, Cambridge University Press, New York.

Ostrom, E. and Roy Gardner (1993). "Coping with Asymmetries in the Commons: Self Governing Irrigation Systems Can Work", *Journal of Economic Perspectives* 7(4), pp. 98-112.

Pandit, M.K. (1997). "Ecological Economics – Towards a Synthesis of Two Disjunct Disciplines", *Current Science* 72(3), pp. 119-123.

Pangare, Ganesh and Pangare V. (1992). "From Poverty to Plenty, The Story of Ralegaon Siddhi", Indian National Trust for Art and Cultural Heritage.

Perrings, C. (1987). *Economy and Environment: A Theoretical Essay on the Interdependence of Economic and Environmental Systems*, Cambridge University Press, Cambridge, U.K.

Pigou, A.C. (1932). *The Economics of Welfare*, Macmillan, London.

Reitveld, P. and R. Janssen (1989). "Sensitivity Analysis in Discrete Multiple Criteria Decision Problems: On the Citing of Nuclear Power Plants", Research memorandum 66, Vrije-Universitiet, Amsterdam.

Saint, Kishore (1993). *Social Dynamics of Natural Resource Management – A Case Study in South Rajasthan Aravallis*.

Schotter, A. (1981). *The Economic Theory of Social Institutions*, Cambridge University Press, Cambridge, U.K.

Seibert, H. (1981). "Okonomische Theorie Naturlicher Ressourcen: EIN Uberblick", *Z. Wirtsch. Soc. Wiss.*, 18 pp. 267-298.

Sengupta, R.P. (1999). "Ecology and Economics: Interrelation and the Concept of Sustainability", mimeo, Indian Institute of Management, Calcutta.

Sethi, Rajiv and E. Somanathan (1996). "The Evolution of Social Norms in Common Property Resource Use", *The American Economic Review,* 86 (4), pp. 767-788.

Shogren, J.F. (1998). "A Political Economy in an Ecological Web", *Environmental and Resource Economics,* 11 (3-4), pp. 557-570.

Society for Promotion of Wasteland Development (1989). *A Study of Jawaja Project*, New Delhi.

Turner, K., C. Perrings and C. Folke (1996). "Ecological Economics: Paradigm or Perspective", CSERGE Working Paper, GEC 95-17.

Wade, R. (1987). *Village Republic: Economic Conditions for Collective Action in South India,* Cambridge University Press, Cambridge, UK.

6

Hidden Dimensions of Community Forestry in South Asia

A Gender Analysis[1]

BINA AGARWAL

1. Introduction

Community forestry groups, managing State or community-owned forest resources, represent one of the most rapidly growing forms of collective action in the developing world. This paper focuses on South Asian experience to illuminate how such groups, ostensibly set up to operate on principles of cooperation, and meant to involve and benefit all members of the rural community, can effectively exclude significant sections, such as women. While seemingly participatory, equitable and efficient, they can cloak substantial gender-related inequities and inefficiencies. The paper also analyses what underlies such unfavourable outcomes and how the outcomes could be improved.

The paper is based largely on fieldwork I undertook during 1998-1999 in 87 community forestry sites across five states of India (Gujarat, Karnataka, Madhya Pradesh, Orissa, and the Uttar Pradesh hills) and two districts (Kaski and Dang) of Nepal.[2] These are supplemented by existing case studies and some earlier visits to selected sites. Information was obtained mostly through unstructured interviews with villagers, at times with women and men in separate groups, at other times with both sexes jointly, in addition to individual interviews with key informants, especially office bearers in the community forestry groups.

---

1. This is a condensed version of a paper published under a different title (see Agarwal, 2002).

2. In India, 'state' relates to administrative divisions, while the term 'State' is used throughout in the political economy sense of the word. In Nepal 'districts' are the biggest administrative divisions, while in India, districts are sub-divisions of states.

2. Background

In rural South Asia, forests and village commons have always been important sources of basic necessities and supplementary livelihoods, providing villagers with firewood, fodder, small timber, and various non-timber products. Especially for the poor and women who own little private land, they have been critical for survival. In India's semi-arid regions in the 1980s, for instance, the landless and landpoor procured over 90 per cent of their firewood and satisfied 69-89 per cent of their grazing needs from common pool resources (Jodha, 1986). At that time, firewood alone provided 65-67 per cent of total domestic energy in India's hills and desert areas and over 90 per cent in Nepal as a whole (Agarwal, 1987). This situation remained largely unchanged even in the early-1990s when community forestry programmes were formally launched in both countries. Firewood was then still the single most important source (and for many the only source) of rural domestic energy in South Asia, and was still largely gathered, not bought. In 1992-93, for instance, 62 per cent of rural India's domestic energy came from firewood. In most Indian states over 80 per cent of rural households used some firewood as fuel; and, taking an all-India average, only about 15 per cent of the firewood so used was purchased (Natrajan, 1995).

Over time, however, people's ability to fulfill their needs had been eroding with the decline in communal resources, due both to degradation and to shifts in property rights away from communities to the State and to individuals. The push toward community forest management represented a small but notable reversal in these processes of statisation and privatisation, toward a re-establishment of greater community control over forests and village commons. Indeed there is now a mushrooming of community forestry groups (CFGs) in South Asia.[3]

In India, these CFGs include: (i) State-initiated groups formed under the Joint Forest Management (JFM) programme launched in 1990, in which village communities and the government share the responsibilities and benefits of regenerating degraded local forests; (ii) self-initiated groups, started by a village council, youth club or village elder, and concentrated mainly in Bihar and Orissa; and (iii) groups with a mixed history, such as the *van panchayats* or forest councils in the hills of Uttar Pradesh (UP) initiated by the British in the 1930s.

3. I will be using the term CFG to cover all types of community forestry groups.

Some of these have survived or been revived by NGOs. JFM groups are the most widespread, both geographically and in terms of forest area. To date, almost all Indian states have passed JFM resolutions. These allow participating villagers access to most non-timber forest products and to 25-50 per cent (varying by state) of any mature timber harvested. There were approximately 63,000 JFM groups in 2001, covering 14.2 million hectare (mha) or 18.6 per cent of the 76.5 mha administered as forest land (Sehgal, 2001). In addition, there are a few thousand groups of the other types.

Nepal's community forestry programme launched in 1993 is largely State-initiated. Here the State transfers even good forest to a set of identified users who form a forest user group (FUG) and are entitled to all of the benefits.[4] In 2000, there were 9100 FUGs involving one million households and 0.66 mha or 11.4 per cent (the target being 61 per cent) of the country's 5.8 mha of forest land (Government of Nepal, 2000). In both India and Nepal, NGOs can act as catalysts in group formation and functioning.

Unlike the old systems of communal resource management which typically recognised the usufruct rights of all village residents, the new CFGs represent a more formalised system of rights. Usually these rights are based either on membership (as in the state-initiated groups), or on rules specified by selected (often self-selected) community members (as in the self-initiated groups). Hence, membership, or some other formal system, is replacing village citizenship as the criterion for establishing rights in the commons.

This raises some critical questions, such as: how are the CFGs performing in terms of participation, equity and efficiency from the perspective of women, especially the poor? Are the emerging systems of rights in communal property inclusive and equitable, or are they replicating the patterns of elite and male centredness that characterise rights in private land? The section below focuses on these concerns.

3. Gendered Outcomes: Participation, Equity and Efficiency

In terms of forest regeneration, many CFGs have had notable success. Often all that is involved is restriction of entry and protection, although in some cases replanting is also done. Even with

4. The government, however, retains the right to reclaim any forests seen to be mismanaged by the FUGs.

simple protection, natural revival is often rapid if the rootstock is intact. Within five to seven years, many of the severely degraded tracts in semi-arid India have been covered with young trees; and areas with some vegetation, but notably declining, show encouraging signs of regeneration. In addition, in many ecological zones, there are reports of higher incomes and employment, lower seasonal out-migration, improvement in the land's carrying capacity, and enhanced biodiversity.[5]

Viewed from a gender perspective (and especially that of poor women) however, these results look less impressive on several important counts: effective participation; equity in the sharing of costs and benefits; and efficiency in functioning.

3.1 Participation

In both India and Nepal, the State-initiated groups generally have a two-tier organisational structure, consisting of a general body with members drawn from the whole village and an executive committee (EC) of some 9-15 persons. Both bodies, interactively, define the rules for forest use, punishments for breaking rules, the methods of protection and benefit distribution, and so on. Which category of persons has a voice in decisions bears critically on CFG functioning, and who gains or loses from them.

Women's effective participation in CFG decision-making would require not only that they become members, but that they attend and speak up at group meetings, and can sway at least some decisions in their own favour. To what extent do women in general, and poor women in particular, so participate?

3.1.1 Participation in Management

Women usually constitute less than 10 per cent of the general bodies in most JFM groups;[6] they are typically absent in the self-initiated groups;[7] and are few or none in the *van panchayats*.[8] Their presence in Nepal's FUGs is similarly sparse.

---

5. Viegas and Menon (1993), Arul and Poffenberger (1990), and my field vists in 1995, 1998-99.
6. Roy *et al.* (1992), Guhathakurta and Bhatia (1992), and Narain (1994); also my field visits 1998-99.
7. Kant *et al.* (1991), Singh and Kumar (1993), and my fieldwork in 1998-99.
8. Sharma and Sinha (1993), Tata Energy Research Unit (TERI, 1995); also my fieldwork in 1998-99. In the TERI study, only nine out of 50 *van panchayats* examined had any women members.

In India, the membership criteria in the JFM general body and the EC vary by state. Eight of the 22 states for which information is currently available restrict general body membership to one person per household. This is almost always the male household head. In eight other states, due to rule amendments, both spouses, or one man and one woman, can now be members, but this still excludes other household adults. Only three states allow membership to all village adults. In the self-initiated CFGs, the customary exclusion of women from village decision-making has been replicated. In Nepal's FUGs, again, the household is the unit of membership (Seeley, 1996). Without being general body members, women usually hear little about what transpires at meetings. Many women complain: "Our husbands don't tell us about meetings" or "When we ask them what happened at the meeting, they say: what will you gain by knowing?" (women to author, Orissa, 1998).

Women's representation in the ECs is also typically low. Although in many states, recent JFM resolutions require the inclusion of two or three or even $1/3^{rd}$ women in the EC, the women so included are rarely chosen by other women as their representatives. Such women are seldom active or effective. In Nepal again, women's presence is nominal, most are poorly informed about the FUG's activities, and some are even unaware that they are EC members (Moffatt, 1998).

Due to lack of awareness or other constraints discussed later, only a small percentage of the female general body or EC members usually attend the meetings. Those who attend rarely speak up, and if they do speak they say their opinions carry little weight: "Men don't listen, except perhaps one or two. Men feel they should be the spokespersons." (author's fieldwork in Nepal, 1998). Having a voice in the EC is important since this is the site for discussions and decisions on many critical aspects of CFG functioning. As matters stand, women are not party to many crucial decisions.

Although there are some contrasting examples of all-women CFGs and mixed CFGs with a high female presence, these remain a typical. There are no consolidated figures for India, but in Nepal, in 2000, all-women FUGs constituted less than 3.8 per cent of all FUGs, controlling only 1.1 per cent of FUG land. Typically this is degraded land, while mixed FUGs commonly control a few hundred hectares and usually of natural forest.[9]

9. Calculated from Government of Nepal (2000).

3.1.2 Participation in Protection

Despite their limited presence on CFG bodies, many women play an active role in protection. In formal terms, the bounded forest area is usually protected by employing a guard, with CFG members contributing the wage, or by forming a patrol group from among member households. A male guard or an all-male patrol characterised 45 per cent and 18 per cent respectively of the 87 sites I visited. Only a small percentage of patrols were constituted by both sexes, or by women alone, and there was a rare female guard. More commonly, women patrol informally. Women's informal vigilance improves protection in important ways. In fire fighting, likewise, women join in enthusiastically; and in several instances their alertness alone saved the forest.

On the one hand, therefore, most women are excluded from CFG membership and management; on the other hand, many women contribute notably to protection efforts, indicating their stake in forest regeneration. However, women's limited involvement in the decision-making process has implications for both equity and efficiency.

3.2 Equity

How equitable are the CFGs in cost and benefit sharing?

3.2.1 Cost Bearing

The costs of forest closure are broadly of two types: those associated with protection and management and those associated with forgoing forest use. The former usually includes membership fees, the forest guard's pay, the opportunity cost of patrolling time, and so on. These types of costs are borne largely by men. The costs of forgoing forest use include the opportunity cost of time spent in finding alternative sites for essential items such as firewood and fodder, other costs (identified below) associated with firewood shortages, the loss of livelihoods based on non-timber forest products, and so on. These types of costs fall largely on women.

Consider the firewood-related effects. Firewood is an everyday need, obtaining which is mainly women's responsibility (compared with, say, small timber that is needed occasionally for agricultural implements, *etc.*, and is mainly men's responsibility). Typically when protection begins, all human and animal entry is banned, especially in semi-arid regions. Where the land was barren anyway this caused no extra hardship. But where earlier women could fulfill at least part of their firewood needs from the protected area, after closure they were forced to travel to neighbouring sites, involving additional time, energy, and (where those sites were also protected) the risk of being caught and fined. As a result, in the early years of JFM, Sarin (1995) found that in some protected sites in Gujarat and West Bengal, women's collection time and distances traveled increased several fold. When neighbouring villages too started protecting, many women faced severe shortages. Most made do with the limited firewood available from trees on their home fields, supplemented by inferior fuels with additional negative consequences (described below). The poorest (with no land or cattle) were compelled to continue collecting clandestinely. Such gendered consequences were widespread, causing considerable resentment among the women.

In most places, this picture has remained largely unchanged even after several years of protection. Of the 87 CFGs I visited in 1998-99, firewood was available in 80. Of these 45 (60 per cent) still had a ban on firewood collection, with 21 not opening the forest at all and 24 opening it for a few days annually for drywood collection and/or cutback and cleaning operations. The remaining CFGs allowed some collection, usually only of fallen twigs and branches. Even after years of protection, women thus reported a persistence of firewood shortages in most of the sites I visited, and complaints especially from poor women were common, such as: 'We go in the morning and only return in the evening. Since the end of the rainy season, we have been going every day... Earlier too there was a shortage but not as acute' (woman to author, Karnataka, 1998). The exceptions were some parts of Orissa, Karnataka and Madhya Pradesh which had thicker forests and where the rules were more lenient.

Where possible, women substitute other fuels. A fortunate few have biogas but most turn to twigs, dung cakes, agricultural waste, or even dry leaves. Fire from these inferior fuels needs careful tending to keep the flame alive which increases cooking time and prevents women from simultaneously attending to other work. Moreover, these fuels generate more smoke, with negative health effects. In several villages women also report economising and bearing associated hardships.

Usually women from both middle and poor peasant households report such domestic energy problems, since even in the better-off homes firewood is typically gathered and not purchased. Women of landless or landpoor households are, however, the worst off, since without private land they also have no crop waste or trees of their own, and few cattle for dung. As a poor woman in Khut village (UP hills) told me: 'We don't know in the morning if we will be able to cook at night'.

As the forests have regenerated, at best these hardships have been alleviated; they have not disappeared. Firewood shortages, for instance, continue to be reported even 8-10 years after protection in many regions, despite the quite large areas being protected and considerable fuelwood being available for extraction. Estimates suggest that much more can be sustainably extracted than is currently being done (Ravindranath, 2000). Also other solutions (biogas, fuelwood plantations) could be found by the community. Hence the scarcities that women are experiencing in many places do not appear to be due to inadequate availability or a lack of potential solutions, but to women's limited bargaining power, whereby their problems are seen as individual/private rather than as warranting community attention.

3.2.2 Benefit Sharing

There are also gender inequities in benefit sharing. In some cases the benefits are not distributed at all. Among Orissa's self-initiated groups, for example, many all-male youth clubs have completely banned forest entry and have been selling forest produce, and using the quite substantial funds so obtained on religious festivals or on club functions (Singh and Kumar, 1993; my fieldvisits, 1998). In other types of CFGs, the money is normally put in a collective fund to be used as the group deems fit. Women typically have little say in how the fund is used.

Where the CFGs distribute the benefits, say as firewood or grass (as among some of the JFM groups), women of non-member households usually receive none, since entitlements are typically linked to membership. Often these are poor households whose members have migrated for work, or are out all day on wage labour and cannot easily contribute to patrolling or to the guard's wages. Even in member households usually men alone can claim the benefits directly, either because only they are members, or because entitlements are on a household basis, so that even if both spouses are members they get only one share. At best, women can benefit indirectly in some degree where the benefits are in kind (such as firewood), or where member households continue to enjoy the right to collect drywood from the protected area.[10] But where the CFGs distribute cash benefits, money given to men is often spent in large part on gambling, liquor, or personal items.[11]

3.3 *Efficiency*

Women's lack of participation in CFG decision-making, and gender inequities in the sharing of costs and benefits from protection, can have a range of efficiency implications. Some initiatives, for example, may fail to take off at all; others may not sustain the gains, or there may be a notable gap between the gains realised and those realisable (in terms of resource productivity and diversity, satisfying household needs, enhancing incomes, *etc.*). Inefficiencies can stem from one or more of the following problems (see also, Agarwal, 2000).

First, there are rule violations. In almost all the villages I visited there were at least some cases of rule violation, and at times this was a frequent occurrence. Violations by men usually involve timber for self-use or sale (the latter in areas with commercially valuable trees). Violations by women typically involve firewood. Where a CFG bans collection without consulting women or addressing their difficulties, many women are under pressure to break the rules, given their daily need for fuelwood. In Agrawal's study (2001) of a *van panchayat* village, women constituted 70-80 per cent of reported offenders between 1951 and 1991, many of them belonging to poor and low caste households.

A second source of inefficiency lies in inadequate information sharing with women. Information about rules, conflicts, or other aspects of forest management, does not always reach women (my fieldvisits, 1998-99). Similarly, male forest officials seldom consult women or seek their feedback when preparing micro-plans for forest development. Some women hear about the plans through their husbands, others not at all (Guhathakurta and Bhatia, 1992).

Third, inefficiencies can arise if the male guard or patrol fails to notice resource depletion. During my 1995 fieldvisit to Gujarat, a women's informal patrol in Machipada village took me to the protected site, and, pointing out the illegal cuttings which the men

10. Kant *et al.* (1991), ISO/Swedforest (1993), and Arul and Poffenberger (1990); also author's fieldwork in 1998-99.

11. Guhathakurta and Bhatia (1992), and my fieldwork in 1998-99.

had missed, noted: 'Men don't check carefully for illegal cuttings. Women keep a more careful lookout'. This gender difference, at least in part, arises because women, as the main and most frequent collectors of forest products, are more familiar with the forest than men.

Fourth, and relatedly, there are problems in catching transgressors. Typically, all-male patrols or male guards cannot deal effectively with women intruders because they can be charged with molestation. Threats to this effect, or the filing of false police cases against patrol members, especially by women from neighbouring villages and their families, are not uncommon. Equally, however, women on their own have difficulties in night patrolling or confronting aggressive male intruders. The most efficient solution appears to be a patrol team consisting of both sexes, but these are rare. When women voluntarily set up informal patrols, even where there is a male patrol, the efficiency of protection can improve notably (Sharma and Sinha, 1993).

Fifth, and relatedly, efficient functioning requires effective methods of conflict resolution. This is made difficult with women's virtual exclusion from the formal committees, even where the conflict involves women, as is not infrequently the case with firewood-related intrusions.

A sixth form of inefficiency stems from ignoring women's knowledge of plants and species when preparing plans for forest regeneration. Women as the main fuel and fodder collectors can often explain the attributes of trees and grasses better than men (Pandey, 1990; Chen, 1993). In general, women are better informed about the local environment in which they gather and collect and men about species found in distant areas (Gaul, 1994). Women's systematic exclusion from decision-making and management of new planting programmes can thus have negative efficiency implications, by failing to tap women's knowledge of diverse species for enhancing biodiversity.

A seventh form of inefficiency can arise from ignoring possible gender differences in preferences, say regarding when grass should be cut or which trees should be planted. I found that in the rare cases when women were consulted, they often came up with more suitable suggestions on when the forest should be opened for forest produce collection. Women's greater involvement in forest planning would thus better fulfil household needs and increase their commitment to the initiative.

Basically, from a gender perspective clearly the CFGs are violating many of the conditions deemed by several scholars as necessary for building enduring institutions for managing common pool resources. This includes conditions such as ensuring that those affected by the rules participate in framing and modifying the rules; that the rules are simple and fair; that there are effective mechanisms for monitoring the resource and resolving conflicts; and so on.[12]

Despite women's low involvement, forests might regenerate, but some of the initiatives might not sustain, and others might produce less than the full potential benefits.

4. What Determines Gendered Outcomes?

The gender-related efficiency outcomes discussed above are in large part *secondary* outcomes, stemming from women's low participation in the CFGs and from inequities in the rules of forest use, benefit sharing, *etc*. Hence it is important to examine what underlies women's low participation and the inequities in cost and benefit sharing.

In broad terms, the degree of participation and the distribution of costs and benefits can be seen to depend especially on the following factors: rules, norms, perceptions, the person's individual endowments and attributes, and their household endowments and attributes (which define where they fall within the structural hierarchies of class, caste, etc).

4.1 Factors Affecting Women's Participation

4.1.1 Rules

In formal CFGs, such as JFM groups in India or FUGs in Nepal, rules determine membership in the general body or the EC. As noted earlier, where the rule restricts membership to only one person per household, the male household head tends to join. Full inclusiveness would require that all adults be allowed to join. This is rare.

In addition, lack of awareness of rules can also constrain women's participation. In West Bengal, a study of 19 CFGs showed that even four years after the state order was amended to allow women's inclusion, barely two-fifths of the members knew of the change (Raju, 1997).

---

12. See, especially, Ostrom (1990), and Baland and Platteau (1996).

4.1.2 Social Norms

Even when membership rules are favourable and women join, they seldom attend or speak up at meetings because social norms restrict their visibility, mobility, and behaviour. These norms, whether internalised by women or imposed on them by threat of gossip, reprimand, or even violence, impinge directly on women's autonomy and ability to participate effectively in CFGs dominated by men.

Some communities have quite strict female seclusion norms. But more pervasive is the subtle gendering of physical space and social behaviour. For instance, norms often dictate a gender segregation of public space. Women of 'good character' are expected to avoid village spaces where men congregate, such as tea stalls and the market place (Agarwal, 1994). For older women, the restriction is less, but never fully absent. Many women thus feel uncomfortable attending CFG meetings.

The gender division of labour is another pernicious norm. The fact that women bear the main responsibility of childcare and housework, in addition to the load of agricultural work, cattle care, *etc.*, makes for high work burdens and logistical constraints. This seriously restricts women's ability to attend lengthy meetings held at inconvenient times.

Norms also reduce women's participation by creating subtle gender hierarchies, such as by requiring women to sit on the floor while men sit on cots, or requiring women to sit at the back of the meeting space where they are less visible and effective. Moreover, where senior male family members are present, women either do not attend meetings, or do not oppose men publicly. The hierarchy that marks 'respectful' behaviour in the family also marks community gatherings.

4.1.3 Social Perceptions

Incorrect perceptions about women's abilities impinge on men's willingness to include women in the CFGs. Men often view women's involvement as serving no useful purpose and tend to downplay their potential contributions. Some men's direct responses to questions are indicative: "There is no advantage in having women in the EC." Or "Women are illiterate. If they come to meetings, we men might as well stay at home (author's fieldwork, 1998). In some cases, I found that the men who were decrying my interviewing the women on the grounds that they were illiterate, were themselves illiterate!

4.1.4 Entrenched Territorial Claims

Men oppose women's inclusion much more strongly once their own claims are entrenched. For instance, where CFGs start out with only male members, or where men feel they have a prior claim to the land, they resist new claimants. 'Why do we need women? What we are doing is ok' (author's fieldwork, 1999).

4.1.5 Personal Endowments and Attributes

Women's lesser access to personal property or political connections reduces the weight of their opinions. In addition, limited experience in public interaction undermines their effectiveness in public forums. Some of these disadvantages can be overcome by older, married women, with leadership qualities and the self-confidence to speak up. In many CFGs, the few women members are typically widows, or older married women living in their parental homes who tend to be less socially constrained (Narain, 1994; Britt, 1997).

4.1.6 Household Endowments and Attributes

Finally, factors such as the class and caste of the woman's household tend to matter where the village is multi-caste and dominated by the upper-caste, or where the CFG is constituted of several villages that are caste/class homogeneous in themselves, but differ hierarchically from other villages in the CFG.[13] The effect of caste is complex, however. While being low-caste and poor can adversely affect a person's ability to bargain for a better deal within an upper-caste community, low-caste women are also less restricted by social norms than upper-caste women.

4.2 Factors Affecting Distributional Equity

Similar (*but not identical*) factors affect gender inequitable outcomes in terms of costs and benefits. The principal factor underlying gender differences in cost sharing appears to be social norms governing the gender division of labour. As already discussed, women's primary responsibility for firewood and fodder means that women bear the bulk of the costs of forgoing forest use.

Benefit sharing is likely to be affected by a number of factors. One, there are the rules regarding entitlements to benefits. As noted, access

13. Author's fieldwork in 1998-99. See also, Sarin (1998) and Hobley (1996).

to some types of benefits is linked to membership. However, even if both spouses are members, the woman may not get a separate or additional share if the CFG has decided that the household rather than the individual will be the unit of distribution.

Two, perceptions about contributions and deservedness matter (Agarwal, 1997, Sen, 1990). Tasks such as collecting firewood and fodder, stall-feeding animals, storing and processing grain, *etc.*, done mainly by women, are usually economically invisible since they seldom bring in cash returns. Also household chores done within the home are rendered physically invisible. All this negatively affects perceptions about women's contributions. Women seen to be participating in forest management would be better placed to claim equal benefits with men in that their contributions would be better recognised.

Three, whether or not the outcome is equitable depends on pre-existing personal endowments and attributes. Since women as a gender (even if not all women as individuals) have fewer private economic endowments, CFG shares given only to male members typically result in inequitable outcomes for women in both rich and poor households.

Four, as we've noted, the degree to which women are affected by forest closure or shortages is linked to their household's economic endowments and social attributes, in particular to their household's class, caste, *etc.* For instance, women in households that own land and animals can get some fuel and fodder from private assets, although, as noted, social constraints can also limit their options with respect to alternative collection sites.

5. Improving Outcomes for Women: The Bargaining Framework

How can the factors outlined above be acted upon to improve outcomes? A promising analytical framework for examining the possibilities for change on all these counts is that of bargaining. Women's ability to change rules, norms, perceptions and endowments in a gender-progressive direction would depend on their bargaining power with the State, the community and the family, as the case may be. What would affect women's ability to bargain effectively in these three arenas?

5.1 Bargaining: Some Conceptual Issues[14]

5.1.1 The State

We would expect women's bargaining strength with the State to depend on a complex set of factors, such as, whether they function as a group or as individuals; and the cohesiveness and strength of the group. The bargaining power of such a group is likely to be higher the larger and more unified it is; the greater the political weight carried by the castes of which it is composed; the greater its command over economic resources; the more the support it gets from NGOs, the media, academics, and international donors; and the more State officials are influenced by gender-progressive norms and perceptions.

Moreover, the State itself can be seen as an arena of bargaining at multiple levels (*e.g.* state-level and centre), between multiple parties (*e.g.* policymaking and policy implementing bodies), and between different elements of the State structure (*e.g.* different ministries), with varying commitments to gender equality. There could also be contestation between gender-progressive and conservative government officials.

5.1.2 The Community

The second important arena of bargaining is the community. Implicit or explicit bargaining can occur between an individual (or a subset of individuals) and the community over the rules and norms governing, say, economic resource use and social behaviour, and over the enforcement of those rules and norms. Non-compliance with CFG rules could be seen as a form of implicit bargaining.

As with the State, women's bargaining power within the community would be enhanced if they had support from external agents such as NGOs and the State. Group cohesiveness and strength is also important. For instance, an individual woman breaking seclusion norms could easily be penalised, say by casting aspersions on her character. Such reprisals are less possible if women decide to transgress social norms as a group (Agarwal, 1994).

In addition, in a multi-caste/class-heterogeneous village, we would expect women's bargaining power to depend on the socio-economic composition of their group and their ability to command funds. In the sharing of communal resources, for instance, the negotiating strength

14. For elaboration, see Agarwal (1997).

of low-caste or poor women, even if they formed a group, is likely to be weaker than that of high-caste or rich peasant women whose caste or class as a whole commands greater power in the village.

5.1.3 The Family

The third major arena of bargaining is the family. Intrafamily bargaining for a more equitable sharing of benefits or tasks, or for greater freedom to participate publicly, is perhaps the most complex aspect of bargaining (Agarwal, 1994, 1997). Broadly four types of factors are likely to impinge on a woman's bargaining power in the home: her personal endowments and attributes (education, whether she earns an income, property ownership, age, marital status, *etc.*); her ability to draw upon extra-household support from friends, relatives, women's groups and NGOs, and the State; social norms (which define who gets what, or who does what in the household); and social perceptions (about her deservedness).

Some common determinants of bargaining power in all three arenas are support from external agents, social norms and perceptions, and group strength. Norms, perceptions, and group strength require some elaboration.

Social norms can affect bargaining power both directly and indirectly. For instance, norms that restrict women's presence in public spaces directly reduce women's ability to bargain for rule changes within CFGs. In addition, they do so indirectly by reducing women's ability to build contacts with NGOs or State officials. Social norms can also influence how bargaining is conducted: *e.g.* covertly or overtly; aggressively or quietly. In cultures or contexts where social norms stifle explicit voice, women may be pushed into using covert forms of protest, such as persistent complaining or withdrawing into silence (Agarwal, 1994). Moreover, attempts to change social norms can themselves constitute a bargaining process.

Social perceptions can affect women's bargaining power in so far as women's contributions and abilities diverge from perceptions about their contributions and abilities. As noted earlier, much of what women do is rendered invisible and therefore undervalued by both families and communities. To the extent that women internalise these perceptions, they can self-restrict their options or what they seek to change and bargain over. To enhance women's bargaining power, a necessary step would thus be to change women's own perceptions about their potential options and abilities, as well as the perceptions of their families, the community and the State regarding their abilities and the legitimacy of their claims.

Group strength can be a critical factor at all levels of bargaining and in all forms of bargaining (including over social norms and perceptions). Here village women's group strength derives not merely from the number of women who want a change in rules and norms, but also from their willingness to act collectively in their common interest. In other words, it depends on whether gender is a basis of group identity, over and above the possible divisiveness of caste or class. The creation of such group identity may thus need to be part of the process of improving outcomes for women.

Let us now consider ground experience in attempts to improve women's participation and distributional equity in CFGs. These experiences do not illustrate all elements of the bargaining framework, but they reveal some key elements.

5.2 Bargaining: Ground Experience

5.2.1 The State

JFM experience indicates that successfully bargaining with the State for changing the initial rules of entry is not very difficult. Pressure from external agents such as gender-progressive NGOs and key individuals, for instance, has led a number of Indian states to make JFM membership rules more women-inclusive. Here village women did not have to explicitly bargain for changes, but the women's movement in South Asia has brought about a sufficient shift in perceptions regarding gender inequalities to make such issues easier to resolve through outside intervention. Village women, on this count, thus start from a position of some bargaining strength.

5.2.2 The Community

Bargaining with the community to ensure that more women-inclusive membership rules are implemented, and to increase women's effective voice in CFGs, has proved more difficult. On the positive side, some of the gender-progressive NGOs, forest officials and donors have used their bargaining power with the community to bring about changes in women's favour, sometimes on their own initiative, at other times when village women approached them.

For instance, some Indian NGOs have made high female membership in mixed groups a condition for forming the groups. In

Gujarat, one NGO insists on 50 per cent women when starting new CFGs. Similarly, some state-level officials in India have increased women's membership in mixed groups, by stipulating that there should be at least 30 per cent women in the general body, or by refusing to start meetings unless the men also invite the women (Viegas and Menon, 1993; Sarin, 1998). For distributional equity, likewise, the staff of a Gujarat-based NGO took up women's complaints about firewood shortages at a CFG meeting. This resulted in a shift from total closure of the forest to its opening for a few days annually. Sometimes, small changes in rules occur due to women's persistent complaining. However, for a larger and sustained impact, an active input is required from women themselves, in terms of more formal involvement in rule making and the bargaining power to ensure changes in their favour.

Ground experience suggests that to bring this about, for a start, a critical mass of vocal women is necessary. This can give women more voice in mixed forums, and help them challenge restrictive social norms and perceptions. As some women interviewed by Britt (1993: 146) in the UP hills stressed: 'without a good majority of women present it is impossible to express opinions.' There is a growing consensus among gender-progressive NGOs and elements of the State that for bringing together a critical mass of vocal women within CFGs, separate women's groups will need to be formed, as a first step.

There is less consensus, however, on what type of group this should be. Where all-women CFGs have been formed, many have done well in terms of protection and increasing women's self-confidence. However, so far, all-women CFGs, have usually arisen in special circumstances, and are still marginal in terms of numbers and area protected. Also, they cannot solve the problem of women's low presence and lack of effective voice in the more typical all-male or mixed CFGs. For this, other kinds of efforts are needed. Toward this end, some rural NGOs have been forming all-women savings-and-credit groups, which, unlike CFGs, do not involve a resource over which there is a generalised community claim. In some regions, more multi-functional women's groups, such as *mahila mangal dals* in the UP hills, or *amma samuhs* in Nepal, are also doing well.

Such separate women's groups (organised around savings, *etc.*) have enhanced women's self-confidence and experience in collective functioning and promoted a sense of collective identity. They have also increased women's ability to deal with government agencies, improved male perceptions about women's capabilities, and influenced some social norms which earlier confined women to the domestic space. The response below is fairly typical:

> Men used to shut us up and say we shouldn't speak. Women learned to speak up in a *sangathan* (group). Earlier we couldn't speak up even at home. Now we can be more assertive and also go out. I am able to help other women gain confidence as well (village woman leader to author, Gujarat, 1999).

These experiences are similar to those of many other rural women's groups across South Asia, which too indicate that group strength, external agency support, and activities that enable women to make a visible contribution (especially monetary) can alter social norms and perceptions, and increase the social acceptance of women in public roles. But in many villages, separate women's groups have also sharpened gender segregation in collective functioning. Often women's savings groups are seen as 'women's groups' and the CFGs as 'men's groups'.

To overcome this divide, more concerted efforts to integrate women's groups into CFGs appear necessary. For instance, an NGO in rural Karnataka encourages women's savings groups to discuss CFG functioning, collect CFG membership dues, and persuade women to join the CFG. As a result, in several of its villages, over 80 per cent of the women in the savings groups are now in the CFG general body (author's fieldwork, 1998). Another approach (yet to be tried) could be to form a women's sub-group within each mixed CFG, that would separately discuss and subsequently represent women's forest-related concerns in the full CFG meeting.

5.2.3 The Family

Bargaining within the family, as noted, is the most complex and few rural NGOs directly intervene here. Forming all-women groups can, however, help. For instance, during my fieldvisits I found several cases where a women's group had supported individual women in their negotiations with husbands, or where joining a group had improved women's situation at home. As one such group told me:

> There are one or two men who objected to their wives attending our meetings, and said you can't go. But when our women's association came to their aid, the men let their wives go (village women to author, Gujarat, 1998).

In other words, group strength and women's visible contributions can weaken restrictive social norms, and improve a man's view of his wife's deservedness, although some norms, such as the gender division of domestic work, can prove more rigid.

Finally, CFGs are affected by the wider context of structural and social inequalities within which they are located. Both participation and distributional equity are affected by the pre-existing inequalities predicated on the caste and class of women's households, as well as on gender. These inequalities are unlikely to decline substantially within the parameters of CFG functioning. To change these would need more wide-ranging measures to enhance the access of women in general, and of poor and low-caste households in particular, to land and other assets.

6. Conclusion

CFGs are a significant example of group functioning. While many have done quite well in regenerating the environment, they have been less successful in ensuring women's participation in decision-making, or gender equity in the sharing of costs and benefits from forest protection. As a result, they have also failed to tap the full potential of the collective effort. Improving participation and equity is thus important both in itself and because it can prove complementary to effective functioning.

This analysis shows that for more participatory, equitable, and efficient outcomes, it is necessary to change factors such as rules, norms and perceptions, and the pre-existing structural inequalities in endowments and attributes of women's households and of women themselves. Such change will require strengthening women's bargaining power with the State, the community and the family. This has been achieved to some degree through the intervention of external agents, such as NGOs, forest officials and donors. But long-term changes will need enhancing women's self-confidence and collective strength. Forming separate women's groups can help, but to ensure that these do not cause greater gender segregation, their conscious integration into mixed CFGs will be needed. Forming women's sub-groups within each CFG could provide another way forward. In either case, these are only a few steps among the many that will be needed to transform mixed CFGs into more gender egalitarian institutions.

References

Agrawal, A. (2001). "State Formation in Community Spaces: The Forest Councils of Kumaon", *Journal of Asian Studies*, 60 (1): pp. 1-32.

Agarwal, B. (2002). "The Hidden Side of Group Behaviour: A Gender Analysis of Community Forestry in South Asia", in Heyer, J., F. Stewart & R. Thorp (eds) *Group Behaviour and Development: Is the Market Destroying Cooperation*? Clarendon Press, Oxford.

————. (2000). "Conceptualising Environmental Collective Action: Why Gender Matters", *Cambridge Journal of Economics*, 24 (3), pp. 283-310.

————. (1997). "Bargaining and Gender Relations: Within and Beyond the Household", *Feminist Economics*, 3 (1), pp. 1-51.

————. (1994). *A Field of One's Own: Gender and Land Rights in South Asia*, Cambridge: Cambridge University Press.

————. (1987). "Under the Cooking Pot: The Political Economy of the Domestic Fuel Crisis in Rural South Asia", *IDS Bulletin*, 18 (1), pp. 11-22.

Arul, N.J. and Poffenburger, M. (1990). "FPC Case Studies", in Pathan, R.S., N.J. Arul and M. Poffenburger (Eds): *Forest Protection Committees in Gujarat: Joint Management Initiative*, Ford Foundation, New Delhi, Working Paper No. 7, pp. 13-25.

Baland, J.M. and Platteau, J.P. (1996). *Halting Degradation of Natural Resources: Is there a Role for Rural Communities?*, Oxford: Clarendon Press.

Britt, C. (1993). *Out of the Wood? Local Institutions and Community Forest Management in Two Central Himalayan Villages*, Cornell University, Ithaca, draft monograph.

Chen, M. (1993). "Women and Wasteland Development in India: An Issue Paper", in Singh, A. and N. Burra (eds) *Women and Wasteland Development in India*, Delhi: Sage Publishers, pp. 21-90.

Dahal, D.R. (1994). *A Review of Forest User Groups: Case Studies from Eastern Nepal*, Kathmandu, ICIMOD.

Gaul, K.K. (1994). "Negotiated Positions and Shifting Terrains: Apprehension of Forest Resources in the Western Himalaya", PhD dissertation, Department of Anthropology, University of Massachusetts, Amherst.

Government of Nepal (2000). *Forest User Group Statistics*, Community and Private Forestry Division, Department of Forests, Kathmandu.

Guhathakurta, P. and K.S. Bhatia (1992). *A Case Study on Gender and Forest Resources in West Bengal*, World Bank, Delhi, June 16.

Hobley, M. (1996). *Participatory Forestry: The Process of Change in India and Nepal*, London: Overseas Development Institute.

ISO/Swedforest (1993). *Forests, People and Protection: Case Studies of Voluntary Forest Protection by Communities in Orissa*, New Delhi: Swedish International Development Agency (SIDA).

Jodha, N.S. (1986). "Common Property Resources and the Rural Poor", *Economic and Political Weekly*, 21 (27), pp. 1169-81.

Kant, S., Singh, N.M. and Singh, K.K. (1991). *Community-based Forest Management Systems: Case Studies from Orissa*, Delhi: SIDA; Bhopal: Indian Institute of Forest Management; and Delhi: ISO/Swedforest.

Moffatt, M. (1998). "A Gender Analysis of Community Forestry and Community Leasehold Forestry in Nepal with a Macro-Meso-Micro Framework", M.A. dissertation in Development Policy Analysis, Department of Economics and Social Studies, University of Manchester.

Narain, U. (1994). "Women's Involvement in Joint Forest Management: Analysing the Issues", Draft paper, May 6.

Natrajan, I. (1995). "Trends in Firewood Consumption in Rural India", *Margin*, 28 (1), pp. 41-45.

Ostrom, E. (1990). *Governing the Commons*, Cambridge: Cambridge University Press.

Pandey, S. (1990). "Women in Hattidunde Forest Management in Dhading District", Nepal, *MPE Series* No. 9, International Centre for Integrated Mountain Development (ICIMOD), Kathmandu, Nepal.

Raju, M. (1997). "Seeking Niches in Forest Canopy: An Enquiry into Women's Participation", mimeographed report, Ford Foundation, Delhi.

Ravindranath, N.H., K.S. Murali, and K.C. Malhotra (2000). *Joint Forest Management and Community Forestry in India: An Ecological and Institutional Assessment*, New Delhi: Oxford and IBH Publishing Co. Pvt. Ltd.

Roy, S.B., R. Mukerjee, and M. Chatterjee (1992). *Endogenous Development, Gender Role in Participatory Forest Management*, IBRAD, Calcutta.

Sarin, M. (1998). *Who is Gaining? Who is Losing? Gender and Equality Concerns in Joint Forest Management*, Society for Promotion of Wasteland Development, New Delhi.

————. (1995). "Regenerating India's Forest: Reconciling Gender Equity and Joint Forest Management", *IDS Bulletin*, 26 (1), pp. 83-91.

Seeley, J. (1996). "Who benefits from Participatory Forest Management", *Banko Janakari*, 6 (1), pp. 38-39.

Sehgal, S. (2001). "Joint Forest Management: A Decade and Beyond", paper presented at the workshop on Policy Implications of Knowledge with Respect to Common Pool Resources in India, The Institute of Economic Growth, Delhi, September 14.

Sen, A.K. (1990). "Gender and Cooperative Conflicts", in Tinker, I. (Ed): *Persistent Inequalities: Women and World Development*, Oxford University Press, pp. 123-49, New York.

Sharma, A. and A. Sinha (1993). "A Study of the Common Property Resources in the Project Area of the Central Himalaya Rural Action Group", mimeo, Indian Institute of Forest Management, Bhopal, Madhya Pradesh.

Singh, N. and Kumar K. (1993). "Community Initiatives to Protect and Manage Forests in Balangir and Sambalpur Districts", mimeo, SIDA, New Delhi.

Tata Energy Research Institute (TERI) (1995). "Community Participation in *Van Panchayats* of Kumaon Region of Uttar Pradesh", Paper No.1, Part I, TERI, Delhi.

Viegas, P. and G. Menon (1993). "Bringing Government and People Together: Forest Protection Committees of West Bengal - Role and Participation of Women", in Singh, A. and N. Burra (Eds): *Women and Wasteland Development in India*, New Delhi: Sage Publications, pp. 71-210.

7

Cost Benefit Analysis of Cleaning Ganges

Some Emerging Environment and Development Issues[1]

A. MARKANDYA
M.N. MURTY

1. Introduction

The Ganges is one of the most important river systems in the world. This 2,510 kilometre (km) long river has a basin covering 861,404 square km. Currently, half a billion people, almost one tenth of the world's population, live within the river basin, at an average density of over 500 square km, and this population is projected to increase to over one billion people by the year 2030. There are about 52 cities, 48 towns, and thousands of villages in its basin. Nearly all the sewerage from these populations goes directly into the river, totalling over 1.3 billion litres per day, along with a further 260 million litres of industrial waste, runoff from the six million tonnes of fertilisers and 9,000 tonnes of pesticides used in agriculture within the basin, and large quantities of solid waste, including thousands of animal carcasses and several hundred human corpses released into the river every day for spiritual rebirth. The inevitable result of this onslaught onto the river's capacity to receive and assimilate waste has been an erosion of river water quality, to the extent that, by the 1970s, large stretches (over 600 km) of the river were effectively dead from an ecological point of view.

The "Ganga Action Plan (GAP)" an important environmental project to clean the Ganges, originated from the personal intervention and interest of the late Indira Gandhi. The GAP was launched in February 1985. The final investment cost of the GAP has been

---

1. This paper is mainly drawn from Markandya and Murty, 2000, "Cleaning-up the Ganges: The Cost Benefit Analysis of Ganga Action Plan", Oxford University Press, New Delhi. It is an abridged version of paper published under the same title in Environmental and Development Economics 9: 61-81 Cambridge University Press, February, 2004.

estimated at Rs. 7657.37 million at 1995-96 prices during 1985-86 to 1996-97. The operating costs of the programme are estimated as Rs. 480.264 million[2] during the same period. The GAP has been perhaps the largest single attempt to clean up a polluted river anywhere in the world. Although a number of other international scale river basin clean-up programmes have been effectively implemented in other countries, none has the full spectrum of geographical, ecological and socio-cultural complexities which faced the Indian Government during implementation of the GAP. The sums of money referred to above are large by any standards, and were committed with the main objective of raising the river water quality to bathing standard. As a result of GAP, the quality of water in the Ganges has shown varying improvements in absolute terms since 1985. The dissolved oxygen levels have been improving in the areas of Kanpur, Allahabad and Varanasi after 1992. In the lower stretch, at Nawabganj, however, dissolved oxygen levels have continued to decline. Similar improvements in phosphate and nitrate concentrations have been observed since the early-1990s.

The assessment of river quality changes as a result of the GAP could be correctly made by comparing the conditions of river in the late-1990s without the GAP with the conditions with the GAP. Such a comparison has to be carried out using a sophisticated water quality model. The results of such a model in the case of the Ganges show that some improvements in water quality (measured in terms of dissolved oxygen and biochemical oxygen demand (BOD) were observed everywhere, *albeit* quite small ones in some places. It is also worth noting that a total stretch of about 437 km still violates the permissible level of 3.0 mg/l of BOD. In terms of dissolved oxygen the level throughout the river is now more than 5.0 mg/l. Without the GAP, more than 740 km would have violated the BOD limit, with about 1000 km violating having BOD levels in excess of 10 mg/l. So, in summary, some improvements in water quality have been achieved. The important question is, what are these worth in money terms, taking account of the broadest set of values placed on cleaner water? It is this question that is addressed in this paper.

The GAP is a good example of how environmental federalism works. Co-operation among the riparian countries or provinces in a

2. The average exchange rates in 1995 were Rs. 54.5 to the pound sterling and Rs. 35.2 to the US dollar. Hence the investment costs amount to £ 205 million or $ 318 million. The operating costs are £ 6.4 million or $ 10mn.

federal country is a pre-requisite for any river cleaning programme. A polluted river causes damages to countries down stream and, as a consequence, benefits from river cleaning up stream accrue to the countries down stream. Therefore, a contract among the riparian states agreeing on the principles to share the cost of cleaning is an essential first step for any river cleaning programme. A programme to clean the Ganges, a river flowing through three provinces (Uttar Pradesh, Bihar and West Bengal) of the Indian federation requires co-operation between the centre and provinces and among the provinces themselves. In fact, all the three levels of government (central, provincial and local) are involved in the construction and maintenance of GAP programmes.

According to the polluter pay principle, the cost of cleaning Ganges should be mainly borne by households and industries, the main polluters, in its basin. The entire capital cost of the GAP, however, is met by the central government while the operation and maintenance cost is shared by central and provincial governments. The various schemes for cleaning Ganges include projects for interception and diversion of sewage, sewage treatment plants, low cost sanitation projects, and river front development projects. In the current cost sharing arrangement, the households, the main polluters of Ganges are paying for cleaning Ganges to the extent they pay sewerage charges to local governments. These payments meet only a small part of operation and maintenance cost of sewage treatment plants. As per the current environmental regulations in India, all the water polluting industries have to meet the effluent standards fixed by the central and state pollution control boards. Therefore, industries located in the Gangetic basin and polluting the Ganges have to incur the cost of meeting the prescribed standards. This cost, incurred by the industries, becomes part of cost of cleaning Ganges in India. Almost the entire cost of treating household borne effluents has to be met by the Government out of general taxes it collects from the public.

2. Benefits and Beneficiaries from Cleaning Ganges

There are multiple benefits from cleaning the Ganges[3]. Table 7.1 describes the benefits and the beneficiaries of the river cleaning

---

3. See Mitchell and Carson (1989), Figure 3.1, p.61 for a classification of benefits from an improvement of fresh water quality.

programme. There are benefits accruing to people who stay near the river or visit the river for pilgrimages or tourism. These will be in the form of recreation and health benefits and are called user benefits. The other category of benefits are those accruing to the people who are not staying near the river but gain welfare from knowing the river is clean. This category of people can be both Indians and foreigners. These are called non-user benefits arising out of people's preferences for the bio-diversity or the aquatic life the Ganges supports and the religious significance of the river. Other beneficiaries include fishermen, farmers and those for whom employment is created as a result of the project. Fishermen get benefits of improved fish production. Farmers get some type of irrigation and fertiliser benefits by using treated water and sludge from the sewage treatment plants of GAP. The investment projects for cleaning Ganges provide employment to unemployed or underemployed unskilled labour in India. Also, the cleaning Ganges contributes benefits in the form of cost savings to water supply undertakings along the river. Hence the beneficiaries from cleaning Ganges can be classified as users, non-users, health beneficiaries, farmers, unskilled labour, and fishermen. The non-user benefits of the Ganges arise out of motives people have to bequeath the bio-diversity the river supports to the future generations (bequest motive), for getting reassured about the conservation of Ganges with the knowledge that the river is kept clean and the aquatic life is protected (existence motive), and to protect the people living in the river basin from water borne deceases (altruistic motive).

Table 7.1

Identification of Benefits and Beneficiaries from Cleaning Ganges

Benefits Class	*Benefit Category*	*Beneficiaries*
User	Instream Withdrawal	Recreation Users Farmers, Fisher men, Industries and Households (Agriculture, Industrial and Commercial)
	Aesthetic Ecosystem	Recreation Users General Ecosystem Support (Food Chain)
Non-user	Vicarious Consumption and Stewardship (Existence and Bequest values)	Indian Public and International Communities

The Ganges supports 25,000 or more of species of bio-diversity ranging from micro-organisms to mammals. There are a number of international species comprising of mammals, reptiles and birds supported by the Ganges ecosystem. The Ganges dolphin, irrawady dolphin, finless porpoise, and a variety of ottars are some of the important mammals found in the river. In the case of bird life, osprey, ring tailed fishing eagle, and Indian skimmer are important species. A variety of crocodiles including *Gharial*, marsh crocodile or *Maggar*, and salt-water crocodile and a number of turtles unique to the Ganges are the reptiles supported by the Ganges. The GAP has helped in preserving these species in four ways. First, there are some for which there have been *in situ* conservation and captive breeding programmes. Second, the GAP has raised awareness and encouraged conservation efforts through information dissemination *etc*. Third, the GAP has facilitated the collection of information on species and their habitat, something that will contribute in an important way to their conservation. Finally, the general improvement of the quality of water of Ganges has helped most of the above species.

The international significance of many species mentioned above can result in placing substantial non-use values on the Ganges by the international communities. Therefore, the international communities can potentially contribute money for cleaning the Ganges if India desires such a support. The resource constraints and the very high opportunity cost in terms of foregone development benefits from the conservation programmes of Ganges may make this option attractive to India for the river cleaning programmes in future.

3. Estimation of Benefits and Costs of GAP

3.1 User and Non-user Benefits

The user and non-user benefits of cleaning Ganges are estimated using the contingent valuation methods of survey of households.[4] These benefits are described as people's willingness to pay for cleaning the river. The CV survey instrument has three components: (i) Scenario specification, (ii) Elicitation, and (iii) Socioeconomic characteristics of the respondents. In the scenario specification, the information about the environmental good provided is given to the

4. See Freeman III, 1993 and Mitchell and Carson, 1993 for a detailed description of contingent valuation methods.

respondent. The environmental good provided in this case is the clean Ganges and the flow of environmental services from it. First, an overview of GAP including its year of inception and target (uniform bathing quality in the river) is given. Second, a brief summary is provided of basic causes for pollution in the river, pointing out that the domestic sewage from large cities is the single largest cause for pollution. Third, a brief account is made of activities of GAP, ranging from the setting up of sewage treatment plants to constructing electric crematoria.

For value elicitation, respondents were shown a certain map of water quality of Ganges (either of uniform bathing quality, or river water quality as it was in 1995 or in 1985) and were then asked to evaluate the benefits they perceived themselves. Three payment vehicles were considered: (i) payment to government, (ii) payment to a reputable charitable organisation, and (iii) payment to a local citizen group (of which the respondent could become a member). The first option was rejected outright at the pre-testing stage, given the prevailing lack of confidence in government. The other two options were tried in pre-testing and found the reputable charitable organisation was the most acceptable payment vehicle. The elicitation format chosen is an open ended bidding game. The respondents were asked two follow-up questions to their initial bid, one of which is a closed ended question.

Socio-economic details of households for which information was collected are age, education and occupation of the respondent, the size of the household, and the gross annual household income from all sources. For measuring non-user benefits, the target population is restricted to urban literate population in the major cities (population one million and above) in India. First, contingent valuation involves considerable hypothetical reasoning that would be difficult for illiterate respondents to follow. Second, willingness to pay for non-user benefits is constrained by income, if incomes are at subsistence levels, it will be difficult to respondents to reveal positive values. Cities were selected to achieve maximum geographical coverage. With in each city, the sampling scheme was designed to control for geographical spread and income categories. Accordingly, the city was divided into four geographical zones, and households in three income categories of high-income, middle-income, and low-income groups were sampled. The sampling in each geographical zone and income group was done by taking every alternative household along a street or in a complex of residential flats. There are 2000 households surveyed in ten cities in India. For measuring user benefits, especially amenity benefits from Ganges, the sample is limited to residents, tourists, and pilgrims (at bathing *ghats*). The sample is drawn from three cities, Allahabad, Varanasi, and Calcutta on the Ganges. Within each city, the sampling scheme is designed to cover residential areas within half-a-kilometre on either side of the river, and major pilgrimage centres with control for geographical spread and income categories. Again for the residential sample, only literate households are chosen. Each household was asked to place a value on the three scenarios of river quality: (a) quality before the river cleanup, (b) the current quality, and (c) bathing quality. The willingness to pay function relating to these values to socio-economic characteristics of households and the river quality was then estimated.[5] Table 7.2 provides estimates of mean willingness to pay for users and non-users based on the estimated willingness to pay functions.

Table 7.2

Mean Willingness to Pay for Non-users and Users
(Rupees per Household Per Annum at 1995-96 Prices)

Levels of Water Quality	*Bathing Quality*	*1995 Quality with GAP*	*1985 Quality*	*1995 Quality Without GAP*
Non-users	557.94	192.81	101.48	97.51
Users	581.59	167.23	93.28	71.12

Source: Markandya and Murty (2000)

The extrapolation of household willingness to pay for user and non-user benefits to the beneficiary population requires the information about the size of the population given the estimates of household mean willingness to pay. The beneficiary population for the non-user benefits constitutes the urban literate population in India. An estimate of urban literate population of households in 23 cities having population one million and above in India is made as 8.733 million (Markandya and Murty, 2000). The beneficiary population of user benefits is assumed to constitute the urban literate households located within 0.5 km of the river. The population of user households

5. See Markandya and Murty, 2000; 2004 for details about the estimated willingness to pay equations.

is estimated as 37213 (Markandya and Murty, 2001). Table 7.3 provides the estimates of annual aggregate incremental user and non-user benefits from GAP. If the pilgrims to various *ghats* of the river are also considered as users of Ganges, the users benefits could be very high running into several thousands of millions.[6]

Table 7.3

Aggregate Willingness to Pay for Changes in Ganges Water Quality

(Rs. million at 1995-96 prices)

Change in water Quality level	*Non-user Benefits*	*User Benefits*
1985 to bathing quality	4021.1	32
1985 to 1995 quality	797.7	5
Simulated to bathing quality	3986.5	33
Simulated to actual 1995 quality	832.3	6

Source: Markandya and Murty (2000)

3.2 Health Benefits

The health benefits could be estimated using the cost of illness approach, dose response function, and the health production function. The dose response function and the cost of illness approaches may underestimate the health benefits from the pollution abatement for they could not account for the expenditures incurred by the households on mitigating (using medicines, and consulting a doctor) and averting activities (using water purifiers and staying indoors) in response to environmental pollution. The household health production model accounts for these expenditures. The estimates of health benefits from the reduction in river pollution made here using the cost of illness approach could therefore underestimate health benefits.

The health benefits are estimated by a study conducted by the All India Institute of Hygiene and Public Health (AIIH&PH, 1997), Calcutta. Data was collected about the health of a sample of population living along the Ganges in the two scenarios of with and

6. This method of estimating benefits of hypothetical values of water quality is, to the best of our knowledge, not one that has been used before. Markandya and Murty (2000) provide a rough estimate of annual user benefits (benefits to those living along the riverbanks and to pilgrims) as Rs. 6680 million by improving the river quality to the bathing quality standard.

without river cleaning. Since cross section data are used in estimating the health benefits, the data about the health of the population in the control region are used for the scenario without river cleaning. The health benefits are estimated as the improvement in user income due to reduction in working days lost due to illness from water borne diseases.

Both recreational and health benefits are regarded as user benefits. The recreational benefits to the literate households living along the Ganges are estimated using the contingent valuation method as described above. The health benefits are estimated as increased income due to the reduced number of working days lost from illness to the river users belonging to lower income groups. There is a possibility that the willingness pay responses of literate households in the contingent valuation survey may capture the health benefits to them along with the recreational benefits. However, care is taken while designing and implementing the CV method for measuring recreational benefits from the cleaning Ganges to avoid the possibility of willingness to pay responses from the respondents containing both health recreational benefits.

A study conducted by AIIH&PH (1997) presents 'before' and 'after' the GAP data on the health population living along the Ganges river. The benefits from the improved water quality from the GAP are estimated based on (a) increases in the users income due to reductions in working days lost, (b) savings in the cost of treatment of raw water drawn from the river for the public supply due to the GAP. A health survey was conducted in selected areas affected by the Ganges pollution in six towns on the Ganges and corresponding studies were conducted among a group of control areas in the same towns, except that they have not been affected by the GAP. These towns are Haridwar, Kanpur, Chandannagar, Titagarh, Patna, and Nabadwip. Morbidity and mortality data were collected respectively for six month and twelve month periods. Using the data from the survey, the yearly benefits of improvements in water quality of the river due to GAP was estimated in terms of increases in household incomes for each of the six study areas (where average numbers in household is assumed to be five). This is based on the difference between the number of working days lost due to sickness for the pre-project site or the control area and the number lost in post-project study areas. These figures for decreases in the number of household days lost are multiplied by the average daily income of households in each study area. The results are given in Table 7.4.[7] The total number of users in the six study areas is 473,550 and the total benefits estimated are Rs. 34.84 million. Hence the average annual benefit of improvements to water quality based on reductions in working days lost through sickness is calculated as Rs. 73.57 million per million users.

Table 7.4

Health Benefits from Reduced Loss of Working Days

Town	*Average No. of Working Days Saved Yearly Family*	*Regular Users of Ganges in Town (No. of Families)*	*Individual Daily Income (Rs.)*	*Total Value (Rs. mn.)*
Haridwar	6.09	41,300	64	16.00
Kanpur	3.42	15,560	35	1.86
Patna	6.58	22,480	88	12.94
Chandannagar	6.44	5,690	38	1.37
Nabadwip	7.37	4,760	65	2.28
Titagarh	2.61	4,920	31	0.39

Source: AIIH&PH (1997)

The sewage from towns and cities along the Ganges is used for irrigation by small farmers. There could be health benefits to sewage farm workers from the GAP projects. A study by AIIH&PH of health conditions of the sewage farm workers of Titagarh town before and after water quality improvement schemes indicated that worm and protozoal infestation was reduced in workers in the post-project period. These results were used as a basis for a notional estimate of a reduction of four days per month in working days lost per sewage farm worker due to these improvements. Therefore the total monetary benefit was calculated as Rs. 480,000/year/100 sewage farm workers.

In order to estimate the total annual health benefits of GAP, the loss of working days in the Ganges river area are calculated as follows:

7. The data provided by AIIH&PH was for household incomes. Since the losses of days are for person-days, the value of per person can be estimated by dividing the household income by the size of the household. It is assumed that individual incomes are half household incomes — i.e. there are two full time earners per household.

Gain in value of working days due to GAP per user	Rs. 73.57
Area within 0.5 km of river	252 Square Km.
Average density	500/square Km.
Hence total population affected	1,262,500
Hence total value of gain in working days	Rs. 92.88 million.

Thus the annual gain in health benefits by avoiding the loss of working days is estimated as Rs. 92.88 million. The other category of health benefits considered in this paper are for sewerage farm workers. These benefits work out to be Rs. 4800 per worker per year. Assuming that there are 100 workers for each of the 35 GAP sewage treatment schemes, this would amount to a total benefit of Rs. 16.8 million.

3.3 Benefits to Water Supply Undertakings

The AIIH&PH study also looked at the likely costs of the treatment of water for public supply had water quality not been improved by the implementation of GAP. It is likely that without the GAP, the present system of water treatment followed after the GAP would be inadequate to provide water quality for drinking purposes. To reach this standard would require the upgrading of treatment technology by at least introducing activated carbon absorption techniques for the removal of toxic chemicals and heavy metals. The additional cost of this technology was calculated for the six towns in the study based on the assumption of the cost of activated carbon absorption techniques of Rs. 3,000 per million litres. The results are given in Table 7.5 and show a total benefit per year from implementation of GAP of Rs. 731.29 million for the six towns. This indicates that in Calcutta, where water supply from the Ganges is 900 MLD (*million litres per day*), the yearly benefit of improved water quality through GAP is Rs. 985.5 million.

Although the above estimates are useful information, they cannot be included in the cost benefit analysis as such. The reason is that the study is measuring the improvements in health and other factors resulting from the improvements in water quality. If one then adds the costs of an alternative method of improvement as a benefit, one is double counting. If there had been no GAP, the health and other benefits would not have materialised. Of course if water treatment costs fall compared to what they were before GAP, those savings are correctly to be added to GAP benefits. But the above cost savings are relative to a technique that is an improvement in water treatment which achieves the goals of GAP.[8]

Table 7.5

Benefit of GAP Water Quality Improvements as Measured by Savings in Water Treatment Expenditure

Town	*Population*	*Water Supply* (MLD)*	*Benefit per Year (Rs. mn.)*
Titagarh	114085	17.11	18.74
Chandannagar	120378	18.06	19.78
Nabadwip	104533	15.68	17.17
Patna	1376701	206.51	226.13
Kanpur	2037333	305.60	334.63
Haridwar	699230	104.88	144.84
Total			**731.29**

3.4 Agricultural Benefits

Benefits to farmers are estimated using the data from a survey of farmers using water from sewage treatment plants (STPs) of GAP. Benefits to farmers are estimated as value of incremental farm output due to irrigation and savings in the cost of conventional fertilisers from making use of the partly treated water from sewage treatment plants. The GAP has 35 STPs with a capacity to treat waste water volume of 919.82 million litres a day. For estimating irrigation benefits of GAP projects, a survey of 108 farmers around STPs in Kanpur and 116 farmers around STPs in Varanasi was conducted in August, 1996. The survey collected information about the cropping pattern, crop productivities, input use, and the sources of irrigation for the farms around the STPs, and the socio-economic characteristics of farmers' households.

Given the volume of waste water treated by the STPs and an estimate of waste water capacity per day required to irrigate one hectare of land, the annual irrigation potential of STPs can be

8. An earlier reviewer of this study has noted that, for the seven cities along the Ganga the annual cost 'savings' are higher than the total benefits calculated in this study. This implies that, in a situation where water supplies have to come from the river, it is likely to be more cost effective to invest in water treatment plants to clean up polluted river water. There would be merit in examining this issue further.

estimated. An estimate based on the data collected through the survey of farms shows that to irrigate 1000 hectare of land, a STP of 74.3 MLD capacity is needed. On the basis of this estimate, it is calculated that the 919.82 MLD waste water capacity of STPs of GAP can irrigate 12,380 hectare of land. The estimate of average annual yields per hectare of cropped area based on the survey data for GAP and non-GAP farms are respectively given as Rs. 16837 and Rs. 9518. Therefore, the incremental benefits per hectare of irrigated land in GAP farms is estimated as Rs. 7319. The annual incremental benefits from irrigating 12,380 hectare of land by the GAP projects can now be estimated as Rs. 90.61 million at 1995-96 prices.[9]

Savings in conventional fertilisers to the GAP farmers could be obtained by comparing the estimates of conventional fertilisers used by the GAP farmers and non-Gap farmers. The estimated cost of conventional fertilisers per hectare of GAP and non-GAP farms based on the survey data are respectively given as Rs. 150 and Rs. 687. Therefore, the per hectare incremental benefits for savings in fertiliser cost due to GAP projects is estimated as Rs. 535. The annual incremental benefits from the savings in the fertiliser cost can now be estimated as Rs. 6.6 million at 1995-96 prices.

The sludge generated in the process of treating waste water by STPs has been found to have fertiliser potential. The data for waste water volume in terms of MLD and the annual quantity of sludge generated for STPs at Mirzapur and Kankhal at Haridwar shows that for a waste water volume of one MLD, about 8.036 (MT) of sludge can be generated annually. Given the total waste-water volume of 919.82 MLD from all STPs of GAP, the total amount of sludge generated annually by the GAP projects can be estimated as 73914.30 MT. NEERI, 1996 provides the chemical analysis of sludge from some STPs from the Varanasi and Kanpur areas. According to the NEERI analysis, the average concentration of fertilisers in the sludge are estimated as 18.37 Kg/MT, 5.08 Kg/MT and 4.68 kg/MT respectively for Nitrogen, Phosphorous and Potassium. Given these estimates, annual fertiliser potential of sludge from GAP projects can be

9. An earlier reviewer of this work has questioned the valuation of the benefits in terms of gross value of returns rather than the net values after deduction of expenses. Taking the gross values is correct when the change in the environmental variable is small and when allowance is made for the fact that farmers can optimise with respect to crop mix, inputs etc. In that case it can be shown that the benefits of an improvement in an external factor such as water quality is the gross increase in yield.

estimated as 1357.805 MT of Nitrogen, 375.485 MT of Phosphorous and 345.919 MT of Potassium.

The retail prices of fertilisers, Nitrogen, Dai & Phosphatic (D.A.P) and Potash are respectively given as Rs. 4000, Rs. 12000 and Rs. 6000 per MT during the year 1995-96 in the surveyed areas. Given these prices, the value of fertilisers in the total sludge are estimated as Rs. 5.43 million for Nitrogen, Rs.4.51 million for Phosphorous and Rs. 2.08 million for Potash. Therefore, the total value of fertilisers in the sludge annually generated by the GAP projects is estimated as Rs. 12.02 million at 1995-96 prices.

3.5 Fisheries Benefits

GAP could contribute to the increased supply of fish and reduce the risk of fish infection or contamination. For estimating the benefits from the improved fish supply from Ganges, the data are needed about fish species caught and catch volume, catch effort, fish prices, and the significant non-GAP changes and GAP changes that could affect fish catch. Unfortunately, the reliable data on these various items are not available so that the fisheries benefits from the GAP could not be estimated. Given that the incremental fisheries benefits mainly accrue to fishermen in the Gangetic basin belonging to a very low income group in the Indian economy, these benefits assume importance from the point of view of income distributional effects of GAP in the estimation of social benefits.

3.6 Benefits to Unskilled Labour

There are employment benefits to unskilled labourers due to GAP. Empirical studies about the employment in the Indian economy show that there is surplus unskilled labour, especially in the rural or agricultural sector. The construction and the operation and maintenance of GAP projects create employment to these unemployed labourers and contribute to the increase in their real incomes. Out of total investment of Rs. 7657.37 at 1995-96 prices made on the GAP projects during its first phase, Rs. 1837.77 million were paid as the wage bill to the unskilled labour. Out of annual expenditure of Rs. 355.703 million on the operation and maintenance cost of GAP projects, Rs. 81.645 million were paid as the wage bill to unskilled labour.

There is empirical evidence to show that the shadow wage rate or the incomes foregone by the unskilled labourers by switching from the employment in agriculture to the industrial projects is negligible. Also with the presence of underemployment or disguised unemployment in agriculture, the cost to the Indian economy (loss in national income) by shifting unskilled labourers from the farm employment to the industrial employment could be zero. Therefore there are social benefits from the employment of unskilled labourers on the GAP projects first due to increased income due to employment and second due to the redistribution of income to the unskilled labourers belonging to the low income group in the Indian economy.

3.6 Costs of Cleaning the Ganges

3.6.1 Costs to Government

The total funds released by the Government of India for the investment expenditure of GAP (under both GAP Phases I & II) at 1995-96 prices were Rs. 7657.37 million during the period 1985-86 to 1996-97. Of the total funds released, Rs. 7045.40 million is under GAP Phase I and the remaining Rs. 611.97 million are under GAP Phase II. However, the total actual investment under GAP Phase I is Rs. 6397.25 million. This includes Rs. 2769.88 million in Uttar Pradesh, Rs. 2782.94 million in West Bengal and Rs. 844.43 million in Bihar. Table 7.6 also provides information about the time phasing of investment expenditures for GAP Phase I during the period 1985-86 to 1996-97. These expenditures cover a large number of water pollution abatement projects contributing to clean up Ganges. They have also created employment for a large number of surplus unskilled labourers in the states of Uttar Pradesh, Bihar and West Bengal in the Gangetic basin.

Estimates based on the detailed data on the construction of three Sewage Treatment Plants (STPs) show that the expenditures on skilled and unskilled labour constitute respectively 22 per cent and 24 per cent of the total capital cost of GAP projects. Out of total capital cost of Rs. 7657.37 million at 1995-96 prices, the unskilled labour and skilled labour employed for the construction of GAP projects amount to Rs. 1837.77 million and Rs. 1684.62 million respectively. Table 7.6 provides details of the composition of the capital cost of GAP in terms of domestic material, and skilled and unskilled labour.

Expenditures on the operation and maintenance of projects under GAP Phase I during the period 1986-87 to 1996-97 at 1995-96 prices was Rs. 355.70 million. This breaks down to Rs. 231.36 million (66

Table 7.6

Domestic Material, Skilled Labour and Unskilled Labour Components of the Capital Cost of GAP

(Rs. Million at 1995-96 Prices)

Year	*Domestic Material*	*Skilled Labour*	*Unskilled Labour*	*Total Capital Cost*
1985-86	83.09	33.85	36.93	153.87
1986-87	310.68	126.58	138.08	575.34
1987-88	478.33	194.88	212.59	885.80
1988-89	589.84	240.30	262.15	1092.29
1989-90	579.96	236.28	257.76	1074.00
1990-91	452.62	184.40	201.17	838.19
1991-92	381.94	155.61	169.75	707.30
1992-93	374.01	152.37	166.22	692.60
1993-94	416.47	169.67	185.10	771.24
1994-95	181.26	73.85	80.56	335.66
1995-96	144.30	58.79	64.13	267.21
1996-97	142.49	58.05	63.33	263.87
Total	**4134.99**	**1684.63**	**1837.77**	**7657.37**

Source: Markandya and Murty (2000).

per cent) for Uttar Pradesh, Rs. 67.87 million (19 per cent) for West Bengal and Rs. 56.48 million (15 per cent) for Bihar. Data on the operation and maintenance expenditure of GAP-II is not available and, therefore, the estimates of these expenditures are obtained by assuming that the ratio of operation and maintenance cost and capital cost of GAP-II is same as that of GAP-I. An estimate of operation and maintenance cost of GAP projects created so far under Phase I and Phase II is made as Rs. 480.264 million. Estimates of share of skilled and unskilled labour in the total operating cost of GAP projects based on the detailed data of three STPs and three Municipal Pumping Stations (MPSs) show that they form respectively 4 per cent and 17 per cent of operation and maintenance cost. Table 7.7 provides the time phasing of operation and maintenance expenditure of GAP, at 1995-96 prices. Out of total operation and maintenance cost of Rs. 480.26 millions at 1995-96 prices, skilled and unskilled labour account for Rs.19.21 million and Rs. 81.65 million respectively as given in Table 7.7.

Table 7.7

Domestic Material, Skilled Labour and Unskilled Labour Components of O&M Cost of GAP

(Rs. Million at 1995-96 Prices)

Year	*Domestic Material*	*Skilled Labour*	*Unskilled Labour*	*Total O&M Cost*
1986-87	5.088	0.258	1.095	6.440
1987-88	10.391	0.526	2.236	13.153
1988-89	22.021	1.115	4.739	27.875
1989-90	29.693	1.503	6.390	37.586
1990-91	20.008	1.013	4.306	25.327
1991-92	38.297	1.939	8.241	48.477
1992-93	38.288	1.939	8.239	48.465
1993-94	46.865	2.373	10.085	59.322
1994-95	42.272	2.140	9.097	53.509
1995-96	82.580	4.181	17.770	104.532
1996-97	43.906	2.223	9.448	55.577
Total	**379.409**	**19.211**	**81.645**	**480.264**

Source: Markandya and Murty (2000).

3.6.2 Cost to Industry

The international experience of river cleaning programmes including that of Ganges in India shows that a combination of instruments and institutions have to be used to achieve the river cleaning objectives. The environmental regulation requires the polluters to comply with safe environmental standards. The compliance to the environmental standards requires both private and public investments. In the case of cleaning Ganges, there is public investment through the project GAP and there is private investment by industries in the Gangetic basin. It is mandatory for the industries to make investments in pollution control to meet the national standards for the water quality. There are 68 heavily polluting industries in Gangetic basin generating 2.6 million kilolitres of effluent every day. The data about the pollution abatement cost collected for a sample of 18 water-polluting industries in the river basin that are meeting the effluent standards provides an estimate of Rs. 0.39 per kilolitre of water treated at 1993-94 prices (Murty *et al.*, 1999). The daily cost of treating 2.6 million kilolitre of effluent is Rs. 1.014 million. The annual cost of effluent treatment for the water polluting industries in the river basin is estimated as Rs. 370.11 million.

4. Estimates of Social Benefits of GAP

Estimates of time flows of benefits and costs at market prices described in the earlier section could be used to estimate the social benefits of cleaning Ganges. For estimating the social benefits of GAP using the methods of social cost benefit analysis of investment projects (Dasgupta, Marglin and Sen, 1972; Little and Mirrlees, 1974) one requires the estimates of social rate of discount and the shadow prices of investment and unskilled labour for the Indian economy. The social cost of investment in GAP could be greater than the cost at market prices or the financial cost because of scarcity of capital. The social cost of employing unskilled labour on the project could be lower than the wage bill paid at market wage because there is surplus unskilled labour in the Indian economy. Similarly, the social rate of discount is lower than the market rate of interest because of the presence of economic externalities in the accumulation of capital; the society will have lower time preference rate for savings than the rate individuals have in the free market. Murty *et al.,* (1992) provides the estimates of social rate of discount and shadow prices of capital and unskilled labour for the Indian economy. These estimates are 10 to 12 per cent range for the social rate of discount, 40 per cent premium for capital (the shadow price of capital is 40 per cent higher than the market price), and 50 per cent of market wage as shadow wage rate.

The criteria of net present social value, internal rate of return and the benefit-cost ratio could be used to estimate the social benefits of GAP. Considering the estimates of benefit and cost flows of GAP during the period 1985-2020, Table 7.8 provides estimates of present value of benefits and costs to various agents in the Indian economy from cleaning Ganges at 10 per cent rate of discount. The net present value of GAP at 10 per cent rate of discount is estimated as Rs. 4147.51 million at shadow prices of investment and unskilled labour. The internal rate of return on investments on GAP is as high as 15.4 per cent. The benefit cost ratio is estimated as 1.68.

The pollution free Ganges provides benefits to both rich and poor people. It is a source of livelihood to fishermen, farmers and to the people using it for drinking and bathing. Unskilled labour get employment benefits from the GAP projects. The non-user benefits and the benefits from recreational and amenity services accrue mostly to rich people. From the equity point of view, the benefits from river cleaning accruing to poor people assume importance and contribute to the increased social benefits. If the estimates of income distributional weights to benefits accruing to various classes of beneficiaries from the Ganges are available, the social benefits from cleaning Ganges from the equity point of view can be estimated.

Table 7.8

Estimates of Present Value of Benefits of Cleaning Ganges for Various Beneficiaries at Market Prices and with Income Distribution Effects

(Rs. million at 1995-96 prices)

	At Shadow Prices	*With Income Distribution Effects*	
		$\varepsilon = 1.75$	$\varepsilon = 2.0$
1. Users	29.11	2.79	1.98
2. Non-users	6871.03	439.74	295.45
3. Farmers	574.93	1709.84	1997.88
4. Health beneficiaries	826.93	2549.29	2873.58
5. Fishermen	NA	NA	NA
6. Unskilled labour	1919.42	5708.36	6670.00
7. Industrial units	–1504.59	–144.44	–102.31
8. Government	–4569.32	–4569.32	–4569.32
9. Net present value	4147.51	5696.26	7167.26
10. Benefit cost ratio	1.68	2.21	2.53

Source: Markandya and Murty. 2000.

Note: Rate of discount is taken as 10 per cent. The cost to the government is the present value of costs incurred up to the year 1996-97.

Suppose the social welfare function for the Indian economy is of the following form Atkinson (1970):

$$W = \sum_{i-1}^{N} \frac{AY_i^{1-\varepsilon}}{1-\varepsilon} \quad ...(1)$$

where

W: Social welfare function

Y_i : Income of individual i

e : Elasticity of social marginal utility

A: a constant

The social marginal utility of income is defined as

$$\frac{\partial W}{\partial Y_i} = AY_i^{-\varepsilon} \quad ...(2)$$

Taking per capita national income $\overline{Y}$ as the numéraire, and giving it the value of one, it can be written from (2)

$$\frac{\partial W}{\partial Y_i} = A\overline{Y}^{\varepsilon} \equiv 1$$

$$A = \left(\overline{Y}\right)^{\varepsilon}$$

Substituting $\left(\overline{Y}\right)^{\varepsilon}$ for A in (1), the social marginal utility of income to the individual i (**SMU$_i$**) can be written as

$$\frac{\partial W}{\partial Y_i} = SMU_i = \left[\frac{\overline{Y}}{Y_i}\right]^{\varepsilon} \qquad \text{...(4)}$$

The SMU$_i$ is in fact the weight to be attached to the costs and benefits to group i relative to costs and benefits to the person with income equal to the national *per capita* income. In order to compute these weights, data about $\overline{Y}$, Y_i and ε are needed. Some recent studies in India about the estimates of ε have suggested a range of 1.75–2.0 for its value (Murty *et al.* 1972). The Economic Survey, 1995-96, Government of India suggests an estimate of per capita Gross Domestic Product for the Indian economy of Rs. 9321 at 1995-96 prices. The estimates of social marginal utility for various beneficiaries from cleaning Ganges are given in Table 7.9.

Table 7.9

Estimates of Income Distributional Weights for the Incomes of Beneficiaries from Cleaning Ganges

Beneficiary Group	*Annual Per Capita Income (Rs.)*	*Income Distributional Weights*	
		ε = 1.75	*ε = 2.00*
Unskilled labour, farmers and health beneficiaries	5000	2.974	3.475
Urban users	35000	0.096	0.068
Non-users	44705	0.064	0.043
Industrial owners	44705	0.064	0.043
Government	9321*	1.000	1.000

Note: Per capita incomes of urban users and non-users are estimated from the survey data. The per capita income of industry owners is assumed to be same as that of non-users.

* National per capita Gross Domestic Product in 1994-95.

The estimate of net present social value of GAP increases from Rs. 4147.51 million to Rs. 5696.26 million while the benefit cost ratio goes up from 1.68 to 2.21 if income distributional benefits are accounted.

5. Sustainability of Processes of Cleaning Ganges

A number of different mechanisms can be considered to raise the resources for sustaining the cleaning of Ganges. They are a polluter-pays principle, a user-pays principle (with government involvement), a user-pays principle (without government involvement), and funding from the general tax system.

The polluter-pays principle would mean a water charge per kilo litre collected as a tax, or more likely as part of the water tariff from households and industries. Given the general interest in employing market-based instruments to deal with water pollution, this would make a good case study and would assist in the design of a suitable tax system. A particular problem to be resolved would be to ensure that the tax is collected efficiently and passed on to the authority with responsibility for cleaning the Ganges.

The user-pays principle with government involvement places a tax on both user and non-user beneficiaries. An alternative to the involvement of the government is to set up a charitable commission for the Ganges with the responsibility to collect payments from user and non-user beneficiaries. The commission would have autonomy from the government but would be accountable to the public through the Commission for Charities or a similar body. It would have regional offices, which would not only collect money but would also be responsible for disseminating information about the Ganges and changes in its water quality.

Finally there is the possibility of using general taxes. This may not be a feasible instrument, given the extreme pressures on such tax revenues and the uncertainties created for future revenue flows to maintain the Ganges water quality. Of course there is no reason why only one of these options has to be implemented. It may be in fact possible to have a combination of an effluent tax and a voluntary payment scheme of the kind outlined above. The details have, of course, to be worked out, but the prospects of success are good.

6. Conclusion

Many environmental and development issues have to be dealt with in the river cleaning programmes. They under score the importance of co-operation of riparian states against non co-operation to deal with cross boundary pollution, the need for institutions and instruments to sustain the cleaning process, and the high values people place on river conservation with the accrual of benefits from the preservation of bio-diversity and aquatic life to both national and international communities.

The experience of river cleaning programme including the programme to clean Ganges suggests that a mix of instruments and institutions have to be used to achieve the objectives. They comprise direct public and private investments, economic instruments, and the institutions facilitating local community participation.

There are multiple benefits from the river-cleaning programme. As shown in this paper, the estimation of these benefits requires the market and non-market valuation. Due to data problems, all the benefits from the GAP could not be estimated. With whatever benefits quantified, the GAP has significant positive net present social benefits at 10 per cent social rate of discount for the Indian economy. The internal rate of return is as high as 15 per cent.

The environmentally sustainable agricultural and industrial development in India requires the continuation of processes of cleaning Ganges in future. Given that the international communities get benefits as non-users from cleaning Ganges, if required, India can get financial support from these communities to sustain the river cleaning.

References

AII&PH (1997). *A Study of Health Impacts of Ganga Action Plan.*

Atkinson, A.B. (1970). "On the Measurement of Inequality", *Journal of Economic Theory,* 2, pp. 244-63.

Dasgupta, P.S., and S.A. Marglin, and A.K. Sen (1972). *Guide Lines to Project Evaluation,* United Nations, New York.

Freeman, A.M. III (1993). "The Measurement of Environmental and Resource Values", *Resources for Future,* Washington DC.

Little, I.M.D., and J.A. Mirrlees (1974). "Project Appraisal and Planning for Developing Countries", London, Heinemann Education Book.

Markandya, A. and M.N. Murty, (2000). "Cleaning-Up Ganges: The Cost Benefit Analysis of Ganga Action Plan", Oxford University Press, New Delhi.

Mitchell , R.C. and R.T. Carson, (1989). "Using Surveys to Value Public Goods", *Resources for Future,* Washington DC.

Murty, M.N. *et al.,* (1992). "National Parameters for Investment Project Appraisal in India", Working Paper No. E/153/92, Institute of Economic Growth, Delhi-11007.

Murty, M.N., A.J. James and Smita Misra (1999). *Economics of Industrial Pollution: The Indian Experience,* Oxford University Press, New Delhi.

Section III

Globalisation, Liberalisation and Trade

8

Host Country Policies and Quality and Quantity of Foreign Direct Investments: Implications for India

NAGESH KUMAR

1. Introduction

One of the most striking aspect of the current trend of globalisation is the exponential growth of foreign direct investment (FDI) flows or the multinational enterprises (MNEs) activity. Expanding magnitudes of FDI inflows over the 1990s have prompted governments—in both developed as well as developing countries alike—to attract MNEs with various incentive packages to access their resources *viz.* capital, technology, skills, market access, among others, to expedite the process of their development. Developing countries, in particular, constrained as they are in expediting their development by the paucity of resources of all types—financial capital, entrepreneurship, technological know-how, efficient managerial techniques, access to markets abroad—have looked to FDI as a panacea for all their scarcities especially in the context of drying up of official transfers of resources. In the race for seeking more and more FDI inflows, however, the countries have overlooked the fact that all the flows of FDI do not benefit their host countries similarly. There is indeed a great variation in the extent of capital, entrepreneurship, technology, market access brought by them. Some may actually bring pretty little, if at all. While in general, it is admitted that the host governments' policies may play an important role in extracting the benefits of FDI for their development (see for instance, UNCTAD, 1999), a more exact analysis of relative role of

---

• This paper is adapted, updated and shortened version of an earlier one published under the title "Host Country Policies, WTO regime and the Global Patterns of FDI Inflows: Recent Quantitative Studies and India's Strategic Response", *Economic and Political Weekly*, 6 January 2001: 39-50. The views expressed are personal and should not be attributed to RIS.

different policy measures in shaping the patterns of magnitudes and quality of FDI inflows is not available.

In this background, this paper summarises some findings of our recent comprehensive attempt to quantitatively analyse the role of structural, geopolitical and policy factors in shaping the patterns of MNE activity, using an exclusive four dimensional data-set. The focus here would be to summarise the findings pertaining to the role of host government policy factors. The structure of the paper is as follows. Section 2 briefly outlines the analytical frameworks that have been developed to analyse the patterns of FDI especially pointing out hypotheses pertaining to the role of host government policies. Section 3 presents a summary of findings pertaining to the host government policy factors. Section 4 concludes it with some remarks on a possible response of India to the emerging challenges.

2. Role of Host Country Policies on Different Aspects of MNE Activity: A Note on Analytical Frameworks and Hypotheses

The inter-country variation in affiliate sales as a measure of intensity of operation of Japanese and US MNEs in a particular country, in a particular sector and at a particular point of time was sought to be explained in the framework of an Extended Model of Location of Foreign Production formulated by us drawing upon the complementary approaches of gravity model of international trade and the theory of international operations of firms. This model explains the affiliate sales in terms of some demand (or gravity) factors in the host country captured by population, per capita national income, the geographical distance between the home and the host country, the extent of cultural affinity (proxied by linguistic homogeneity) between the home and host country, and the extent of urbanisation. The model also includes a few variables in tune with the theory of foreign operation of firms that make local production preferable to exporting. These include wage rates, an index of quality of infrastructure and a vector of variables capturing different elements of host country's policy framework. The policy factors included the relative openness of country's trade regime, performance requirements imposed by host countries on foreign affiliates, the extent of investment incentives provided by host governments, the extent of tax incentives extended by host governments and the tax rates [see Kumar, 2002, for more details].

The above framework was then adapted to explain affiliate activity in modern and traditional industries. Taking cue from the new location theory, it was posited that the MNE activity in modern or knowledge intensive activities may be driven by created assets localised in particular countries. Similarly, the agglomeration economies may affect the MNE activity in different industries differently.

The next step is to explain why foreign operations in some countries are more export-oriented than in others. Although a large volume of literature has addressed itself to the phenomenon export-platform production by MNEs in general and in the context of East Asian countries, in particular [see Nayyar, 1978; Frobel, *et al.*, 1980; Kumar, 1994a, among others], it focuses on the operations that feed back the home countries of MNEs. However, the exports to third countries by MNE affiliates have grown in the recent years faster than those directed to home countries. We contended that the two types of export-oriented production are of different nature and developed a conceptual framework that took into account the destination of exports (see Kumar, 1998a). A stylised view of the home market oriented production abroad is that it is essentially cost saving in nature that is rationalised abroad to benefit from international differences in factor prices and raw material costs for home market consumption by MNEs. The home market oriented FDI generally involves production of intermediate goods which are often custom made [Kumar, 1998a].

The third country oriented production abroad, on the other hand, results from the strategy of MNEs to assign the responsibility for serving specific regional or even global markets in particular product lines to certain affiliates. This strategy is some times called product mandating and results from the efficiency seeking restructuring or specialisation within the MNE. This strategy helps the corporation to internalise the economies of specialisation and scale by focusing the attention on the production of a specific product line. Global product mandating as a strategy has been made possible by the recent trend of liberalisation of economies world-wide. The recent trend of regional economic integration has contributed greatly to the process of internal restructuring of enterprises by eliminating the tariff and non-tariff barriers across the participating countries and thus removing the need to maintain horizontal national operations for MNEs. The Single

Market Plan of the European Union, for instance, has prompted not only the European MNEs but also the American and Japanese MNEs operating in the Common Market to restructure their operations on a pan-European basis [see Kumar, 1994b, for illustrations]. Third country-oriented ventures, therefore, produce final goods for serving the mandated markets that generally cover host country local market.

Based on these stylised views of the two types of export-platform production, potential factors that would be relevant for the two situations were identified and predictions were formulated.

Finally, we explain why affiliates in some countries conduct R&D and not in others. Here, an analytical framework is developed that takes into account the recent writings on the internationalisation of R&D of MNEs and the factors that act as centripetal and centrifugal forces. The size of the host market, availability of technological infrastructure and resources, among other factors may affect the decision-making pertaining to location of R&D in a particular country (see Kumar, 2001, for more details).

2.1 Role of Host Country Policy

2.1.1 Trade Policy Regime

The relative openness of a host country's trade regime may have two counteracting influences on the extent of foreign presence. Firstly, a country with a more open liberal trading environment may be a better place to do business for foreign enterprises and FDI inflows may increase. On the other hand, the bulk of FDI inflow in most countries is of the tariff (or non-tariff trade barrier) jumping type. Protection accorded to the local industry by host governments is known to have prompted MNEs to set up local production as confirmed by a number of studies that reported the favourable effect of protection in explaining FDI patterns (see Caves, 1996 for a review of evidence). In more recent times, industrialised countries in the EU, for instance, have used protectionist measures such as voluntary export restraints (VERs), quotas, screw driver regulations, rules of origin, and various anti-dumping measures to encourage foreign-based MNEs, especially Japanese based, to increase domestic content in their sales (see e.g. Belderbos, 1994; Moran, 1998). Hence, the depth or extent of localisation may be inversely related with the openness of the trade regime. In part this is because a restrictive trading regime may raise the costs of imported inputs and may encourage to localise a greater extent of production in the host country. Therefore, the openness of the trade policy regime (*OPENNESS*) was expected to affect the affiliate sales in general favourably and inversely related with the depth of their manufacturing activity.

However, export-orientation of production may be positively related with the *OPENNESS*. This is more so for export-oriented production that is geared to third country markets. This is because the latter are organised on the basis of overall efficiency unlike the efficiency based on the factor costs as in the case of the home market oriented ventures. Hence, inputs and components may be sourced from different places depending upon the cost. Furthermore, many developing country governments have established export processing zones in an explicit effort to attract MNEs to set up export-platform ventures by offering them a more liberal trading environment in an otherwise closed economy. Besides they also provide a more efficient infrastructure, port facilities, and privileges such as tax holidays and sometimes even more harmonious industrial relations by curbing or restricting strikes *etc*. These zones have been used by MNEs for labour intensive processing mainly for home markets. Hence, size of export processing zones (*EPZONES*) was expected to particularly favour home market export orientation of affiliates.

Finally, the location of R&D may also be influenced by policy environment within the host countries with respect to overall international orientation, although its role is less straight forward. An economy protecting local industry may create a greater demand for technological inputs by increasing the need for indigenisation by making imports relatively more expensive. On the other hand, a restrictive trade regime may discourage MNEs from undertaking R&D activity in the economy because of perceived difficulties in importing R&D inputs such as equipment, personnel, components *etc*. and for other handicaps of a restrictive atmosphere. Hence, *OPENNESS*, was included among potential explanatory variables without a prediction of the direction of impact.

2.1.2 Investment Policy Regime

Several aspects of government policy regime may contribute to the perceived investment climate in the country including some elements of policy that apply to foreign enterprises such as performance requirements and fiscal incentives meant for industrial investments.

Performance Requirements: A large number of host governments impose a variety of performance requirements on MNEs to pattern their operations in consonance with the country's development objectives (see Guisinger *et al.*, 1985; UNCTC, 1991). These requirements are often concerned with the transfer of production and technology to the host country. These requirements tend to make the conditions of investment restrictive and hence may adversely affect foreign sales. If they are effective, however, they may improve the quality of foreign sales favourably in the sense of enhancing the depth of whatever output foreign affiliates produce in their host country. The incidence of different types of performance requirements as imposed in the country *viz.* transfer of technology, export commitments, and local content regulations, is measured by $PRFREQ_{it}$.

The extent of overall performance requirements imposed by host countries are predicted to adversely affect the attractiveness of a country as a potential host for MNEs. However, those MNEs that still locate in countries imposing some performance requirements may have their operations affected by them. Some of the performance requirements are actually meant to promote a greater localisation of production of affiliates. In particular, a large number of host governments have imposed local content regulations on foreign affiliates at the time of entry to deepen their commitment to the host country. The host governments have been concerned with often enclave nature of foreign affiliates' operations in particular, the weak nature of backward linkages. Local content regulations have, therefore, been widely used by the host governments to increase the extent of backward linkages of MNE affiliates. Hence, the extent of local content requirements ($LOCONTREQ_{it}$) was expected to favourably affect the depth of foreign affiliates' production.

Finally, sometimes the host country governments, especially of countries with relatively large domestic markets, have allowed to MNEs access to their domestic market subject to their accepting certain export commitments. These regulations could be specially relevant in situations where domestic market sales are at the cost of exports as in the case of third country exports. If export commitments are effective, a positive relationship is expected between intensity of export commitments imposed (*EXCOMT*) and third country export intensity.

Investment and Tax Incentives: A larger number of governments especially of developed countries, compete among themselves by offering a variety of fiscal incentives to attract FDI (see for instance, UNCTAD, 1995). Earlier studies have found incentives to be affecting the pattern of location of FDI (see for instance, Loree and Guisinger, 1995). Hence, investment incentives ($INCENT_{it}$) and tax incentives ($TAXINCENT_{it}$) were expected to favourably affect foreign affiliate sales. Investment and tax incentives offered by host governments are meant to attract MNEs to locate production in their countries. Very often these incentives are linked to employment or value addition created. Hence, they should also have a favourable effect on the extent of localisation of production.

2.1.3 Patent Regime

Recently, there has been a lot of controversy on the role of intellectual property protection in determining inward FDI flows. Stronger protection may reduce the transaction cost of transfer of knowledge by MNEs to foreign countries. Hence, it may encourage arm's length licensing of the knowledge and reduce the need for undertaking FDI (see for instance Brewer, 1993). On the other hand, it has been argued that poor IPR regime tends to adversely affect the investment climate and hence the probability of MNE investments (Mansfield, 1994). Relatively little empirical verification of these contentions that has been made has generally shown an insignificant influence of the extent of intellectual property protection on inward FDI (Ferrantino, 1993; Kondo, 1994; Correa, 1997). Lee and Mansfield (1996), on the other hand, in a sample of 14 countries (observations pooled over three years) find the perceived weakness of intellectual property protection adversely affecting the volume as well as the composition of US FDI inflows to the countries. However, given the small size of sample, a rather subjective measurement of intellectual property regime (based on firm's perception), and low t-values of the coefficients, the findings could be considered only as indicative unless replicated in larger samples. Hence, the possible effect of an index of strength of patent protection in the country (*PATENTRIGHT)* on the foreign affiliate operations and their depth was examined without the benefit of *a priori* prediction.

The issue of intellectual property protection links more directly with R&D activity. MNEs may be apprehensive of locating their key R&D centres in countries with weak patent regimes. Therefore, the relative strength of patent protection available in a country may be a factor in determining the overseas R&D activity by MNEs. On the other hand, in the case of overseas R&D directed to local adaptations and providing other support to the local production of the MNE, and not directed to new product development, the patent regime may not be of much consequence to it. Kumar (1996a) found a mixed evidence of the role of intellectual property protection on R&D activity of US MNEs in that it had a significant positive effect for the industrialised country sub-sample but an insignificant effect for the developing country sub-sample. It was rationalised in terms of possible differences in the nature of R&D done in the two groups of countries. Subsequent case studies have shown that relatively soft patent regime that has prevailed in India since the 1973, has not prevented a large number of MNEs from locating R&D bases in the country (Kumar, 1999).

3. Quantitative Analysis and Findings

A Note on Data Sets and Methods: The empirical verification of the above propositions was performed with the help of an exclusive database, as indicated earlier, that covered four dimensions *viz.* two home countries, 74 host countries, seven branches of manufacturing and three points of time between 1982-94 period. Estimations for US and Japanese affiliates were made separately while the observations were pooled across the other three dimensions. Hence, appropriate controls were included in the estimations. Furthermore, the estimations were repeated for sub-samples of developing countries, of specific sectors and points of time if tests indicated structural change. Finally, we have examined if additional considerations apply in explaining the patterns of FDI in modern or knowledge intensive industries. These industries have been defined following in the light of UNCTAD classification to include chemicals and products, non-electrical machinery, electrical and electronic equipment; and scientific instruments (that is subsumed in Other Manufacturing in our classification).

The variable measurements of the dependent and policy variables are summarised in Annex I. The data source is the Glob-Ted Database compiled at the UNU/INTECH on the basis of the Benchmark Surveys of the US Direct Investment Abroad conducted by the US Department of Commerce and unpublished data from MITI Basic Surveys of Overseas Operations of Japanese Corporations and many other published and unpublished sources as indicated in Kumar (2002, Data Appendix).

The models were estimated using OLS method in all the cases except for the *AFR&D* where GLS estimations were made in the framework of a Tobit model given a large proportion of limit observations. Heteroskedasticity correction was applied besides normalisation of most of the variables for scaling down the variation.

3.1 Summary of Findings Pertaining to the Host Country Policy Variables

The role of various parameters of policy covered in the quantitative exercises is summarised in Table 8.1 and is discussed below.

3.1.1 Openness of Trade Regime

The affiliate output in all industries as well as in modern industries is positively associated with the extent of openness of trade regime. However, the depth of production in the host country is inversely related with the openness of trade regime especially in modern or technology intensive industries. The implication of these findings is that although a country with a freer trade regime is more attractive location for operations of MNEs, a more open trade regime discourages a deeper integration of their operations with the domestic economy. Hence, if the objective is to make MNEs generate a greater proportion of output within the host country, a somewhat restrictive trade regime is more conducive although it may cost some inflows. The openness of trade regime, however, is more conducive to export-orientation of production especially that geared to third countries. This is because a more open regime facilitates sourcing of inputs from different places. Setting up more export processing zones as a tool of policy which create more liberal enclaves within economies with more restrictive policy regime might also help host countries in attracting the home market oriented FDI inflows. In a related finding the export-orientation of MNE affiliates was associated with a relatively smaller generation of value added per unit of sales, corroborating the evidence on the enclave nature of export-oriented production as observed in many countries. A challenge for the host country policies is to ensure that export-platform production bases set up by MNE affiliates are integrated in the host economy and are not operating as enclaves.

The openness of trade regime, however, discourages the R&D investments by MNE affiliates. This is to be explained in terms of the opportunity for adaptations that a relatively restrictive trade regime offers by placing a premium on local content of production. The role

Table 8.1

Role of Policy Characteristics of Host Countries in Shaping the Patterns of MNE Operation: A Summary of Quantitative Findings

Variable	*Affiliate Output*		*Depth of Production*		*Export-orientation*		*R&D Investment*
	All Manf.	*Modern Industries*	*All Manf.*	*Modern Industries*	*Home Market Oriented*	*Third Country Oriented*	
Openness of Trade Regime	+++i	+++i	-,-ii	-,-,-,+	+i	++	-,i-,
Export Processing Zones					++		
Performance Requirements	-,-,ii	-, ii					
Local Content Requirements			++ii	++ii			
Export Commitments						++	
Investment Incentives	+i++	+++I	+++i	+++i			
Tax Incentives	+++I	+++	i+ii	+iii			
Patent Protection	i,i,+,-	iiii, +,-	iiii	i+ii			iiii
Other Factors Controlled or specified in the Model	Population, Income, Distance, Culture, Urbanisation, Infrastructure, Tax Rate; Sector, time and regional controls		Population, Income, Distance, Sector, time and regional controls		Infrastructure, Distance, North America, Caribbean, sector and time controls	Infrastructure, Market Size, EU, NAFTA, EFTA and Lome, sector and time controls	Market size, R&D manpower, R&D wages, scale of R&D activity, techno. Specialisn., sector, time
N	500 (US); 728 (Japan)	varies across sectors	375 (US), 484 (Jap)	varies	432/450	397/442	184/407
F- value	51.92 (US); 40.02 (Japan)	-do-	7.14/ 7.78	-do-	17.01/6.73	27.17/9.77	n.a.
Adjusted R^2	0.70 (US); 0.53 (Japan)	-do-		-do-	0.36/0.15	0.51/0.25	n.a.

Source: Kumar (2002).

Note: + indicates significant positive effect; -, a significant inverse effect; i, indicates an insignificant relationship.

of trade policy regime is, therefore, characterised by a number of trade-offs; between the extent and depth of affiliate production, between domestic *versus* export-oriented production, and for relative technological independence of the affiliates.

3.1.2 Performance Requirements

The imposition of performance requirements by host countries at the time of entry, in general, makes them less attractive for MNEs to locate operations. However, specific types of performance requirements are effective in improving the quality parameters they intend to achieve. Local content requirements, for instance, have been found to be associated with a greater extent of localisation of production. Export commitments have been found to be effective in prompting MNEs to export a greater proportion of output to third countries. Therefore, a more restrictive FDI policy regime (in terms of imposing performance requirements) too, like trade regime, affects the investment climate in general but may improve the quality of inflows that come. It is a challenge for developing country policy-makers to resolve this trade-off between the breadth and depth or possibly quantity and quality of MNE activity by fine tuning these policies to their best advantage in light of their other attractions as locations for production by MNEs.

3.1.3 Investment and Tax Incentives

Investment incentives offered by host governments are specifically designed to attract MNEs to locate production in their territories. They have been found to be favourably associated with MNEs' operations in the country. Since these incentives are generally proportional to the extent of employment created in the host country, they are also favourably associated with the depth of affiliates production. Tax incentives were found to have a greater effect on the affiliate output than on the extent of their localisation. The role of investment incentives has been debated in the literature in light of their role in distorting the global pattern of investments. Because developing countries are constrained in their capability to offer cash incentives for attracting FDI, such incentives further perpetuate the concentration of these inflows in industrialised countries which are known to offer large handouts for attracting FDI inflows. Hence, an international intervention to curb investment incentives is required.

3.1.4 Patent Regime

The strength of patent protection regime of a host country generally has an insignificant relationship with the magnitude of affiliate output or its depth. It remains so even in the modern industries. Finally, the strength of patent protection offered by a host country does not affect its attractiveness as a location for R&D activity. Other recent work and case study evidence has also corroborated that the lack of adequate patent protection does not adversely affect the attractiveness of a country otherwise well suited for R&D activity. This is because MNEs are able to obviate the constraints placed by the host country's patent regime by registering patents in their home countries. Hence, there seems to be no empirical basis for the presumption of the Uruguay Round Negotiations that stronger patent regimes improve investment climate in the host countries and hence will encourage inflows of FDI.

To sum up therefore, the host government policy plays an important role in augmenting a country's attractiveness for MNEs' operations and to shape their quality. There appear to be considerable trade-off between quantity and quality of FDI inflows. Hence, a more specific targeting of FDI inflows may be more effective. For instance, there is a trade-off between the magnitude and the depth of affiliate production in that former is favoured by openness of trade and investment policy regime while the latter is adversely affected. Similarly export-orientation is favourably affected by openness of trade regime while R&D intensity is inversely related with it. This analysis may help policymakers in developing countries to evaluate their comparative advantages in attracting various types of FDI inflows and formulate a policy package in order to optimise FDI inflows in accordance to their development policy goals.

4. Concluding Remarks: India's Response to Globalisation and WTO

We may now conclude the paper with some remarks for policy options before India in the context of the emerging WTO regime and in the light of the quantitative findings presented above.

4.1 A Strategic Approach to Industrial Competitiveness Policy

Our quantitative findings have revealed that MNE investment especially in modern or knowledge industries has favoured locations that provide them complementary location bound created assets especially for the knowledge intensive value adding activities. Other scholars, notably Dunning (1998) have also argued that the countries that are able to create 'a strong nucleus of flagship national firms' will be better placed to tap the MNEs' value adding resources than others, especially in the internationally oriented sectors. It comes very close to what we prefer to call 'national champions'. The national champions can enter into mutually beneficial alliances with foreign multinationals and could also give visibility to national capabilities in those industries.

Taking cues from this discussion, it is imperative that India should also use the emerging world trading system to her advantage rather than confine to passively implementing the schedules of liberalisation and commitments of its markets. Otherwise we run the risk of further marginalisation in the global economy. This requires a strategic response and concerted action by the government and the industry. It would mean that the government and (domestic) industry together cooperate in implementing an 'industrial competitiveness policy (ICP)' rather than a conventional industrial policy. The ICP could cover identifying a list of niche areas of strategic interest, identification of potential national champions, encouraging corporate consolidation and restructuring, support and provide necessary assistance to potential national champions, protect them from hostile take-overs by foreign rivals, among other measures. It would involve identifying the various safe guards such as anti-dumping and counter veiling duties, technical standards, among others and grey area measures in different WTO Agreements that are not inconsistent with them and exploit them. These include direct R&D subsidies, subsidies for building brand names and trade marks, venture capital firms. This would also call for providing infant industry protection to fledgling domestic industry in select industries for limited period, by giving them assured access to domestic market so that they could grow to certain size and muster confidence to enter international markets and globalise their operations. Besides encouraging consolidation of domestic enterprises through take-overs by the emerging national champions, they could be allowed to take-over foreign enterprises in other countries and undertake outward FDI to strengthen their presence outside. Their technological capability, giant scale of operations, combined with increasing international visibility will facilitate mutually beneficial alliances with major global corporations. A couple of Indian enterprises have been able to achieve such distinction *e.g.* Ranbaxy which is now much sought after by the global pharma majors like Eli Lilly, Bayer, among others. Many more examples can be replicated.

4.2 Focusing on Maximising the Contribution of FDI Inflows rather than their Maximising the Magnitudes of Inflows

The findings of the quantitative studies suggest considerable trade-offs between the quantity and quality of FDI inflows. In a developing country such as India that seeks FDI as a development resource, the focus of the FDI policy should be on maximisation of its contribution to the India's development rather than on maximisation of the magnitude of inflows by itself. One respect where substantial potential remains to be exploited with respect to MNEs' contribution to India's development is expansion of her exports. MNEs have so far come to India primarily for exploiting her large domestic market and their contribution to India's exports is negligible. In contrast, MNEs account for nearly 40 per cent of China's manufactured exports. Our findings suggest that imposing export commitments on MNEs at the time of entry could be important means of prompting them to explore possibilities of integrating a host country especially those with larger domestic markets, into their regional or global sourcing strategies. Many countries, including China, have successfully tapped these policies formally or informally to push MNEs to contribute to the development of their export capabilities (see Kumar 2003a). The export commitments are not inconsistent with the TRIMs Agreement and hence can still be imposed. The evidence also suggests that export-oriented FDIs bring to the host country best practice technology and also cause beneficial information spillovers on the export opportunities and hence could facilitate exporting activity of domestic enterprises as well (see Aitken *et al.*, 1994, for evidence from Mexico).

4.3 Bringing a Strategic Element in the FDI and Technology Import Policies for an Autonomous Path of Expansion

The experience of East Asian countries has highlighted that selective approach to FDI may provide a necessary condition for charting an autonomous path of internationalisation. Evidently, the East Asian newly industrialising economies have consciously sought technology, as much as possible, unaccompanied by ownership with a selective policy. As documented very well in the literature [see for instance, Kim, 1997; Kumar and Siddharthan, 1997], such policy has allowed to the technology importing domestic firms independence of decision making so important for pursuing an autonomous path of expansion. The emergence of Japanese, and of late, Korean and Taiwanese corporations as multinational enterprises in their own right would not have been possible with technology acquisition under FDI route. It must be emphasised, however, that market transfers alone do not guarantee such outcomes. They only provide necessary conditions and are effective only in the presence of responsive (and perhaps aggressive) local entrepreneurship willing to complement imported knowledge with extensive in-house technological effort on absorption, adaptation, continuous updating and eventually on innovation.

FDI policy needs to have a strategic perspective particularly in relation to the strategic sectors identified as a part of the industrial competitiveness policy for building local capability. It will have to be pursued in a manner that the foreign entry does not threaten the existence of national champions in an unfair manner.

4.4 Policies for Diffusion of Knowledge Brought in by MNEs

Another sphere where governmental intervention may be required to maximise gains from globalisation is in diffusion of knowledge brought in by foreign enterprises. An important channel of diffusion of knowledge brought in by MNEs in the host economy is vertical inter-firm linkages with domestic enterprises. A rather slow progress has been observed in terms of generation of vertical linkages with local firms in developing host countries by affiliates of either US or Japanese MNEs (see Lipsey, 1998) and Urata, 1998). In addition, Japanese MNEs tend to transplant the vendor-OEM links prevailing in the home country in that the traditional component suppliers of Japanese equipment manufacturers follow their overseas investments. This pattern tends to limit the generation of local linkages. Therefore, policies promoting generation of vertical inter-firm linkages between MNE affiliates and local enterprises will help in diffusion of knowledge brought in by them. Our quantitative analysis has highlighted the potential role that local content regulations could play in pushing the MNE affiliates to deepen their commitment to their host countries. However, these regulations are no longer permitted under the TRIMs Agreement. The host governments could consider employing proactive measures that encourage foreign and local firms to deepen their local content as a number of countries e.g. Singapore,

Taiwan, Korea and Ireland have done so successfully (Battat, *et al.*, 1996). The knowledge diffusion could also be accomplished by creating sub-national or sub-regional clusters of inter-related activities which facilitate the spillovers of knowledge through informal and social contacts among the employees besides traditional buyer-seller links.

4.5 Fostering Enterprise Level R&D in the Post-TRIPs Regime

The findings reported above have shown that IPR regime does not affect the investment climate in a host country. However, strengthening of IPR regime in tune with TRIPs Agreement's obligations in India has the prospect of adversely affecting the domestic R&D activity especially in the chemicals and pharmaceuticals industry by choking the domestic industry's access to knowledge spillovers from the R&D activity in other countries in the form of product development which formed the basis of process innovative activity of Indian enterprises. Hence, the Indian pharmaceutical industry runs the risk of getting marginalised in the global market because of its inability to compete on the basis of cheaper processes alone in the new regime. It might lead to an international division of labour where Indian companies will concentrate on the price competitive lower end of the market comprising off-the-patent drugs and leaving the monopolistic and more value adding parts of the market to the developed country based MNEs. The government might play a useful role in consolidating the innovative capability in the domestic pharmaceutical industry and help it to nurture through subsidies, protection and building mutually reinforcing linkages between enterprises - public funded laboratories, institutions of higher learning, among others, to foster product innovations. It may now be possible to upgrade the innovative capabilities of some domestic enterprises which had embarked on the process innovations in the wake of the Indian Patents Act 1970 to cover product development rather than allowing it to die. Some steps to promote R&D activity in the pharmaceutical industry have been taken by the government recently with creation of a Rs. 150 crore fund.

4.6 Competition Policy

The policy to support and protect national champions as proposed above has a possible pitfall as it could lead to rent seeking by national champions. So the challenge for policymakers is to ensure that the national champions do not abuse their market power. Some competitive pressure is also necessary for them to sharpen their efficiency and to prompt them to pursue innovation based rivalry. The competition policy could take several forms depending upon the relative strength of local enterprises and the extent of monopoly. East Asian countries, for instance, have pushed competitiveness of national champions with intense domestic competition and exposing them to international markets by imposing and rigorously monitoring export targets.

The increasing domination of technologies by few large corporations globally as observed by Kumar (1998b: Chapter 2) coupled by technoprotectionism in industrialised countries and recently strengthened and harmonised international regime of intellectual property protection also emphasise the need for effective anti-trust regulations in developing countries. The new norms of patent protection treat importing as working of patents and provide to the patent holders greater freedom to opt for exporting to particular markets and choosing not to transfer technology. Furthermore, the recent spurt of the cross-border merger and acquisition activity between large MNEs has adverse effects on the market concentration in many host countries where the affiliates of the merged enterprises operate as competitors. While most industrialised countries are equipped with effective anti-trust regulations to deal with possible abuse of monopoly power of patent holders and anti-competitive effects of international mergers, most developing countries either lack anti-trust legislation designed to deal with such situations or their implementation is poor.

Another aspect of competition policies is to provide a level playing field for local enterprises *vis-a-vis* subsidiaries of MNEs which enjoy access to their parent's brand and trade names besides a number of other intangible assets especially in the context of liberalisation of national economies to MNEs. An affiliation with established global chains of companies having a wide range of products and services lends a formidable edge to MNE affiliates over the national firms in the host markets. To use their advantages most effectively, MNE affiliates tend to adopt non-price modes of rivalry characterised by a heavy reliance on marketing and advertising to differentiate their products. These strategies raise barriers for the entry of new firms and are referred to as 'contrived entry barriers' in the industrial organisation literature. The empirical studies have revealed that the advantages enjoyed by MNE affiliates in the form of access to brand names *etc.* either pushes host country local firms to serve the price competitive lower ends of the markets or to seek alliances with MNEs to buy access to their brand names [see Kumar and Siddharthan, 1997, Chap. 7 for a review]. The competition policy to promote a healthy competition between local firms and MNE affiliates could take the form of either offsetting the monopoly power of MNE affiliation and foreign brands through fiscal measures or assisting national firms to build their own brands and technological capability. It is in view of this that some countries attempt to restrict the use of foreign brand names for domestic operations and instead encourage national enterprises to develop local brand names. In the case of pharmaceutical industry, for instance, some countries encourage the use of generic rather than brand-names to curb the market power of MNEs' brand names.

4.7 Approach to the WTO Negotiations

Finally, in light of the above, it is clear that it is of critical importance for the host governments to preserve the policy flexibility to pursue selective policy or impose performance requirements on FDI, if necessary. Some of the performance requirements have already been outlawed by the WTO's TRIMs Agreement. Attempts are being made by developing countries to expand the scope of international trade rules beyond what is covered under TRIMs and GATS and further limit the policy flexibility available to developing countries by creating a WTO's multilateral framework on investment.[1] India was part of the Group of 16 developing countries that firmly opposed the negotiating mandate on investment at the Cancun Ministerial Conference of WTO held in September 2003. The Conference, however, could not be concluded successfully because of inability of the member countries to arrive at a consensus on different contentious subjects including investment.

Secondly, India along with like-minded countries, should try to recover the policy space lost in the TRIMs Agreement. The TRIMs Agreement had a provision for a Review within five years of its implementation. In a joint submission to the WTO's Committee on TRIMs in October 2002 with Brazil, India has argued that the TRIMs

---

1. see Kumar (2003b) and Correa and Kumar (2003) for a more detailed discussion on this.

Agreement should be amended in order to incorporate specific provisions that will provide developing countries necessary flexibility to implement development policies. In particular, they have proposed that developing countries should be allowed to use investment measures or performance requirements to promote domestic manufacturing capabilities in high value-added sectors, stimulate transfer and indigenous development of technology, promote domestic competition and correct restrictive business practices.

Furthermore, Investment and tax incentives appear to have significantly distorted patterns of foreign production by MNEs in favour of developed countries. The distorting effects of these incentives are similar to those of trade barriers. The governments—both federal as well as local—need to be brought under some international discipline to curb the use of incentives that distort the patterns of location of production by MNEs just as trade barriers and subsidies to domestic industries are regulated by WTO. Because of 'prisoners dilemma' inherent in the incentives competition, an international agreement to limit the investment distorting incentives would collectively maximise the welfare of participating countries. India could take a proactive initiative in seeking an International Discipline on Investment Incentives with a built-in exception based on level of industrialisation.

References

Aitken, Brian, Gordon H. Hanson and Ann E. Harrison (1994). "Spillovers, Foreign Investment and Export Behaviour", NBER Working Paper 4967, Cambridge, MA: NBER.

Battat, Joseph, Isaiah Frank and Xiaofang Shen (1996). *Linkage Programs to Strengthen Local Companies in Developing Countries*, Foreign Investment Advisory Service, Occasional Paper 6, Washington, DC.

Belderbos, René (1994). *Strategic Trade Policy and Multinational Enterprises: Essays on Trade and Investment by Japanese Electronics Firms*, No. 68, Tinbergen Institute Research Series, Erasmus University, Rotterdam, and Thesis Publishers.

Brewer, Thomas (1993). "Government Policies, Market Imperfections, and Foreign Direct Investment", *Journal of International Business Studies*, 24(1): pp. 101-120.

Caves, Richard E. (1996). *Multinational Enterprise and Economic Analysis*, Second Edition, Cambridge: Cambridge University Press.

Correa, C.M. (1997). "New International Standards for Intellectual Property: Impact on Technology Flows and Innovation in Developing Countries", *Science and Public Policy* 24(2): pp. 79-92.

Correa, Carlos and Nagesh Kumar (2003). *Protecting Foreign Investment: Implications of a WTO Regime and Policy Options*, London, New York and New Delhi: Zed Press and Academic Foundation for RIS.

Dunning, John H. (1998). "Changing Geography of Foreign Direct Investment: Explanations and Implications", in Nagesh Kumar *et al.*, *Globalisation, Foreign Direct Investment and Technology Transfers: Impacts on and Prospects for Developing Countries*, London and New York: Routledge.

Ferrantino, Michael J. (1993). "The Effect of Intellectual Property Rights on International Trade and Investment", *Weltwirtschaftliches Archiv*, 129: pp. 300-31.

Frobel, F.J. Heinrichs, and O. Kreye (1980). *The New International Division of Labour*, Cambridge: Cambridge University Press.

Guisinger, Stephen E. *et al.*, (1985). *Investment Incentives and Performance Requirements: Patterns of International Trade, Production and Investment*, New York: Praeger.

Kim, Linsu (1997). *Imitation to Innovation: The Dynamics of Korea's Technological Learning*, Boston, MA: HBS Press.

Kondo, Edson Kenji (1994). "Patent Laws and Foreign Direct Investment: An Empirical Investigation", PhD dissertation, Boston: Harvard University.

Kumar, Nagesh (1994a). "Determinants of Export-Orientation of Foreign Production by U.S. Multinationals: An Inter-Country Analysis", *Journal of International Business Studies* 25(1), pp. 141-56.

————. (1994b). "Regional Trading Blocs, Industrial Reorganisations and Foreign Direct Investments – The Case of the Single European Market", *World Competition* 18(2): pp. 35-55.

————. (1996a). "Intellectual Property Protection, Market Orientation and Location of Overseas R&D Activities by Multinational Enterprises", *World Development*, 24(4): pp. 673-688.

————. (1998a). "Multinational Enterprises, Regional Economic Integration, and Export-Platform Production in the Host Countries: An Empirical Analysis for the US and Japanese Corporations", *Weltwirtschaftliches Archiv*, 134(3): pp. 450-483.

————. (in collaboration with John Dunning, Robert Lipsey, Jamuna Agarwal and Shujiro Urata) (1998b). *Globalisation, Foreign Direct Investment and Technology Transfers: Impacts on and Prospects for Developing Countries*, London and New York: Routledge.

————. (1999). "Multinational Enterprises, Overseas R&D Activity and the Global Technological Order", Occasional Paper #56, RIS, New Delhi; ISBN 81-7122-070-3.

————. (2000). "Explaining the Geography and Depth of International Production: The Case of US and Japanese Multinational Enterprises", *Weltwirtschaftliches Archiv*, 136(3): pp. 442-477.

———. (2001). "Determinants of Location of Overseas R&D Activity of Multinational Enterprises: The Case of US and Japanese Corporations", *Research Policy,* 30: pp. 159-174.

———. (2002). *Globalisation and the Quality of Foreign Direct Investment.* Oxford University Press.

———. (2003a). "Performance Requirements as Tools of Development Policy: Lessons from Experiences of Developed and Developing Countries", paper presented at the International Conference on Trade, Investment and Development organised by Government of India and UNCTAD, New Delhi, 18-20 May 2003. New Delhi: RIS (revised version available as RIS Discussion Paper # 52) available at www.ris.org.in.

———. (2003b). "Investment on the WTO Agenda: A Developing Country Perspective and the Way Forward for the Cancun Ministerial Conference", Discussion Paper #56, RIS, available at www.ris.org.in.

Kumar, Nagesh and N.S. Siddharthan (1997). *Technology, Market Structure and Internationalisation: Issues and Policies for Developing Countries.* London and New York: Routledge.

Lee, Jeong-Yeon, and Edwin Mansfield (1996). "Intellectual Property Protection and US Foreign Direct Investment", *The Review of Economics and Statistics,* 78(2): pp. 181-186.

Lipsey, Robert E., "The Internationalisation of US MNEs and its Impact in Developing Countries", in Nagesh Kumar, *et.al., Globalisation Foreign Direct Investment and Technology Transfer: Impact on and Prospects for Developing Countries,* London: Routledge, pp. 146-174.

Mansfield, Edwin (1994). *Intellectual Property Protection, Foreign Direct Investment, and Technology Transfer,* Discussion Paper 19, International Finance Cooporation, The World Bank, Washington, D.C.

Moran, Theodore (1998). *Foreign Direct Investment and Development,* Washington, DC: Institute of International Economics.

Nayyar, Deepak (1978). "Transnational Corporations and Manufactured Exports from Poor Countries", *Economic Journal,* 88:59-84.

UNCTAD (1995). *Incentives and Foreign Direct Investment,* TD/B/ITNC/Misc.1, Geneva: United Nations.

UNCTAD (1999). *World Investment Report 1999,* New York: United Nations.

UNCTC (1991). *The Impact of Trade-related Investment Measures on Trade and Development: Theory, Evidence and Policy Implications,* New York: United Nations.

Urata, Shujiro (1998). "Japanese Foreign Direct Investment in Asia: Its Impact on Export Expansion and Technology Acquisition of the Host Economies", in Nagesh Kumar, *et al., Globalisation Foreign Direct Investment and Technology Transfer: Impact on and Prospects for Developing Countries,* London: Routledge, pp. 146-174.

9

India's Agro Export Performance and Competitiveness in Changed International Scenario

RAMESH CHAND

Historically agriculture in India has played significant role as foreign exchange earner through export of traditional items like tobacco, tea, coffee, cashew nuts, spices, raw cotton, basmati rice, sugar *etc*. Agriculture contributed more than 44 per cent of total export earnings of India during 1960-61. During 1970s this share remained around 30 per cent. Agricultural exports remained stagnant during 1980s (Figure 9.1), though there was some growth towards the end of the decade. This reduced the share of agro exports in total exports of India to 17.17 per cent by 1989-90. India's agro export got a big boost with the economic reforms started during the year 1991 because of three factors. One, economic reforms sought to reverse the adverse terms of trade for agriculture by reducing protection to industry (Manmohan Singh 1995). This was expected to increase flow of resources to agriculture, which was further expected to raise output and share of output available for exports. Two, economic reforms corrected overvalued exchange rate which raised export price and thus rendered exports more attractive. Third, the new economic policy relaxed/ removed several restrictions on exports.

In a short span of four years after 1992-93 agricultural export doubled in $ value. Though, both, agricultural as well as non-agricultural exports witnessed impressive growth with progress of economic reforms, the impact was relatively higher on agricultural exports. As a result, share of agricultural exports in total exports increased from 16.3 per cent in 1992-93 to 20.5 per cent by 1996-97. This generated lot of optimism and euphoria about prospects of agricultural exports from India and frequent assertions were made about the vast export potential of Indian agriculture.

The situation took a sudden turn after 1996-97 (Figure 9.1) when agro exports started moving on a downward trend showing decline of 3.41 per cent in 1997-98 and around 9 per cent each in 1998-99 and 1999-00. The setback to India's agro export started a year after WTO Agreement on agriculture was implemented. This raises serious concerns about implications of trade liberalisation and competitiveness of Indian agriculture.

Figure 9.1

India's Agro Exports During 1997-2002

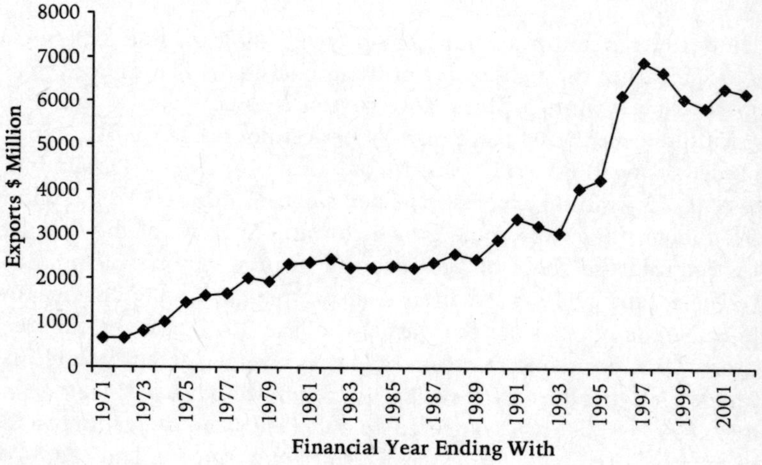

Questions are being asked whether present situation has become adverse to agriculture trade due to implementation of WTO commitments, lower efficiency of Indian agriculture, or, lack of suitable trade policy and strategy. This requires looking at various factors which determine export competitiveness of Indian agriculture. We need to understand why export competitiveness of Indian Agriculture declined suddenly? What are the domestic and international factors that influence export competitiveness and which are responsible for sharp decline in India's agricultural exports. There is a need for thorough study to identify commodities in which India has advantage. In this background the present paper focus on following objectives:

1. How the performance of agriculture exports has been affected by recent international environment?
2. What are the real cost of exports and competitiveness of important agricultural commodities and how they have been affected by post-WTO competitive global liberalisation?
3. What are the trade trends in selected commodities and groups?
4. What is the behaviour of international prices and their influence on export?
5. What should be the strategy to maintain continuity and to promote agricultural exports?

The remaining paper is organised into five sections. The first section describes analytical tools and other details about methodology. Section II discusses export performance of Indian agriculture during the last decade and changes in real cost of exports and export competitiveness for various agricultural commodities. The section also looks at trend in quantity of various products traded in global market. Section IV examines the behaviour of world prices of selected agricultural commodities and discuss their implications for India's export. The main findings, strategy for export and policy implications are presented in the last section.

1. Analytical Tools and Methodology

The paper use only two measures namely Nominal Protection Coefficient (NPC) and Domestic Resource Cost (DRC) to analyse export competitiveness and to find comparative advantage in export of different commodities. NPC is the simplest indicator of domestic protection and export competitiveness and is given by the ratio P_i^d/P_i^w, P_i^d is domestic price of commodity 'i' and P_i^w is world reference price (border price-equivalent) of commodity i, adjusted for transportation, handling and marketing expenses. NPC greater than unity indicates effective incentives to producers compared to free trade scenario and NPC lower than 1 indicates that the commodity is disprotected. Similarly, NPC<1 indicates that private trade would find it profitable to export the commodity whereas NPC>1 indicates the situation where private trade would find it profitable to import the commodity. As prices of output and inputs often do not capture true opportunity cost therefore NPC based on nominal prices does not indicate true competitiveness or worth of a tradable commodity to a producing country.

Real value of resources that go into production of a tradable commodity is estimated by DRC. DRC is not used by private trade but it reveals real cost of export (to the society or country) to earn given amount from export. It is used to find out whether it is worthwhile to use domestic resources for producing a commodity for export. Domestic Resource Cost (DRC) is the value of domestic resources needed to earn a unit of foreign exchange through export or save a unit of foreign exchange through import substitution by production of the commodity under consideration. The domestic resources included primary non-traded factors of production such as land, labour and non-traded capital. In DRC calculations, value of domestic resources is estimated at their opportunity cost or shadow prices. DRC was computed as under:

$$DRC_i = \frac{\sum_{j=k+1}^{j} A_{ij} P_j^s}{P_i^w - \sum_{j=1}^{k} A_{ij} P_j^w}$$

In this expression P_j^s refer to shadow price of jth primary input; A_{ij} is quantity of jth input required to produce a unit of commodity i and P_j^w is world price of jth tradeable input. Fertilisers, seeds, insecticides/pesticides and cost of fuel used in agricultural machinery have been treated as tradable inputs while land, human labour, bullock labour and capital have been treated as primary non-tradable inputs. Irrigation was also used as non-tradeable input and its cost was computed net of subsidy on electricity and water.

The study provides estimates of NPC and DRC for selected commodities which are important for export and for which Cost of Production data was available from Commission on Agriculture Costs and Prices (CACP) reports and from Ministry of Agriculture publications. The coverage is shown in Table 9.1. As there are large variations in cost and regional resource endowments, infrastructure and other factors the comparative advantage in producing various commodities would differ from state to state. It is therefore appropriate to prepare estimates of DRC at regional level.

Second, estimating cost of export or competitiveness using a few years data can lead to misleading results as the years may not be representing the situation. This could happen both due to abnormal situation in domestic production or international prices corresponding only to specific situation. To overcome these, estimates of competitiveness have been prepared for a period of five years.

Table 9.1

Commodities and States for which DRC Estimates are Prepared

Commodity	*States*
Paddy/rice	West Bengal, U.P., Andhra Pradesh, Punjab
Wheat	Uttar Pradesh, Punjab and Madhya Pradesh
Groundnut	Gujarat, Karnataka
Sugarcane	Uttar Pradesh
Soyabean	Madhya Pradesh and Maharashtra

Cost of cultivation data as reported by Economic and Statistics Advisor to Government of India has been used as available for the recent three years to estimate various indicators of competitiveness. But this data is published with a gap of 2-3 years. In order to assess the competitiveness in the most recent years the present study projected cost of cultivation for the years 2000-01 and 2001-02 using variable input price index, published by Commission on Agricultural Costs and Prices, for the recent years for the concerned crops. Similarly, output prices in the concerned states for the corresponding period have been used in estimating value of output.

1.1 Selecting World and Domestic Prices

Credibility and comparability of NPC and DRC depend upon choice of appropriate domestic and world prices for inputs and output. For rice, FoB price Bangkok, was considered as the price relevant for export of Indian rice. There are five kinds of international prices quoted for rice. Out of these, price of 100 per cent B Thai white rice was found to be closely related to the prices which India received for export of non-basmati rice. It was assumed that India would get this price for its rice exports.

Export competitiveness of rice was estimated for four states namely Punjab, Uttar Pradesh, West Bengal and Andhra Pradesh. Price of common rice or coarse rice in Amritsar market in Punjab, Kanpur in Uttar Pradesh, Santhia in West Bengal, and Kakinada in Andhra Pradesh were used to represent domestic prices. For Punjab and U.P. rice world reference price was adjusted for domestic marketing and transportation cost between port (Mumbai) and Delhi. For Andhra Pradesh and West Bengal domestic marketing cost and local transport cost were deducted from international price to arrive at domestic reference price.

Export competitiveness of wheat has been studied for three states *viz*. Punjab, Uttar Pradesh and Madhya Pradesh. International prices of US HRW No. 2 wheat were used as the world reference price. The export data for the last ten years show that India realised 10 per cent lower price than US HRW wheat, because Indian wheat varieties are somewhat inferior compared to US HRW wheat. Accordingly, 90 per cent of US HRW wheat was considered as FoB price for wheat export. However, in the case of Madhya Pradesh wheat, which is of superior quality and always fetches higher price in domestic market compared to the wheat produced in North-West India, international price was not discounted. These prices were further adjusted for domestic transportation and marketing cost between port and producing region. Domestic prices were taken from Hapur in U.P., Ludhiana in Punjab and Indore in Madhya Pradesh. As the wheat importing countries are located around the world it was assumed that FoB price relevant for US wheat would be relevant for Indian wheat.

There was very wide variation in international prices of groundnut due to quality grades. To overcome this, price received by Indian exporters for groundnut in shell, which is exported in large quantity, was used as international price. For domestic market, prices obtaining in Hyderabad were used. For Soyabean seed, prices for US Soyabean CIF Rotterdom were used as international prices. It was assumed that India would be able to sell soyabean at the same rate as the CIF prices at Rotterdom without deducting for freight. The major suppliers of soyabean and soyabean products are USA, Argentina and Brazil, major buyers are located in East Asia and Europe. India sells soyabean products to East and South east Asian countries. The oceanic freight between US ports and East Asian countries is higher than the freight between India and the east Asian countries by about same amount as the freight between US gulf ports to Rotterdom. So there is no need to calculate back from CIF Rotterdom price the US FoB price and to use the same as FoB price for India. Prices prevailing in Dewas, Madhya Pradesh were taken to represent domestic prices.

In the case of sugarcane the traded product is not sugarcane but sugar. Thus, beside cost of production of sugarcane, data on cost of processing sugarcane to sugar or traded product was also required. As sugar in the world is traded largely as raw sugar (jaggery) in this study we used cost of production of jaggery to estimate DRC. A quick survey was conducted to get hand on information from farmers in West U.P. on cost of making jaggery.

2. Trade Performance

Two broad indicators of performance of export are share of export in country's GDP and share of the country's export in world export. The information on these two indicators, since the beginning of economic reforms, is furnished in Table 9.2. The Table reports data on exports based on Indian sources and U.N. sources. The former is used to present share in GDP while the latter is used to estimate share in global trade. As there are variations in coverage and definitions, for sake of uniformity, the share in global trade is estimated by using data from the same source.

Table 9.2

India's Agriculture Export in Post-Reforms and Post-WTO Period

	Based on India's Data Sources@		*Based on U.N. Statistics#*		
	India's Exports $ Million	*Share in GDP Agriculture %*	*India's Export $ Million*	*World Export $ Million*	*India's Share in World Export %*
1990-91	3352	3.76	4396	477223	0.921
1991-92	3203	4.22	4170	477902	0.873
1992-93	2950	4.34	4351	509940	0.853
1993-94	4013	5.20	4842	493732	0.981
1994-95	4211	4.74	5057	567001	0.892
1995-96	6098	6.73	7041	664453	1.060
1996-97	6806	6.66	7818	672050	1.163
1997-98	6685	6.42	7518	666456	1.128
1998-99	6064	5.77	6744	630377	1.070
1999-00	5842	5.50	6241	605944	1.030
2000-01	6273	6.07	6875	614864	1.118
2001-02	6183	—			

Source: @: 1. Agricultural Statistics at a Glance, Ministry of Agriculture, GoI.
2. Economic Survey, Ministry of Finance, GoI.

Source: # United Nations Trade Statistics Yearbook, 1995, 1998 and 2000. Refer to export in the preceding year. Includes export of food and live animals, beverage and tobacco, crude material including textile fibres, vegetable oils/fats and oilseeds etc.

During early-1990s, agricultural exports constituted around 4 per cent of GDP agriculture. The policy of reducing control over exports and exchange rate adjustments boosted growth of exports that raised share of exports in GDP agriculture close to 7 per cent by 1996-97. However, this turned out to be the peak year, and per cent of GDP sold overseas declined thereafter, not only as a share but also in absolute value in US $. This decline, to some extent, was keeping with the decline in global agricultural trade, the reason for which is decline in international prices of agricultural commodities and not the decline in physical quantity of export (Chand 2002a and Chand and Jha 2001).

India's share in world export of agricultural commodities witnessed an increase upto 1996-97 but India could not maintain its share at this level when global trade started declining under the influence of fall in global prices. These results show that decline in value of India's agricultural exports in post-WTO period is much more than the decline in world trade in agriculture. This shows that India's agricultural exports are highly elastic to the price received for export. When price was favourable, India's export grew faster than world export, and when prices turned adverse then India's export declined faster than world trade. This has important implications for maintaining continuity in export.

2.1 Export of Important Commodities

Changes in export are seen some time from changes in value and some time from changes in quantity. Both serve specific purpose. While value indicates earnings from export, quantity provides better indicator of export performance.

In value terms marine products topped the list of agricultural export during early-1990s followed closely by export of oilmeal (Table 9.3). Marine product export was valued at $ 590 million during 1991-92 and it increased to $ 1127 million by 1994-95. Oilmeal export was valued at $ 377 million during 1991-92 which increased to $ 534 million during 1992-93 and $ 740 million during 1993-94. Other important items of export were tea, cashewnut, basmati rice, spices and tobacco with value ranging between $ 122 to $ 495 million. Liberalisation of export of non-basmati rice in mid-1990s provided big boost to its export. As a result, earnings from rice export figured at the top during 1995-96 and during 1998-99, exceeding the export of marine products. Out of the two grades of rice, basmati rice showed a steady upward trend whereas non-basmati rice showed violent year to year fluctuations in export.

Table 9.3

Export of Selected Agricultural Products During Reforms and Post-WTO Period

($ million)

Commodity	*1991/92*	*1992/93*	*1993/94*	*1994/95*	*1995/96*	*1996/97*	*1997/98*	*1998/99*	*1999/00*	*2000/01*	*2001/02*
Basmati rice	204	276	338	276	255	352	454	446	411	472	387
Non-basmati rice	105	60	72	108	1113	543	454	1046	311	170	279
Wheat	52	3.5	0.07	13.5	110	197	0.11	*	*	91	280
Cotton raw inc. waste	125	63	208	45	61	444	221	49	18	48	9
Pulses	**	18	23	29	39	37	97	53	97	118	77
Oilmeal	377	534	740	573	703	985	925	461	378	448	474
Sugar and mollases	64	122	57	20	152	304	69	6	9	111	375
Marine products	590	602	813	1127	1012	1129	1207	1038	1184	1396	1218
Groundnut	3	3	54	32	69	92	153	33	86	69	53
Spices	152	136	182	195	238	339	380	388	408	355	312
Tea	495	337	337	311	351	292	505	538	412	392	360
Coffee	136	130	174	335	450	402	457	411	332	260	229
Tobacco Mfd. &	154	164	147	81	134	213	288	181	233	190	170
Cashew	274	257	333	369	370	362	377	387	568	449	374
Castor oil	57	40	92	141	222	177	155	160	247	209	131
Guargum meal	38	36	45	45	68	100	147	173	188	130	84
Poultry & dairy prod.	**	**	**	**	18	35	32	23	28	47	73
Meat & prep.	94	89	110	128	188	200	218	187	189	322	251
Floriculture product	6	5	6	10	18	18	23	25	27	26	27
Fresh fruits	**	**	**	60	69	69	75	63	71	85	85
Fresh vegetables	143	108	132	79	89	94	84	65	77	100	121
Processed fruit/veg.	36	41	49	79	104	92	105	109	129	172	152

* Less than 0.5 million $. ** Data not available.

Source: Agricultural Statistics at a Glance, Ministry of Agriculture, GoI, various issues.

During the recent years oilmeal exports have been worst affected. After witnessing 90 per cent growth between 1992-93 and 1996-97, oilmeal exports dwindled to less than 40 per cent by 1999-00 compared to the peak attained in 1996-97. There is some recovery in the last two years but still the export earnings are less than half of those during 1996-97.

Exports of cotton have almost dried up in the changed international scenario. Earnings from cotton exports declined from $ 444 million in 1996-97 to mere $ 18 million in 1999-2000, and dropped further to half during the year 2001-02. Almost similar has been the case with the exports of sugar during 1996-97 and 1999-00. However, sugar exports have recovered considerably during the years 2000-01 and 2001-02 and have reached a new peak. Decline in export has also been witnessed in the case of groundnut, tobacco and meat till 1999-00. All these items have shown some improvement during the year 2000-01.

India has been quite consistent in export of marine products with export remaining around $1.1 billion. Export of traditional items like tea, cashew and spices maintained their status in post-WTO trade liberalisation but coffee export has been hit badly. Castor oil and guargum meal are emerging as important items of export. Export of horticultural items showed modest to large growth even during the post-WTO period.

In order to see whether the changes in value of export are purely price phenomenon or quantity phenomenon we also need to see the changes in quantity of export. This information for different groups of products is provided in Tables 9.4 to 9.6.

Table 9.4

Export of Rice, Wheat, Sugar and Cotton

('000 tonnes)

Year	*Non-Basmati Rice*	*Basmati Rice*	*Total Rice*	*Wheat*	*Sugar*	*Cotton*
1990-91	273	232	505	139	191	374
1991-92	411	267	678	658	446	160
1992-93	255	325	580	37	485	64
1993-94	240	527	768	ng	204	297
1994-95	448	442	891	87	51	71
1995-96	4541	373	4914	1091*	734	33
1996-97	1989	523	2512	1848*	1716	269
1997-98	1796	593	2389	22	248	165
1998-99	4366	598	4964	2	23	42
1999-00	1258	638	1896	ng	144	16
2000-01	683	852	1534	813	769	30
2001-02	1541	667	2208	2649	1677	8
2002-03	4076	595	4671	3570	1692	11

* Includes wheat flour

Like their value, exports of non-basmati rice and wheat in terms of quantity showed sharp fluctuations. When exports of rice were first liberalised during 1995-96 India's exports suddenly rose to more than four million tonnes. After a fall in the next two years India again exported more than four million tonnes of rice and became second most important exporter in the world after Thailand. However, in the following years export remained below 1.5 million tonnes despite the fact that India was accumulating large surplus in government stock much above what was genuinely needed. India is constantly improving its performance of export of basmati rice whose export rose from 2.32 lakh tonnes during 1990-91 to 5.23 lakh during 1996-97 and 8.52 lakh tonnes during 2000-01.

In the case of wheat, till recently India sometime used to import big lot and sometime it used to have large surplus for export depending upon the domestic production and stock management (Chand and Jha 2001). Of late, India has not experienced shortage of wheat that could necessitate imports. Rather, like rice, India has faced problem of vast accumulation of wheat stock after the year 1998 (Chand 2003a).

In the last three years attempts have been made to liquidate excess stock of rice and wheat in the international market. But due to depressed international prices and sharp rise in domestic prices of rice and wheat, brought out by government policy of raising procurement prices (Chand 2003b), India could not sell large amount of surplus grains in the international market[1]. This shows that generation of surplus in the domestic market does not guarantee that export would take place. The second important factor for export to take place is that domestic prices must be sufficiently lower than international prices. During the years 2001-02 and 2002-03 India has set a new record of exporting 2.65 and 3.57 million tonnes of wheat but this was made possible by providing large subsidy (Chand 2002b).

Exports of cotton have almost dried up in the recent years. India exported 3.74 lakh tonnes of cotton (lint) during 1990-91 which remains the highest level since then. The current level of export is only ten thousand tonnes. The main reasons for decline in cotton export are stagnancy in its production during the last ten years and rising demand from domestic textile industry.

---

1. For more details see Chand (2001) and Chand 2003a.

Sugar export followed the usual pattern of some time very big export and some time meager export. However, one redeeming feature of sugar export has been the rising trend during last four years. During the years 2001-02 and 2002-03, India exported more than 1.6 million tonnes sugar which is only slightly lower than the previous peak attained during 1996-97.

Export of horticultural products, meat and preparation and processed food have generally moved on rising trend after 1994-95.

3. Trade Competitiveness and Prospects

3.1 Rice

Estimates of trade competitiveness and domestic resource cost alongwith domestic and international prices are reported in Table 9.5 for the states of West Bengal, Andhra Pradesh and Punjab. Andhra Pradesh and West Bengal are coastal states, and exporting rice from these states would require only internal movement and marketing cost. Whereas, in the case of Punjab, additional cost of transport from Punjab to the port in Gujarat or Mumbai has to be reckoned to arrive at relevant world reference price. This is the reason that in some cases despite domestic price in Punjab being lower than the domestic price in Andhra Pradesh and West Bengal, NPC in former state turns out to be higher than the latter.

NPC, which purely indicate export competitiveness at existing prices and is guiding indicator for private trade, show that export from Andhra Pradesh and Punjab were competitive during 1997-98 and 1998-99. Subsequently, as international prices declined export did not remain attractive from these two states. However, in the case of West Bengal as domestic prices also behaved in the same way as the international prices, exports remained competitive.

DRC indicates the cost to society in terms of opportunity cost of non-tradeable inputs like land, labour and capital *etc.* to earn one Rupee from export in terms of value added. For instance, DRC of magnitude of 0.40 for rice indicates that to earn one rupee of foreign exchange through export of rice a country would be using domestic resources only worth Rs. 0.40. Thus, DRC below one indicate that allocating more resources to a commodity to promote its export is socially desirable. Out of the five years since 1997-98 only in last year DRC in Andhra Pradesh and Punjab turned out to be above one. In

West Bengal it remained below one throughout. These results indicate that it is highly paying for the country to promote export of rice though in some years private trade may not find it profitable to go for export due to high level of domestic prices or low level of international price.

Table 9.5

Domestic and International Prices and Estimates of Competitiveness and Domestic Resource Cost for Paddy/Rice under Exportable Hypothesis

State	*Particulars*	*1997-98*	*1998-99*	*1999-2000*	*2000-01*	*2001-02*
West Bengal						
	Domestic price Rs./qtl	785	986	853	791	741
	World price Rs./qtl	1174	1325	1096	946	844
	NPC	0.707	0.789	0.832	0.903	0.957
	DRC	0.404	0.551	0.606	0.743	0.879
Andhra Pradesh						
	Domestic price Rs./qtl	910	1085	1032	913	1054
	World price Rs./qtl	1174	1325	1096	946	844
	NPC	0.824	0.872	1.015	1.024	1.390
	DRC	0.640	0.559	0.760	0.950	1.183
Punjab						
	Domestic price Rs./qtl	733	783	858	812	813
	World price Rs./qtl	1174	1325	1096	946	844
	NPC	0.737	0.694	0.975	1.137	1.370
	DRC	0.441	0.457	0.620	0.870	1.180

3.2 *Wheat*

Measures of export competitiveness were estimated for Uttar Pradesh, Punjab and Madhya Pradesh. Out of these U.P. and Punjab are the top two states in terms of production while Madhya Pradesh is picking up particularly in terms of production of better quality wheat in the country which fetches much higher price than the wheat produced in North West Indian states.

During the last five years domestic prices in all the states ruled higher than international prices implying that wheat producers have received much higher prices in domestic market than what they would receive from international market. In other words, wheat produced in India has been found to enjoy very high level of protection under exportable hypothesis. These indicators suggest that export of wheat at domestic and world price structure prevalent during last five years is highly uncompetitive (Table 9.6).

Table 9.6

Domestic and International Prices and Estimates of Competitiveness and Domestic Resource Cost for Wheat under Exportable Hypothesis

State	*Particulars*	*1997-98*	*1998-99*	*1999-2000*	*2000-01*	*2001-02*
Uttar Pradesh						
	Domestic price Rs./qtl	526	598	653	676	617
	World price Rs./qtl	475	454	437	526	545
	NPC	1.513	1.908	2.315	1.887	1.682
	DRC	1.056	1.253	1.627	1.289	1.353
Punjab						
	Domestic price Rs./qtl	514	612	626	608	610
	World price Rs./qtl	475	454	437	526	545
	NPC	1.682	2.304	2.700	1.995	2.003
	DRC	1.389	1.487	1.903	1.608	1.696
Madhya Pradesh						
	Domestic price Rs./qtl	590	677	779	792	758
	World price Rs./qtl	528	505	485	585	606
	NPC	1.342	1.667	2.077	1.694	1.572
	DRC	1.319	1.440	1.739	1.510	1.582

DRC was also more than one in all the cases. This implies that earning one rupee of value added from export of wheat costs the nation more than one rupee of domestic resource. Therefore, unless efficiency of wheat production improves or international prices go very high, it is not desirable to grow wheat for export purposes.

Out of the three major wheat producing states, DRC was lowest in Uttar Pradesh. Sensitivity analysis shows that if international prices during the year 2000-01 and 2001-02 were 17 and 21 per cent higher than their actual level than it becomes profitable to allocate resource to wheat for export purpose.

3.3 Groundnut

Domestic prices of groundnut in shell of average quality were significantly lower than the FOB prices India got for export. As we have used same set of prices for all the three states all of which also have similar access to port so NPC is same for all the states (Table 9.7). DRC was lowest and below one for the state of Gujarat.

Table 9.7

Domestic and International Prices and Estimates of Competitiveness and Domestic Resource Cost for Groundnut under Exportable Hypothesis

State	*Particulars*	*1997-98*	*1998-99*	*1999-2000*	*2000-01*	*2001-02*
Andhra Pradesh						
	Domestic price Rs./qtl	1763	1800	1835	1875	1841
	World price Rs./qtl	2266	2175	2280	2179	2293
	NPC	0.819	0.874	0.849	0.912	0.849
	DRC	0.621	0.621	0.666	0.749	0.738
Gujarat						
	Domestic price Rs./qtl	1763	1800	1835	1875	1841
	World price Rs./qtl	2266	2175	2280	2179	2293
	NPC	0.819	0.874	0.849	0.912	0.849
	DRC	0.400	0.443	0.439	0.479	0.475
Karnataka						
	Domestic price Rs./qtl	1763	1800	1835	1875	1841
	World price Rs./qtl	2266	2175	2280	2179	2293
	NPC	0.819	0.874	0.849	0.912	0.849
	DRC	0.791	0.662	0.815	0.928	0.941

Estimates of DRC have sharply increased over the last five years in Karnataka but still remain below one. In Andhra Pradesh domestic resource cost to earn one rupee of foreign exchange from groundnut varied between 62 to 75 Paise. In Gujarat DRC remains below Re. 0.48 in all the years. Thus, from social point of view it is highly desirable to promote export of groundnut in all the three states with best returns from Gujarat, moderate returns from Andhra Pradesh and relatively low return from Karnataka.

3.4 Soyabean

Soyabean is grown mainly in Madhya Pradesh while Uttar Pradesh and Maharashtra also grow it on some area. As far as soyabean seed is concerned its price in domestic market remained higher than international price in all the five years representing high as well as low level of international prices. Accordingly, NPC was also found to be higher than one for Madhya Pradesh and Maharashtra (Table 9.8).

Table 9.8

Domestic and International Prices and Estimates of Competitiveness and Domestic Resource Cost for Soyabean under Exportable Hypothesis

State	*Particulars*	*1997-98*	*1998-99*	*1999-2000*	*2000-01*	*2001-02*
Madhya Pradesh						
	Domestic price Rs./qtl	1077	1001	880	940	998
	World price Rs./qtl	1098	1032	865	965	932
	NPC	1.094	1.091	1.174	1.119	1.253
	DRC	0.668	0.770	1.032	0.904	0.982
Maharashtra						
	Domestic price Rs./qtl	1077	1001	880	940	998
	World price Rs./qtl	1098	1032	865	965	932
	NPC	1.056	1.047	1.110	1.059	1.175
	DRC	0.771	0.705	1.087	1.000	1.089

In contrast to NPC, DRC remained below one in all the years for MP except one year when international price of soyabean was abnormally low. In the case of Maharashtra, when international prices are high than DRC is below one otherwise above one. On an average DRC for soyabean produced in Maharshtra remains below one.

These results indicate that based on market prices export of soyabean is not attractive and competitive. But when resources are valued at opportunity cost and value added is estimated at international prices of output and inputs than soyabean production is found to be highly competitive. In other words it is a paying proposition to go for export of soyabean and promoting its production in the states of Madhya Pradesh and Maharashtra; the advantage is greater in MP as compared to Maharashtra.

3.5 Sugarcane

Uttar Pradesh is the largest sugarcane producing state of India accounting for little more than one third of sugarcane production in the country. Like wheat and paddy, government intervention in terms of affecting sugarcane prices for the producers is quite strong. If government imposes a price for sugarcane which is higher than that would be determined by market forces than price of sugar or raw sugar would obviously be higher than that dictated by market forces. This ultimately affects the competitiveness of sugar for export by private trade. Because of sharp decline in international prices of sugar attractiveness for export got further eroded.

Domestic price of jaggery in UP was higher than price of raw sugar in international market (Table 9.9). Accounting for internal cost of marketing and transport to port further reduces FoB export price as relevant for producers in the state of Uttar Pradesh. However, DRC presents entirely different picture than what emerges from measures like NPC, EPC, ESC which are considerable affected by domestic price. It may be noted that DRC does not take into account domestic price of final product but it takes into account cost of resources. DRC reveals that except year 1999-00 which was very abnormal for international prices, it was socially paying and beneficial proposition to devote resources to sugarcane production for export of raw sugar. For every one rupee earned from value added in sugarcane production for export there was a cost of Re. 0.73 during 1997-98 and Re. 0.845 during the year 2001-02.

Table 9.9

Domestic and International Prices and Estimates of Competitiveness and Domestic Resource Cost for Sugarcane, Gur under Exportable Hypothesis

State	*Particulars*	*1997-98*	*1998-99*	*1999-2000*	*2000-01*	*2001-02*
Uttar Pradesh						
	Domestic price Rs./qtl	896	881	956	963	1028
	World price Rs./qtl	933	828	598	808	858
	NPC	1.138	1.309	2.233	1.539	1.559
	DRC	0.731	0.772	1.228	0.875	0.845

Note: Prices refer to *gur* in domestic market and raw sugar in international market.

4. Behaviour of International Prices

Annual series on nominal international prices of wheat, rice, soyabean seed, cotton, sugar and groundnut are plotted in Figure 9.2 to Figure 9.7. A cursory look at the plotted series show sharp cyclical pattern in almost all the series. Most of the series do not show any rising or falling trend in nominal $ prices. During the last three decades first peak in wheat prices was recorded during 1974 when international price touched $ 187 per tonne. This was followed by trough during 1977 when the price dropped to $ 107. The second peak occurred during 1981 and was lower than the previous peak. Similarly, second trough occurred after ten years and was higher than the previous trough. After this, the duration of cyclical pattern got narrowed down for some time. During the decade of 1990s wheat prices peaked during 1996 to reach level of 210 which was highest so far. The prices fell more sharply than the rise in next three years which took the series to $ 112 in 1999, the lowest level after 1977. Once again the cycle appears to have taken upward turn as the prices during the years 2000, 2001 and 2002 have steadily risen to $ 115, 128 and 148. This way, the decade of 1990s witnessed more spread in the prices than the previous decades. Second, implementation of WTO agreement did not seem to have altered cyclical behaviour of prices – rather it has taken nominal prices to the lowest level in more than quarter of the last century.

Figure 9.2

International Prices of Wheat UH HRW

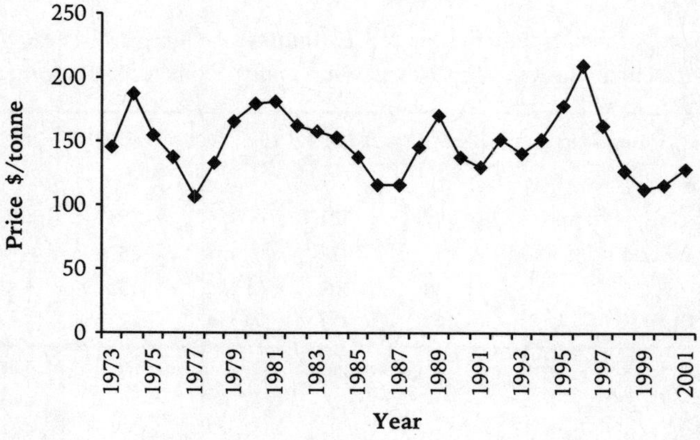

Figure 9.3

International Prices of Rice Thai

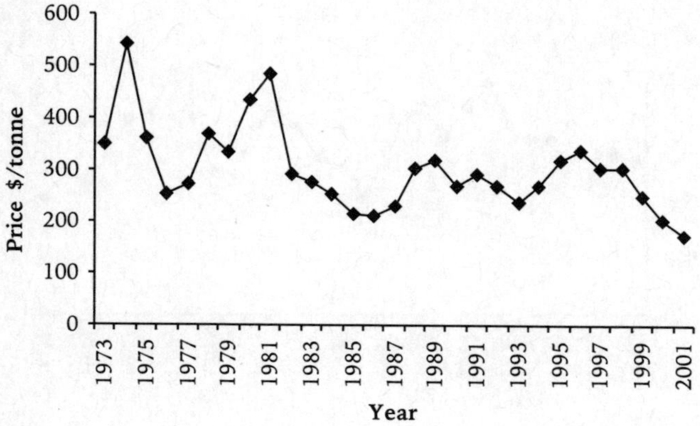

Figure 9.4

International Prices of Sugar, Carribean Port

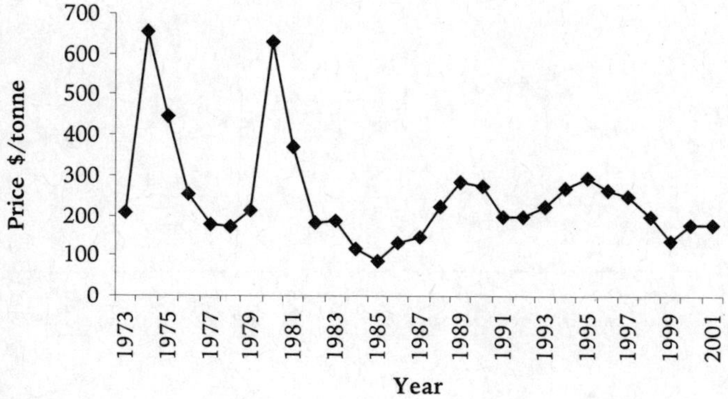

In the case of rice international prices, represented by Thai rice, showed violent fluctuations before 1982 but then somewhat stabilised. Normal cyclical pattern started from 1982 when the price was $ 293/tonne. The trough was reached in 1986 when prices dropped to $211. The next peak was during 1989 which carried rice price to $320. As the cycle would imply, the prices were rising before WTO and reached peak level of $ 338 during 1995. As was the case

Figure 9.5

International Prices of Cotton, Liverpool Index

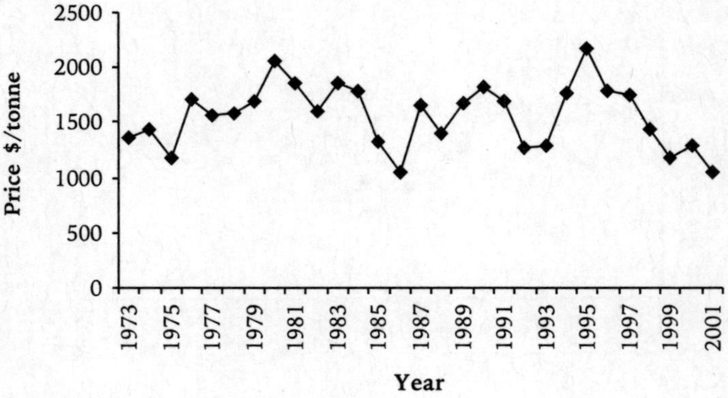

Figure 9.6

International Prices of Soyabean Seed, US CIF Rotterdam

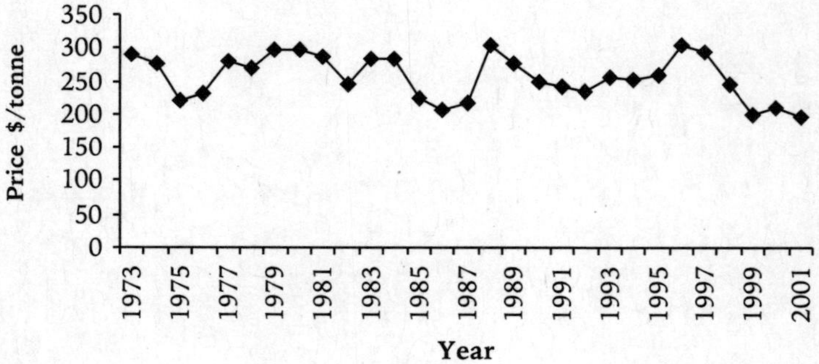

with wheat rice prices in next four years dropped to almost half by 2001. The year 2002 show some recovery and might mark upward movement in the cycle.

Similar behaviour is exhibited by price series on sugar, cotton and soyabean. Price series of groundnut exhibit slightly different pattern. Beside fluctuation the overall trend was moving upward till early 1990s. During 1990s the trend in nominal prices show downward movement.

Figure 9.7

International Prices of Groundnut Nigerian, London

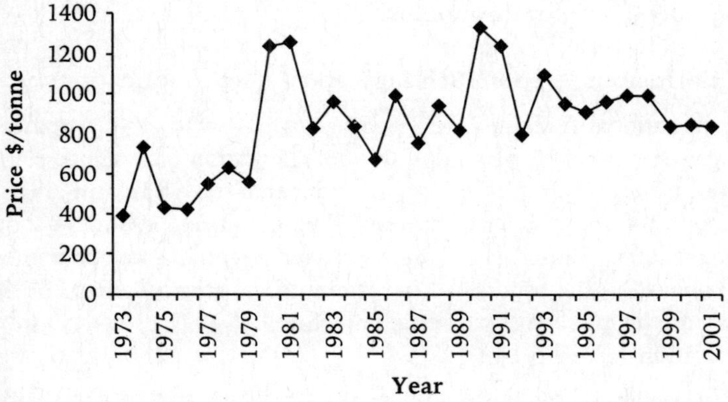

What can be concluded from the price behaviour is as follows. Prices of several commodities considered to be important for export from India show neither rising nor a declining trend in $ value. In other words, year to year movements in agricultural prices are mainly of cyclical nature without any secular trend. Thus, to compete in international market, real cost of production in agriculture must decline, or at least it should not increase. Otherwise any country would loose its competitive edge.

Very low level of international prices experienced during 1998 to 2001 is partly due to cyclical behaviour of prices and partly due to competitive liberalisation of post-WTO period. There are no indications that in future prices would not show similar fluctuations. This has important implications for export depending upon level of domestic prices *vis à vis* international prices. Some commodities, where domestic prices remain lower than international prices, even when international prices are low, the cyclical movement towards trough only narrow down the margin from export but the commodities remain exportable. The more serious problem is with those commodities where international prices at their low level turns lower than the domestic prices as is the case with rice, wheat, sugar and soyabean.

There are only two options in such cases. One, improve efficiency of production and other market related operations such that supply price does not turn higher than the international prices when they are low. The second option is to support export during low international prices through mechanisms like price stabilisation funds. Such funds can raise money by taking a part of margin from export when international prices are high and using the same to support export when international prices are low.

5. Conclusions, Export Strategy and Policy Implications

International trade and prices scenarios have witnessed important changes during recent years due to implementation of Uruguay round of General Agreement on Trade and Tariff (GATT) and due to economic reforms followed by developing countries, including India, during 1990s. While global markets have become somewhat more open almost all the countries have attempted to take advantage of this situation by pushing exports. This has led to increased global competition for exports.

The policy of reducing control over exports and exchange rate adjustments boosted growth of farm exports. However, subsequently the export share as well as absolute value in US $ followed decline. This happened mainly due to unusual decline in international prices as global agricultural trade also showed some decline in value term. The decline in India's agro export was much higher than the decline in global agro trade. When price is favourable, India's export grow faster than world export, and when prices turn adverse then India's export decline faster than world trade. This affects India's image as a reliable supplier in global markets and adversely affect the prices fetched by India's export.

In the new international trade environment India performed much better in exporting horticultural, livestock, processed and other products whose demand is more income elastic. This has taken place despite several odds. One, SPS has become big issue in the post-WTO period and SPS issues are more serious in the case of horticultural, processed and livestock products than raw and bulk products like wheat, rice, cotton, coffee *etc*. Two, India was said to be not well equipped to ensure high level of SPS standards. It shows that where adequate returns and incentives are available, Indian exporters overcome the domestic infrastructural weaknesses. Another evidence of this is available from the experience of export of rice and wheat. India has accumulated vast stock of wheat and rice but not able to compete in the international market.

India has advantage and potential for promoting export of rice, groundnut, soyabean and sugar but it is in a disadvantageous position to compete and benefit from export of wheat. There is a clear advantage in export of cotton based on all indicators. In the case of soyabean and sugarcane, market prices do not reveal competitiveness but from social or country's point of view it is beneficial to promote their export. In sugarcane government intervention in prices has eroded competitiveness to a large extent.

Prices of several commodities considered to be important for export from India show neither rising nor a declining trend in $ value and year to year movements in agricultural prices are mainly of cyclical nature. This implies that to compete in international market, real cost of production in agriculture must decline.

Domestic factors are the key to improve export. The most important is improvement in efficiency that helps in cutting prices for export. Under the liberalised environment, export requires paradigm shift from "output growth" to "efficient growth or growth accompanied with improvement in efficiency". Further, improvement in efficiency does not involve only the reduction in cost of production. Equally important are the other costs and processes which reflect into price like cost of marketing, cost of transport and cost of processing.

Raising productivity in already agriculturally advanced regions would involve more cost in terms of inputs compared to underdeveloped regions as the developed regions are at a higher level on the production frontier. The twin goal of increase in productivity and efficiency can be achieved by harnessing potential of underdeveloped regions and through development of specialisation pockets. The best suited enterprises should be identified for different agro-ecological settings and these should be supported by physical as well as institutional infrastructure. The focus must shift to area specific enterprises.

India's producers are at a disadvantage in respect of infrastructure compared to their counterparts in developed world from where most of competition comes. Development of infrastructure is essential to improve efficiency in production and marketing. Beside physical infrastructure, technological improvement is the most important source of growth in total factor productivity and in improvement of efficiency. Competitive global liberalisation has thrown new and formidable challenge to compete with international technologies.

Facing this challenge would require vigorous efforts in domestic R&D. Some countries have very effectively applied tools of biotechnology to raise yield, reduce cost of production, and improve quality. India needs to learn from the experience of such countries and should encourage new technologies yield enhancing and cost reducing technologies without getting bogged down in the debates on transgenics and genetically modified products.

References

Chand, Ramesh (2001). "Emerging Trends and Issues in Public and private Investments in Indian Agriculture: A Statewise Analysis", *Indian Journal of Agricultural Economics*, Vol. 56 No.2, 161-184, April – June 2001.

———. (2002a). "Indian Agriculture and WTO: Looking Beyond Doha", Keynote Paper, IX Annual Conference Proceedings, *Agricultural Economics Research Review*, 17-42.

———. (2002b). *Trade Liberalisation, WTO and Indian Agriculture: Experience and Prospects*, Mittal Publications, New Delhi, 2002

———. (2003a). "Government Intervention in Foodgrain Markets in the Changing Context", Policy Paper 19, National Centre for Agricultural Economics and Policy Research, New Delhi.

———. (2003b). "Minimum Support Price in Agriculture: Changing Requirements", *Economic and Political Weekly*, V.38 (29):3027-3028, July 19, 2003.

Chand, Ramesh and Jha D. (2001). "Trade Liberalisation, Agricultural Prices and Social Welfare", in S.S Acharya and D.P. Chaudhri (ed.) *Indian Agricultural Policy at the Crossroads*, Rawat Publications, Jaipur, pp.17-126.

Singh, Manmohan (1995). "Inaugural Address delivered at the 54th Annual Conference of the Indian Society of Agricultural Economics", *Indian Journal of Agricultural Economics*, 50 (1), January – March.

10

Liberalisation, Multinational Enterprises and Export Performance: Evidence from Indian Manufacturing

ARADHNA AGGARWAL*

1. Introduction

In the globalised world of the 1990s, MNEs have assumed a major role in international trade. According to an estimate (UNCTAD, 1999) two-thirds of total world trade was accounted for by MNEs in 1996; over a third was intra-MNE. Besides, foreign affiliates of MNEs are estimated to account for more than one-fifth of world exports and one-third of developing country exports. The process of increasing global integration, reinforced by the renaissance of the market economy, the emergence of new, generic and core-knowledge technologies as the vital competing resources and a growing tendency for techno-protectionism and strengthening of the international IPR [e.g. Dunning and Narula 1997; Kumar 1998a, Dunning 1998] has intensified the technology-based competition in world markets in the 1990s.

In this new environment MNEs have an edge over local firms due to their access to proprietary assets, location-specific endowments of countries and regions in which they operate and their strategies to deploy and integrate these assets. The nature and character of FDI has also undergone substantial changes with MNEs pursuing more globally integrated production and marketing strategies having greater trading prospects [Dunning 1994, 1998; Aggarwal 1997; Papanastassiou and Pearce 1999]. It is therefore expected that MNEs would play a key role in international trade, particularly in high-tech industries in this period.

---

* My thanks to Professors N.S. Siddharthan, B.N. Goldar and Nagesh Kumar for their useful comments. The paper was presented at a national seminar organised in the honour of Prof. K.L. Krishna. Comments of discussants are gratefully acknowledged. Thanks to two anonymous referees of the journal. Usual disclaimer applies.

The impact of recent globalisation trends on the export-enhancing role of MNEs, particularly in developing countries, has been discussed extensively in many recent studies [Dunning 1994, 1998; UNCTAD 1999]. Empirical studies however on this issue are scarce. A recent cross-country analysis for 52 countries [UNCTAD 1999] suggested a positive relationship between FDI and manufactured exports; the relationship was stronger for developing than developed countries and in high- and low- tech industries than in medium-tech ones. Individual country-level studies are however, scarce. Against that background, this paper analyses the Indian experience in the 1990s. It attempts to answer two questions. The first is: do MNE affiliates export more than the domestic firms in the open regime of the 1990s in Indian manufacturing? The second is: do MNE affiliates have comparatively greater advantage in high-tech than in low- and medium-tech industries? These questions are addressed in the paper through a firm-level analysis of the determinants of export intensity in the late-1990s.

A structural adjustment programme in India was initiated in the mid-1980s with a massive dose of liberalisation being administered in 1991. As a result, the average effective rate of protection which was as high as 126 per cent during 1984-90 came down to 86 per cent over 1991 (Das 2002). The average nominal tariff rate in the manufacturing sector declined from 116.6 per cent in 1987-88 to 53 per cent by 1994-95 and the peak rate of tariff was lowered from 110 per cent to 65 per cent over the same period (Saleem, 1996). The import weighted average tariff rate (inclusive of basic, special and additional custom duties) declined from 102.3 per cent in 1993-94 to 38.12 per cent by 1998-99 (Mehta 1997). There have been reductions in quantitative restrictions as well. The share of imports under OGL in the manufacturing sector was only 20 per cent in 1987; it increased to around 55 per cent by 1994-95 (Saleem 1996). By 1997-98 over 90 per cent of imports in the manufactured group were free from non-tariff barriers and less than 20 per cent items in this sector were under non-tariff-barriers (Mehta 1999). Beside trade liberalisation, the 1990s also witnessed substantial relaxation in FDI policies. In the initial phase of liberalisation (1993-95) the inflows of FDI and foreign technologies increased tremendously (the ratio of FDI to gross domestic investment rose over four-fold during 1993-98). Manufactured exports also increased rapidly during the same period with their share in total exports rising from around 75 per cent in 1989-90 to around 81 per cent by 1999. This study using firm level data examines whether the FDI and export performance were related positively during this period.

The outline of the paper is as follows. Section II sets out the theoretical framework of linkages between the policy regime, MNEs and exports. Section III describes the model and the methodology; Section IV discusses the empirical results while Section V concludes the analysis.

2. MNE Affiliates, Exports and Policy Regime: Hypotheses

The theoretical literature suggests that liberal trade regimes attract export-oriented FDI. Bhagwati (1973), using the framework of the international trade theory, argued that exogenous FDI inflows are essentially to exploit local cost conditions *a la* H-O model and are, therefore, attracted to industries where the country has comparative advantages. Tariff barriers distort this pattern and induce tariff-jumping FDI in import-substituting industries. Vernon (1966) in his product cycle theory suggested that cost competitiveness concerns drive production abroad in the maturing stages of production. Foreign production, therefore, is to exploit the location-specific advantages to achieve cost-efficiency. Its objective is to service the host country market and export to other countries. Thus, export-oriented FDI takes place in maturing stages of production. High tariffs, however, offer a locational advantage for tariff-jumping, import-substituting FDI in the early stages of production. Thus protected regimes are likely to attract import-substituting FDI.

Dunning (1993) argued that firms' ownership advantages and the host country's location-specific advantages interact with the internalisation advantages to determine the nature and consequences of FDI. Artificially high exchange rates, government regulations and protected economic environment within a restrictive trade regime induce FDI that is of market seeking variety. Open regimes that facilitate intra-firm trade, allow greater freedom to MNEs and are export-friendly may, on the other hand, attract resource seeking, efficiency seeking and/or asset acquiring FDI, all of which have a significant impact on trade.

The literature on exports and technology treats FDI as a mode of technology transfer. It argues that due to easy access to proprietary technology of their parents, MNE affiliates are likely to be more competitive in international markets. Their export-competitiveness however, depends upon the kind of technology actually transferred by their parents. In a protective regime, MNEs may not be motivated to transfer new technologies to their affiliates due to the absence of competition and government regulations regarding foreign equity ownership holdings and local content requirements on FDI (Balasubramanyam and Salisu 1991, Wang and Blomstrom 1992). The *initial* technology advantages continue to provide these affiliates with an edge over the local firms (see also Papanastassiou and Pearce 1999). Opening up of the economy spurs competition from importers, other foreign firms as well as new and modernising indigenous firms. To maintain their profitability in the face of mounting competition, parents update the technologies of their affiliates to strengthen their national and international competitiveness (Blomstrom *et al.*, 1994, Kokko 1992).

While the arguments set out above describe the links between the export-promoting role of MNE affiliates and trade regime in a given economy, many recent studies [see e.g. Dunning 1994,1998; Kumar 1998b; Papanastassiou and Pearce 1999] have focused on the impact of the recent process of globalisation on the export-role of MNEs. These studies argue: most MNEs tended to be of 'stand alone' type or truncated miniature replica (TMR) of their parents reaping monopolistic profits in a protected economic environment. The process of globalisation has induced them to restructure their operations to avail economies of scale and scope by internalising the economies of specialisation through the integration of assets, production and marketing activities across countries to advance the core competencies in the global markets. They are locating different stages of production in different countries according to factor costs and capabilities and/or distributing similar production activities across affiliates in countries with similar capabilities to reap scale economies. These strategies have shifted the focus from market-seeking to efficiency-seeking export-oriented production.

The theoretical literature summarised above suggests that MNE affiliates are likely to be more outward oriented, and are associated with more competitive technology, better management techniques and better marketing skills in a globalised world. The first hypothesis therefore is that the export intensity of MNE affiliates is greater than that of local firms in the 1990s.

There are reasons to believe that MNEs play a greater export-role in high-tech than in low- and medium-tech industries. High-tech industries are characterised by rapidly changing and complex technologies. Such technologies, as the theory of internalisation (Magee 1977; Teece 1977; Davidson and Mcfetridge 1984; among many others) suggests, may not be transferred to unaffiliates in host countries through markets due to high incidence of market failures such as inefficient pricing, the risk of leakage, information asymmetry and uncodifiability of knowledge in their transfers. Internal hierarchies are preferred to transfer such technologies. Therefore, MNE affiliation confers a distinct advantage on firms in these industries. On the contrary, relatively older and codifiable technologies prevailing in low- and medium-tech industries may be transferred through markets also. Besides, it is also argued that the importance of delivery and effective marketing *etc.* increases with technological complexity of the products (UNCTAD 1995,1999). Marketing-based advantages therefore, provide a competitive edge to MNEs over local firms in high-tech industries. Evidence suggests (UNCTAD 1999) that despite their broad technology base, firms in the newly industrialising economies [NIEs] have begun using strategic alliances with leading MNEs for rapid entry into complex activities due to increasing competition. Finally, highly integrated production systems raise barriers-to-entry for developing countries into high-tech export markets. MNE affiliation provides close integration into global markets and networks. The second hypothesis, therefore, is that MNE Affiliates have greater competitive advantages over local firms in high-tech industries than in low and medium-tech industries.

3. The Model

To test the above two hypotheses, the existing studies that relate export performance of firms to technological capabilities, variable costs and the scale of operation are drawn upon. While adapting this framework to the present context, the following explanatory variables are identified.

3.1 Multinational Affiliation

The discussion above suggests that MNE affiliates have an edge over their local counterparts in international markets and are likely to enjoy a higher export intensity. However, many authors postulate a positive relationship between foreign equity stake and exports. They argue that MNEs prefer to control their export-oriented affiliates closely through high ownership stakes treating their marketing network as their proprietary asset (see UNCTAD 1999). Besides, the empirical evidence suggests that more complex and advanced technologies are transferred to closely held affiliates (Behrman and Willander 1976, Teece 1977). In view of the theoretical literature, a positive effect not only of multinational affiliation (FS) but also of foreign equity stake (FE) on firms' export intensity is postulated.

3.2 Technology Imports

Technology imports is one of the most important sources of knowledge acquisition by enterprises in developing countries. Technology import may be disembodied in the form of blue prints or embodied in capital goods. While the disembodied technology imports involve arms' length purchase of technology [MT], embodied technologies are acquired through imports of capital goods [IMPK]. The two modes of technology imports are differentiated on the basis of the age, nature, complexity and packaging of technologies that are involved and hence, are likely to have differential impact on firms' export performance.

3.3 Local R&D Activity

Technology acquisition through external sources does not confer competitive advantages on all firms automatically and equally. Firm-specific technology absorption and development capabilities are crucial in determining performance-enhancing effects of technology acquisition and improving international competitiveness (Lall 1992; Mowery and Oxley 1997). These capabilities are reflected in R&D intensity [RDS], which is expected to affect their export performance positively.

3.3.1 Skills of Labour Force

Most studies in the evolutionary literature have emphasised learning as an important determinant of firms' competitiveness (Mowery and Oxley 1997). In the process of learning, the most crucial input is the presence of skilled labour force. It is argued that acquisition of technology may be a key factor but it is the effective utilisation of technology that makes it valuable and there are two requirements for this. First, the firm must hire skilled persons and train them and two; the firms must organise to make use of employees' skills effectively (Lazonic 1993, Lall 1999). To capture the effect of the two, I use efficiency of labour force as a measure of SKILL and expect a positive relationship between export performance and SKILL.

3.4 Imports of Raw Materials

Early studies on the cost competitiveness of Indian industry (see, World Bank 1984, CEI 1986 for engineering industries[1] and Doraiswamy 1992 for chemical industry) suggested that in the protected regime high tariff rates on inputs affected cost competitiveness of Indian products adversely. If that is the case, one may expect low tariffs and easy importability of raw materials and components to confer cost competitiveness on firms in the post-liberalisation period of the 1990s. Besides, firms using imported materials would also compete on the basis of superior quality of products, particularly in markets where consumers are more quality conscious (Lall 1986). Thus, the import intensity of raw materials (IMRS) is postulated to affect firms' export performance positively.

3.4.1 Firm Size

Theoretically, size (SIZE) is predicted to affect export performance of firms positively (see Bonaccorsi 1992 for a survey). The new trade theory posits a positive impact of market size in view of economies of scale. It argues that the scale economy provides cost advantages in production, R&D and marketing efforts (Kumar and Siddharthan 1994). The literature associated with export marketing, on the other hand, suggests that large firms have greater resources to gather information on markets in foreign countries and to cover uncertainties of a foreign market (Wakelin 1997). It is therefore, hypothesised that large firms are likely to be more export-oriented.

3.4.2 Industry-specific Effects

Considering that the industries differ vastly in terms of the organisational structure, policy environment, technological characteristics and historical development, one may expect that industry specific differences are significant. To take account of these differences, industry specific effects are controlled in the empirical analysis. The model for inter-firm variations in export performance, therefore, is given by [1]:

$$EXP = [FE/FS, MT, IMPK, RDS, SKILL, IMRS, SIZE, D_1, ---, D_n] \quad ...(1)$$

Where EXP denotes the export intensity of a given firm and D_1, - - -, D_n are industry specific dummies for n industries.

---

1. This study was commissioned by the Confederation of (Indian) Engineering Industry (CEI) and has been cited by K.C. Khanna, 'Why Industry Stagnates', Times of India, 28 October, 1986.

3.5 Data Base and Methodology for Empirical Testing

For the empirical testing of the above hypotheses, the study uses the CAPITAL LINE database. This database provides financial statistics of firms listed on the stock exchange. For each company, the industrial activity accounting for at least half of its turnover is specified. The database includes firms engaged in both manufacturing and non-manufacturing activities. The empirical analysis here was to be confined to the manufacturing sector firms. Therefore, manufacturing firms' data are extracted from the database for five years that is from 1996 to 2000. This yielded 4211 observations of 970 firms. The firms were classified into 33 industries. Since the data span was five years, it was necessary to control year-to-year variations. To even out such variations, yearly averages were worked out. Firms that were producing primarily for the export markets (exporting more than 60 per cent of their sales in overseas markets) were excluded from the sample. These were 48 firms. In a sample where the average export intensity is 6 to 7 per cent, the inclusion of such firms could introduce sampling bias. Firms with missing observations were also dropped. After eliminating these firms, we were left with a panel data set of 916 firms across 33 industries. Since some firms did not export at all, a Tobit Model was fitted to the data. To capture the unobserved industry-specific effects both fixed effect and random effect models were estimated. Since a fixed effects model cannot be estimated in a tobit framework, thirty-three industries were re-classified into 16 broad industries to capture industry-specific effects. Tobit model estimates were then obtained with dummy variables for these 16 industries. These estimates are presented as fixed effect tobit models (FEM). However, tobit random effect models were estimated with all 33 industry groups (REM) using the STATA statistical package.

The empirical testing of the second hypothesis required classification of industries in different technology groups. For this, we used the revised classification provided by the OECD (see, Hatzichronoglou 1997). In this classification, four different technology-groups are identified. These are namely, high-tech, medium-high-tech, medium-low-tech and low-tech industries. Since our sample provided information on the main product of each firm, it was easy to classify firms and then industries according to this classification (Appendix 1). Fixed and random effects tobit models were estimated for each industry group separately.

4. Empirical Results

The results based on fixed and random effects tobit models are presented in Tables 10.1 and 10. 2. While Table 10.1 presents results for the entire data set, Table 10.2 provides results for different industry groups.

Table 10.1 shows that FS turned out to be significant at 10 per cent with a positive sign; FE was insignificant in all equations. The results suggest that MNE affiliates performed better than local firms though there is no evidence of the positive relationship between foreign equity stake and export performance of firms in Indian manufacturing. Most studies directed at the pre-1990s period in India found MNEs to have either the same or an even lower export intensity than that of local firms (Lall and Streeten 1977, Subrahmanian and Pillai 1979, Lall 1986, Kumar 1990, Pant 1993, Kumar and Siddharthan 1994). Jain (1998) in her analysis of selected industries found that the impact of foreign holding on firms' export performance was not significant in the early-1980s in any industry; in the late-1980s it improved in some of the industries. Findings of the present study therefore appear to be supporting my first hypothesis that liberalisation measures of the 1990s enhanced the export-role of MNE affiliates in the late-1990s. However, this inference may be drawn with two caveats (1) the relationship between FS and export intensity is not strong enough to suggest that India is attracting efficiency seeking FDI on a significant scale; (2) contrary to our expectations, firms with higher foreign equity stake are not more export oriented than those with smaller stake.

Industry-group-wise results do not lend support to the second hypothesis of the paper. Both FE and FS emerged insignificant for the high-tech industry group. The results could partly be explained by the Patent Regime followed in India since 1970. This regime abolished product patents and relaxed the terms of process patents. The absence of patent protection may have restricted the inflows of more advanced technologies in high-tech sectors, particularly drugs and pharmaceuticals. It could also be that much of FDI in this group is concentrated in EPZs. If that is so, it may not necessarily be conducive to building dynamic export capabilities in high-tech sectors. In general it is argued that FDI in EPZs is resource seeking and that its benefits in terms of technology diffusion and upgradation of competitiveness are at best limited (Balasubramanyam 1988).

Table 10.1

Determinants of Inter-firm Variations in Export Intensity: Tobit Model Analysis

	Fixed Effect				Random Effect			
Variable	*Coefficient*	*z-Statistic*	*Coefficient*	*z-Statistic*	*Coefficient*	*z-Statistic*	*Coefficient*	*z-Statistic*
FS	0.0149 [c]	1.6480	—	—	.0141[c]	1.655	—	—
FE	—	—	0.0002	1.3276	—	—	.0003	1.294
SIZE	0.0119 [a]	5.3360	0.0120 [a]	5.3608	.0128 [a]	5.680	.0128 [a]	5.703
MT	−0.1083	−0.9347	−0.1072	−0.9269	—	—	—	—
IMRS	0.2107 [a]	5.0802	0.2106 [a]	5.0671	.2059 [a]	4.985	.2059 [a]	4.979
SKIL	−0.0005	−0.5947	−0.0004	−0.5676	—	—	—	—
RDS	0.9832 [c]	1.6534	0.9581 [c]	1.6122	.7958	1.530	.7742	1.595
IMPK	0.1342 [b]	2.3660	0.1304 [b]	2.2957	.1374 [b]	2.425	.1338 [b]	2.361
CONSTANT	—	—	—	—	-.0347	.0123	−.0344	-2.796
SCALE	0.1135	36.561	0.1135	36.558	—	—	—	—
L-likelihood	385.337	—	384.926	—	367.56	—	366.629	—
NOB	916	—	916	—	916	—	916	—

a – significant at 1 per cent, b – significant at 5 per cent and c – significant at 10 per cent.

Table 10.2

Industry Group-wise Determinants of Export Intensity

	High-Tech Industries							
	Fixed Effect				Random Effect			
Variable	Coefficient	z-Statistic	Coefficient	z-Statistic	Coefficient	z-Statistic	Coefficient	z-Statistic
FS	–0.006	–0.2709			.00298	.122		
FE			–0.0066	–0.2709			–8.2e06	–.015
IMPK	–0.4880	–1.3926	–0.4880	–1.3926				
MT	–0.1718	–0.3941	–0.1718	–0.3941	–.2559	–.603	–.2491	–.591
IMRS	0.4261 [a]	4.9618	0.4261 [a]	4.9618	.3999 [a]	4.560	.3996 [a]	4.558
RDS	0.8773	1.0107	0.8774	1.0107	.9876	1.122	.9761	1.110
SKIL	0.0080 [a]	2.6405	0.0080 [a]	2.6405	.0078 [a]	2.537	.0077 [a]	2.506
SIZE	0.0065	0.8808	0.0065	0.8808				
CONSTANT					–.0458	–1.441	–.0448	–1.403
SCALE:C(12)	0.1036	13.554	0.1036	13.554				
L-L	67.511		67.902		62.266		62.259	
NOB	111		111		111		111	

Contd...

...*Contd*...

	Medium High-Tech Industries							
	Fixed Effect				*Random Effect*			
	Coefficient	*z-Statistic*	*Coefficient*	*z-Statistic*	*Coefficient*	*z-Statistic*	*Coefficient*	*z-Statistic*
FS	0.0191 [c]	1.7261	—	—	.01734 [c]	1.686	—	—
FE	—	—	0.0002	0.9404	—	—	.00018	.781
IMPK	0.1221	1.6855 [c]	0.1184	1.5261	.1169	1.537	.1143	1.627
MT	–0.1007	–0.5132	–0.1004	–0.5106	–.1259	–.633	–.1249	–.626
IMRS	0.1310 [b]	2.3883	0.1367 [b]	2.4829	.1193 [b]	2.144	.1253 [b]	2.234
RDS	0.9550	1.6882 [c]	0.8383	1.6053	.8538	1.217	.7881	1.138
SKIL	0.0010	0.6674	0.0010	0.6605	.0005	.312	.0004	.293
SIZE	0.0107 [a]	3.5214	0.0109 [a]	3.5708	.0091 [a]	2.996	.0093 [a]	3.067
CONSTANT	—	—	—	—	–.0157	–.923	–.0142	–.832
SCALE	0.1013	25.604	0.1015	25.599	—	—	—	—
L-L	229.3824	—	228.34	—	226.159	—	225.209	—
NOB	442	—	442	—	442	—	442	—

Contd...

...Contd...

	Medium Low-Tech Industries							
	Fixed Effect				*Random Effect*			
	Coefficient	*z-Statistic*	*Coefficient*	*z-Statistic*	*Coefficient*	*z-Statistic*	*Coefficient*	*z-Statistic*
FS	–0.0059	–0.2682	—	—	–.0012	–.057	—	—
FE	—	—	–6.72E-05	–0.1572	—	—	.00006	.145
IMPK	0.1197	1.0004	0.1203	1.0054	.1371	1.146	.1380	1.154
MT	–0.3847	–1.1870	–0.3863	–1.1895	–.3127	–.991	–.3146	–.993
IMRS	0.2211 [a]	2.6534	0.2208 [a]	2.6384	.2521 [a]	3.087	.2508 [a]	3.062
SKIL	9.51E-05	0.0730	0.0001	0.0797	.00097	.765	.0010	.787
SIZE	0.0145 [a]	3.6483	0.0145 [a]	3.6448	.02103 [a]	4.830	.0210 [a]	4.832
CONSTANT	—	—	—	—	–.07934	–3.611	–.0803	–3.621
SCALE	0.1067	17.373	0.1067	17.372	—	—	—	—
LL	91.525	—	91.502	—	96.310	—	96.139	—
NOB	216	—	216	—	216	—	216	—

Contd...

...Contd...

	Low-Tech Industries							
	Fixed Effect				*Random Effect*			
	Coefficient	*z-Statistic*	*Coefficient*	*z-Statistic*	*Coefficient*	*z-Statistic*	*Coefficient*	*z-Statistic*
FS	0.0585	1.5215	—	—	.05199	1.319	—	—
FE	—	—	0.0014 [c]	1.8680	—	—	.0013 [c]	1.772
IMPK	0.4472 [a]	4.4332	0.4440 [a]	4.4231	.4494 [a]	4.433	.3867 [a]	2.805
MT	–0.1456	–0.5634	–0.1417	–0.5505	–.1496	–.571	–.2051	–.689
IMRS	0.1031	0.5433	0.0997	0.5277	.0828	.430	.1050	.542
RDS	–6.1319	–0.3173	–5.8810	–0.3055	–5.416	–.260	–4.865	–.412
SKIL	—	—	—	—	—	—	—	—
SIZE	0.0139 [c]	1.9108	0.0135 [c]	1.8682	.01428 [c]	1.927	.0131 [c]	1.759
CONSTANT	—	—	—	—	–.0101	.0369	–.0087	–.233
SCALE	0.1779	14.482	0.1739	14.506	—	—	—	—
L-L	7.921	—	8.5033	—	2.4136	—	2.521	—
NOB	153	—	153	—	153	—	153	—

a – significant at 1 per cent, b – significant at 5 per cent and c – significant at 10 per cent.

FS did emerge significant in medium high-tech industries. However the statistical significance at 10 per cent is rather weak. In low-tech industries, FE (and not FS) turned up significant indicating that firms with higher foreign equity are likely to export more. The results are in conformity with those reported in UNCTAD [1999]. It is argued there that many MNEs are setting up wholly owned production facilities in low-tech industries (textiles, food processing) in low-wage countries. They set up more sophisticated facilities to produce higher quality products which they export to other countries using their marketing networks [UNCTAD 1999]. Our results are in line with this explanation suggesting that India's competitive advantage still lies in low wages.

MT is not significant in any equation. Theoretically, it is argued that market transactions that transfer only standard and codified technologies may not confer competitive advantages on firms, particularly in high-tech industries. However, countries such as Japan and Korea acquired competitiveness on the basis of imported technologies even in high-tech industries in the early phase of their development. In the Indian context also, previous studies showed that licensing did confer competitive advantages on firms in engineering industries [Lall 1986, Kumar and Siddharthan 1994, Jain 1998]. However, with growing technology-based competition and relaxation of conditions for MNE entry the world over, this strategy appears to be getting less attractive in acquiring competitive advantages abroad. There may be cases of success but it appears that these cases may not be generalised.

IMPK emerged significant for all firms combined. However, a disaggregated analysis suggests that imports of capital goods provide distinct advantages in low-tech industries only where IMPK is significant at 1 per cent level. This could be because technologies in these industries are widely diffused and are mainly embodied in capital goods [Lall 1998].

IMRS came up significant at 1 per cent with a positive sign for all firms pooled together and in each sub-sample except the low-tech industry group. Lowering of tariff and non-tariff barriers on raw materials and components facilitated imports of raw materials and components from the cheapest possible sources available, which gave a distinct cost competitiveness to firms in Indian manufacturing.

RDS is positive though not quite significant at 10 per cent level in the sample of all firms. It is generally feared that relaxation in the restrictions on technology transfers would enhance firms' dependence on foreign technologies reducing the role of domestic R&D (Subrahmanian, 1991). However, the findings here support the evolutionary school of thought, which maintains that building up technological capabilities through own R&D efforts are crucial in creating competitiveness. A disaggregated analysis shows that R&D variable was significant only in medium-high-tech industries. In others, it turned insignificant. It could be that in high-tech industries R&D efforts may not match the world standard and, in medium- and low-tech industries its levels are negligibly small.

SKILL variable emerged insignificant in the sample for all firms (Table 10.2). In high-tech industry group however, this variable turned out to be significant at 1 per cent with a positive sign. Our results indicate that skill creation is crucial for creating competitiveness in high-tech sectors. Porter (1999) finds a one-to-one relationship between R&D workforce and innovative capacity. Most existing studies on India do not find skill to exert significant influence on firms' competitiveness. However, these studies used either the share of highly paid employees in total wage bill (Kumar 1990, Kumar and Siddharthan 1994) or average wage rates (Lall and Mohammad 1983) as a measure of skill intensity. While these variables need not reflect skill intensity, the efficiency variable used in this paper reflects not only the skills of labour force but also the way the productive system uses it.

Firm size turned significant with a positive sign in all the equations. Most previous studies found smaller firms to be more export oriented in the restrictive regime (Lall and Kumar 1981, Patibandla 1995). Kumar and Siddharthan (1994) found very large firms to be domestic market oriented. The present study however, shows that intensified competition and exchange rate correction favoured large firms in the world markets in the 1990s.

5. Conclusion

This paper analysed the inter-firm determinants of export performance in Indian manufacturing in the late-1990s. The objective was to test two hypotheses: first, that in a liberalised regime, MNE affiliates perform distinctly better than local firms in export markets and second, that MNE affiliates have greater comparative advantages in high-tech than in low- and medium-tech industries. For the empirical analysis, export models with technology, cost and scale variables were estimated for a sample of firms drawn from Indian manufacturing. Tobit model estimations conducted on all the sample firms pooled together supported the first hypothesis. However, the evidence of the better performance of MNEs is not strong enough to suggest that India is attracting efficiency-seeking outward-oriented FDI. Even firms with higher foreign equity stakes have not performed distinctly better than others.

The results also show that high-tech industries are not attracting efficiency seeking FDI as had been expected. In medium-high-tech sectors their performance is somewhat better. However, even in this group the results are not robust. In low-tech industries, however, firms with high foreign stake are found to be performing better. Two important implications of the results are: one, it appears that the economy is not fully integrated with the global economy and that the existing industrial and technological capabilities need reorientation to attract efficiency seeking FDI; two, India's competitive advantages still lie in low-tech sectors. There have not been dynamic changes in the export structure even after liberalisation (see Lall 1999 also). The results also suggest that in technology-based sectors own technological capabilities of firms are crucial determinants of export performance of firms. Finally, it was found that the export performance of firms was linked strongly with firm size and imports of raw materials and component in almost all technology groups.

A few policy remarks follow from the findings of this paper. The liberalisation of markets and technological changes taking place has changed the kind and determinants of trans-border activities engaged in by MNEs. MNEs are increasingly looking for a physical and human infrastructure, which enables them to create and exploit their ownership specific core competencies. However, for such efficiency seeking FDI they prefer locations, which have well developed R&D base, a good physical infrastructure, skilled labour and well developed economic clusters. In the absence of such assets, developing countries may fail to attract such FDI. It is therefore, crucial for the countries to upgrade the competitiveness of their own resources and capabilities. Government may also need to revise their policies with respect to FDI regulations and intellectual property rights. The results also suggest that the lowering of tariff walls on the imports of capital goods and inputs have had desirable impact on firms' competitiveness. This policy may further be rationalised. Finally, it may be suggested that deliberate government policies should promote a strong nucleus of flagship indigenous firms in internationally oriented sectors policies to compete in the world markets.

References

Aggarwal, Aradhna (1997). "Liberalisation, Internationalisation advantages and Foreign Direct Investment : The Indian Experience in the 1980s", *Transnational Corporations*, Vol. 6, No. 3, pp. 33-57.

———. (2000). "De-regulation, Technology Imports and Local R&D Efforts: An Analysis of the Indian Experience", *Research Policy*, Vol. 29, No. 9, pp. 1081-1093, Elsevier Science, North Holland.

Alam, G. (1985). "India's Technology Policy and its Influence on Technology Imports and Technology Development", *Economic and Political Weekly*, Vol. 20, Nos. 45,46,47 (Special No.), pp. 2073-2080.

Amemiya, T. (1973). "Regression Analysis When the Dependent Variable is Truncated Normal", *Econometrica*, Vol. 41, No. 6, pp. 997-1016.

Athukorala, P. *et al.* (1995). "Multinational Firm and Export Performance of firms in Developing Countries: Some Analytical Issues and New Empirical Evidence", *Journal of Development Economics*, Vol. 46, No. 1, pp. 109-122.

Balasubramanyam, V.N. (1988). "Export Processing Zones" in Greenway, D. (ed.) *Economic Development and International Trade*, London, Macmillan.

Balasubramanyam, V.N. and M. Salisu (1991). "Export Promotion, Import Substitution and Direct Foreign Investment in Less Developed Countries" in A. Koekkoek and L. Mennes (eds) *International Trade and Global Development*, London: Routledge.

Behrman, J. and H. Willander (1976). '*Transfer of Manufacturing Technology Within Multinational Enterprises*', Cambridge Mass Ballinger.

Bhagwati, J.N. (1973). "The Theory of Immeserising Growth: Further Applications", in Micheal B. Connolly and A.K. Swoboda (eds) International Trade and Money, Toronto, University of Toronto Press.

Blomstrom, M., A. Kokko and M. Zezan (1994). "Host Country Competition, Labour Skill and Technology Transfer by Multinationals", in *Weltwirtschaftliches Archiv*, Vol. 130, No.3, pp. 521-533.

Bonaccorsi, A. (1992). "On the Relationship Between Firm Size and Export Intensity", *Journal of International Business Studies*, Vol. 23, No. 4, pp. 605-35

Caves R.E. (1996). *Multinational Enterprise and Economic Analysis 2nd ed.* Cambridge: Cambridge University Press.

Chen C., L.Chiang and Y. Zhang (1995). "The Role of Foreign Direct Investment in China's Post 1978 Economic Development", *World Development*, Vol. 23, pp. 691-703.

Das (2002). "Some Aspects of Productivity, Growth and Trade in Indian Industries", Ph.D. dissertation, University of Delhi, Delhi.

Davidson W.H. and D.G. Mcfetridge (1984). "International Technology Transactions and the Theory of Firms", *Journal of Industrial Economics*, Vol. 32, No. 3, pp. 253-64

Doraiswamy, L.K. (1992). "Technology Development and Transfer in India: The Agony and the Ecstasy", *Indian Chemical Industry-Emerging Scenario*, Indian Chemical Manufacture Association (ICMA).

Dosi, G. (1988). "Sources, Procedures and Micro Economic Effects of Innovation", *Journal of Economic Literature*, Vol. 26, No.3, pp. 1120-71.

Dosi G., K. Pavitt and L. Soete (1990). *The Economics of Technical Change and International Trade*. London: Harvester Wheatsheaf

Dunning, J.H. (1993). *Multinational Enterprises and the Global Economy, Reading*: Addison-Wesley

———. (1994). "Re-evaluating the Benefits of Foreign Direct Investment", *Transnational Corporations*, Vol. 3, No. 1, February pp. 23-52.

———. (1998). "Changing Geography of Foreign Direct Investment: Explanations and Implications" in Nagesh Kumar *et al. Globalisation, Foreign Direct Investment and Technology Transfers: Impacts on and Prospects for Developing Countries*, London and New York: Routledge.

Dunning, J.H. and R. Narula (1997). "Developing Countries *Versus* Multinationals in a Globalising World: The Dangers of Falling Behind", in P. Buckley and Pervez Gauri (eds.), *Multinational Enterprises and Emerging Markets: Managing Increasing Interdependence*, London: Dryden Press (Harcourt Publishers).

Fritsch, W. and F.Gustavo (1991). *Foreign Direct Investment in Brazil: Its Impact on Industrial Restructuring*, OECD.

Hatzichronoglou, T. (1997). "Revision of the High-Technology Sector and Product Classification", STI Working Paper OECD/GD(97)216, OECD Paris.

Jain, Aradhna (1998). "MNEs, Technology and Industrial Structure: Indian Experience in the 1990", Ph.D. dissertation, Delhi School of Economics, Delhi University [unpublished].

Krugman, P. (1985). "A Technology Gap Model of International Trade" in K. Jungfelt and D. Hague (eds) *Structural Adjustment in Development of Open Economies*, Proceedings of the Conference of the International Economics Associations held at Yxtaholm, Sweden, London, The Macmillan Press Ltd.

Kokko, A. (1992). *Foreign Direct Investment and Host Country Characteristics and Spillovers*, Stockholm, Economic Research Institute, Stockholm, School of Economics.

Konrad, N. and D. Wahl (1985). "Scientific and Technology Potential in Developing Countries as National and International Factors", *Economic Quarterly*, Vol. 20, No. 3, pp. 3-18.

Kumar, N. (1990). *Multinational Enterprises in India: Industrial Distribution, Characteristics and Performance*. London and New York Routledge.

———. (1998a). "Technology Generation and Technology Transfer in the World Economy: Recent Trends and Implications for Developing Countries", in Nagesh Kumar *et al. Globalisation, Foreign Direct Investment and Technology Transfers: Impacts on and Prospects for Developing Countries*, London and New York: Routledge.

———. (1998b). "Multinational Enterprises, Regional Economic integration and Export Platform Production in the Host Countries: An Empirical Analysis for the US and Japanese Corporations", *Welwirtschaftliches Archiv*, Vol. 134, No. 3, pp. 450-3.

———. and N.S. Siddharthan (1994). "Technology, Firm Size and Export Behaviour in Developing Countries: The Case of Indian Enterprises", *Journal of Development Studies*, Vol. 31, No. 2, pp. 289-309.

———. and N.S. Siddharthan (1997). *Technology, Market Structure and Internationalisation: Issues and Policies for Developing Countries*. UNU INTECH Studies in New Technology and Development, published in association with Routledge, London and New York.

Lall S. (1985). *Multinationals, Technology and Exports*, London: Macmillan.

———. (1986). "Technological Development and Export Performance in LDCs: Leading Engineering and Chemical Firms in India", *Weltwirtschaftliches Archiv*, Vol. 122, No. 1, pp. 80-91.

———. (1987). *Learning to Industrialise: The Acquisition of Technological Capability by India* London: Macmillan Press.

———. (1992). "Technological Capabilities and Industrialisation", *World Development*, Vol. 20, No.2, pp pp. 165-186.

———. (1998). "Exports of Manufactures by Developing Countries: Emerging Patterns of Trade and Location", *Oxford Review of Economic Policy*, Vol. 14, No. 2, pp. 54-73.

———. (1999). "India's Manufactured Exports: Comparative Structure and Prospects", *World Development*, Vol 27, No. 10, pp. 1769-1786.

———. and R.Kumar (1981). "Firm-Level Export Performance in an Inward Looking Economy: The Indian Engineering Industry", *World Development*, Vol. 9, No. 5, pp. 453-463.

———. and S. Mohammad (1983). "Multinational in Indian Big Business: Industrial Characteristics of Foreign Investment in a Heavily Regulated Economy", *Journal of Development Economics*, Vol. 13, No.1, pp. 143-57.

———. and P. Streeten (1977). *Private Investments, Transnationals and Developing Countries*, London: Macmillan.

Lazonic, W. (1993). "Learning and the Dynamics of International Competitive Advantage", in R.Thomson (eds) *Learning and Technological Change*, St. Martin's Press, pp. 172-200.

Magee S.P. (1977). "Information and Multinational Corporations: An Appropriability Theory of Direct Foreign Investment", in Bhagwati (eds) *The New International Economic Order,* Cambridge, MA MIT Press, pp. 317-340.

Mehta, R. (1999). "Tariff and Non-tariff Barriers of Indian Economy: A Profile", monograph, Research and Information Systems for Developing Countries, New Delhi.

Mowery, D.C. and J.E. Oxley (1997). "Inward Technology Transfer and Competitiveness: The Role of National Innovation System", in D. Archibuigi and Michie Jonathan (eds) *Technology, Globalisation and Economic Performance,* Cambridge University Press.

Nunez, W.P. (1990). *Foreign Direct Investment and Industrial Development in Mexico,* OECD.

Pant, M. (1993). "Export Performance, Transnational Corporations and the Manufacturing Sector: A Case Study of India", *The Indian Economic Review,* Vol 28, No. 1, pp. 41-54.

Papanastassiou, M. and R. Pearce (1999). *Multinationals, Technology and National Competitiveness,* Edward Elgar.

Patibandla, M. (1995). "Firm Size and Export Behaviour: An Indian Case Study", *Journal of Development Studies,* Vol 31, No. 6, pp. 868-882.

Pavitt, K. (1984). "Sectoral Patterns of Technical Change: Towards a Taxonomy and A Theory", *Research Policy,* Vol 13,No. 6, pp. 343-373.

Porter, M.E. (1999). "Innovative Capacity and Prosperity: The Next Competitiveness Challenge", *The Global Competitiveness Report.*

Saleem, H.N. (1996) "India: Tariff Policy Reform and Impact on Protection 1987-88 to 1994-95", monograph, National Institute of Public Finance and Policy, New Delhi.

Subrahmanian, K.K. (1991). "Technological Capability under Economic Liberalism: Experience of Indian Industry in Eighties", *Economic and Political Weekly,* August 31[35], M87-89.

Subrahmanian, K.K. and P. Pillai (1979). *Multinationals and Indian Exports,* New Delhi: Allied.

Teece, D.J. (1977). 'Technology Transfer by Multinational firms - The Resource Cost of Transferring Technological Know-how' *Economic Journal* 87, [346], June pp. 242-61.

UNCTAD 1995 *World Investment Report 1995,* UNCTAD.

UNCTAD 1999 *World Investment Report 1999,* UNCTAD.

Urata, S. (1999). "Intra firm Technology Transfer by Japanese Multinationals in Asia", in D.J. Encarnation (eds) *Japanese Multinationals in Asia: Regional Operations in Comparative Perspective,* Oxford University Press.

Vernon, R. (1966). "International Investment and International Trade in the Product Cycle", *Quarterly Journal of Economics,* Vol 80, No. 2, pp. 190-207.

Wakelin, K. (1997). *Trade and Innovation: Theory and Evidence,* Edgar Publishing Inc. 1997, Cheltenam, U.K., Northanmpton, USA.

Wang, Y.J. and M. Blomstrom (1992). "Foreign Investment and Technology Transfer—A Simple Model" *European Economic Review,* Vol 36, No. 1, pp. 137-155.

World Bank (1984) "India: Non-electrical Industrial Machinery Manufacturing - A Subsector Study", *Report No. 5095-IN,* 2 August.

Appendix 1

Industry-group	*Industry*		*R&D Intensity*	*Export Intensity*		
				All Firms	*MNE*	*DOM*
All Firms		Mean	0.000897	0.070225	0.071	0.063
		Std. Dev.	0.006450	0.111684	0.102	0.099
		Observations	916	916	234	682
Hi-tech	Pharmaceuticals,	Mean	0.002436	0.072413	0.064	0.076
	Telecommunication, Computer	Std. Dev.	0.011688	0.109059	0.081	0.118
	Photocopying machines	Observations	111	111	31	80
Med-high	Sc. Instruments,	Mean	0.001245	0.057791	0.069	0.052
	Other engineering & Chemical	Std. Dev.	0.007179	0.087558	0.099	0.0810
	Industries	Observations	442	442	141	301
Med-low	Rubber & Plastic products	Mean	Neg.	0.059793	0.051	0.058
	Metal & Metal products	Std. Dev.	–	0.094289	0.065	0.091
	Non metallic minerals	Observations	215	215	30	185
Low-tech	Paper, Textiles, Food	Mean	Neg.	0.109313	0.110	0.089
	Beverages, Tobacco, wood	Std. Dev.	–	0.158578	0.147	0.132
		Observations	153	153	32	116

Variables

Dependent Variable

Export intensity [EXP] : Total export as a proportion of firms' sales.

Independent Variables

Foreign Affiliation: Two alternative variables are used to proxy foreign affiliation in the present analysis. These are,

FS : =1 if foreign equity >25 per cent and

=0 otherwise;

FE: The share of foreign firms in total equity holding.

Intensity of Market Transactions of Technology [MT]: technical fee and royalties paid abroad as a proportion of firms' sales.

Intensity of Imports of Capital Goods [IMPK] : imports of capital goods as a proportion of firms' sales.

R&D Intensity [RDS]: Expenditures incurred on in-house R&D labs and equipments as a proportion of firms' sales.

Skill Intensity [SKILL] : Value added per unit of wage bill.

Intensity of Imports of Raw Materials and Components [IMRS] : Imports of components and raw materials as a ratio of firms' sales.

SIZE: Log of total sales of firm i.

11

Import Liberalisation and Productivity Growth in Indian Manufacturing Industries in the 1990s

BISHWANATH GOLDAR
ANITA KUMARI

1. Introduction

Since 1991, India has undertaken a major economic reforms programme. Under the programme, significant and far-reaching changes have been made in industrial and trade policy. Import liberalisation has been a principal component of the economic reforms undertaken. Tariff rates have been brought down considerably and quantitative restrictions on imports have been by and large removed. These reforms in import policy, along with complementary changes in industrial policy, technology import policy and foreign direct investment policy, were aimed at making the Indian industry more efficient, technologically up-to-date and competitive, with the expectation that efficiency improvement, technological up-gradation, and enhancement of competitiveness would enable Indian industry achieve rapid growth. Given that the main object of import liberalisation was to improve industrial productivity, it is appropriate to ask how far has import liberalisation contributed to the better productivity performance of Indian industry in the post-reform period. The present paper addresses this issue.

The estimates of total factor productivity (TFP) growth are presented for Indian manufacturing and major industry groups for the period 1981-82 to 1997-98. The objective is to compare the growth rate in TFP in Indian manufacturing industries in the 1990s, i.e. the post-reform period, with that in the 1980s. This is followed by an econometric analysis of inter-temporal and inter-industry variations in productivity growth rates, aimed at assessing the effect of import liberalisation on productivity growth in Indian manufacturing industries in the 1990s. Another aspect that receives specific attention in the econometric analysis is the effect of capacity utilisation on measured productivity growth.

2. Effect of Import Liberalisation on Industrial Productivity

There are reasons to expect a favourable effect of import liberalisation on industrial productivity. This is expected to occur through several channels: (a) import liberalisation will provide to industrial firms greater and cheaper access to imported capital goods and intermediate goods (embodying advanced technology), which will enable the firms improve their productivity performance; (b) greater availability of imported intermediate goods will enable the firms to exploit better the productivity enhancing potential of imported technology; (c) the increased competitive pressure on industrial units in a liberalised import regime will force them to be more efficient in the use of resources (which can be achieved through better organisation of production, improved managerial efficiency, more effective utilisation of labour, better capacity utilisation, *etc.*); (d) the increased competitive pressure coupled with expanded opportunities for importing technology and capital goods will bring greater technological dynamism in industrial firms; (e) as the competitive business environment forces inefficient firms to close down, the average level of efficiency of various industries should improve; (f) greater access to imported inputs and a more realistic exchange rate associated with a liberalised trade regime would enable industrial firms compete more effectively in export markets. This would allow them to increase their sales and reap economies of scale with concomitant gains in productivity.

Evidently, there are persuasive theoretical arguments for contemplating a positive effect of import liberalisation on industrial productivity. However, this view or hypothesis does not have a strong empirical support. There have been a number of empirical studies for developing countries, including the countries of Asia, in which econometric models have been estimated to assess the effect of import liberalisation on industrial productivity.[1] Some of them have found a significant favourable effect of import liberalisation on industrial productivity. But, some have found no significant effect, while some

1. For a review of this literature, see Das (2002).

others have found an adverse effect of import liberalisation on industrial productivity. Thus, on the whole, the empirical evidence on the relationship between import liberalisation and industrial productivity in developing countries is mixed and no definite conclusion can be drawn.

As regards Indian industry, there are two recent studies, which have examined the effect of economic reforms on industrial productivity. These are by Krishna and Mitra (1998) and Balakrishnan, Pushpangadan and Suresh Babu (2000). Both studies have used firm-level data taken from Centre for Monitoring Indian Economy (CMIE) database. Also, there is similarity in the method of econometric analysis applied in the two studies. But, the studies come up with conflicting results. Krishna and Mitra find evidence of a significant favourable effect of reforms on industrial productivity. Balakrishanan *et al.*, on the other hand, find an adverse effect of economic reforms on industrial productivity. One serious limitation of both studies is that they have not used explicit trade liberalisation variables in the econometric model estimated. Rather, a dummy variable approach has been taken to distinguish between the pre- and post-reform periods.

This study differs from the above two studies in several respects. The analysis of productivity is undertaken at the industry level rather than at the firm level. The source of data is also different. More important, an attempt is made here to incorporate explicitly variables representing trade liberalisation in the econometric model estimated.

3. Productivity Growth in Indian Manufacturing

This section presents estimates of total factor productivity growth in Indian manufacturing and 17 two-digit industry groups in the period 1981-82 to 1997-98. Two other studies in which estimates of productivity growth in Indian manufacturing have been presented for the 1990s are Trivedi, Prakash and Sinate (2000) and Srivastava (2000). Srivastava has carried out a careful and detailed econometric analysis of productivity growth and technical efficiency in manufacturing firms in India for the period 1980-81 to 1996-97, using data for about 3,000 companies. Trivedi *et al.* have presented estimates of productivity growth for aggregate manufacturing and five major industry groups for the period 1973-74 to 1997-98. They have used industry-level data taken from the *Annual Survey of Industries* published by the Central Statistical Organisation (CSO), Government of India.

The basic data source used for the present estimates of industrial productivity is the same as used by Trivedi *et al.*, (2000). Also, the methodology of productivity measurement adopted here is similar to the one used by them. However, greater care has been taken in the measurement of output and inputs, so as to obtain better estimates of productivity growth.

3.1 TFP Estimation Method

A three-input framework has been used for the TFP estimates presented in the paper, as done in several earlier studies including Trivedi *et al.*, (2000). The translog index of TFP has been used for the measurement of TFP.

Under the three-input framework, the translog index of TFP growth is given by the following equation:

$$\Delta \ln TFP(t) = \Delta \ln Q(t) - \left[\frac{SL(t)+SL(t-1)}{2} \times \Delta \ln L(t)\right] - \left[\frac{SK(t)+SK(t-1)}{2} \times \Delta \ln K(t)\right]$$

$$- \left[\frac{SM(t)+SM(t-1)}{2} \times \Delta \ln M(t)\right] \qquad ...(1)$$

In this equation, Q denotes gross output, L labour, K capital and M materials (including energy) input. $\Delta \ln Q(t) = \ln Q(t) - \ln Q(t-1)$. In the same way, $\Delta \ln L(t)$, $\Delta \ln K(t)$ and $\Delta \ln M(t)$ are defined. SL, SK and SM are respectively the income shares of labour, capital, and materials input. These add up to unity. $\Delta \ln TFP$ is the rate of technological change or the rate of growth of TFP.

Using the above equation, the growth rates of TFP have been computed for each year. These have then been used to obtain an index of TFP. Having obtained the TFP index for different years, estimates of TFP growth rate have been made for two sub-periods, 1981-82 to 1990-91 and 1990-91 to 1997-98, and for the entire period 1981-82 to 1997-98. The estimation of TFP growth rate for the entire period has been done by fitting an exponential (or semi-log) trend equation to the TFP index. To obtain the growth rates for the sub-periods, the kinked exponential model has been used.

3.2 Data Sources

The basic source of data used for the productivity estimates is the *Annual Survey of Industries*, which has been the principal data source in most earlier studies on industrial productivity in India. For making price corrections to the reported data on gross output and intermediate input, suitable deflators have been constructed with the help of the official series on wholesale price indices (*Index Number of Wholesale Prices in India*, prepared by the Office of the Economic Advisor, Ministry of Industry). These have been taken from the official publications and the publications of the Centre for Monitoring Indian Economy (CMIE). For a few specific items, other sources of data have been used to construct price indices for those items. The construction of deflator for intermediate input requires that the price indices for various categories of items be combined using appropriate weights (representing their shares in the intermediate input cost). For this purpose, the weights have been taken from an input-output table for 1989-90, prepared by the Central Statistical Organisation (CSO). For constructing the capital input series for manufacturing industries, estimates of net fixed capital stock (for the benchmark year) and gross fixed capital formation (for different years) made by the CSO have been used. These have been taken from the *National Accounts Statistics* (NAS).

3.3 *Measurement of Output and Inputs*

Details of the methods employed for the measurement of output and inputs are given in the Appendix of the longer version of the paper published in the *Developing Economies* (December 2003). Suffice it to note here that deflated gross output is taken as the measure of output. Number of persons employed is taken as the measure of labour input. Deflated fixed capital stock is taken as the measure of capital input. To obtain a measure of materials input, the time series on value of materials (including energy) consumed has been deflated by a price index formed by taking into account the cost structure as given in the input-output matrix for 1989-90. The estimates of deflated gross output and deflated material input have been worked out for the individual two-digit industries. These have then been added to obtain the estimate for aggregate manufacturing.

3.4 *TFP Estimates*

Estimates of TFP growth in the aggregate manufacturing sector are shown in Table 11.1. Growth rates are presented for the periods 1981-82 to 1990-91 and 1990-91 to 1997-98, and for the entire period 1981-82 to 1997-98. The Table also shows, for comparison, TFP growth rates for these periods computed from the TFP indices presented in the study of Trivedi *et al.*, (2000). It would be noticed that the two sets of estimates are quite similar.

Table 11.1

TFP Growth in Indian Manufacturing, 1981-82 to 1997-98

Period	TFP Growth Rate (per cent per annum)	
	This Study	Trivedi et al. (2000)
1981-82 to 1990-91	1.89	1.26
1990-91 to 1997-98	0.69	0.63
1981-82 to 1997-98	1.40	1.00

Note: The growth rates for sub-periods are estimated by fitting a kinked exponential model.

The estimated growth rate of TFP for the period 1981-82 to 1990-91 is 1.89 per cent per annum, which indicates a significant growth in TFP in Indian manufacturing in the 1980s. Also, there is a clear indication of a fall in the rate of growth of TFP in the 1990s as compared to the growth rate in the 1980s. The estimated growth rate of TFP in Indian manufacturing for the 1990s is 0.69 per cent per annum as against 1.89 per cent per annum for the 1980s. This finding of a decline in TFP growth in Indian manufacturing in the 1990s is in concurrence with the TFP estimates of Trivedi *et al.*, (2000).

For the entire period 1981-82 to 1997-98, the growth rate of TFP in manufacturing is estimated at 1.4 per cent per annum. This estimate of TFP growth rate is by and large in line with the estimates of Trivedi *et al.*, (2000).

TFP estimates for two-digit industries are shown in Table 11.2. The estimated growth rate of TFP for the period 1981-82 to 1990-91 is positive for twelve out of the seventeen groups. For the period 1990-91 to 1997-98, the growth rate of TFP is positive for eleven groups out of seventeen. In most cases, the growth rate for the latter period is relatively lower (11 out of 17 groups). This is consistent with the finding of a decrease in the growth rate of TFP in the 1990s as compared to the 1980s at the aggregate manufacturing level.

Why did TFP growth in Indian manufacturing decelerate in the 1990s? Was this due to a negative effect of import liberalisation on productivity of domestic industry, as a few studies for other developing countries have found? Or, were there other reasons for a slowdown in productivity growth? One possible explanation, at least a partial one, may lie in gestation lags. There was a spurt in investment activity in the 1990s in response to economic reforms.

This step-up in investment activity in manufacturing might have had an immediate adverse effect on productivity due to gestation lags.[2] A more detailed analysis of these issues is taken up in the next section.

Table 11.2

Estimates of TFP Growth Rates, Two-digit Industries, 1981-82 to 1997-98

NIC Code	*Description*	*Growth Rate of TFP (% per annum)*		
		1981-90	*1990-97*	*1981-97*
20-21	Food products	1.04	0.03	0.62
22	Beverage & tobacco	–0.61	–1.66	–1.04
23	Cotton textiles	2.44	–1.09	0.99
24	Wool, silk and manmade fibre textiles	3.04	1.86	2.55
25	Jute textiles	–0.24	0.81	0.19
26	Textile products	1.45	–1.15	0.38
27	Wood, wood products, furniture	2.81	–9.86	–2.41
28	Paper, paper products, printing and publishing	–0.91	0.92	–0.16
29	Leather, leather products	–0.87	1.54	0.12
30	Chemicals, chemical products	3.14	1.15	2.32
31	Rubber, plastic, petroleum and coal products	3.58	–2.01	1.28
32	Non-metallic mineral products	3.18	–0.41	1.70
33	Basic metals and alloys	0.59	2.57	1.41
34	Metal products	–0.07	1.07	0.40
35+36 +39	Machinery	2.06	1.22	1.72
37	Transport equipment	1.37	2.64	1.89
38	Other manufacturing	6.55	3.32	5.22
	All Manufacturing sector	**1.89**	**0.69**	**1.40**

Note: 1. The TFP estimates are based on the three-input framework.
2. NIC = National Industrial Classification.

2. Uchikawa (2001) has discussed about the investment boom in Indian industries in the first half of the 1990s and drawn attention to the adverse effect it had on productivity. He notes (p. 3253) that as a result of the reforms the Indian manufacturing sector had an investment boom in the first half of the 1990s. The boom was over by the mid-1990s. Although lumpy investment raised output sharply, demand did not expand as much as capacity. This led to underutilisation of capacity and thus had an adverse effect on productivity. See also Uchikawa (2002, p. 48).

4. Econometric Analysis of Productivity Growth Rates

This section presents the results of a multiple regression analysis applied to study the effect of import liberalisation and gestation lags on industrial productivity. The analysis is based on pooled cross-section and time-series data. Growth rates of TFP computed for the 17 two-digit industries for different years during the period 1981-82 to 1997-98 are pooled for the regression analysis. The regression equation is specified as:

$$TFPG_{it} = \alpha + \beta_1 GO_{it} + \beta_2 ERP_{it} + \beta_3 NTB_{it} + \beta_4 (ERP_{it} \times NTB_{it}) + \beta_5 IKR_{it} + \beta_6 REER_t + \beta_7 GAGR_t + \gamma DUMLIB + u. \quad ...(2)$$

In this equation, $TFPG_{it}$ is the growth rate of TFP in industry i in year t, GO_{it} is the growth rate of output (deflated gross value of production) in industry i in year t, ERP_{it} is the effective rate of protection accorded by tariff to industry i in year t, NTB_{it} is the extent of non-tariff barriers on imports in respect of industry i in year t, IKR_{it} is the ratio of recently made investments to existing capital stock in industry i in year t, $REER_t$ is the real effective exchange rate in year t, and $GAGR_t$ is the growth rate of agricultural output in year t. *DUMLIB* is a dummy variable for the post-liberalisation period (taking value one for 1991-92 onwards and zero for earlier years) and u is the error term.

In the cross-sectional regression analysis of productivity growth, output growth is commonly used as an explanatory variable (see, for example, Goldar 1986, and Ahluwalia, 1991).[3] This is the reason for including output growth in the regression equation specified.

Since agriculture is an important source of demand for industrial products (both as intermediate inputs and as final consumer goods), agricultural growth is expected to have a demand-side effect on industrial productivity. Agricultural growth has therefore been included as an explanatory variable in the regression analysis.

The ratio of recent investment to capital stock has been taken as an explanatory variable with a view to capturing the effects of gestation lags in investment projects on productivity. Other explanatory variables used in the model include effective rate of protection (*ERP*), non-tariff barriers on imports (*NTB*) and real

3. This captures the effect of output growth on productivity through technological advance and scale economies.

effective exchange rate (*REER*). These variables are expected to capture the effect of trade policy reforms and changes in exchange rate on industrial productivity performance. It should be pointed out that while lowering of tariff and non-tariff barriers exposes domestic industry to greater import competition, a depreciation of exchange rate would to some extent neutralise the effects of reduced imports barriers. This has indeed been the case with Indian manufacturing in the 1990s. To assess the effect of trade reforms on productivity, it is important therefore that the real effective exchange rate be included in the regression equation as an explanatory variable.

In the regression equation specified, an interaction term involving *ERP* and *NTB* has been included. The purpose is to allow the effect of tariff reduction on productivity growth to be different for different industries or different periods of time depending on the extent of quantitative restrictions on imports. It may be argued that if the extent of quantitative restrictions on imports is low (high), then the effect of tariff reduction on productivity will be larger (smaller).

The regression equation given above has been estimated by the Ordinary Least Squares (OLS) method. However, to take into account industry-specific factors, intercept dummy variables, one for each industry, have been used, which amounts to applying the fixed-effects model.[4]

4.1 Data Sources on Explanatory Variables

Goldar and Saleem (1992) presented estimates of the effective rate of protection (ERP) for various input-output sectors (manufacturing industries) for the years 1980-81, 1983-84 and 1989-90. In a recent study, Nouroz (2001) has presented estimates of ERP for various input-output sectors (manufacturing industries) for the years 1987-88, 1992-93, 1994-95 and 1997-98, using a methodology similar to that used by Goldar and Saleem (1992). To get a complete series on ERP for the period 1980-81 to 1997-98, the ERP estimates made by Goldar and Saleem for 1980-81, 1983-84 and 1989-90 have been combined with the estimates of Nouroz for 1992-93, 1994-95 and 1997-98, and then these have been interpolated. Next, the input-output sectors

---

4. The random-effects model was also tried. But, the results were found poor as compared to the results of the fixed-effects model – the coefficients of several explanatory variables turned out to be statistically insignificant. Therefore, for presentation in the paper and for drawing inferences from the econometric analysis, the results of the fixed-effects model were chosen.

have been mapped into the two-digit industry groups. For each two-digit industry group, an estimate of ERP for different years have been formed by taking a weighted average of the estimates for the constituent input-output sectors (value added weights).[5]

As regards non-tariff barriers on imports (NTB), the estimates presented in a report of the National Council of Applied Economic Research have been used for the analysis (NCAER, 2000). These are estimates of the import coverage ratio, that is the percentage of imports covered by non-tariff barriers. The estimates of the import coverage ratio could be obtained for various input-output sectors for the years 1988-89, 1995-96 and 1997-98. The estimates for the input-output sectors were aggregated to yield estimates for the two-digit industry groups in the same way as done for ERP. The estimates for 1988-89 were used for all the years from 1981-82 to 1990-91, assuming thereby that the extent of non-tariff barriers changed very little in this period. The estimates for 1990-91 (same as 1988-89) and 1995-96 have been interpolated to obtain estimates for the in-between years. Similarly, the estimates for 1995-96 and 1997-98 have been interpolated to obtain the estimate for 1996-97.

The real effective exchange rate (REER) has been taken from a publication of the Reserve Bank of India (*Handbook of Statistics on Indian Economy*). The index is based on 36 country bilateral trade weights, base 1985=100.

Agricultural growth has been measured as the rate of change in gross domestic product of the agriculture and allied sectors at constant prices of 1980-81. The data have been taken from Reserve Bank of India, *Handbook of Statistics on Indian Economy, 1999*.

To capture the effect of gestation lags on productivity, the ratio of investment in fixed assets made in the previous two years to the existing fixed capital stock has been taken as an explanatory variable. Here, the assumption is that investments in plant and machinery need about two years' time to be able to achieve fully their potential output. This does not seem to be an unrealistic assumption to make.

The investment ratio variable described above has, however, a shortcoming. The construction of the variable is such that it should

5. The ERP estimates used in the paper have been measured by taking the tariff-based approach. This methodology assumes that tariffs are the only source of distortion, implying that there are no quantitative restrictions (QRs) or other non-tariff barriers. For details, see Goldar and Saleem (1992) and Nouroz (2001).

be highly correlated with the growth rate of capital input. Since in the computation of TFP growth, a weighted combination of the growth rate of capital input and growth rates of other inputs get subtracted from the growth rate of output, a spurious negative relationship may arise between the investment ratio variable and the rate of TFP growth. In view of this possibility, in some regressions, a different variable has also been tried for capturing the adverse effects of gestation lags on productivity. This is constructed as the ratio of investments made in two previous years to the investments made in the previous five years, and denoted by I2/I5. If there is a spurt in investment, this ratio should go up.

4.2 Regression Results

Table 11.3 presents the results of regression analysis. Regressions (1), (2) and (3) differ in regard to the investment ratio variable. In regression (1), the effect of the gestation lag is captured by the ratio of recent investment in fixed assets to existing capital stock (*IKR*). In regression (2), *IKR* is replaced by *I2/I5* (for reasons given earlier). In regression (3), neither of the two investment-ratio variables is included in the equation. The specifications used in regressions (4), (5) and (6) are similar to those in regressions (1), (2) and (3), except that in these regression equations *NTB* and dummy variable for the post-liberalisation period (*DUMLIB*) have been dropped (since the coefficients of these variables are found to be statistically insignificant).

The regression results presented in Table 11.3 clearly show a significant positive relationship between output growth and TFP growth. The coefficient of the output growth is positive and statistically significant at the one per cent level in all the equations estimated. Such a relationship between output growth and productivity growth has been found in a large number of earlier studies, including studies for Indian industries (Goldar 1986; Ahluwalia 1991).

The coefficient of agricultural growth is positive and significant at the five per cent or one per cent level in all the regression equations estimated. This may be interpreted as showing the effect of agricultural growth on industrial demand and hence on industrial productivity.

Table 11.3

Determinants of Productivity Growth
(Dependent Variable: TFP Growth Rate)

Explanatory Variables	*Regressions* (1)	(2)	(3)	(4)	(5)	(6)
GO	0.360*** (10.91)	0.357*** (10.62)	0.345*** (10.29)	0.354*** (10.93)	0.350*** (10.60)	0.339*** (10.30)
GAGR	0.195*** (2.96)	0.196*** (2.89)	0.160** (2.39)	0.182*** (2.84)	0.181*** (2.75)	0.151** (2.32)
IKR	–25.718** (–3.65)			–25.52*** (–3.68)		
I2/I5		-7.980** (-2.35)			–7.609** (–2.27)	
ERP	–0.109** (–2.56)	–0.083* (–1.92)	–0.095** (–2.19)	–0.109*** (–2.74)	–0.090** (–2.19)	–0.103** (–2.53)
NTB	0.012 (0.30)	0.028 (0.73)	0.030 (0.78)			
ERP×NTB	0.0008* (1.80)	0.0007 (1.42)	0.0008* (1.70)	0.0008** (2.10)	0.0007* (1.89)	0.0009** (2.39)
REER	0.088** (2.05)	0.108** (2.45)	0.090** (2.05)	0.058** (2.03)	0.076*** (2.60)	0.068** (2.33)
DUMLIB	1.699 (0.95)	1.917 (1.05)	1.367 (0.75)			
Adjusted R^2	0.357	0.337	0.325	0.360	0.339	0.328
No. of Observations	272	272	272	272	272	272

Notes: 1. Figures in the parentheses are t-ratios.
2. GO= growth rate of output; GAGR= growth rate of output of agriculture and allied activities; IKR= ratio of recent investment in fixed assets to existing fixed capital stock; I2/I5 = ratio of investments made in two previous years to the investments made in the previous five years; ERP= effective rate of protection; NTB= non-tariff barriers on imports; REER= real effective exchange rate; DUMLIB= dummy variable for the post-liberalisation period.
3. The estimated equations include a constant term and 16 industry dummies.

* Significant at 10 per cent; ** Significant at 5 per cent; *** Significant at 1 per cent.

The coefficients of the variables representing the pace of investment activity, *IKR* or *I2/I5*, are found to be negative and statistically significant at the five per cent or higher level. These variables have been used in the regression to capture the effect of gestation lags on productivity, and a negative relationship is expected.

Turning to the variables representing import liberalisation, the coefficient of *ERP* is found to be consistently negative and it is statistically significant at ten per cent or higher level in the estimated regressions. In some equations, the coefficient is statistically significant at the one per cent level. This may be interpreted as showing the productivity enhancing effect of tariff reform (through increased competitive pressure on domestic industry).

The coefficient of *REER* is found to be positive. It is statistically significant at the five per cent or higher level in the regressions. Since there is a negative relationship between *ERP* and TFP growth, a positive relationship should arise between *REER* and TFP growth. This is so because a depreciation of exchange rate (a decline in *REER*) will counter the effects of tariff reduction.

The coefficient of the *NTB* variable is found to be positive. This is contrary to the expected relationship. However, in none of the regressions shown in the Table, is the coefficient statistically significant. The coefficient of the interaction term involving *ERP* and *NTB* (i.e. the product of these two variables) is found to be positive. It is statistically significant in most equations. This may be interpreted as showing that the effect of tariff reform on productivity is stronger if there is less quantitative restriction on imports.

The coefficient of the dummy variable for the post-liberalisation period (*DUMLIB*) is found to be positive, but statistically insignificant. This variable is expected to capture the net effect of all factors connected with economic reforms other than those directly included in the equation. Any differences between the pre- and post-reform periods unconnected with the reforms also get reflected in the coefficient of *DUMLIB*. Since a statistically insignificant coefficient is found, it may be inferred that this group of factors did not on balance have an adverse effect on productivity growth in Indian manufacturing.

Interestingly, when the investment ratio variable and all the trade liberalisation related variables (*ERP*, *NTB* and *REER*) are dropped from the equation, the coefficient of *DUMLIB* becomes significantly negative. This shows that in order to obtain a proper assessment of the effect of reforms one should include in the econometric model variables reflecting the reforms process, rather than use of a dummy variable for the post reform period and expect that this will capture the effect of reforms as some earlier studies for Indian industries have done.

To sum up, the results of the regression analysis do not indicate any significant adverse effect of import liberalisation on productivity growth in Indian manufacturing industries. Rather, there are indications that a lowering of tariff may have contributed positively to productivity growth. Also, it seems that the explanation for lower industrial productivity growth in the 1990s may partly lie in gestation lags in investment projects.

It should be pointed out here that the average growth rate of agricultural output was lower in the post-reform period (2.3 per cent per annum during 1990-91 to 1997-98) as compared to the pre-reform period (3.4 per cent per annum during 1981-82 to 1990-91). The slower agricultural growth may have led to a slow growth in demand for industrial product, which in turn may have caused under-utilisation with an adverse effect on productivity. Thus, the deceleration in productivity growth in Indian industry in the 1990s may in part be attributed to a slowdown in the growth of agriculture in this period.

5. Capacity Utilisation and Productivity

Regression analysis presented above suggested that gestation lags in investment projects was one of the factors that caused slowdown in TFP growth in Indian manufacturing in the 1990s. This, however, needs to be qualified because if gestation lags had seriously constrained industrial production in the mid-1990s, output growth should have picked up after 1997-98 because of accelerated investment during 1994-95 to 1996-97, which did not happen. Rather, the growth rate of real gross value added in registered manufacturing came down from 9.5 per cent per annum during 1990-91 to 1996-97 to 4.3 per cent per annum during 1997-98 to 2000-01.[6] Thus, gestation lags cannot provide an adequate explanation of the fall in the growth rate of TFP in manufacturing in the 1990s, though on the basis of the results obtained it seems this factor did make a contribution.

Uchikawa (2001, 2002) has pointed out that while the investment boom of the mid-1990s raised production capacities substantially, demand did not rise which led to capacity under-utilisation. He notes that under-utilisation of capacity manifested itself first in consumer

6. Growth rates based on gross domestic product of registered manufacturing at 1993-94 prices given in the National Accounts Statistics.

durable and non-durable goods industries and then in capital goods and intermediate goods industries (Uchikawa, 2002: 40).

In consideration of the above points, there is clearly a need to incorporate capacity utilisation into the regression analysis. It should be taken as an explanatory variable in the regression equations estimated to explain variations in productivity growth. Another variable that should be included in the regression equations is man-days worked per employee since it reflects effective utilisation of the manpower available.

Table 11.4 presents the regression results obtained by including rates of change in capacity utilisation and man-days worked per employee as explanatory variables. Data on employment and man-days worked are available in the *Annual Survey of Industries*, which were used to compute man-days per employee.[7] Capacity utilisation rates were estimated for each two-digit industry for the period 1981-82 to 1997-98 using the minimum capital-output ratio method, applied earlier by Sastry (1984) and Uchikawa (2001, 2002), and several other studies. The estimates of capacity utilisation obtained by this method are rather crude, but these had to be employed for the analysis as no better estimates of capacity utilisation were readily available.

A strong positive relationship is found between the rate of change in capacity utilisation and the rate of growth in productivity. This is obviously expected. On the other hand, the coefficient of the rate of change in man-days per employee is not statistically significant. The explanation for not finding a significant relationship between productivity growth and changes in man-days per employee probably lies in the fact there has not been much change in man-days worked per employee in most industries, especially in the 1990s.[8]

The average rate of change in capacity utilisation (across industries and years) was 2.37 per cent per annum in the pre-reform period and –1.39 per cent per annum in the post-reform period. Since the coefficient of the variable is about 0.25, changes in capacity utilisation would account for about one percentage point difference in the growth rate of TFP between the pre- and post-reform period. Thus, the fact that capacity utilisation in industries was growing in the

7. Data on man-days are not available for 1997-98. The figures for 1996-97 were therefore repeated for 1997-98.

8. Average growth rate in man-days per employee was 1.03 per cent per annum in the 1980s and 0.16 per cent per annum in the 1990s.

1980s and falling in the 1990s can explain most the observed difference in the growth rate of TFP between the two periods.

Table 11.4

Determinants of Productivity Growth, Additional Regression Results (Dependent Variable: TFP Growth Rate)

Explanatory variables	Regressions					
	(1)	(2)	(3)	(4)	(5)	(6)
GO	0.206*** (2.69)	0.161** (2.38)	0.135** (2.18)	0.212*** (2.78)	0.160** (2.36)	0.136** (2.20)
GAGR	0.209*** (3.18)	0.215*** (3.20)	0.203*** (3.08)	0.193*** (3.00)	0.195*** (2.99)	0.186*** (2.89)
IKR	–13.900 (–1.58)			–14.67* (–1.69)		
I2/I5		–3.446 (–0.96)			–3.132 (–0.87)	
ERP	–0.104** (–2.44)	–0.091** (–2.14)	–0.097** (–2.28)	–0.106*** (–2.65)	–0.096** (–2.38)	–0.102** (–2.54)
NTB	0.018 (0.46)	0.026 (0.68)	0.026 (0.70)			
ERP×NTB	0.0008* (1.73)	0.0007 (1.55)	0.0008* (1.68)	0.0007** (2.03)	0.0007* (1.92)	0.0008** (2.11)
REER	0.096** (2.20)	0.107** (2.42)	0.100** (2.30)	0.057** (1.98)	0.064** (2.20)	0.060** (2.09)
DUMLIB	2.212 (1.23)	2.461 (1.36)	2.334 (1.29)			
CCU	0.190** (2.20)	0.244*** (3.27)	0.272*** (3.94)	0.173** (2.04)	0.234*** (3.16)	0.260*** (3.82)
CMD	0.007 (0.08)	0.010 (0.11)	0.005 (0.06)	0.024 (0.26)	0.026 (0.29)	0.021 (0.24)
Adjusted R^2	0.365	0.361	0.361	0.366	0.361	0.361
No. of Observations	272	272	272	272	272	272

Notes: 1. Figures in the parentheses are t-ratios.

2. GO= growth rate of output; GAGR= growth rate of output of agriculture and allied activities; IKR= ratio of recent investment in fixed assets to existing fixed capital stock; I2/I5 = ratio of investments made in two previous years to the investments made in the previous five years; ERP= effective rate of protection; NTB= non-tariff barriers on imports; REER= real effective exchange rate; DUMLIB= dummy variable for the post-liberalisation period; CCU = rate of change in capacity utilisation; CMD = rate of change in man-days per employee.

3. The estimated equations include a constant term and 16 industry dummies.

* Significant at 10 per cent; ** Significant at 5 per cent; *** Significant at 1 per cent.

As regards the other explanatory variables, the results reported in Table 11.4 are by and large similar to those reported in Table 11.3. A significant negative relationship is found between *ERP* and TFP growth and a significant positive relationship between agricultural growth and industrial productivity growth. Two important differences that may be noted in the regression results after inclusion of capacity utilisation among explanatory variables are: (a) the coefficient of the output growth variable decreases in numerical value (but remains statistically significant), and (b) the coefficients of variables representing gestation lags become statistically insignificant (barring one equation). It may be argued that the capacity utilisation variable captures the effect of gestation lags (due to the manner of estimation of production capacity). Hence, after inclusion of capacity utilisation variable in the regression equation, the variables representing gestation lags may become statistically insignificant in explaining TFP growth.

5.1 TFP Estimate for Manufacturing Adjusted for Capacity Utilisation

Since the above analysis clearly shows that capacity utilisation had a major effect on productivity growth in Indian manufacturing, it is important that an estimate of TFP be made corrected for changes in capacity utilisation. This has been done and is discussed further below.

Estimation of capacity utilisation in manufacturing has been done on the basis of electricity consumption, using a methodology applied earlier by Mulega and Weiss (1996).[9] The ratio of electricity consumption to capital stock is first computed for different years in the period under study. A trend line is fitted to the data, which is then shifted up so that it passes through the point having largest positive residual. The actual ratio of electricity to capital is then compared with the ratio indicated by the trend line (adjusted) to compute capacity utilisation. The estimates of capacity utilisation in Indian manufacturing obtained by this method are shown in Figure 11.1. An alternate estimate based on the minimum capital-output ratio is also shown in the figure for comparison. This series on capacity

9. Data on electricity sold to industry by utilities have been used for this purpose. These data have been taken from Energy, Centre for Monitoring Indian Economy, Mumbai, April 2002. Since detailed industry-wise electricity consumption data are not available, this methodology could not be applied to the two-digit industries.

utilisation in manufacturing is obtained as a weighted average of the capacity utilisation estimates for the various two-digit industries.

Figure 11.1

Capacity Utilisation in Indian Manufacturing

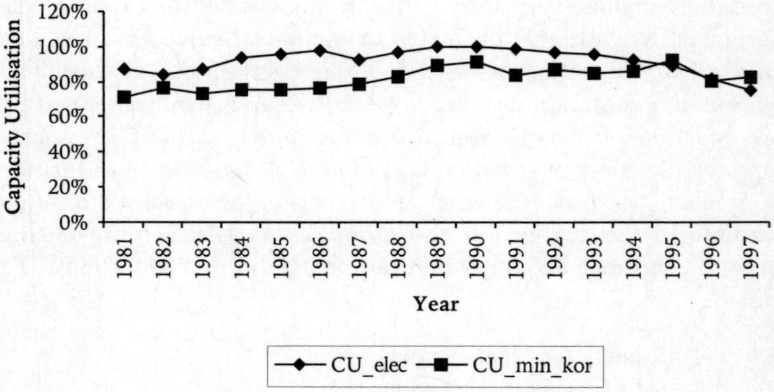

CU_elec = capacity utilisation estimated based on electricity consumption;
CU_min_kor = capacity utilisation estimated by the minimum capital-output ratio method.

The capacity utilisation series based on electricity consumption as well as that based on minimum capital-output ratio indicate an upward trend in capacity utilisation in Indian manufacturing in the 1980s and a downward trend in the 1990s. For the 1990s, the estimates based on electricity consumption show a steeper fall in capacity utilisation than the estimates based on minimum capital-output ratio.

The estimates of TFP growth in the manufacturing sector obtained after correcting for capacity utilisation are shown in Table 11.5. The trend growth in TFP adjusted for capacity utilisation was 1.3 per cent per annum in the period 1990-91 to 1997-98, only marginally lower the growth rate of TFP of 1.6 per cent per annum in the period 1981-82 to 1990-91. The difference between the growth rates of the two periods is not statistically significant.

Based on the results of regression analysis presented in Table 11.4 and the estimates of TFP presented in Table 11.5, it may be concluded that the deceleration in TFP growth in Indian manufacturing in the 1990s observed in several earlier studies was essentially a consequence of capacity under-utilisation in Indian manufacturing in this period. Once that is corrected for the growth rate of TFP in the 1990s was about the same as that in the 1980s.

Table 11.5

TFP Growth in Indian Manufacturing, 1981-82 to 1997-98–Estimates Corrected for Capacity Utilisation

Period	*TFP Growth Rate (Per cent per annum)*	
	Corrected for Capacity Utilisation	*Not Corrected*
1981-82 to 1990-91	1.6	1.9
1990-91 to 1997-98	1.3	0.7
1981-82 to 1997-98	1.5	1.4

Note: The growth rates for sub-periods are estimated by fitting a kinked exponential model.

6. Conclusion

The paper examined trends in total factor productivity in Indian manufacturing in the 1980s and the 1990s. The estimates obtained indicated that during the 1990s, a decade of major industrial and trade reforms, there was a deceleration in TFP growth in manufacturing, corroborating the findings of several earlier studies. However, a closer examination revealed that (a) capacity utilisation was a significant factor influencing productivity growth in industries and (b) there was an increase in capacity utilisation in manufacturing in the 1980s and a fall in the 1990s. After making corrections for changes in capacity utilisation, the TFP growth estimates for the 1990s were found to be about the same as in the previous decade.

Multiple regression analysis was carried out to study the factors influencing TFP growth in manufacturing industries. The results showed a significant favourable effect of tariff reforms on industrial productivity. The analysis revealed that under-utilisation of industrial capacity was an important cause of the observed productivity slowdown in the post-reform period. The regression results also indicated that slower growth of agriculture in the 1990s and gestation lags in investment project may have had an adverse effect on TFP growth in Indian manufacturing in this period.

References

Ahluwalia, I.J. (1991). *Productivity and Growth in Indian Manufacturing*, Delhi: Oxford University Press.

Balakrishnan, P., K. Pushpangadan and M. Suresh Babu (2000). "Trade Liberalisation and Productivity Growth in Manufacturing: Evidence from Firm-level Panel Data," *Economic and Political Weekly*, October 7, 35(41): pp. 3679-82.

Das, D.K. (2002). "Trade Liberalisation and Industrial Productivity: An Assessment of Developing Country Experience", *ICRIER* Working Paper No. 77, New Delhi: Indian Council for Research on International Economic Relations (available on line at: www.icrier.res.in/pdf/deb.pdf).

Goldar, B.N. (1986). "Import Substitution, Industrial Concentration and Productivity Growth in Indian Manufacturing," *Oxford Bulletin of Economics and Statistics*, May, 48(2): pp. 143-64.

Goldar, B.N. and Hasheem N. Saleem (1992). "India's Tariff Structure: Effective Rates of Protection of Indian Industries," *Studies in Industrial Development*, Paper No. 5, Ministry of Industry, Government of India.

Krishna, P. and D. Mitra (1998). "Trade Liberalisation, Market Discipline and Productivity Growth: New Evidence from India," *Journal of Development Economics*, 56(2): pp. 447-62.

Mulega, G. and J. Weiss (1996). "Trade Reform and Manufacturing Performance in Malawi 1970-91", *World Development*, 24 (7): pp. 1267-78.

National Council of Applied Economic Research (NCAER) (2000). *Protection in Indian Industry*, New Delhi: NCAER.

Nouroz, H. (2001). *Protection in Indian Manufacturing: An Empirical Study*, Delhi: MacMillan India.

Sastry, D.U. (1984). *The Cotton Mill Industry in India*, Delhi: Oxford University Press.

Srivastava, V. (2000). "The Impact of India's Economic Reforms on Industrial Productivity, Efficiency and Competitiveness", Report of a project sponsored by the Industrial Development Bank of India, New Delhi: National Council of Applied Economic Research.

Trivedi, P., A. Prakash, and D. Sinate (2000). "Productivity in Major Manufacturing Industries in India: 1973-74 to 1997-98," Development Research Group Study No. 20, Mumbai: Department of Economic Analysis and Policy, Reserve Bank of India.

Uchikawa, S. (2001). "Investment Boom and Underutilisation of Capacity in the 1990s", *Economic and Political Weekly*, August 25, 36(34): pp. 3247-54.

————. (2002). "Investment Boom and the Capital Goods Industry", in S. Uchikawa (ed.), *Economic Reforms and Industrial Structure in India*, New Delhi: Manohar Publishers.

12

Liberalisation and Growth of Firms in India

N.S. SIDDHARTHAN
K. LAL

1. Introduction

The objective of this study is to analyse the impact of the liberalisation policies introduced by the Government of India since 1991 on the growth of firms in India. The study covers the period 1994 – 2000 and includes all the manufacturing firms covered by the *Capital Line* data set.[1] Earlier studies on the impact of liberalisation on growth (growth of productivity/sales turnover) yielded ambiguous results (Bartelsman and Doms 2000 and Tybout 1992, 2000, Liu 1993 for a survey of the literature). By and large, the literature blames the use of aggregate production functions and regressions based on a cross-section of sectors and a cross-section of nations for the confusing findings. These studies argue that liberalisation results in the entry of new enterprises with a more recent vintage of technology which could result in the exit of some of the existing firms that cannot compete with the new entrants using a different technological paradigm. Therefore, due to the phenomenon of entry and exit of firms, the sector's overall growth rate need not be high. In other words, liberalisation and introduction of new technologies could result in the Schumpeterian turmoil of creative destruction. Some of the studies (Bartelsman and Doms 2000 and Tybout 1992, 2000, Liu 1993, Nelson and Winter 1977, Nelson and Pack 1999) emphasise the

1. The Capital Line data set is being marketed and maintained by M/s Capital Market Pvt. Ltd. It covers the data of all the firms that are registered with various stock exchanges in India. There are about 8000 firms in the data set. The data set includes the information on about 300 attributes such as financial, collaboration with MNE: technological as well as financial, type of raw material used i.e. imported and local, historical data of firm, product mix, and performance indicators of firm. Although Capital Market maintains data from the mid-eighties, we have used the data of the post-liberalisation period.

heterogeneity of firms and technology and for this reason do not favour industry level or country level studies and the use of methodologies that assume uniform production functions, a representative firm for an industry, homogeneity of enterprises and the measurement of total factor productivity growth as a residual. In this study, we analyse the inter-firm differences in the growth rates over a seven-year period. The basic unit is the firm and we allow for the entry and the exit of firms during the sample period.

2. Analytical Framework

The neo-classical theory of the firm is not designed to explain the growth of firms (Hay and Morris 1991). Hence, following our earlier works (Siddharthan and Lall 1982; Siddharthan *et al.*, 1994), we will be following the Marris (1964) managerial framework to explain inter-firm differences in the growth of capital stock. The text book version (Hay and Morris 1991) of the Marris model has the following structure of equations:

Growth of demand: $D_g = \gamma_1(d^*)$ ...(1)

Growth of Supply: $S_g = \frac{I}{K} = \alpha \frac{\Pi}{K} = \alpha\rho$ ...(2)

Where $\alpha \leq \alpha^*$

Cost of expansion: $d = \gamma_2 \frac{1}{\rho} q$ ...(3a)

Where it can be shown that $\rho = \frac{\pi}{v}$

$$d = \gamma_2\left(\frac{1}{\pi} v\right) \quad \text{...(3b)}$$

The equilibrium point can be represented by Eq. 4

$$D_g = S_g \quad \text{...(4)}$$

Substituting (3a) in (1) $D_g = \gamma_3\left(\frac{1}{\rho}\right)$ ...(5)

where D_g is the demand for growth, d^* is the rate of successful diversification, S_g supply of growth, I investment, K capital stock, α

the amount of new investment financed per unit of profit earned, α^* the maximum value α can take, Π Profits, π profit margin, v capital output ratio, and ρ is the profit rate.

The model, as is well known, is not concerned with short-term fluctuations in growth but deals with long-term trends. In the model, the growth of demand is a non-linear function of the profit rate (equation 5) and the curve, also referred to as the profit-growth frontier, takes an inverted "U" shape and the growth of supply (equation 2) is a linear function of the profit rate. The equilibrium point is at the intersection of the growth of demand and supply curves. Empirically only the equilibrium points are observable and not the whole growth of demand curve. The profit-growth frontier is fixed for the given environment under which a firm operates. However, the environment (Marris also refers to it as the super environment) could change with the changes in technology resulting in the introduction of new products and processes and with changes in the policies of the government. With the change in the super environment, the growth of demand curve will shift. An individual firm's shift in the profit-growth frontier, which is a function of firm specific variables such as multinational affiliation, international orientation and intangible assets like technology, brand name and goodwill and which enables the firm to exploit the changes in environment to its advantage/disadvantage is represented by $\Phi(\varepsilon)$. The growth function can then be rewritten as:

$$D_g = \Phi(\varepsilon)\gamma_3\left(\frac{1}{\rho}\right) \qquad \ldots(6)$$

If the shift is favourable, that is, $\Phi(\varepsilon) > 0$, then the firm could enjoy both higher profit and growth rates. Furthermore, because of multi-products, different firms could face different environments and different growth of demand curves. For the losers, however, the term $\Phi(\varepsilon)$ is expected to be negative. Consequently the profit-growth frontier of such firms could experience an inward shift. Equation 5 represents the relationship between growth and other variables in a given environment. In this paper we intend to examine the growth of firms over a period of policy changes. Hence, we derive the equation that captures the policy changes during the time period, Δt. The change in growth rate due to policy changes can be represented by the following equation:

$$\frac{\partial}{\partial t}Dg = \frac{\partial}{\partial t}\Phi(\varepsilon) + \frac{\partial}{\partial \rho}\gamma_3\left(\frac{1}{\rho}\right) * \frac{\partial \rho}{\partial t} \qquad ...(7)$$

Here, $\frac{\partial}{\partial t}$ represents the impact of policy changes on the annual growth rate of firms. That is, policy changes influence the environment under which the firm functions and the firm specific variables expressed by ε determine the annual shifts in the firm's growth-profit frontier.

We argue in this paper that with the liberalisation measures introduced in India during the early-1990s, the super environment facing Indian firms changed. Earlier, Indian firms were not allowed to expand capacity, change product mix, introduce new products and processes and import machinery and technology without obtaining an industrial/import license. With the change in policy, firms were allowed to enter into joint ventures with multinational enterprises (MNEs) more freely, import technology from MNEs, import capital goods and expand capacities and introduce new products without obtaining an industrial license. In the early-1990s the Indian rupee was made convertible in the current account and imports were more freely allowed. Nevertheless, not all firms would have benefited from the liberalisation measures. There would have been gainers and losers (Pandit and Siddharthan 1998). For the beneficiaries of the liberalisation measures the growth of demand curve would have shifted favourably while for the victims it would have contracted. We have identified firm-specific variables which would have determined the shift in the growth-profit frontier and enabled the firms to grow faster/ slower. These are the size of the firm, MNE affiliation as measured by the share of foreign equity in the total equity of the firm, import of technology, import of machinery, export orientation, vertical integration, and capital intensity. Furthermore, we argue that the impact of these determinants on growth will not remain constant over the years but will change during the process of liberalisation over the years.

2.1 Firm Size (Size)

The environment faced by large and small firms could be different. Larger firms have more options compared to smaller ones with regard to choice of technology, products and markets. By and large, smaller firms may not be able to produce goods where minimum size economies are significant and they may also be serving the more restricted local markets. As per this argument size is a definite advantage for growth and larger firms operate in a different environment in the sense used by Marris. However, most studies that tested for the importance of size on the growth of firms (Rowthorn 1971; Buckley *et al.*, 1978; Siddharthan and Lall 1982), did not find size an advantage for growth. Their samples, however, consisted mainly of very large firms (top 500 Fortune companies). Thus among the very large corporations size was not an advantage for growth. Size could be an advantage if the sample consisted of both small and large firms. For the Indian sample during the period of liberalisation, we expect the size advantages to get pronounced as the liberalisation process progresses. During the initial stages, size may not be important, but over the years due to increases in competition and import penetration size advantages will get pronounced. Larger firms may also be better positioned to enter into joint ventures with MNEs.

2.2 MNE Affiliation (MNE)

MNE affiliation can help firms to push the growth-profit frontier favourably as the MNEs enjoy a superior endowment of intangible assets, which includes technology, global networks, brand names and superior managerial practices (Caves 1996; Dunning 1993). Several studies show that MNEs and their affiliates enjoy higher productivity levels compared to local firms (Bartelsman and Doms 2000; Tybout 1992, 2000; Liu 1993). However, there is no evidence in literature that MNEs grow faster than the local firms.

2.3 Technology Imports (Royalty)

For modernisation and technological up-gradation and introduction of new products and processes, intra-firm transfer of technology through FDI need not be the only option. Firms can also import technology at arms length against royalty and lump sum payments. The liberalisation measures introduced in India during the 1990s made technology imports at arms length easier. Several Indian firms adopted this route to license technology and modernise their units (Siddharthan and Pandit 1998).

2.4 Import of Machinery (MK)

Though India liberalised import of machinery to modernise plants, all firms may not have succeeded in importing the appropriate machines. There are imperfections in the international machinery market and the MNEs would be reluctant to sell them to unrelated third parties (Siddharthan and Safarian 1997). Furthermore, computer-integrated manufacturing systems are less standardised and in these systems software and tacit elements are integrated with the machinery. Hence in these systems the scope for unpacking of technology is limited (Radosovic 1999, pp. 70-72). Therefore, while some firms succeeded in importing the right type of machines, others did not. Those who succeeded introduced new products and processes and could shift the frontier and grow faster. We expect this variable to be very important in explaining the growth of firms in the post-liberalisation period.

2.5 Export Orientation (Exports)

One of the important constraints for growth is the demand constraint and in particular the domestic demand constraint. Firms that are export oriented could overcome the domestic demand constraint and grow faster. The relationship between exports and growth is a complex one. There could be simultaneity in the relationship between the two variables. In the Indian case, however, the firms are not export intensive. Most firms serve the domestic market and the average export intensity of Indian firms is about 10 per cent and for the modern sector it is about 8 per cent. Hence we have considered this variable as an independent variable. That is, exports influence growth but not the other way around.

2.6 Vertical Integration (VI)

In the pre-liberalisation period most of the firms did not specialise and invest in improving the quality of inputs and other components, as that would have involved applying for a fresh industrial license. During the 1980s any change in product specification or improvement required the obtaining of a fresh industrial license. Under these circumstances, the firms sourced components from other Indian firms. Third party and market sourcing could create problems relating to non-compliance of delivery schedules and maintenance of high quality of the inputs. Under a protected environment these might not affect the performance of firms but in a liberalised regime, maintenance of product quality and reduction of inventory costs assume importance. Hence we expect vertical integration to increase in the post-liberalisation years.

2.7 Capital Output Ratio (COR)

In the Marris model (equation 3b) capital output ratio and growth are positively related. Accordingly we also hypothesise a positive relationship.

In the model the Dependent Variable is the **Growth of Capital stock (GK).**

The Model:

$$GK_{it} = \alpha_t + \beta_{1t} \text{ Log Size}_{it} + \beta_{2t} \text{ MNE}_{it} + \beta_{3t} \text{ Royalty}_{it} + \beta_{4t} \text{ MK}_{it} + \beta_{5t} \text{ Exports}_{it} + \beta_{6t} \text{ VI}_{it} + \beta_{7t} \text{ COR}_{it} + U$$

where i refer to the firm and t to the year. As hypothesised we expect α and β to change over the years. We capture the changes in the regression coefficients over the years by introducing intercept and slope year dummies.

3. Sample and Variables

For estimating the model we use the *Capital Line* data set. The data set covers about 8000 firms, which include firms from the service sector, trading firms and banks. In our sample, firms belonging to the service sector have been excluded. Thus the sample consists of only manufacturing firms. The study allows for the entry and exit of firms and therefore we have not kept the number of firms fixed for the sample period. While considering new entrants, we have included them in the sample only after they had started their manufacturing activities. Thus firms that were in the initial stages of setting-up of their plant and machinery and had not yet commenced their selling activities have been excluded. On an average new firms take about two to three years to commence manufacturing activities. The sample consists of 7444 observations covering about 1369 manufacturing firms for the period 1994-2000. The sample covers the following industrial sectors: automobiles and their components (115 firms), cables (33), chemicals (108), electrical goods (61), engineering (106), electronics (67), fertilisers (26), food (68), glass (17), leather (34), metal products (28), paper products (58), personal care (17), pharmaceuticals (173), plastic goods (75), rubber (22), and textiles (361).

3.1 Variables: Dependent Variable

GK_{it}. Percentage growth rate of gross fixed assets per annum of the firm. Subscript $_i$ refers to the firm and $_t$ to time.

Independent Variables

Size$_{it}$. Size of the firm as measured by sales turn over.

MNE$_{it}$. Percentage share of the foreign collaborator's equity in the total equity. In a wholly owned subsidiary it will be 100 per cent.

Royalty$_{it}$. Royalty and technical fee payments made abroad as a ratio of sales turnover.

MK$_{it}$. Payments made for import of capital goods as a ratio of sales turnover.

EXPORTS$_{it}$. Export of goods as a ratio of sales turnover.

VI$_{it}$. Vertical Integration, ratio of value added to sales turnover.

COR$_{it}$. Capital output ratio, ratio of gross fixed assets to value added.

Certain other variables like the import of components, materials and leverage were also tried as independent variables. Since they did not emerge significant they have not been reported.

The variables are in current prices and have not been deflated by the price index. However, time dummies (both slope and intercept), have been given to capture annual price and other policy changes. This method was preferred for the following reasons. During the period of liberalisation new products and processes were introduced and the price index does not capture the quality changes and the introduction of new products. Prices of products of different vintages in industries with fast technological change are not comparable. Since the impact of liberalisation was mainly on the quality of the products, it was considered more appropriate to introduce time dummies. In other words, we are mainly dealing with a cross-section of firms and expect the value of the coefficients to change over the years and we capture the changes by introducing intercept and slope time dummies.

4. Statistical Results

Table 12.1 presents results that are corrected for heteroskedasticity. We also introduced industry dummies to capture the possible differences in the behaviour of the 17 industries and they are presented in the Appendix 1. Since most of the industry dummies were not statistically significant they will not be discussed in the text. In addition to the determinants presented in the Table, we tried other variables like the leverage ratio, import of components and raw materials but none of these turned out to be significant.

Table 12.1

Determinants of Growth of Capital Stock of Indian Firms (All Firms)

	Constant	*Log Size*	*MNE*	*Royalty*	*MK*	*Exports*	*VI*	*COR*	*W-Test:* p value
Base Sp	189.85*	-25.61*	-0.35*	9.82@	-2.55	156.28	-163.14*	-1.20*	
"t"	(3.72)	(-2.77)	(-2.49)	(1.83)	(-0.16)	(1.44)	(-2.98)	(-1.21)	
Var*95	-65.84	-0.88	-0.18	-1775.5#	-12.29	4.50	26.13	42.34@	0.00*
	(-0.45)	(-0.04)	(-0.33)	(-0.74)	-(0.06)	(0.02)	(0.31)	(1.64)	
Var*96	-127.11*	15.45	0.33@	-691.56@	706.65*	-165.18	158.57*	3.32	0.00*
	(-2.39)	(1.59)	(1.62)	(-1.79)	(3.27)	(-1.49)	(2.89)	(1.00)	
Var*97	-185.92*	25.44*	0.44@	44.09	5.45	-174.19	166.35#	10.14	0.015#
	(-3.33)	(2.65)	(1.64)	(0.14)	(0.31)	(-1.57)	(2.22)	(1.51)	
Var*98	-188.35*	28.91*	0.13	921.91	29.71	-158.02	162.55*	2.92*	0.012*
	(-3.67)	(3.11)	(0.78)	(1.34)	(1.39)	(-1.45)	(2.97)	(2.40)	
Var*99	-181.06*	25.84*	1.09@	-6.55	531.27#	-156.60	161.94*	1.28	0.005*
	(-3.53)	(2.77)	(1.84)	(-0.01)	(2.10)	(-1.44)	(2.96)	(1.29)	
Var*00	-164.55*	23.31*	0.27@	-121.44	272.53*	-157.89	161.46*	0.88	0.003*
	(-3.14)	(2.46)	(1.71)	(-1.14)	(2.89)	(-1.45)	(2.95)	(0.73)	
Mean	44.38	3.57	5.46	0.0044	0.032	0.11	0.39	3.30	
SD	310.38	1.70	14.64	0.23	0.64	0.23	1.09	8.10	

Note: No. of observations 7442; R^2 = 0.1188; F = 18.10. * significant at 1%, # at 5% level and @ at 10% level. Equations are estimated using *Eviews* package and are corrected for heteroskedasticity.

Base Sp refers to the base year, that is, 1994 specification. Var*95 refers to the respective variable given in the columns multiplied by the time dummy. Mean refers to the arithmetic mean of the variables and SD is their respective standard deviations. Under the column constant the mean and SD of the dependent variable is given. We also tried other determinants like leverage ratio, import of components and raw materials and did not find them significant and hence have not reported in the table. W-Test refers to Wald Test of joint significance of the variables interacted with a given year dummy.

Table 12.1 presents the estimates of the model specified in Section II. In the table, independent variables are given in the columns and the intercept and slope dummies are presented in the rows. The base year specification (for the year 1994) is presented in the first row. Under the column "Constant" the intercept dummies for the respective years are presented. Other columns from the row "Var*95" onwards present the values of the slope dummies for the respective years. The last column gives the probability values of the Wald Test of joint significance of the variables interacted with a given year dummy.[2] The test supports the validity of our using intercept and slope time dummies. There have been significant changes in the value of the coefficients over the years.

Table 12.1a

Growth of Gross Fixed Assets 1994-2000 (All Firms)

Year	*Mean Growth*	*Standard Deviation*
1994	59.71	241.33
1995	125.09	751.06
1996	51.24	178.99
1997	21.63	173.34
1998	19.27	50.32
1999	18.38	82.99
2000	15.19	70.08
Entire period	44.38	310.38

In Table 12.1, the intercept dummies have negative signs for all the years indicating a declining investment rate after taking into account the influence of the determinants specified in the model. The actual decline in the percentage growth of gross fixed assets is presented in Table 12.1a. This behaviour is mainly due to the policy changes introduced during the 1990s. Soon after the introduction of liberalisation policies there was a rush of investment by the corporate firms. This was mainly because during the earlier regime, firms were not allowed to expand capacities and import capital goods and technology without obtaining an industrial and import license. Once the restrictions on capacity expansion were removed there was a rush for investment. During 1995 the growth rate was more than 100 per cent. Such high growth rates are not sustainable in the long run and the growth of capital stock should settle down to more realistic levels. The average growth rate for the entire period has been very high, about 40 per cent. Along with the decline in the mean growth rate from the unrealistically high to more realistic levels, the standard deviation of the growth rates has also declined significantly.

The slope coefficients of the size variable have also been changing over the years. During the earlier period, size was not an advantage

2. See Appendix 2 for details of Wald Test.

for growth. In the base specification the sign of the coefficient was negative and significant. For 1995 the coefficient was not significant indicating that the 1995 behaviour was not different from the 1994 behaviour. However, since 1996, the sign of the size coefficient has turned positive and is significant for most of the years. Thus in the liberalised regime size advantages have emerged important to withstand global competition.

MNE affiliations in terms of equity participation also show a similar (though weaker) trend to the firm size. In the base specification it is significant with a negative sign at 1 per cent level. The sign of the MNE coefficients turn positive after 1996 and the value of the coefficients for 1997 and 1999 are large enough to offset the negative impact of the base specification value. However, the post-1997 coefficients are significant at only the 10 per cent level. This could be because the liberalisation regime has not increased foreign direct investments (FDI) in India. Since 1997 FDI inflows into India have been declining steadily. They have declined from $3577 million in 1997 to $2635 million in 1998 to $2168 million in 1999. Moreover, India's share in world FDI inflows is a mere 0.5 per cent. FDI's role in gross capital formation in India is also meagre, less than 3 per cent. Under these conditions the relatively low level of significance (at 10 per cent level) of the MNE variable in the table is not unexpected. The coefficient of Royalty was positive in the basic specification and was significant at the 10 per cent level. However, the sign turned negative during 1995 (significant at the 5 per cent level) and 1996 (significant at the 10 per cent level). Since 1997 the slope coefficients of Royalty have not been significantly different from the base specification coefficient. Therefore, it is possible to conclude that in recent years technology imports have been having a (weak) positive influence on growth. Furthermore, exports also did not contribute to growth. During this period, the growth of Indian firms depended mainly on domestic sales and not on exports. On an average the sample firms exported about 11 per cent of their sales.

Import of capital goods, on the other hand, has turned out to be an important determinant of growth during recent years. The main source of technology transfer and the chief mode of modernisation of manufacturing units have been import of capital goods (Siddharthan and Safarian 1997). Thus while expenditures on royalty and technical fee accounted for hardly 0.4 per cent of the sales revenue, capital goods imports amounted to more than three per cent of the sales revenue. An earlier study using neo-Schumpeterian investment function also found capital goods imports important in explaining investment (Pandit and Siddharthan 1998). The importance of technology transfer through the import of machinery with their embodied software and tacit components is emphasised in literature (Radosovic 1999, pp. 70-72).

The roles of vertical integration and capital output ratio changed significantly over the years. During the initial years—1994-95—vertically integrated firms did not grow. On the other hand firms that subcontracted grew faster. However, during the post-1996 period vertically integrated firms grew faster. This radical change in the influence of vertical integration on the growth of firms could be due to the increased importance of factors like product quality, reduction of uncertainty in production processes, better management of demand fluctuations, timely delivery and the need to reduce inventory costs due to global competition. Therefore, firms started manufacturing high quality components in-house rather than buying them from third parties. The removal of licensing restrictions also helped these firms to increase in-house production. This feature has also got reflected in the capital output ratios. During 1994 COR had a negative sign. Since 1995 it has turned positive indicating capital intensity and higher in-house content. Nevertheless, value addition to sales ratio is less than 40 per cent and about 60 per cent of sales is still sourced from outside vendors.

5. Conclusion

The neo-classical economic theory does not have a model to analyse the growth of firms. Therefore, this paper follows the Marris framework and introduces certain important modifications in the Marris (1964) model to analyse the impact of the series of liberalisation measures introduced by the Government of India since 1991 on the growth of Indian corporate firms. In particular, using the Marris framework, the paper argues that policy changes introduced since 1991 would result in a change in the environment under which the firms functioned. Nevertheless, the ability of the firms to shift their growth-profit frontier will depend on firm specific characteristics like international orientation, affiliation and strategic alliances with multinational enterprises, size of the firm, capital intensity and vertical integration. Furthermore, the impact of firm-specific determinants will vary over the years in accordance with the progress of the liberalisation measures. Thus all the coefficients of the determinants will vary with time. This is an important feature of the model. The results of the study show that during the initial years, firm size, MNE affiliation, capital intensity, vertical integration and import of capital goods had a negative impact on growth. However, in recent years the impact of these variables has turned positive and significant indicating the important changes brought about by globalisation.

Soon after the introduction of liberalisation measures there was a surge in the investment and expansion programmes of the sample firms. The average growth in capital stock during 1995 was more than 100 per cent. This was mainly due to the removal of shackles by the government and the desire of the firms to reap early entrant advantages in introducing new and better quality goods. However, this extraordinarily high investment rate could not be sustained and the investment rate settled down to more realistic levels. During the controlled regime, since expansion of capacity in a given product line was not easily granted, firms opted for product diversification rather than specialisation. After liberalisation, expansion activities became more focussed and firms turned to vertical integration aimed at improving product quality and delivery schedules. The sign of the coefficient of vertical integration changed to positive after 1995. Arm's length purchase of technology against lump-sum and royalty payments also influenced inter-firm differences in investment rates, though its impact was not strong. Perhaps liberalisation policies with regard to arm's length purchase of technology affected all firms more or less equally thereby reducing its impact. Furthermore, the sums involved in technology payments were not large. However, inter-firm differences in the import of capital goods were substantial and this variable significantly influenced the investment behaviour of the sample firms. In the case of computer aided numerically controlled machines, the software and the tacit components were inbuilt and the machines were also activity specific. Thus unlike for the machines of the earlier vintage, the search, acquisition and transaction costs are high for the purchase of new machines. Firms that were successful in acquiring these machines grew faster. Thus liberalisation policies had different impacts on different sets of firms. Values of the determinants of the firms' shift in their respective growth-profit frontiers differed. Also, the impact of the determinants changed over time.

References

Bartelsman, E.J. and Doms, M. (2000). "Understanding Productivity: Lessons from Longitudinal Microdata", *Journal of Economic Literature*, Vol. 38, pp. 569-594.

Buckley, P.J., J.H. Dunning and R.D. Pearce (1978). "The Influence of Firm Size, Industry, Nationality, and Degree of Multinationality on the Growth and Profitability of the World's Largest Firms, 1962-1972", *Weltwirtschaftliches Archiv*, Vol. 114, No. 2, pp. 243-57.

Caves, R.E. (1996). *Multinational Enterprise and Economic Analysis*, (Second Edition), Cambridge Survey of Economic Literature, Cambridge: Cambridge University Press.

Davidson, R. and J.G. Mackinnon (1993). *Estimation and Inference in Econometrics*, Oxford: Oxford University Press.

Dunning, J.H. (1993). *Multinational Enterprises and the Global Economy*, Reading: Addison-Wesley Publishing Company.

Hay, D.A. and D.J. Morris (1991). *Industrial Economics and Organisation: Theory and Evidence*, 2nd edition, Oxford: Oxford University Press.

Liu, L. (1993). "Entry-exit, Learning, and Productivity Change: Evidence from Chile", *Journal of Development Economics*, Vol. 42, pp. 217-242.

Marris, R. (1964). *The Economic Theory of Managerial Capitalism*, London: Macmillan.

Nelson, R.R. and S. Winter (1977). "In Search of a Useful Theory of Innovations", *Research Policy*, Vol. 6, No. 1. pp. 36-77.

Nelson, R.R. and H. Pack (1999). "The Asian Miracle and Modern Growth Theory", *The Economic Journal*, Vol. 109. pp. 416-436.

Pandit, B.L. and N.S. Siddharthan (1998). "Technological Acquisition and Investment: Lessons from Recent Indian Experience", *Journal of Business Venturing*, Vol. 13, No. 1, pp. 43-55.

Radosovic, S. (1999). *International Technology Transfer and Catch-up in Economic Development*, Cheltenham: Edward Elgar.

Rowthorn, R. (1971). *International Big Business 1957-1967: A Study of Comparative Growth*, Cambridge: Cambridge University Press.

Siddharthan, N.S. and S. Lall (1982). "The Recent Growth of the Largest US Multinationals", *Oxford Bulletin of Economics and Statistics*, Vol. 44, pp. 1-13.

Siddharthan, N.S. and B.L. Pandit (1998). "Liberalisation and Investment: Behaviour of MNEs and Large Corporate Firms in India", *International Business Review*, Vol. 7, No. 5, pp. 535-548.

Siddharthan, N.S., B.L. Pandit and R.N. Agarwal (1994). "Growth and Profit Behaviour of Large Indian Firms", *The Developing Economies*, Vol. 32, No. 2, pp. 188-209.

Siddharthan, N.S. and A.E. Safarian (1997). "TNCs, Technology Transfer and Import of Capital Goods: Recent Indian Experience", *Transnational Corporations*, Vol. 6, No. 1, pp. 31-49.

Tybout, J.R. (1992). "Linking Trade and Productivity: New Research Directions", *World Bank Economic Review*, Vol. 6, No. 2, pp. 189-211.

————. (2000). "Manufacturing Firms in Developing Countries: How Well do They do, and Why?", *Journal of Economic Literature*, Vol. 38, pp. 11-44.

APPENDIX I

Table A1

Dependent Variable: Growth of capital stock
Method: Least Squares
Sample: 7444
Included observations: 7442
Excluded observations: 2

Variable	*Coefficient*	*Std. Error*	*t-Statistic*	*Prob.*
Constant	67.74823	15.22851	4.448776	0.0000
Log Size	–6.661423	2.328466	–2.860863	0.0042
MNE	–0.256331	0.258379	–0.992074	0.3212
Royalty	–3.674731	15.78795	–0.232755	0.8160
MK	23.01728	5.589370	4.118046	0.0000
Exports	38.27576	16.38164	2.336504	0.0195
VI	–5.986694	3.355085	–1.784364	0.0744
COR	2.853528	0.454196	6.282586	0.0000
Y1995	61.96813	14.38255	4.308563	0.0000
Y1996	–11.65815	14.07556	–0.828255	0.4076
Y1997	–33.63885	13.84641	–2.429428	0.0151
Y1998	–45.53346	13.79479	–3.300772	0.0010
Y1999	–47.58414	13.90259	–3.422681	0.0006
Y2000	–44.35645	15.26978	–2.904851	0.0037
AUTO	2.494048	13.78944	0.180866	0.8565
CABLE	1.713212	23.77401	0.072062	0.9426
CHEM	–13.32472	14.60206	–0.912523	0.3615
ELECTRI	–1.343384	18.06679	–0.074357	0.9407
ELECTRONICS	4.308772	17.51674	0.245980	0.8057
ENGG	–1.027387	15.01550	–0.068422	0.9455
FERT	–1.255620	26.16537	–0.047988	0.9617
FOOD	29.76008	18.65884	1.594959	0.1108
GLASS	–27.83602	31.71765	–0.877619	0.3802
LEATHER	38.45951	25.49481	1.508523	0.1315
METAL	10.38549	26.18356	0.396642	0.6916
PAPER	–10.20724	19.27121	–0.529663	0.5964
PCARE	1.784154	31.37219	0.056871	0.9546
PHARMA	43.25606	12.26994	3.525369	0.0004
PLASTIC	7.188701	17.47422	0.411389	0.6808
RUBBER	139.0020	28.89818	4.810062	0.0000
R-squared	0.031122	Mean dependent var		44.37484
Adjusted R-squared	0.027331	S.D. dependent var		310.3836
S.E. of regression	306.1127	Akaike info criterion		14.28981
Sum squared resid	6.95E+08	Schwarz criterion		14.31768
Log likelihood	-53142.37	F-statistic		8.209776
Durbin-Watson stat	1.994032	Prob(F-statistic)		0.000000

Appendix II

Wald Test is basically used for testing specification and dynamic structure of the relationship between the variables. Other tests such as Chow can also be used for specification and stability test. However, F-statistics reported in the Chow test have an F-distribution only if the errors are independent and identically normally distributed. This restriction implies that the residual variance in two sub-samples must be equal, whereas we can compute a Wald statistics (see Davidson and Mackinnon 1993 for details) for structural change with unequal sub-sample variances. Hence the Wald Test was considered to be the most appropriate to test the year-wise specification and the relationship between the variables. In this paper we have tested the specification for individual years. For model specification test of a year, the data were split into two groups, that is, data for that particular year and the data for other years. For instance, to test the specification of the model for 1995, the data were split in two groups, namely: (1) data for 1995 of all the firms, and (2) the entire dataset excluding 1995. Then the Wald statistics was computed for two sub-samples. Similarly the test statistics was computed for other years.

Section IV

Macro Models and Growth

13

Five Decades of Macroeconometric Modelling Research for India: A Synoptic View

K. KRISHNAMURTY

1. Introduction

Macroeconometric Modelling research has been a long march ever since its start in mid-fifties but in an environment not so encouraging for research on Tinbergen-Klein type macroeconometric models for India in the earlier decades. But it was not a lonely trail. Several researchers joined the march despite heavy odds and low returns. There are several reasons for poor encouragement for such research. Foremost among them was that they were the hey-days of I-0 techniques and planning models. The attitude towards macroeconometric models has now turned favourable under the new policy regime.

We now turn *first,* to an outline of evolution of econometric models for India, *second,* to some theoretical and empirical issues relevant to macromodelling, *third,* to use of models in forecasting, policy analysis and planning, *fourth,* to future agenda of research with some suggestions and finally, concluding observations.

It is necessary to note at the outset that there is neither anything profound nor new in what is stated here but only a recapitulation of the progress achieved in the past, current status and potential trends.

2. Evolution of Econometric Models

India has perhaps been among the first few developing countries for which economy-wide econometric models were estimated. The earliest work dates back to the mid-fifties when macromodelling as a professional academic activity even in many developed countries was still in its infancy. The earliest model for India was estimated by Narasimham under the guidance of Nobel Laureate Professor Jan

Tinbergen. The hazards in attempting to model an underdeveloped economy at that time are self evident. Problems arising from the absence of comprehensive and empirically feasible theoretical framework relevant to developing countries, weak and inadequate data base, and lack of perspective as regards the role of such models in LDCs are quite evident from the early models. Since then there has been considerable progress.

Broadly speaking, models for India can be grouped into five generations. Fifth generation models are now on line.[1] A good number of models belong to the earliest generation. These were obviously the most severely constrained by a variety of data problems on top of the usual hurdles and disadvantages associated with new explorations. Most of the First Generation models were Ph.D. dissertations many of which were prepared under the supervision of Nobel Laureate Professor Lawrence R Klein. Time and resources, apart from data availability, were severe constraints on the researchers. Unlike their counterparts working on developed countries, researchers on Indian models have had very little to draw upon in term of sectoral econometric studies. Therefore, it is not surprising that they had to be small, simple and often rather close to the text book macroeconomic theory.

Nevertheless, these models served well as explorations in an important branch of economic analysis. They uncovered the weaknesses of the available data base - many of which have been reduced since then and also prompted further quantitative research at the sectoral level. Even though models belonging to the First Generation were simple, they were by no means routine. Despite considerable odds, each model had a specific focus and innovated wherever it dealt with problems common with other models. To be specific, the major focus in different models belonging to this generation (early-sixties to mid-seventies) includes issues such as price behaviour (Choudhry, Marwah, Chakrabarty), investment behaviour and endogenous population expansion in a two sector model focussed on growth (Krishnamurty), integration of real,

---

1. Paradigm shift in economic regime and major revisions in the data base in the nineties have necessitated overhaul of even the latest models. They are in the process of being reformulated, re-estimated and being put to test in forecasting and policy analysis. See Econometric Models: Theory and Applications, Eds., D.M. Nachane *et al.*, Allied publishers, New Delhi, 2004; Data, Models and policies, Eds., V. Pandit *et al*. The Indian Econometric Society, Madras School of Economics, Chennai, 2002.

monetary and foreign trade sectors with endogeneous capacity utilisation (Choudhry and Krishnamurty), role of foodgrain output in growth and price stability (Pandit), interaction between monetary and real variables in the monetised component of the economy (Bhattacharya), the structure of monetary and financial markets (Gupta, Mammen), external trade (Choudhary, Dutta) and growth in a dualistic economy (Agarwala).

Among the Second Generation models (mid-seventies to early-eighties) we have the ones by Pani, Ahluwalia, Bhattacharya, Pandit, Srivastava and Rangarajan. The most important feature that distinguishes these models from the earlier ones is their emphasis on policy analysis. Most of the other features follow from this objective. They are more disaggregated and, therefore, much larger. There is an explicit recognition of the mixed nature and some other institutional characteristics of the Indian economy.

They also went one step ahead of their predecessors by allowing for lagged, more varied and somewhat more complex adjustment processes. Unlike their predecessors, the Second Generation models had the advantage of a considerably improved data base, a large variety of rigorous micro and sectoral empirical studies that have emerged since the sixties, and an increased professional interest in applied econometric research. Notwithstanding this, until about the mid-seventies, progress had been in fits and starts.

Progress of macroeconometric research has been considerable in the eighties. Several models were estimated. They are labelled as belonging to the Third Generation. These include (a) Ghose, Lahiri, Madhur and Roy, (b) Pani (c) Bhattacharya, (d) Krishnamurty, (e) Pandit, (f) Bhattacharya and Rao, (g) Ahluwalia and Rangarajan, (h) Narain Sinha, (i) Pandit and Bhattacharya, (j) Bhattacharya, (k) Madhur, (l) Chakrabarty, (m) Krishnamurty, Pandit and Sharma, (n) Kannan, (o) Panchamukhi and Mehta, and (p) Bhattacharya and Guha. Unlike the work in the earlier decades, econometric modelling in the eighties had the benefit of many in depth sectoral econometric studies.

The Third Generation models cited are in many ways similar to those belonging to the Second Generation. But they are larger in size, better disaggregated and seek to carry forward the analysis of policy issues initiated by the Second Generation model builders. The distinguishing features of the Third Generation models are that they explicitly deal with the problems of macroeconomic adjustment and venture to address issues that have not been discussed earlier in formal quantitative terms. Many of these models were put to policy simulations more rigorously than those belonging to the Second Generation. The special focus of each of the Third Generation models is briefly presented in the following Table 13.1.

Table 13.1

Broad Features of Third Generation Models

	Author	*Period*	*Special Focus*
1.	Ghose, Lahiri, Madhur and Roy (1983)	1960-78	General purpose model covering agriculture, industry, government, money and trade with high level of disaggregation.
2.	Pani (1984)	1970-82	Output, demand and prices, and their interaction.
3.	Bhattacharya (1984)	1952-76	Public expenditures, inflation and growth.
4.	Krishnamurty (1984)	1962-80	Inflation and growth; supply side, infrastructure, money and prices public investment and its interrelationship with private investment and fiscal operations and growth-inflation trade-off.
5.	Pandit (1984)	1951-78	Medium term analysis of outputs and prices.
6.	Pandit (1985)	1951-75	Macroeconomic structure, stabilisation policies and growth.
7.	Pandit (1985a)	1955-80	Supply, demand and monetary policy.
8.	Pandit (1986)	1951-80	Growth performance and relative roles of supply and demand; tests made to detect structural break in mid-sixties
9.	Pandit (1986a)	1954-81	External trade in detail and price formation; varying periods for different equations; used in the Global LINK model.
10.	Bhattacharya and Rao (1986)	1967-84	Agriculture-industry interrelationship and public investment.
11.	Ahluwalia and Rangarajan (1986)	1961-80	Agriculture-industry linkages.
12.	Pandit and Bhattacharya (1987)	1961-80	Resource mobilisation, growth and inflation.
13.	Bhattacharya (1987)	1951-85	Effectiveness of monetary policy and inflation.
14.	Madhur (1987)	1952-85	Macro impacts of monetary and fiscal policy changes; *exante* forcasts.
15.	Chakrabarty (1987)	1963-84	Linkages among sectors: real (domestic and foreign), fiscal and monetary sectors.

Contd...

...Contd...

Author	*Period*	*Special Focus*
16. Krishnamurty, Pandit and Sharma (1988)	1962-83	Parameters of growth, productivity, infrastructure, imports, exports, public investment and its interrelationship with private investment, and relative prices.
17. Kannan (1989)	1968-85	Monetary approach to balance of payments: includes trade, invisibles and capital account.
18. Panchamukhi and Mehta (1991)	1970-84	Emphasis on trade flows.
19. Metha and Sinha (1991)	1952-85	External trade and public sector.
20. Rastogi (1991)	1951-87	Two sector rational expectations model with government budget, external trade and debt, and labour market.
21. Bhattacharya and Guha (1992)	1970-89	Public sector resource gap, external trade and public debt - domestic and external.

The Fourth Generation models were developed in the nineties. These models to name a few, are (1) Anjaneyulu, (2) Chakravarty and Joshi, (3) Bhattacharya, Barman and Nag, (4) Rangarajan and Mohanty, (5) Mammen, and (6) Klein and Palanivel. They all address issues relevant to new policy regime and carry out many "what if" policy scenario simulations. These models are large in size, provide emphasis on sectoral details and inter-links and trade-offs between sectors.

Each successive generations of models, needless to add, have benefited from the earlier generation models by avoiding pitfalls of the earlier ones and gaining from the advances made earlier even if such advances were only incremental in character.

It is to be emphasised that most of the modelling exercises in India have been the result of efforts of individual researchers. They were constructed, put to validation tests and useful policy simulations were carried out. However, none of them were maintained and serviced on a sustained basis for policy analysis and forecasting. The trend elsewhere in the world has been towards collective efforts of several scholars working in teams complimenting each other and maintaining the models on a continuous basis. Large size models were the need of the day. The need to comprehend complexities of the functioning of the economy, build comprehensive models incorporating complexities and maintain them are beyond the scope and efforts of one or two individuals.

In tune with the times and the needs, a group of researchers—N.K. Choudhary, Meghnad Desai, D.B. Gupta, K. Krishnamurty, K.L. Krishna—under the leadership of A.L. Nagar with a modest support from the Indian Council of Social Science Research (ICSSR) made an effort to build and maintain a model for India in the early-seventies. The team received substantial academic support from Professor A.M. Khusro in this venture. Considerable time and effort went into building the data base and constructing insightful sectoral models but for locational disadvantages in times not so well endowed with communication network as of today, a complete model could not be put together and analysed.

As the foremost institutional effort, the National Council of Applied Economic Research (NCAER) in mid-eighties built a CGE model. NCAER improved it over the years by updating, supplementing it with behavioural sub-systems and also with anticipatory survey data. They make forecasts and policy simulations regularly. By the very nature of the CGE models, the forecasts are for a year at a time and over time sequential forecasts do not generally imbibe dynamic interlinks. Notwithstanding these factors, this continuing effort is a laudable example of collective attempt with institutional backing.

Professor Klein was a close observer of model building efforts in India. Some of us were his students and he kept abreast of developments in the field. In his Institute of Economic Growth (IEG) Silver Jubilee Lecture (1984), he said:

> "that Indian research on model building for the nation should proceed. The many world class econometricians in India should persevere and keep on trying. Many fine examples of econometric model building, some of a pioneering nature, have been completed for India but none has, up to this point, been regularly maintained........Models go out of date fast. Data bases get revised, new kinds of economic problems come to the fore; and sometimes behaviour changes. A model must be continually administered and kept up to date in order to remain useful. ... . India appears to be in need of a serious model building effort, drawing on the best econometric talent, and designed to function as an ongoing effort, over many years, turning out rolling forecasts every month or two on the most refined time period possible - probably annually at the present time. Such a project should have the form and appearance of the best efforts in Western industrial countries, and I hope that in this academic enclave such a research effort will be launched".

The clarion call from their teacher led Krishnamurty, Pandit and their associates (IEG-DSE Team) to launch macroeconometric modelling for India in early-nineties on a sustained basis with support from the National Science Foundation (US), Industrial Development Bank of India (IDBI) and the ICSSR. The Model research was carried out in the RBI Endowment Unit at the IEG. They were greatly helped by Klein in his role as US Co-operating Scientist for the project. The model has been extensively used for forecasting and policy simulations. The model underwent several revisions with updated data. The project shifted in 1999 to the Centre for Development Economics (CDE) at the Delhi School of Economics (DSE). It is a live project and is now referred to as CDE-DSE model. Several papers were put out in the public domain on the system

About the same time as the launch of IEG-DSE model, the Planning Commission set up the Development Planning Centre at the IEG. The faculty of the Centre, in collaboration with Central Planning Bureau of the Netherlands and the Planning Commission completed a preliminary version of the model in 1998. Subsequently the model seems to have undergone substantial revisions and is being used for forecasting and policy analysis.

With these models *viz.*, NCAER, CDE-DSE and IEG, the macro modelling in India came of age. We have entered what may be called the phase of Fifth Generation models. These models are large, dynamic, incorporate better inter-dependence of sectors compared to many of the earlier models and attempt to incorporate change in policy regime.

From mid-fifties until now about fifty macroeconometric models have been built for India. Tinbergen helped to initiate the process and Klein evinced continued interest and provided intellectual support. The two pioneers and their contributions have signally helped to promote research in this area and assisted in attaining the current status.

Forecasting which was not taken seriously in the early days macroeconometric modelling is now respectable. Apart from the three established research institutions, various private agencies are in the field but the data base and structure of their models on which the forecasts are based are not transparent to the academia as the models are not in the public domain. The pendulum has swung to the other end but the academic profession has to ensure that forecasting and model based policy analysis retain hard earned respectability.

The IEG-DSE Research Team and its members individually and collectively developed several dynamic macroeconometric models of Tinbergen-Klein type since the eighties which have been put to several simulation exercises. They have also been used to provide biannual forecasts of major macro-economic variables and medium-term economic scenarios under alternative assumptions with appropriate adjustment factors to account for recent changes in the economy. The model is a part of the Global LINK Model.[2] The results are regularly presented at the Fall and Spring meetings of Project LINK and subsequently published.

The main characteristics of the latest published version of the model are:[3]

(1) It is the largest of its kind for India with close to 350 equations,

(2) It is disaggregated into five sectors, namely, agriculture, manufacturing, infrastructure, economic services and public administration. Agriculture was further sub-divided into food and non-food agriculture,

(3) The sectoral price levels and capital formation are determined in the system with public sector nominal capital formation being exogenous,

(4) There is a large output sector, a price system and an investment block,

(5) The trade flows are disaggregated into edible products, raw materials, POL products and manufactures,

(6) The quantity of imports and exports is determined with exogenous import prices and endogeneous exchange rate. The export prices are not fixed, so giving rise to an upward sloping supply curve.

This implies that an increase in external demand on account of devaluation will not yield the full benefits since the supply curve is not horizontal. Pass-through effects dampen the increase in export revenues in foreign exchange terms,

(7) In agriculture, prices are determined by flex price system while other prices follow mark-up mechanism with monetary factor and administered prices having their role in both the sectors,

---

2. The LINK Model was initiated by Professor Klein in the late-sixties and initially comprised of largely developed OECD countries. Progressively over time many more countries were brought into the system including a large number of developing countries. The model is now operating under UN auspices and includes close to 100 countries.

3. See Economic Policy Modelling for India, Eds., V. Pandit and K. Krishnamurty, Oxford, New Delhi 2004; also see *Journal of Quantitative Economics*, July 1999.

(8) It has a comprehensive sub-model dealing with public finances and resource gap,

(9) It has also a fairly well disaggregated monetary sector model dealing with financial flows and structure of interest rates,

(10) A comprehensive treatment of saving behaviour of households and corporate sectors is built in,

(11) Crowding-in and crowding-out effects of public investment on private investment are incorporated,

(12) Prices play an important role in domestic resource allocation and foreign trade,

(13) Interest rates and inflation expectations have an important role in determining financial flows and savings, and their composition.

(14) The model provides more emphasis on demand side compared to its earlier versions of the model but supply side continues to be dominant,

(15) The system is driven by weather, public sector nominal investment and its composition, and global trade and external prices, among others, and

(16) All parameters are estimated on the basis of historical data and no benchmark estimates are used.

3. Some Theoretical and Empirical Issues

The theoretical framework for macroeconometric models appropriate for developing countries remains hazy even today. One proposition that held sway for long is the inappropriateness of Keynesian economics to LDCs. Notwithstanding; two points need to be noted in this context. *First*, the debate failed to maintain a distinction between the Keynesian methodology and the Keynesian policy conclusions. *Second*, while there might have been a case against the applicability of the Keynesian theory, no need was felt to explain why classical theory was more relevant to less developed countries and that LDCs suffer more from supply than demand constraints. The belief that demand deficiency is not a problem may be an exaggeration. For instance, India has experienced several episodes of demand constrained growth, including the present one.

Importance of the distinction between the Keynesian methodology and the policy recommendations following from this methodology when combined with specific empirical assumptions has been quite effectively brought out by Chakravarty in late-seventies and early-eighties. The upshot is that one may accept the methodology and, not necessarily the empirical assumptions and the consequences that flow from it. It has also been argued by Pandit and Rakshit that the various assertions rightly made about the nature of markets, and the scarcity of information in LDCs strengthen the case of Keynesian *albeit* quantity adjustments rather than that for classical price adjustments.

Even though these distinctions are well known it is pertinent to identify the basic features of developing economies which appear to be relevant to macroeconomic modelling. Most of these were in fact highlighted by Klein more than three decades ago and again recently in mid-eighties. These features are as follows. *First*, governments in most LDCs besides formulating and executing economic policies, also predominate in many markets as producer, investor and consumer. Consequently, government behaviour is neither fully exogenous nor market oriented.

Second, partly because of the predominance of government intervention say investment and output controls, administered prices and procurements that prevailed earlier, prices may cease to be flexible in a large segment of the economy. This implies a larger role for quantity adjustment than is usually allowed for.

Third, since interest rates were, by and large, policy determined in the organised money markets, equilibrium would partly be attained through price level changes. However, with near abolition of controls on private investment, liberalisation in the financial sector and a significant departure from administered price regime in India, the relative role of quantity and price adjustments may gradually tend to shift in favour of the latter compared to the situation under the earlier policy regime. *Fourth*, credit, as distinct from money may play an important role in production as well as in investment. Thus, credit availability will tend to affect output *via* supply as well as demand. The interdependence between monetary and fiscal policies in LDCs is also very pertinent in this context.

Fifth, the process of liberalisation along with macroeconomic adjustment policies pursued in India since early-nineties has led to fiscal restraint. These measures have a serious actual and potential impact on the role of the state in the development process and in particular on its investment activities. In this context, it is necessary to understand and evaluate the extent to which public and private investments are competitive or complementary and the nature of changes in the relationship that may have taken place and is taking place under the present economic regime.

Finally, it does not appear justifiable to assume away either supply bottlenecks nor demand constraints. Supply constraints may arise from inadequate infrastructure, shortage of imported inputs, poor harvests due to natural factors and capital shortages. All the same, the supply inflexibility should not be exaggerated as has often been done. This constraint is unlikely to be binding in all sectors and at all times. Equally, demand constraints also cannot be ignored. Restraint on public expenditure, as for instance, in the recent years of macro economic adjustment seems to have led to demand induced economic slow down. Shifts between demand and supply constrained regimes have not been an uncommon feature.

A dispassionate and balanced evaluation of the different analytical issues and empirical considerations suggest that the approach for macro-modelling of LDCs would be eclectic in character drawing on various theories relevant to specific structure and changing conditions of the economy under study. In the Indian context, the earlier models laid relatively more emphasis on demand compared to supply while latter models concentrated more on supply constraints and consequently, what is needed is a model that properly emphasises relative importance of supply as well as demand factors and can distinguish regime shifts.

Despite various conceptual and data problems, the issues that need to be addressed in modelling LDCs have been highlighted by Klein in his IEG Silver Jubilee Lecture as under:

(1) the need to emphasise conditions of supply,

(2) demand factors and, enhanced roles of income/wealth distributions and the influence of inequality,

(3) population, its growth and structure,

(4) the extreme importance of trade and its strategic significance, in many cases, of key commodities that are closely tied to world market conditions, especially world prices,

(5) detailed treatment of capital flows, reserves and foreign debt,

(6) exchange rate and its determination,

(7) money supply sensitivity to interrelated twin balances - the internal budget balance of government and the external balance of trade and payments, and its impact on prices,

(8) the necessity of imports, especially of capital equipment, technologies and basic raw materials, making import multipliers positive with respect to these particular type of imports, and

(9) the large size and importance of public sector, responsible for the economy's infrastructure and public goods that meet the basic needs of the poor, such as, wage goods.

It needs to be noted that though several issues raised by Klein have been addressed in the Indian models in varying degrees, no single model so far has focused on all the issues in a comprehensive and well articulated manner.

The introduction of new policy regime in early-nineties has given rise to a number of questions which need to be addressed. In brief, one needs to consider whether macroeconomic models which cover several pre-reform years and few years of post-reform period are of any relevance in dealing with the contemporary policy issues and forecasting as the processes of adjustment are bound to undergo changes. All sectors do not respond to Policy changes with the same speed. At best one can visualise that financial and capital markets and, foreign trade, BOP and exchange rate may experience faster change compared to say productivity, saving and investment behaviour. If this view is correct, then it would follow that some of the segments of the on-going models will have to be checked for possible slow changes while others with faster change may need to be overhauled substantially. The use of econometric models for scenario analysis or for forecasting is not a mechanical job. It is an art requiring judicious judgements about the functioning of the economy. Also, some of the critical relationships need to be put to frequent re-estimation with new information even if they are preliminary in nature to capture changing responses, if any. Many factors of socio-economic and political nature cannot be captured in any mathematical or quantitative models and thus cannot be properly dealt with.

To meet the objectives of macroeconometric modelling highlighted earlier, we should be broadly concerned with disaggregating the economy into sectors, which are more or less homogeneous as regards price and output adjustments keeping in view availability and reliability of data. This will depend partly on whether activities are publicly or privately controlled.

Following these considerations, it appears advisable to disaggregate the real side of the economy into five sectors, namely

(a) 'Agriculture' and related activities and within it, food and non-food sectors,

(b) 'Manufacturing',

(c) 'Infrastructure' consisting of construction, power generation, transport, communications, mining, water supply, *etc*.,

(d) 'Economic Services' including real estate, banking, insurance, trade, hotels, *etc*., and,

(e) 'Public Administration and Defence'.

This extent of disaggregation is, on the one hand, meaningful and manageable and, on the other, reliable in terms of data. This disaggregation permits incorporating interdependence between sectors, say for example, the role of infrastructure in determining level of activity in other sectors such as manufacturing or traditional interdependence between agriculture and manufacturing.

Further, it is now widely agreed that for 'Agricultural' sector, output is largely fixed in the short run but relatively flexible in the medium and the long run. Also, prices in this sector are market clearing subject to rachet effects of procurement and support prices determined by government. For 'Manufacturing' there is general consensus that output may possibly be demand-constrained and that prices are mostly subject to the Kaleckian mark-up on unit costs. For 'Infrastructure' sector output is likely to be resource constrained and prices administered subject to unit production costs. In the case of 'Economic Services' output can safely be assumed to be capable of adjusting to demand and therefore related to the level of economic activity in the commodity-producing sectors including infrastructure. Modelling of price behaviour is difficult but not impossible. For 'Public Administration and Defence' both output and price are hard to disentangle. The nominal value added in this sector is merely determined by expenditure. Any unscrambling of this value into prices and quantities is quite arbitrary. Finally, it is necessary to note that whereas 'Agriculture' is overwhelmingly privately controlled, 'Manufacturing' and 'Economic' services are mixed, and 'Infrastructure' is predominantly in the public sector and likely to remain so even in the wake of economic reforms for some more years to come. The last one, 'Public Administration and Defence' is entirely constituted of government activities. As mentioned earlier, the public sector should preferably not be combined with private sector activities but data availability poses problems in this context.

Further, it may be postulated that unlike other sectors 'Manufacturing' may be either demand-constrained or resource-constrained in the sense that demand may either exceed or fall short of the capacity output. Clearly, the actual output *ex-post* must be equal to the smaller of the two. Thus, the level of activity in this sector and the rest of the economy might switch between two regimes, generating a pattern of cyclical growth. An approach which allows for this would be better than those from the methodologies of "only aggregate demand" or "only aggregate supply". Capacity output needs to be constrained by the stock of capital, raw material supply, and availability of infrastructural facilities.

4. Forecasting and Policy Use of Models

Despite the early start that macro modelling has had for India, we have not gone as far as many other LDCs have in developing, maintaining and using such models for planning, policy analysis and forecasting. In the past the attitude of planners and policymakers as well as of the academic profession at large, has generally been one of scepticism and at best, lukewarm. A few points need to be highlighted in this context.

First, a large segment of policy formulation and evaluation in India, as in other LDCs, is concerned with institutional and structural changes which are rather difficult to deal with in terms of econometric models. *Second*, planning concerns have largely been with long run rather than with short run problems. The long run policy has predominantly taken the form of inter-temporal and inter-sectoral allocation of investment and has been handled in the framework of input-output models. The behavioural segment of the complete model has usually been taken care of by means of simple and isolated relationships. However, this situation has changed in recent years. *Third*, as mentioned earlier, early generation models, which were available till the eighties, were largely exploratory.

They brought out important features of the functioning and inter-linkages between different segments of the economy. But they were not well suited nor intended to be used for practical policy analysis or forecasting. The models that emerged in late-eighties and early-nineties were serious and large scale attempts meant for policy analysis and forecasting. However, they were only used for policy analysis through 'what if' simulations but the modellers generally shied away from using them for forecasting. This may be because there was no serious dialogue among the model builders themselves and between them and others in the profession on the one hand. And on the other, there was also no interaction with planners and policymakers to instil the required confidence. The situation has, however, changed in the nineties with the ushering of new economic regimes. Policymakers have begun to show serious interest by interacting, promoting and collaborating in macroeconometric model building activity with a view to use them as an aid in planning, policy making and forecasting. Thus, the Fifth Generation models have come to assume importance in planning and forecasting and to a limited extent in policy making. Quantification helps in calibrating policy responses. A lot more needs to be achieved before the models could be used with some confidence in policymaking.

The macro modellers can now say with some confidence that to a variety of questions, econometric models can provide answers which are not only plausible and internally consistent but also much better than what the other available techniques can offer. They may relate to planning, policy formulation, policy evaluation or merely to a description of the structure of the economy. For instance, a number of questions relating to the dynamics of price behaviour, consequences of the alternative patterns of public finance on savings and capital formation, choice of an appropriate exchange rate policy and, intersectoral linkages and trade-offs can be handled better with the help of econometric models. However, one needs to note that the macro models are ill-equipped to provide answers to micro issues that policymakers often pose.

We have referred to planning and policy analysis based on econometric models. First, IEG-DSE/CDE-DSE and IEG models were used to make *ex ante* macro-projections for recent Five Year Plans. In the very early years of macro modelling, Krishnamurty and Marwah made *ex ante* projections for the Third Five Year Plan period. Desai in his survey notes that the estimates were in the same ball-park as the realisation compared to Plan projections, which were way away. Another important point to note is that the recent models are regularly used for forecasting and outcomes analysed expost.

The implications of various policies - direction of effects and trade-offs - revealed in different studies are broadly in the same ball-park but differ in some specific details. The broad conclusions that emerged from 'what if' policy simulations on recent models are:

(1) Monetary expansion is an important factor in influencing inflation apart from increases in the costs of critical imports and other domestic inputs; administered prices have a role in inflation management. Relative prices play an important role in the functioning of the economy as several activities are sensitive to price structure.

(2) Monetary expansion is catalysed, given monetary policy stance, largely by Reserve Bank net credit to government and accretion to foreign exchange reserves; in recent years there has been a switch in their relative roles.

(3) Increase in public investment though crowds out private investment in some sectors and for some years, investment particularly in agriculture and infrastructure crowds in private investment. Increase in public investment favours output growth and tones up activity all around leaving aside efficiency aspect. Higher efficiency in public sector infrastructure in particular and in general, other sectors provides a strong push to over all growth.

(4) Increase in fiscal deficit tends to widen balance of payments gap although the extent critically depends how deficit is financed *viz.*, borrowing and deficit financing.

(5) There are trade-offs between growth and inflation on the one hand and, growth and balance of payments on the other.

(6) Liberal monetary policy may not be necessarily desirable. This is due to the fact that higher growth of money supply tends to raises inflation rate. This in turn erodes the real value of public investment, which is set in nominal terms in government budgets. Consequently, any increase in private investment due to easy monetary policy- lower interest rates and larger flow of credit, is out-stepped by reduction in real public investment. The net outcome of complimentarity and crowding out effects of slow down in real public investment tends to over shadow any favourable effects of easy monetary policy on real private fixed investment. Monetary policy combined with fiscal policy is more effective in promoting

growth with moderate inflation. Further, trade policy needs to be supplemented by monetary policy and monetary policy by fiscal policy if benefits in one direction are not at the cost of those in the other direction. Also, downsizing fiscal deficit through public investment has often been a soft instrument. Public investment has, as noted earlier, externalities, which can be repeated by private investment, particularly public investment in infrastructure. Discretionary fiscal stablisers say government current expenditures tends to providė only temporary stimulus to growth. This again emphasis the need for compositional shifts in fiscal expenditures in favour of public infrastructural investment while trying to achieve fiscal consolidation to achieve growth with stability,

(7) Regarding external sector, general tendencies noted are: (a) accelerated growth of the economy is not sustainable unless accompanied by policies to promote larger export earnings, (b) exchange rate depreciation by itself do not considerably change export earnings in dollars - though it promotes an expansion of volume of exports as well as export earnings in rupees, (c) exchange rate adjustments are quite effective in dealing with imports in term of volume, as well as value (in rupees and in dollars). Hence, exchange rate instrument is quite effective if the objective is a reduction in trade imbalance as such and finally, results indicate that reduced import duties and export subsidies are not likely to play havoc with trade deficit if a proper exchange rate adjustment is used. It may be noted that exchange rate depreciation has pass-through effects implying higher domestic prices and this tends to raise export prices.

The above consensus is inspite of the fact that size, structural details and time period of models differ and the studies from which above tendencies are drawn are from both academic and policy-making arena. Substantive progress has been achieved in using models for planning and policy analysis. Yet, there is a long way to go before they could be used in actual policymaking.

5. Future Agenda: Some Suggestions

We can now venture to make some suggestions for future work. We have made considerable progress in recent years yet much more needs to be accomplished to move forward and gain sufficient creditability for macro-modelling. Models have to be made more relevant to the context and times to make them useful in planning, policymaking and forecasting.

Foremost task on the agenda is to search for structural changes in the nineties that may have taken place due to the effect of macroeconomic and structural adjustment policies. Considerable work seems to be currently underway. *Second,* to extract segments of best track record of each of the recent models, comparative evaluation of them needs to be attempted. *Third,* macroeconometric modelling has been 'learning by doing'. We in India have over the years moved from small sized textbook type models to large models. This has helped to capture to some extent complexities of the economy. However, there are diseconomies associated with large size models though modern computing power permits such a venture. Larger the size, the more difficult it is to build comparable and reliable data base for various segments of the economy and to unearth the complexities of the inter linkages. Modern computing power is too fast to comprehend and coherently interpret quickly the result of policy simulations and forecasts. Large models require assumptions on a large number and variety of exogenous variables. To make appropriate and consistent assumptions in forward mode is difficult and time consuming. When forecasts have to be made available quickly atleast on major economic indicators, large models need more time and effort to operate and understand.

At this stage it must be admitted that we are not making a case against large models but only pointing to the need to have moderate sized main frame model with several satellite sub-models for each of the important sectors. This helps to build macromodels with sufficient details to map complex structure of the economy, to enable in-depth understanding of its functioning and to track economy-wide responses to various policy induced or exogenous shocks. Even with moderate sized IEG-DSE/CDE-DSE model with about 450 equations, but large by our standards, it has not been possible to cover within its fold many important elements of the agenda outlined earlier. Specific issues have been dealt in one or the other model in some depth, but they need to be pulled under one umbrella.

Therefore, we advocate fairly large but not too large a main frame model with several sectoral models, which can be operational in 'stand alone' mode and/or within the fold of main frame model. This helps to answer some specific sectoral issues in more detail than the main frame model in its stand 'alone mode'.

At the present time, one would suggest construction of sub-models for the following sectors, to name a few, they are:

a) agriculture to bring out changing cropping pattern and difference in price determination,

b) sub-model for manufacturing to distinguish differential behaviour of important segments with in it say capital, intermediate and, consumer durable and non-durable goods, and, also between private and public sectors within each category; similarly between registered and unregistered sectors.

c) detailed treatment of infrastructure to enable identification of impacts arising from deregulation and privatisation which are currently underway,

d) separate module for service sector to account for heterogeneity and to accord separate treatment for fast growing segments say, as for instance, software industry,

e) on the demand side, a sub-model to enable disaggregation with emphasis on the income/wealth distributions to capture the effect of inequalities. This would help to identify overall and sectoral excess/deficient demand in the system,

f) sub-model for foreign trade, BoP and exchange rate to enable more disaggregation on the goods side of trade with destination-wise focus than has been accomplished so far; to accord more incisive treatment to invisibles particularly software exports which have grown in importance and to permit specific treatment in BoP to private capital flows - direct and portfolio; to allow for more exhaustive analysis of exchange rate determination particularly, the role of private foreign inflows, foreign exchange reserves and RBI intervention in market,

g) detailed sub-models for fiscal, financial and monetary sectors; analysis of capital markets in the financial sector, and the role of the operations of the Reserve Bank of India in influencing interest rates and flows in money-capital markets.

h) sub-models to understand in-depth investment, savings and financing patterns; flow of funds at some stage needs to be integrated in the modelling exercise. Data is not a constraint. RBI has been regularly releasing annual data over the past several years.

The shopping list is large. Scanning the literature, one finds that a lot of very interesting research work has gone-on on several aspects mentioned here and such work is growing. There is a need for an intensive interaction among model builders, specialists, planners and policymakers to sort out issues, priorities, data availability- reliability-susitability, and work out contours of main frame and sub-sectors models. Such an interaction should lead to coordinated and collective effort to bring out well articulated comprehensive model for India.

Fourth, it is time to utilise high frequency data that is now available for many important economic indicators. Most important, NAS data on quarterly basis for the recent years is there now to draw upon. Atleast a modest attempt to construct a quarterly model should be made. This will supplement annual models and will go long way in improving forecasts.

Fifth, considerable and commendable research work is now happening in India in utilising modern time series techniques. Attempt should be made to strengthen and enrich macromodels with latest methodologies and techniques.

6. Concluding Observations

It has been a long and stressful march over many years. Thanks to the efforts of many researchers, macromodeling has come of age in India. The march has to continue. The goal is a shifting one. Data bases gets revised, policy regimes change, new problems emerge and there are many advances in economic and econometric methodologies. The model builders must keep pace with these changes and advances.

At the present stage, attempts to construct new models with several satellite sub-models for important, fast changing and growing sectors to capture structural change is needed. An all rounded effort of this type calls for a co-operative and well coordinated collective effort of several researches and, intensive interaction with and active co-operation of policy-making agencies to make models relevant and useful in practice. The old guard is fading out; it is for the new to take on and push forward the frontiers in this area of empirical research.[4]

---

4. See a very interesting recent study *A Disequlibrium Macroeconometric Model for the Indian Economy* by K. Kalirajan and S. Bhide, Ashgate, Aldershot (UK) 2003. A novelty of the study is specific introduction of regional dimension with regard to agriculture in a disequlibrium macroeconometric model framework.

14

Growth and Macroeconomic Imbalances in India

B.B. BHATTACHARYA
SABYASACHI KAR

1. Introduction

The recent growth performance of the Indian economy has given rise to a lot of hope and excitement. After three decades of sluggish growth of about 3.5 per cent per annum in the post-independence period, the Indian economy attained an impressive growth of 5.6 per cent in the next two decades. Furthermore, during the mid-nineties, the economy grew by more than 7 per cent per annum. This has given rise to a vision of attaining even higher growth rates and joining the club of 'Asian Tigers'. Perhaps the strongest manifestation of this vision lies in the Planning Commission's ambitious growth target of 8 per cent for the Tenth Five Year Plan period. According to the Planning Commission, the target is feasible provided the domestic investment rate could be raised to 32.6 per cent and the incremental capital output ratio (ICOR) is brought down to 4.08. These, as the Planning Commission admits, cannot be achieved with a 'business as usual' approach. A number of reforms, especially at the micro level, would have to be implemented quickly to improve the productivity of investment and reduce the ICOR. The attainment of 32.6 per cent investment rate in turn would require rise in domestic savings rate to 29.8 per cent and the gap would have to be filled up by a fairly high foreign saving or current account deficit rate of 2.8 per cent, see Table 14.1.

In order to achieve this ambitious domestic saving rate, the plan targets public sector saving rate at 4.6 per cent of GDP, against virtually nil at the beginning of the plan period, private corporate saving rate at 5.8 per cent of GDP and household saving rate at 19.4 per cent of GDP. To attain the public saving target, the plan expects the consolidated fiscal deficit of the Centre and the States to decline to 3.3 per cent of GDP from about 10 per cent at the beginning of the plan period. This would require a drastic cut in government revenue expenditure and rise in tax and non-tax current revenues. In the absence of either of them the plan public investment target can be fulfilled only through higher fiscal deficit, in which case there would be a trade-off between growth and fiscal balance. Similarly trade-off may also occur between growth and external balance or current account deficit. Foreign savings augment domestic investment at the expense of higher current account deficit. Two questions emerge in this context: first, is it possible to attain the plan growth target of 8 per cent over the Tenth Plan period, and secondly, if the growth is accelerated through excessive fiscal and external deficits then can it be sustained in the long run. The first issue is evaluated in Bhattacharya & Kar (2004b). This paper addresses the second issue.

Table 14.1

Tenth Plan Targets

Variables	*Target Rates*
GDP Growth Rate (%)	8.00
Gross Investment Rate (% of GDP)	32.60
ICOR	*4.08*
Gross Domestic Saving (% of GDP)	
Public Sector	4.60
Private Corporate Sector	5.80
Household Sector	19.40
Total	29.80
Current Account Deficit (% of GDP)	2.80
Consolidated Fiscal Deficit (% of GDP)	3.30
Consolidated Revenue Deficit (% of GDP)	0.80

The objective of this paper is to examine the nature of the relationship between economic growth and fiscal and external balances in the Indian economy through a macroeconometric model. The model provides a framework for forecasting the growth rate of the economy during the Tenth Plan period under normal (business as usual approach), optimistic and pessimistic assumptions. Although the model explains behaviour of all important macro variables, the focus of attention in this paper is on growth and its relationships with the fiscal and the external balances. The paper is divided into five sections. We begin with an analysis of the causes of trade-offs between growth and the fiscal and external balances in a developing economy followed by a review of literature on this issue in the context of the Indian economy. Next, we discuss the behaviour of growth and the fiscal and the external balances in India during the last three decades. This is followed by an analysis of trade-off between growth and fiscal and current account deficits based on forecasts from a macro model. The forecasts are made on the basis of a macro-econometric model of the Indian economy to analyse the structural changes in the pre- and post-reform periods. The model properties and results are discussed in Bhattacharya and Kar (2002a, 2000b and 2004a).

2. Linkages Between Growth and Fiscal and External Balances

There is a large body of literature on trade-off in macroeconomics. The well-known Phillips Curve shows a trade-off between growth and inflation. The monetarists, while denying the long run Phillips Curve, accept the possibility of short run trade-off between growth and inflation, even under the assumption of rational expectations. In developing countries, Phillips Curve type relationship may not be significant, except probably in the organised manufacturing sector, see Bhattacharya (1984). Instead, in the developing countries trade-off may occur due to structural imbalances in the growth process, particularly when the economy tries to accelerate the overall economic growth. See Taylor (1983) for an analytical discussion on trade-off in developing countries in general and Bhattacharya (1984) for an evaluation of the same in the pre-reform Indian economy.

There are various reasons for which trade-off may occur between growth and fiscal and external balances in a developing economy. First, take the trade-off between growth and fiscal deficit. After the advent of the Keynesian theory, it is now well known that economic growth in general and that of the industry and services in particular are sometimes constrained by the lack of aggregate demand. In such a situation, the government often stimulates aggregate demand by an expansionary fiscal policy resulting in higher growth with higher fiscal deficit. The trade-off may be contained partially by the automatic stabilisation through taxation. But in most developing countries with inelastic tax base, the taxes fail to keep pace with public expenditure resulting in higher growth with greater fiscal deficit. The trade-off may also occur through the supply side. In developing economies, the investment is the single most important factor determining growth. Since private investment is induced by growth of income and other endogenous factors such as the real interest rate, the governments in the developing countries generally try to boost growth through public investment financed by borrowings. In the process growth may accelerate at the cost of fiscal deficit. This has occurred in India during the 1980s, resulting in higher growth and fiscal deficit (Table 14.2). There are numerous other cases where such a trade-off can occur. For example, a higher subsidy on fertiliser can lead to higher agricultural and aggregate growth but at the expense of higher public expenditure and fiscal deficit. Similarly, a rise in salaries and wages of government employees would increase GDP from public administration and aggregate GDP along with higher public expenditure and fiscal deficit. This has happened in India during the 1980s and 1990s (Table 14.2).

Table 14.2

Average Growth of GDP and Fiscal Variables in India

	Seventies (1970-79)	*Eighties (1980-89)*	*Nineties (1990-99)*
GDP Growth Rate (%)	3.39	5.40	6.19
Agricultural Growth Rate (%)	1.74	2.95	3.23
Industrial Growth Rate (%)	4.55	6.67	6.41
Services Growth Rate (%)	4.62	6.77	8.28
Growth Rate (%) of GDP from Public Administration	4.92	7.37	6.23
Fiscal Deficit/GDP Ratio (%)	4.69	8.18	7.71
Public Investment/GDP Ratio (%)	8.19	9.99	7.85
Public Expenditure/GDP Ratio (%)	25.04	31.89	29.72
Salaries & Wages of Public Sector/ GDP Ratio (%)	5.43	6.19	6.77

We may now consider the trade-off between growth and the external deficit as measured by the current account balance. In many developing countries import propensities are usually higher than export propensities and hence, when growth accelerates the trade deficit widens. The import propensity may be higher than the export propensity due to several reasons. First, domestic cost of production may be higher than the import cost. Secondly, as domestic income rises, the propensity to consume imported luxury goods may also rise. Thirdly, growth itself necessitates imports of capital goods like machinery and intermediate products that cannot be produced domestically at competitive costs till the economy reaches a certain stage of development in technology and international competitiveness. Under the fixed exchange rate regime there is no mechanism to automatic correction of the import-export gap. In a market determined exchange rate regime, an excess of imports over exports tends to depreciate the exchange rate, which in turn promotes exports and reduces imports. However, due to structural rigidities and also because of other factors influencing the foreign trade and the exchange rate, the trade gap may not be filled up completely. Thus even in a market determined exchange rate regime, the current account deficit may widen with higher GDP growth.

Apart from trade balance, the current account balance is affected by the factor services. Growth induces foreign capital. If investment financed by foreign capital leads to production of outputs that are consumed more in the domestic market than abroad, then servicing of foreign capital in terms of interest payments and dividends would adversely affect the current account balance. The resultant outcome would be higher growth with worse current account balance. Much would depend on the nature of goods and services produced by foreign funded investments. If such goods and services were exported then the trade-off would be limited.

Let us now compare and contrast the sectoral specifications of some of the macro models of the Indian economy, focusing on the linkage between production sector on the one hand, and the fiscal and the external sectors on the other. A survey of the existing macro models indicates that while there is a consensus on certain aspects of the economy, there are other areas that are less than fully understood. A number of models have focused on the role of fiscal sector. These studies have a detailed model of government receipt and expenditure with most items endogenously determined. In this context, the phenomenon of crowding-in-associated with public investment in India has attracted attention of quite a few model builders. This phenomenon has an important implication on the trade-offs between growth and inflation. Bhattacharya (1984) is one of the early studies that analysed the public sector behaviour at a highly disaggregated level. The focus of the analysis is on the interrelationship between public expenditure, resource mobilisation, inflation and growth. The overall behaviour of the public sector is analysed through a single budget constraint identity, linking public sector expenditure to public sector revenue. This study showed that many conclusions of the Keynesian theory are altered once a budget constraint is introduced in the analysis. Many studies followed thereafter focusing on the public investment and its relationship with the private sector investment and fiscal operations. Krishnamurty, Pandit and Sharma (1988) analysed the public sector investment and its interrelationships with private and relative prices. Madhur (1987) examined the macro impacts of monetary the fiscal policy changes. Rangarajan, Basu and Jadhav (1989) dealt with dynamic interaction of government deficits and domestic debt. Pradhan, Ratha and Sharma (1990) presented an analysis of inter-linkages between public and private investment and its implications for income distribution through input-output based model. Mammen (1999) investigated inter-linkages between the foreign and the government sector. Many researchers have focused on the links between central government budget and its monetised deficit. Bhattacharya and Guha (1992) analysed the interrelationships between public debt, growth and inflations. In another model on stabilisation, Bhattacharya, Barman and Nag (1994) have given an extensive treatment to the linkages between the public sector revenue and expenditures on the one hand, and the real output, prices and foreign exchange on the other. While focusing on the stabilisation programme, the study explicitly included all relevant stabilisation policy instruments in the fiscal and monetary sector and the linkages of these with rest of the economy were analysed extensively.

Though foreign trade is an integral part of the national economy, the treatment given to this sector has been limited. However, there had been some models with focus on the external sector. For instance, Kannan (1985) provides an analysis of foreign trade; Pandit (1986) focused on the external trade and price formation; Marwah (1987) modelled the exchange rate; Ghose, Lahiri and Wadhwa (1986) related quantitative restrictions and imports; Virmani (1991) analysed the role of supply and demand factors in influencing foreign trade. Besides, most general econometric models have estimated import and export functions. In general, exports are determined by the world GDP, domestic prices relative to the world prices and exchange rates, while imports are influenced by the exchange rates, relative prices and the GDP of the country. Different models have adopted different levels of aggregation while specifying export and import equations. While some models have one single equation for exports and imports each, others have more disaggregated specifications for exports and imports. For instance, Bhattacharya (1984) has analysed imports of capital goods and that of raw materials and other commodities separately while Pandit (1986) has a more detailed specification of exports and imports. Krishnamurty and Pandit (1995) employed a small open economy assumption to specify an infinitely elastic import supply function at fixed import price in international currency. Exchange rate then determines the price in local currency. The demand for imports is determined by the domestic level of economic activity (GDP and capital formation). For exports there is a downward sloping demand curve and an upward sloping supply curve. While demand demands on world GDP and relative prices, supply is affected by both relative prices in international currency and domestic level of output. Bhattacharya, Barman and Nag (1994) also gave a detailed treatment to the foreign sector, with imports of goods being disaggregated into the import of food, capital goods and the residual. Import of food is assumed to be exogenous while the import of capital goods is a function of the level of economic activity, price and foreign aid. Residual imports, which are mostly intermediate materials, depend on manufacturing output, the unit value index of intermediate materials imports and on non-food foreign and export earnings.

3. Trends in Fiscal and External Deficits in India

The long run trends in GDP growth rate and the consolidated fiscal deficit of the Centre and States and the current account deficit as per cent of GDP are shown in Figure 14.1, and their decadal averages are shown in Tables 14.1 and 14.2. It may be noted that as such there are no direct relationships between growth rate and fiscal and current account deficit rates. However, a closer examination would reveal that when the twin deficits reached their peaks during the late-1980s, the growth rate of GDP slumped in the next couple of years. After the reform both fiscal deficit and current account deficit rates declined initially till about the mid-1990s. But while the current account balance continued to improve thereafter and became even positive during the early-2000s, the fiscal deficit situation worsened from the late-1990s. In fact the fiscal deficit rate now is as high as it was during the pre-crisis years. The GDP growth rate has also slowed down, *albeit* marginally, during the last few years. But there is no clear evidence that it is due to the rise in fiscal deficit, because during the same period the domestic saving-investment rate has also declined.

Figure 14.1

GDP Growth Rate, Current Deficit and Fiscal Deficit as per cent of GDP (1970-2002)

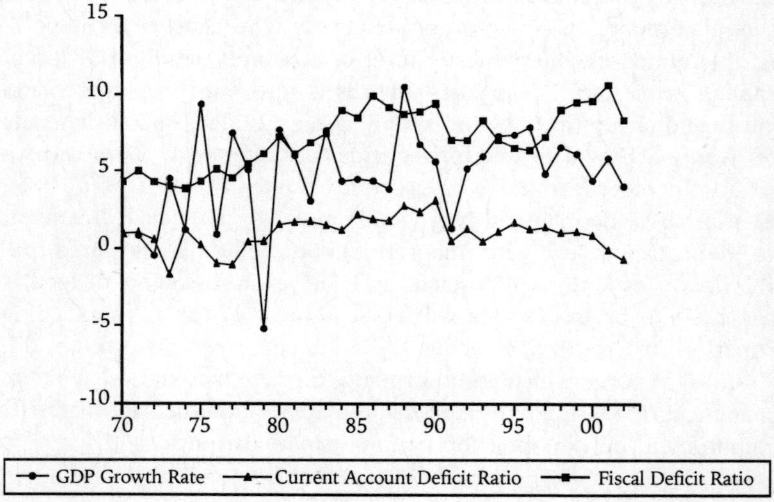

Let us now look at the components of fiscal deficits and their trends over the same period. The pattern of government income and expenditure has changed significantly during the last three decades. Both government revenues and total expenditures (as percentage to GDP) exhibited increasing trends till the mid-eighties, after which they kept falling for the next ten years or so, and have again shown an upward trend after the mid-nineties (Figure 14.2). Another notable aspect is that till the mid-eighties, the revenue income and expenditure approximately moved together and this resulted in very low (and sometimes negative) values of the revenue deficit. After the mid-eighties, however, the expenditure has been significantly higher than the income, leading to high and increasing revenue deficits during this period. The revenue deficit and its determinants are presented in Figure 14.3. Another aspect of the fiscal scenario that has

Figure 14.2

Fiscal Deficit and its Determinants as a Percentage to GDP (1970-2002)

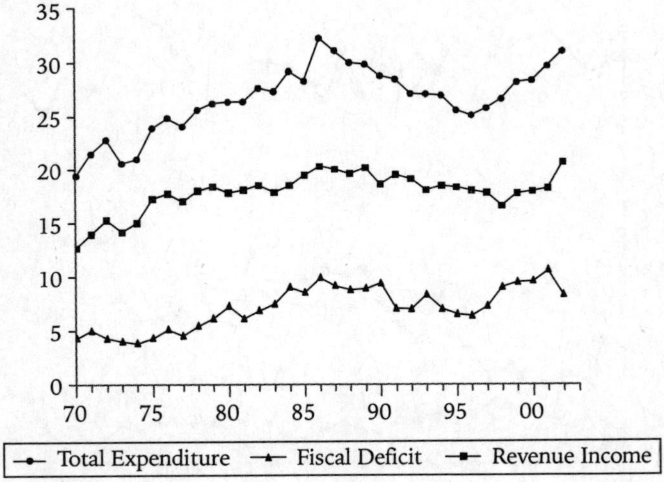

Figure 14.3

Revenue Deficit and its Determinants as a Percentage to GDP (1970-2002)

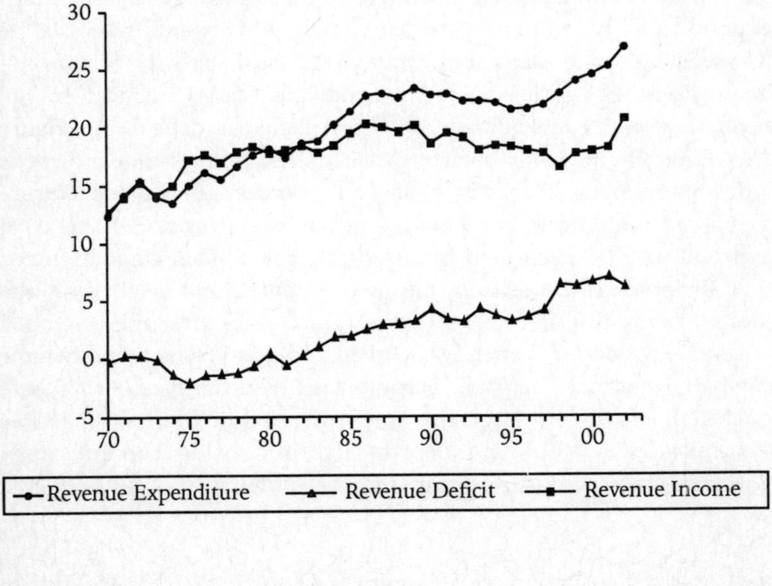

Figure 14.4

Financing of Total Expenditure Tax Revenue, Non-Tax Revenue and Fiscal Deficit as a Ratio to Total Expenditure (1970-2002)

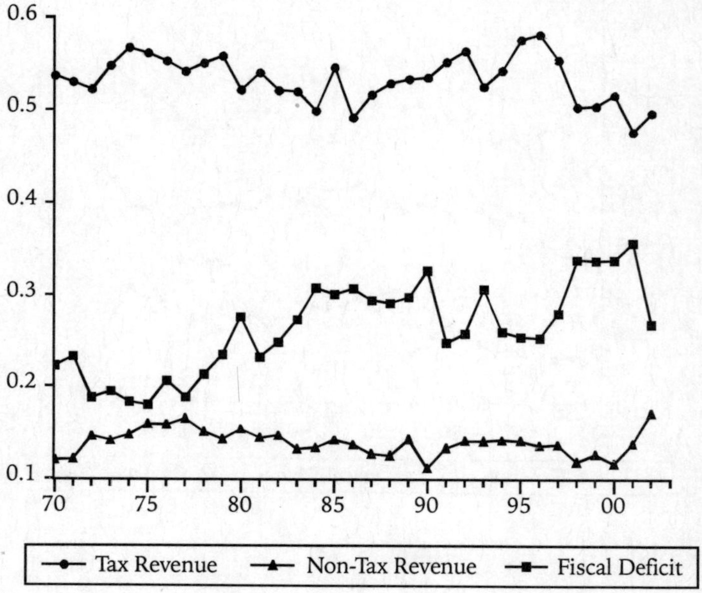

exhibited changing patterns is the mode of financing the total expenditure. At an aggregate level, the total expenditure can be financed by either current revenues (tax and non-tax) or through borrowings. The share of total expenditure that is financed by tax revenue, non-tax revenue and the fiscal deficit is depicted in Figure 14.4. This figure clearly depicts that from the mid-seventies, there is a downward trend in the tax financed proportion of total expenditure and a corresponding upward trend in the proportion of total expenditure that is covered by the fiscal deficit. This amounted to a debt financed growth strategy during the eighties and resulted in high levels of debt-to-GDP ratios. In the initial years after the economic reform, expenditure growth was curbed while the tax revenue became comparatively more buoyant. During this phase the fiscal deficit rate declined. However, after the implementation of the Fifth Pay Commission in 1997, and also the rise in subsidy, the growth of government expenditure began to exceed that of tax and non-tax current revenues. The latter as a ratio to GDP actually fell in the late-1990s and the early-2000s mainly due to a cut in both direct and indirect tax rates. This led to a sharp rise in fiscal deficit rate. The deterioration would have been much worse but for the sharp fall in capital expenditure since the mid-1990s (Figure 14.5).

Figure 14.5

Structural Composition of Total Expenditure Revenue and Capital Expenditure as a Ratio to Expenditure (1970-2002)

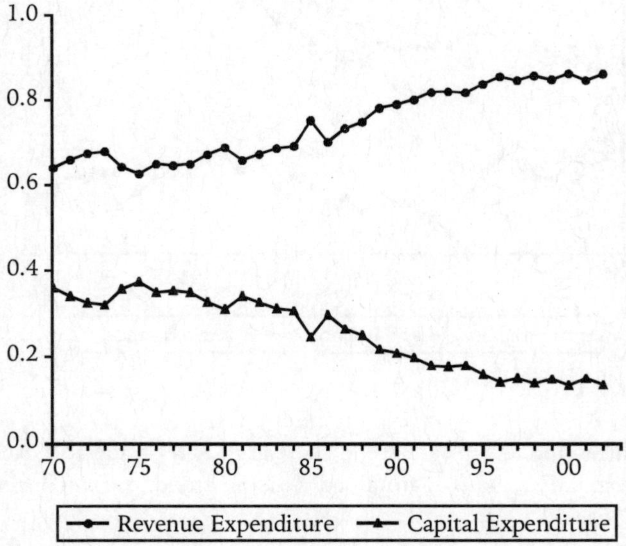

The external balance also changed in the last three decades. Both exports and imports, as ratios to GDP, have grown secularly during these three decades: the former has grown from 3.3 per cent in 1970 to 10 per cent in 2000, and the latter has risen from 3.6 per cent to 11.3 per cent over the same period (Figure 14.6). The exports – GDP ratio exhibited an increasing trend till 1976 and then fell for the next nine years. It started rising again from 1985 onwards, stagnating a little during the Asian Crisis in 1997 and 1998 and recovered sharply thereafter. The imports – GDP ratio also increased very sharply throughout the seventies, particularly after the successive oil shocks in 1974, 1979 and 1990-91. After 1980, both exports and imports—GDP ratios depicted quite similar trends: a downward trend till the

Figure 14.6

Trade Balance and its Determinants as a Percentage to GDP (1970-2002)

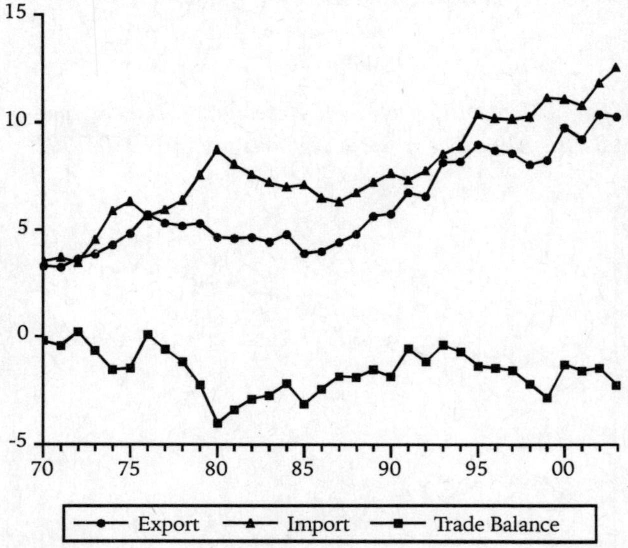

mid-eighties and an upward trend thereafter. After trade and exchange rate deregulation, both maintained a rising trend, except during the Asian Crisis.

Merchandise trade and invisibles determine the Current Account Balance (CAB). In most of the years the net invisibles was positive, and rose sharply in the nineties, thereby restraining the current account deficit (Figure 14.7). Two factors have contributed significantly in this respect: the remittances from abroad and receipts from software services. But for these two factors the current account deficit would have been probably unsustainable even after the economic reform.

4. Analysis Through a Macromodel

To analyse the relationships between GDP growth and the fiscal and the external deficits we have relied on a macro model for the Indian economy depicting the relationships between production, consumption, saving, investment, prices, money, interest, foreign trade

Figure 14.7

Current Account Balance and its Determinants as a Percentage to GDP (1970-2003)

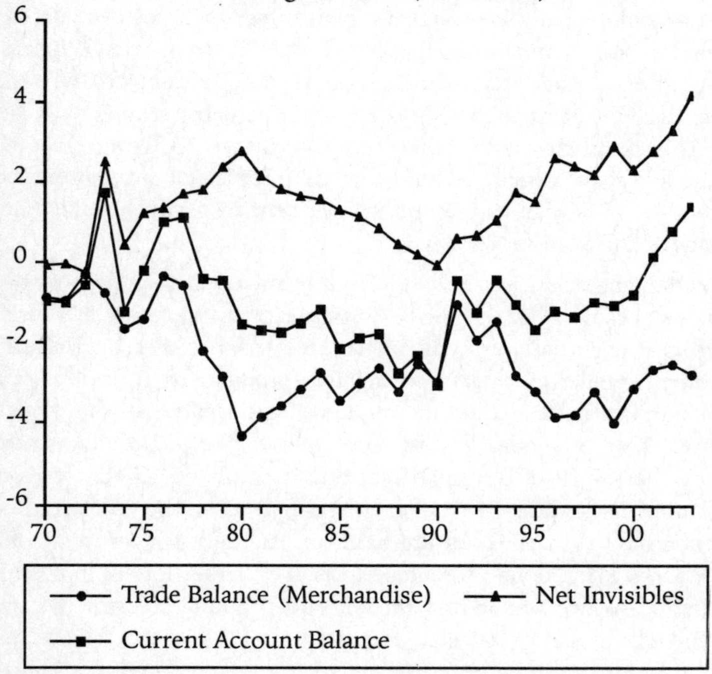

and capital flows and government revenues and expenditures. The theoretical properties of the model and empirical results of structural equations are discussed in details in Bhattacharya and Kar (2002a and 2002b respectively). The model was validated and it was observed that the model predicted quite accurately not only growth rates but also turning points of key variables. Further, it has incorporated fairly successfully macroeconomic impacts of structural changes initiated by on-going economic reforms. In this paper, we shall focus on the tradeoffs between medium run growth and the fiscal and external balances, based on simulations for the base run, optimistic and pessimistic scenarios for the Tenth Plan period. The detailed assumptions about the base run, optimistic and pessimistic scenarios are provided in Bhattacharya and Kar (2004b). In this paper we shall analyse the explicit trade-offs derived from the simulation results from the model.

The base run scenario simulates the economy under the assumption that apart from the normal ongoing changes there would be no major structural change in the economy. The forecast results indicate that the average growth rate of GDP for the Tenth Plan period would be only 6.1 per cent, against plan target of 8 per cent. In the external sector, imports are expected to rise along with exports, leading to an average trade deficit ratio at –1.6 per cent of GDP. The current account balance as a ratio to GDP fluctuates around –0.8 per cent. This is much smaller than the plan target. However, average revenue and fiscal deficits as a ratio to GDP for the Tenth Plan period turn out to be as high as 6.3 and 9.4 per cent respectively, which are well above the plan targets.

Since the base run growth rate is well below the plan target we have simulated the model with four optimistic growth scenarios. It is well known that eventually growth can be accelerated either by a rise in investment rate or by an improvement in productivity of capital or a combination of both. Private investment is endogenous in the model. However there is a great deal of scope to increase public investment through better resource mobilisation. It is observed that public investment as a ratio to GDP has declined after the initiation of economic reform in 1991. In the base run the public investment rate for the Tenth Plan period is assumed to be the average rate of the Ninth Plan period, which implied no further fall in public investment rate. Since it did not yield planners' warranted rate of growth of GDP and aggregate investment rate, the optimistic simulations assume higher public investment rates. In the first optimistic simulation (O1), it is assumed that public investment would be exogenously increased by two per cent of GDP. It is assumed that the sectoral shares of public investment would remain same as before: 20 per cent in agriculture, 50 per cent in industry and 30 per cent in services. The second simulation (O2) assumes an increase in public investment by 4 per cent of GDP with no change in sectoral distribution. These two simulations yield GDP growth rate of 6.8 per cent and 7.4 per cent respectively, still short of plan target of 8 per cent. Since any further rise in public investment may not be feasible under current economic regime, we then simulate with better productivity of capital. The next two simulations measure the combined impact of rise in public investment with improvement in productivity of capital. In the third simulation (O3) and the fourth simulation (O4), the increase in public investment remains the same as in O2, but the output elasticity of capital is raised by 5 per cent and

10 per cent respectively. These simulations yield GDP growth rates of 7.7 and 8.1 per cent respectively. This suggests that the Planning Commission growth target can be attained only with a substantial hike in public investment rate and with a big improvement in productivity of capital (results from O4).

Corresponding to the simulations O1 through O4 the trade deficit (as a ratio to GDP) turns out to be 1.9 per cent, 2.2 per cent, 2.3 per cent and 2.3 per cent respectively. Net invisibles turn out to be positive in all these simulations, and consequently the current account deficit (as a ratio to GDP) turns out to be lower than the trade deficit at 1.1, 1.5, 1.5 and 1.6 per cent respectively. It is assumed that there would no exogenous rise in capital inflows in these simulations. But even without higher capital flows, there appears to be a trade-off between higher growth and trade and current account deficits. But the forecasts from the model turn out to be much lower than the plan target. One reason for this could be that in our model an initial rise in trade and current account deficits lead to rupee depreciation, which in turn improve trade and current account balances in future. Depreciation also improves net invisibles. Thus our results are less pessimistic with respect to current account deficit.

The trade-off between growth and fiscal deficit can occur due to a rise in either government revenue expenditure (consumption and transfer payments) or public investment. In the former case the output would rise only through aggregate demand multiplier effect. In the latter case output would grow on account of both aggregate demand multiplier effect and aggregate supply effect. It may be conjectured easily that the trade-off would higher in the first case. The aggregate demand multiplier would operate till the excess capacity can be utilised by stimulation of demand. From planning point of view the latter is more relevant. Results show that both revenue and fiscal deficits (as a ratio to GDP) fall when the GDP growth is accelerated through higher public investment. The revenue deficit rate in simulations O1 and O2 drops to 4.6 and 2.4 per cent respectively, and the fiscal deficit rate drops to 8.7 and 7.5 per cent respectively. However in productivity led growth (simulations O3 and O4) there is marginal rise: revenue deficit rate rises to 2.5 and 2.7 per cent respectively, and fiscal deficit rate rises to 7.6 and 7.8 per cent respectively. It appears that there is scope to improve the aggregate growth rate through higher public investment. The results are however conditional to the assumption that incremental public investment does not lower the productivity of overall investment rate in the economy.

Having analysed the trade-off involved in the acceleration of growth we may now analyse the trade-off in the lowering of growth. The last two simulations comprise the pessimistic scenario, where we analyse the effects of shocks that have destabilised the Indian economy in the past. In both the simulations we assume severe drought and oil shock during the Tenth Plan period. The difference in the two scenarios lies in their assumption about public investment. In the first pessimistic scenario (P1), there is an increase in revenue expenditure on account of drought with no other budgetary adjustments. In effect it would measure trade-off between growth and fiscal deficit due to rise in government revenue expenditure, *albeit* with a supply shocks. In the second scenario (P2) we assume that an increase in revenue expenditure on account of drought would cut in government investment. This could be the worst case of trade-off between growth and fiscal deficit, except that the quantum of fiscal deficit as such would not rise.

The results indicate that under very adverse circumstances, the average GDP growth rate may decline to 5.5 per cent if public investment is not affected by shocks, and to 5 per cent if public investment falls due to rise in revenue expenditure. Although the growth rate of GDP shows some resilience in the face of these adverse shocks, there are major repercussions in the external and the fiscal sector. In the external sector, the trade deficit (as a ratio to GDP) rises in P1 and P2 to 2.5, and 2.3 per cent respectively. The corresponding current account deficit (as a ratio to GDP) also rises to 1.9 and 1.7 per cent respectively. Thus, the shocks would result in significant deterioration in balance of trade and balance of payments ratios due to lower growth rates (and hence lower outputs). In the fiscal sector, the revenue deficit (as a ratio to GDP) turns out to be 7 per cent in P1 and 7.1 per cent in P2, and the fiscal deficit (as a ratio to GDP) turns out to be 10.1 and 9.9 per cent respectively. Thus while the growth situation remains fairly good the fiscal and external balances deteriorate in these scenarios.

In order to understand the tradeoffs between growth and the fiscal deficit under different plausible circumstances, we have plotted the growth rates for the base run (B), the optimistic simulations (O1, O2, O3 and O4) and the pessimistic simulations (P1 and P2) with the corresponding fiscal deficit ratios in Figure 14.8. It is clear from this figure that the nature and extent of the trade-off depends on the underlying changes taking place in the economy. If the growth rate goes up due to exogenous favourable conditions like, better rainfall and low oil prices (point B compared to P1 and P2), then such increases in growth do not result in higher fiscal deficits (no trade-off). Similarly, increases in the growth rate due to higher public investments (O1 and O2 compared to B) also do not lead to a trade-off. However, productivity led growth (O3 and O4 compared to O2) seem to show some trade-off between growth and fiscal deficits, although the trade-off is relatively mild. However, the trade-off is worse when government revenue expenditure rises.

Figure 14.8

Growth-Fiscal Deficit Tradeoff

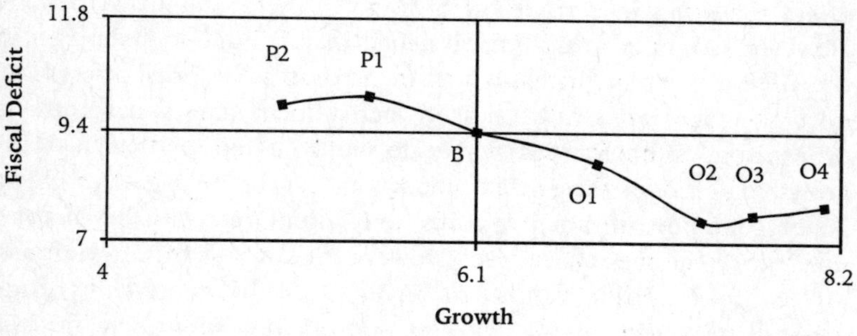

Similarly in Figure 14.9, we represent the trade-off between growth and current account deficit. Here, it is clear that any increase in the growth rate due to an increase in public investments (P1 compared to P2 and O1 and O2 compared to B) lead to a higher current account deficit. However, higher growth rates due to lower supply shocks (B compared to P1) lead to significantly lower current account deficit. On the other hand, productivity led growth (O3 and O4 compared to O2) seem to show negligible impact of growth on the current account deficit.

5. Concluding Remarks

The following inferences may be drawn from this analysis. First, acceleration in aggregate GDP growth can lead to worsening of fiscal deficit depending on how it is financed. Up to a limit, a rise in government expenditure can stimulate both aggregate demand and

Figure 14.9

Growth-Current Account Deficit Tradeoff

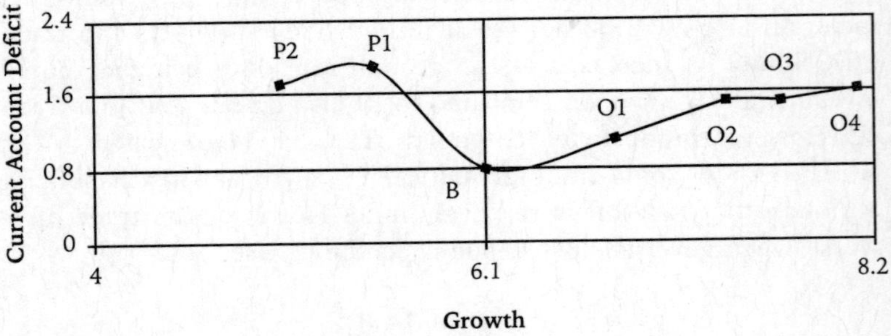

supply, but the demand effect would pre-dominate over the supply effect resulting in a trade-off between growth and fiscal deficit. However as a ratio to GDP fiscal deficit may fall due to faster rise in the GDP at current prices, which incorporates the price effect. But once the capacity is fully utilised then a mere rise in government expenditure cannot increase aggregate supply. It appears that the GDP growth rate under the present conditions can be increased to about 7 per cent per annum if public investment rate can be pushed upwards to the pre-reform level. However this would require vigorous efforts to mobilise funds for investment by curtailing other expenditures and raising tax and non-tax revenues. Any further acceleration in GDP growth would require improvement in productivity of capital.

The current account balance however, is inversely related to GDP growth: a rise in GDP growth stimulates import demand, and given world demand for Indian exports, tends to worsen trade and current balances. However, the current account remains sustainable under normal growth scenario. If however, the international oil prices shoot up dramatically, as it did in some crisis years, and the world trade gets destabilised as a result of both economic and political turmoil, then the current account may become unsustainable, even though growth rate may accelerate. This result would still remain valid even if there were a big influx of capital flows, as witnessed in the second half of 2003. Recent experience elsewhere has shown that a big influx in capital flows can be sustained only if it is accompanied by reasonable current account balance.

References

Bhattacharya, B.B (1975). *Short Term Income Determination*, Macmillan, Delhi

————. (1984). *Public Expenditure, Inflation and Growth—A Macro-Econometric Analysis For India*, Delhi, Oxford University Press.

————. (1987). "The Effectiveness of Monetary Policy in Controlling Inflation: The Indian Experience", 1951-85, *Prajnan*, Vol.XVI (4).

————. (1992). *India's Economic Crises, Debt Burden and Stabilisation*, B.R. Publishing Corporation, Delhi.

Bhattacharya, B.B. and C.H. Hanumantha Rao (1986). *Agriculture-Industry Interrelations: Issues of Relative Growth in the Context of Public Investment*, (mimeo.), Institute of Economic Growth, Delhi.

Bhattacharya, B.B. and S. Guha (1992). "The Behaviour of Public Debt in India: A Macroeconometric Analysis", *Journal of Quantitative Economics*, January.

Bhattacharya, B.B., R.B. Barman and A.K. Nag (1994). "Stabilisation Policy Options: A Macroeconometric Analysis", Development Research Group, Study 8, Department of Economic Analysis and Policy, Reserve Bank of India, Bombay.

Bhattacharya, B.B. and S. Kar (2002a). "A Macro-Econometric Model of the Indian Economy: Some Theoretical Aspects", Discussion Paper, Institute of Economic Growth, Delhi, March.

————. (2002b). "A Macro-Econometric Model of the Indian Economy: Some Empirical Results", Discussion Paper, Institute of Economic Growth, Delhi, March.

————. (2002c). "Short and Medium Run Growth and Stability: A Macro-Econometric Analysis and Forecasts for India", Working Paper, Institute of Economic Growth, Delhi.

————. (2004a). "Nexus Between Growth and Fiscal and External Balances: A Macro-Econometric Evaluation of Post-Reform India", in *Econometric Models: Theory and Applications*, edited by Nachane, Correa, Ananthapadmanabhan and Shanmugam, Allied Publishers, Chennai.

————. (2004b). "Growth and Stability in the Indian Economy in Post-Reform Era: A Macro-Econometric Evaluation", *Journal of Quantitative Economics*, Special Issue in Honour of Prof. Monohar Rao.

Chakravarty, S. (1979). "Keynes, Classics and Developing Economies", in C.H.H. Rao and P.C. Joshi (eds.), *Reflections on Economic Development and Social Change*, Allied Publishers, Delhi.

Desai, M.J. (1973). "Macro Econometric Models for India: A Survey", *Sankhya*, series B, Vol.3, Part 2, pp.169-206.

Ghose, D., Lahiri, A.K. and W. Wadhwa (1986). "Quantitative Restrictions and Indian Exports", *Journal of Development Economics*, Vol. 20.

Kannan, R. (1985). "An Econometric Model of Foreign Trade Sector (1956/57-1979/80)", *Reserve Bank of India Occasional Papers*, Vol.6 (1), June.

Klein, L.R. (1950), *Economic Fluctuations in the United States, 1921-1941*, John Wiley, New York.

————. (1984), *Econometric Models, Planning and Developing Countries: Development Perspectives*, Institute of Economic Growth Silver Jubilee Lecture, B.R. Publishing Co., 1988.

Klein, L. R. and A. S. Goldberger (1955). *An Econometric Model of the United States, 1929-1952*, (Amsterdam: North Holland).

Krishnamurty, K., Pandit, V. and P.D. Sharma (1989). "Parameters of Growth in a Developing Mixed Economy: The Indian Experience", *Journal of Quantitative Economics*, Vol. 5, No.2.

Krishnamurty, K. and V. Pandit (1995). "India's Trade Flows: Alternative Policy Scenarios, 1995-2000", Working Paper, Centre for Development Economics, Delhi School of Economics.

Madhur. S. (1987). "Forecasts and Policy Evaluations Using a Macroeconometric Model for India" (mimeo).

Mammen, T. (1999). *India's Economic Prospects: A Macroeconomic and Econometric Analysis*, World Scientific Publishing, Singapore.

Marwah, K.(1987). "On Managing the Exchange Rate of the Indian Rupee: Modelling Post-Bretton Woods Experience", *Journal of Quantitative Economics*, Vol. 3, No. 1.

Pandit V. (1973). "National Income and the Price Level in India, 1950-51 to 1965-66", *Sankhya*, Ser. B., December.

————. (1984). "Macroeconomic Adjustments in a Developing Economy: A Medium Term Model of Outputs and Prices in India", *Indian Economic Review*, Vol.XIX (1), reprinted in K. Krishnamurty and V. Pandit, *Macroeconometric Modelling of the Indian Economy*, Hindustan Publishing Co., 1985.

————. (1986). "Price Adjustments and India's Trade Performance: A Macroeconomic Analysis", paper presented at meeting of Project Link, Bangkok.

————. (1989). *Macroeconomic Character of the Indian Economy: Theories, Facts and Fancies*, (mimeo.), Delhi School of Economics, September.

Pandit, V. and B.B. Bhattacharya (1987). "Resource Mobilisation, Growth and Inflation: A Trade-Off Analysis for India", *Asia Pacific Economies: Promises and Challenges*, Research in International Business and Management, Vol.6, Part A.

Pani, P.K. (1977). *A Macoreconomic Model of the Indian Economy*, New Delhi, Macmillan.

Pradhan, B.K., D.K. Ratha and A. Sharma (1990). "Complementarity between Public and Private Investment in India", *Journal of Development Economics*, Vol. 33.

Rangarajan, C., A. Basu and N. Jadhav, (1989), "Dynamics of Interaction Between Government Deficit and Domestic Debt in India", *RBI Occasional Papers*, September.

Taylor, L. (1983) *Structuralist Macroeconomics: Applicable Models for the Third World*, Basic Books, New York.

Virmani, A. (1991), "Demand and Supply Factors in India's Trade", *Economic and Political Weekly*, February.

Section V

Population

15

Evolution of Census of India: 1872 – 2001

ASHISH BOSE

1. Importance of Census

India has a proud history of uninterrupted decennial censuses ever since 1881. There were several attempts at census taking in different parts of India and in 1872 a non-synchronous census was conducted all over India. By definition, a census has to be synchronous. India was partitioned in 1947 and the first census after independence was conducted in 1951. This was true of Pakistan also. But subsequently, political events overtook Pakistan, Bangladesh replaced East Pakistan as a new country and decennial censuses got disrupted both in Pakistan and Bangladesh. India continued with decennial censuses right from 1951 to 2001. In 1991, the census enumeration could not take place in Jammu & Kashmir because of disturbances but in 2001, the census enumeration was conducted there. The Census of 2001, the first census in the 21st century is based on a complete enumeration of over one billion people in India.

It is worth recalling at the outset that census data have determined the destiny of the Indian sub-continent in many ways. The partition of India was based on census data on religion. The re-organisation of States on a linguistic basis used census data on languages (mother-tongue). The delimitation of electoral constituencies ever since India held the first general elections in 1952 was based on census data. The constituencies reserved for Scheduled Caste (SC) and Scheduled Tribe (ST) as per the Constitution of India, was also based on census data. India has a proud history of holding regular elections to Parliament and State Assemblies, right from 1952 to 2004. The constituencies are delimited periodically on the basis of census data. The Finance Commission, appointed every five years under the Constitution, recommends allocation of resources between the Centre and States on the basis of population. So does the Planning Commission while preparing five year plans. What is not so well known is the importance of census data in formulating population policy. For example, in 1977 the Population Policy announced by the Emergency Government froze the number of seats in Parliament and State Assemblies as per 1971 census data for the next three decades. This was done to meet the demand from southern States to freeze the seats in Parliament. Otherwise, the representation of these States would have been reduced in Parliament (in terms of number of MPs). This is because of the success of these states in controlling the population growth rate. Otherwise, states, which fail to curb population growth, would be rewarded by giving them more seats in Parliament! In 2000, a National Population Policy was announced by the Government, which extended this freeze by another 25 years, i.e. up to 2026. This was given effect through a subsequent amendment to the Constitution by Parliament.

2. Census Under British Rule

Asok Mitra, the 1961 Census Commissioner who put the Indian Census on the world map by undertaking a very comprehensive census, traces the history of Census as follows:

The British Census series had started in Great Britain in 1801. But the Indian Census, covering a province as a whole, began only in 1851-52, with Madras. The first census was conducted thereafter in the North West Frontier Province, by W.C. Plowden, on 10th January 1865, on "the principle that the population should be determined by an actual house to house enumeration to be made on the same day throughout the province, distinguishing the sexes, the two great creeds, and classifying the people according as they followed agricultural or non-agricultural occupations, the different occupations, and trends of the people, and their various castes." (Mitra 1997)

Mitra makes an interesting observation on the need for census as visualised by the British rulers. He points out:

W.E. Hunter must have been doubly disturbed by the way the East Indian Company was taken unawares by the Sepoy Mutiny of 1857. He published, in 1868, his Comparative Dictionary of the Non-Aryan Languages of India and High Asia and dedicated his publication to Queen Victoria. His preface contains a gem: "The English are now endeavouring to reclaim them. But in order to civilise it is necessary first to understand them." Hunter was appointed Director General of

Statistical Surveys in 1869. In the years that followed, Hunter not only elaborated the statistical system into what came to be known as the Directorate of Commercial Intelligence and Statistics, but also assisted the statistical surveys of districts and provinces that later flowered into the famous Gazetteers. In addition to this, he had much advice to offer in the conducting of the Census of India which undertook exploratory surveys from 1869 to 1872, and thereafter matured into a decennial census which ever since has continued without interruption. (Mitra 1997)

Our research in the history of censuses during the British rule leads us to conclude that the British administrators were fascinated by the diversity of India and the bewildering multiplicity of religions, castes, sub-castes, tribes, languages, dialects and so on. There is convincing evidence in numerous census reports produced by British administrators, many of whom were also good scholars, that the British played up religion, caste and language to divide the people. The British rulers used the census both for satisfying their intellectual curiosity and also for furthering imperialism through their "Divide and Rule" policy which culminated in the partition of India in 1947. In fact, the British also succeeded in giving an excessive slant to caste data to such an extent that Indian sociology often got identified with the sociology of caste. It may however, be argued that India's general elections have reinforced caste and there was a demand for enumerating data on all castes if not only for other backwards castes (OBCs) in 2001 Census. The Government of India did not accept this demand though it was hotly debated in legal, political and academic circles. It may be recalled that Jawaharlal Nehru, the first Prime Minister of India, opted for a secular India and did not want caste data to be collected in the 1951 census except what was required by the Constitution of India, which gave special protection to Scheduled Castes and Schedules Tribes, the most vulnerable sections of India's population.

There is no doubt that the early British rulers in India were fascinated by the phenomenon of castes, sub-castes and tribes in India. The situation was totally new to them and the time and energy they spent in collecting and analysing census data on races, religions, castes, tribes and languages do reflect the intellectual curiosity of the British. However, as empire builders, they were certainly conscious of the use to which these data could be put for tightening the grip over Indian masses. The British fully exploited the divisive tendencies in the country. Perhaps much more than the people of India, the British rulers were more caste-conscious. It is argued that the impact of census enumeration on making people caste-conscious could only be marginal as the real impact was on the enumerators rather than the persons enumerated. This could be so but the fact remains that having collected data on castes, sub-castes, religions, sub-religions, languages, sub-languages, tribes, and so on, the British realised how powerful a tool these data provided for their colonial administration.

Bernard S. Cohn in his paper on "The Census, Social Structure and Objectification in South Asia" says

> The impetus to collect information on caste went way beyond the "intellectual curiosity" of a few officials and was based on widespread and deeply held beliefs about Indians held by the British. Ideas about caste, its origins and functions played much the same role in shaping policy in the latter half of the 19th century as ideas about the village community and the nature of property in the first half of the 19th century. Attempts were made in the first census of 1871-72 to collect information on caste. (Cohn 1970)

Cohn elaborates further:

> It was felt by many British officials in the middle of the 19th century that caste and religion were the sociological keys to understanding the Indian people. If they were to be governed well, then it was natural that information should be systematically collected about caste and religion. At the same time, as the census operations were beginning to collect information about caste, the army was beginning to be reorganised on assumptions about the nature of "martial races", questions were being raised about the balance between Hindus and Muslims in the public services, about whether certain castes or "races" were monopolising access to new educational opportunities and a political theory was beginning to emerge about the conspiracy which certain castes were organising to supplant British Rule. (Cohn 1970)

M.N. Srinivas makes an interesting observation on census as a generator of social mobility. He says:

> "The decennial census, introduced by the British, recorded caste, and it unwittingly came to the aid of social mobility. Prosperous low castes, and even those which were not prosperous, sought to call themselves by new and high sounding Sanskrit names. Getting the names recorded in the census was part of the struggle to achieve a higher status than before".

From caste and religion, we may turn to language. The census authorities had from the beginning a profound interest in language. George Grierson wrote his monumental chapter on "Mother Tongues" in the 1901 Census Report of India, which really was the framework of his great Linguistic Survey which lasted from 1886 to 1928. While we admire these profound scholars, it must be said that language was also used by the British as a convenient handle for their imperial ends. As the States Reorganisation Commission says in its report:

> During the British period, territorial changes were governed mainly by imperial interest. However, as an ostensible factor the linguistic principle figured, for the first time, in a letter from Sir Herbert Risley, Home Secretary, Government of India to the Government of Bengal, dated 3rd December, 1903, in which the proposal for the partition Resolution of 1905, and in the despatch of Lord Hardinge's Government to the Secretary of State, dated 25th August, 1911 proposing the annulment of partition, language was again prominently mentioned. The linguistic principle was, however, pressed into service on these occasions only as a measure of administrative convenience, and to the extent it fitted into a general pattern, which was determined by political exigencies. In actual effect, the partition of Bengal involved a flagrant violation of linguistic affinities. The settlement of 1912 also showed little respect for the linguistic principle in that it drew a clear line of distinction between the Bengali Muslims and Bengali Hindus. Both these partitions thus ran counter to the assumption that different linguistic groups constituted distinct units of social feeling with common political and economic interests. (SRC 1955)

To sum up we may conclude that the British rulers used census as an indispensable tool in governance and also to strengthen their hold on India through a "Divide and Rule" policy.

3. Censuses in Post-independence Era

We shall now briefly describe the salient features of the decennial censuses in the post-independence era. The first such census was conducted in 1951 soon after the partition of India. This census introduced in the questionnaire for the first time a question on 'displaced persons'. A similar question was also introduced in the Census of Pakistan in 1951. Thus we do get estimates from the census of the magnitude of the problem of displaced persons and refugees as a result of the partition of India and the aftermath of the tragic communal rioting. The other highlights of the 1951 census are as follows:

- It gave an economic orientation to the census. It abandoned the earlier practice of cross-tabulating data by religion and introduced new cross-tabulations by livelihood classes. The question on caste was abandoned except for scheduled castes and tribes.
- For the first time in the history of census, it gave rural/urban breakdown for all tables.
- This census introduced for the first time a post-census enumeration check, which gave an idea of the extent of under enumeration in the census.
- The General Report on the census was a happy compromise between the old type of encyclopaedic reporting and the

presentation of bare statistical tables as was done in the 1941 Census. The 1951 Census report gave in brief the main results of this census and at the same time elaborated on one dominating theme – the population – food crisis of India. The report introduced an innovative concept of "improvident maternity."

- The District Census Handbooks gave detailed data for each district in India.

3.1 Highlights of the 1961 Census

- This was a landmark census and one of the most elaborate censuses anywhere in the world, in terms of the questionnaire, tabulations, maps, ancillary studies and publication programme. This census was preceded by intensive preparations, discussions at various levels, consultations with consumers of data and academic scholars, field trials, pre-testing of questionnaires, preparation of notional maps, formulation of elaborate tabulation schemes, concern for micro data right from wards of cities and enumerators' blocks to big cities with population of 100,000 and special tables for individual cities of population of one million and over. Even the house-listing schedule was extended and considerable information on industrial establishment obtained.
- It introduced the concept of "household" and collected valuable data on the household economy, especially in relation to landholdings and system of land tenure. It also introduced a two-fold classification of workers engaged in industries namely:

  (i) household industries

  (ii) manufacturing other than household industries.
- This census introduced rural/urban breakdown of place of birth of migrants, thereby yielding data on all the four migration streams: rural to rural, rural to urban, urban to urban and urban to rural. A great deal of thought was given to tabulation of data on urban population. All this resulted in a clearer picture of urbanisation in India.
- The all-India report was a landmark report, which highlighted the regional variations in the level of living based on a large number of demographic, economic and social indicators,

treating the district as a unit of analysis. Problems of regional development were further analysed in the atlas volumes, special monographs and village studies.

- There were special tables for scheduled caste and scheduled tribe population. A new Social Studies Division was created in the Office of the Registrar General and sociological and anthropological analysis of demographic data received continuous attention from this Division. The work of the Linguistic Unit was also strengthened.
- For the first time, scholars from universities and research institutions were invited to prepare census monographs on demographic subjects of their specialisation and they were given free access to unpublished data and in several cases, special tabulations were undertaken for them. A small honorarium and secretarial and research assistance was also given to these scholars.
- In keeping with the census tradition, the bulk of the enumeration work was done by revenue officials and school teachers but at this census a small honorarium was paid to the enumerators.

3.2 Highlights of the 1971 Census

- This census introduced partial use of electronic computers in processing and tabulating census data. A large number of basic tables for the country as a whole were quickly prepared on a one per cent sample basis.
- The census questionnaire introduced for the first time a direct question on migration (with reference to the last move only) in addition to the usual question on place of birth. This, along with a new sub-question on place of work, yielding data on commutation, was expected to throw new light on internal migration and urbanisation (unfortunately theses data were not tabulated). A question was asked on the 'age at marriage' and also about 'any child born during the last one year', of all currently married women.
- The Vital Statistics Division of the office of the Registrar General has been continuously engaged in collecting data on births and deaths through the Sample Registration Scheme

(SRS). The SRS data are a valuable supplement to census data.

- This census continued to pay considerable attention to the preparation of detailed District Census Handbooks, Census Atlases *etc*. Instead of village surveys, this Census took up socio-economic surveys of over 200 towns and cities.

3.3 Highlights of the 1981 Census

For the first time in the history of Census in India, sampling was introduced at the **enumeration stage** in relation to migration and fertility characteristics. The system of sampling was introduced in consultation with the Central Statistical Organisation and other expert bodies. Ideally, a sample of households would have been desirable but an appraisal of field conditions had indicated that household sampling would not be possible. Therefore, an area sampling approach was adopted. Of the total enumeration blocks in the country, a 20 per cent sample was selected on the basis of systematic sampling and in these blocks, the questions on migration and fertility were canvassed. In other blocks, i.e., in the non-sample blocks these questions were not canvassed. In order to distinguish the records of the sample and non-sample blocks, the Individual Slips in sample blocks were printed in blue with the questions relating to migration and fertility included only in these slips. The Individual Slips canvassed in the non-sample blocks were printed in black and excluded the questions relating to these two topics.

3.4 Highlights of the 1991 Census

- The Houselist was expanded to cover some information relating to housing and household amenities, which was collected during the main enumeration in 1981. By thus advancing the collection of this information during house-listing (which was about 6-10 months ahead of the main census) tabulation of data on housing stock and amenities is expected to be completed earlier than last time.
- A question was canvassed for the first time through the Houselist regarding type of fuel used for cooking by the household. This helps in knowing the impact of the fuel consumption patterns on environment and forest resources and also reveals the extent to which alternative energy sources are being used for domestic cooking.

- In the Houselist, the availability of toilet facility to the household was collected in respect of rural areas also as against only in urban areas in the 1981 Census.
- The Household Schedule was so designed as to record the data on mother tongue and religion of each individual. This schedule was used for the expeditious manual tabulation. The *Primary Census Abstract (PCA)* gives nine-fold industrial categories up to the village level or ward level of a town. The basic census data will be presented for the first time for each Community Development Block in the rural areas all over the country, in addition to data for *Tehsil/Taluka*/District/State or Union Territory.
- A new feature of the Individual Slip of the 1991 Census is a question on ex-servicemen and their status as pensioner or non-pensioner.
- In the 1981 Census, the children in the age group 0-4 were considered as illiterates by definition. At the time of preparation for the 1991 Census, the Department of Education in the Ministry of Human Resource Development and the Planning Commission desired that in the 1991 Census, children in the age group 0-6 should be considered as illiterate since the ability to read and write with understanding is not generally achieved, specially in the rural areas, until a child attains the age of seven or more. Accordingly, in the 1991 Census, children of the age of six years or less were considered as illiterates even if the child was going to school and might have picked up reading and writing a few odd words.
- The concepts and definition relating to economic questions in general and "work" in particular adopted in the 1981 Census were retained for the sake of comparability. However, thought was given to the design and formulation of these questions in the Individual Slip. A sub-group of the Advisory Committee went into this aspect and care was taken to frame the questions in such a way as to help netting the unpaid workers on farm or in family enterprise. In order to ensure that the economic activity of these categories (women and children are the predominant constituents of this workforce) is properly enumerated in the 1991 Census, the instructions to census enumerators were expanded and emphasis was laid on the

need to ask probing questions regarding the work done at any time at all last year or any of the seasons in the reference period, in the case of women. Some of the important suggestions made by the women's organisations with regard to completely netting the economic activity of women were taken into account while drafting the instructions to the enumerators and in designing the training modules for them. Special posters supplied by the United Nations Development Fund for Women (UNIFEM) highlighting the importance of recording women's work were distributed widely to sensitise the enumerators and the respondents.

- In order to provide more detailed tables on the economic activity of the population, it was decided to process in the 1991 Census all the Individual Slips relating to main workers other than cultivators and agricultural labourers, marginal workers and those non-workers seeking/available for work. In the last census this tabulation was based only on a 20 per cent sample of Individual Slips.
- The question on seeking/available for work was asked in the 1991 Census only in respect of non-workers and not for marginal workers also as was done in the 1981 Census. Further, in case of those seeking/available for work, a question on 'whether they had ever worked before' was asked. This would be of help in knowing the number of fresh entrants to the labour force.
- While collecting information on reasons for migration, two more reasons, namely "business" and "natural calamities like drought, floods, *etc*"., were added in the 1991 census by assigning separate codes.

3.5 Highlights of the 2001 Census

The decennial census of 2001 is the first census the 21st century and deserves special attention. To give an idea of the census operation which is a gigantic administrative exercise, comparable to the conduct of general elections in India, we highlight a few facts below about the 2001 census.

- House numbering and house-listing operation carried out from April to September, 2000; Population enumeration undertaken between 9 to 28 February 2001 (both days inclusive): and revisional round from 1 to 5 March 2001; two million enumerators; 220 million households covered. Total population of India as per the final tables was 1,028,737,436 spread in 28 States, seven Union Territories, 593 districts; 5470 sub-districts and 593,732 inhabited villages and 5161 towns and cities. The SC population was 166,635,700 and ST population was 84,326,240.

- In Jammu & Kashmir, unlike in 1991 when the census enumeration did not take place, in 2001, Jammu & Kashmir was covered and the actual census figure included in the all India total (in 1991 the estimated population of Jammu & Kashmir was considered)
- Reference date: 00.00 hours on 1st March 2001.

We may add a few interesting administrative details about this Census:

- Census schedules were printed in 16 languages and the Manual in 18 languages.
- About 7,000 metric tonnes of paper was consumed in printing various Census schedules.
- Video films, audio-cassettes, overhead projectors and power point presentations were used for imparting training to census enumerators.
- Census Help Centres and Census Help Lines/Telephone Help Lines were established for the first time to give assistance to enumerators and also register complaints from the public. In rural areas, Help Centres were opened at *Tehsil/Taluka/*Block headquarters.
- Slum Enumeration Blocks were identified for the first time at this Census, in each town or city having a population of 50,000 and above.
- A system of Permanent Location Code Number (PLCN) was introduced for the first time and each village/ward of town or city was assigned an eight-digit code. Thus each administrative area in any geographical region was uniquely identified. This will help in ensuring comparability of data in future censuses and help in tracking jurisdictional changes in villages/towns.

- A census logo with the motto "people oriented" was introduced by the Census organisation.

3.6 New Features of 2001 Census

The new features of the Houselisting schedule are as follows:

- For the first time, different uses of census houses have been standardised and grouped into ten main uses and assigned code numbers.
- Plastic has been added in the list of material of wall and roof of a census house, as it is often used for shelter in slums and shanties.
- In the previous census, the location of drinking water source was categorised into two locations, *viz.* 'within premises' and 'outside premises'. In the Census of India, 2001, the source 'outside premises' was split into two categorises namely 'near the premises' and 'away from the premises'.
- The scope of question on availability of electricity was expanded to include six sources of lighting. Besides no lighting, this included sources like electricity, kerosene, solar, other oil and any other source.
- In 1991 Census, a question on availability of toilet facilities to the household was canvassed while in Census of India, 2001, specific information on availability of latrine within the house by the type of latrine was sought.

The following new questions were added in the Houselist Schedule:

- If the Census house was used for residential or partly residential purposes, the condition of the census house was categorised as good, liveable or dilapidated based on the perception and response of the respondent.
- A question on number of married couple(s) living in the household was canvassed.
- Information was sought on the number of married couple(s) having independent room for sleeping.
- Information as to whether the waste water outlet of the house is connected to 'closed drainage' or has no drainage was collected.

- A question on availability of bathroom within the house was included.
- Information on availability of kitchen within the house was also sought.
- Availability of certain assets to the households namely, radio/transistor, television, telephone, bicycle, scooter/motor cycle/moped, car/jeep/van were also included.
- It was also enquired whether any banking service was being availed by the household.

3.7 Household Schedule

The following new questions were canvassed in the 2001 Census:

- A question on total disability was canvassed in the 1981 Census. In the 1991 Census, no question on disability was included. At the Census of India, 2001, a question to elicit information on total or partial disability was canvassed. The five types of disability on which information collected are in regard to seeing, speech, hearing, movement and mental disability.
- A new question on 'travel to place of work' was canvassed mainly for workers engaged in non-agricultural activities. Information on distance from the residence to place of work and mode of travel to place of work was also collected under this section.
- The Household Schedule had a new set of questions for households engaged in cultivation/plantation – (i) net area of land under cultivation/plantation, (ii) Net area of land irrigated, and (iii) tenure status. This question was not canvassed at the 1991 Census but was canvassed in the 1981 Census in a slightly different form.
- The signature or thumb impression of the respondent was taken on the House Schedule for the first time in the history of census. This was not only aimed at obtaining correct and complete information but for also giving an opportunity to the respondents to authenticate the information provided by them. The relationship of the respondent with the head of the household was also obtained.

Modification in the 1991 questionnaire adopted in 2001 Census are as follows:

- Age at marriage was collected for males also, while it was collected for only ever-married females until the 1991 Census.
- The type of educational institution attended by a person was enlarged to include school, college, vocational institute, other institute and literacy centre.
- The scope of the definition of 'work' was expanded in the Census of India, 2001 to include production of milk for domestic consumption. In the 1981 Census, cultivation of certain crops even for self-consumption was treated as economic activity. The scope of the term 'Cultivation' was expanded in this Census to include certain other crops such as tobacco, fruits, all types of flowers, roots and tubers, potatoes, chillies and turmeric, pepper, cardamom, all types of vegetables and fodder crops *etc*. This meant that activities related to production of all the above mentioned crops for domestic consumption have been treated as work. Only five crops, *viz*. tea, coffee, rubber, coconut and betel nuts have been classified under 'Plantation' in the Census of India, 2001.
- At the 1991 Census, the question on seeking/available for work was canvassed for only non-workers. At the Census of India, 2001, this question is asked from the marginal workers also. A question to elicit information on secondary work canvassed at the 1991 Census, was dropped.
- From among the categories of non-workers adopted at the 1991 Census, the category 'Inmates of institutions' has been dropped and 'Retired persons and Rentiers' has been replaced by the category 'Pensioners'.
- A new response category "moved after birth' was included in the question on 'reasons for migration' to bring out nuances in migration patterns. Natural calamites or distress migration as a reason for migration for last residence migrants included in the 1991 Census, was covered under category of 'Other'.
- Number of children born alive to currently married women during the last one year was collected for male and female children separately.
- Slum Enumeration Blocks were identified for the first time in census, in each Municipal town having a population of

50,000. Instructions were issued that these Enumeration Blocks do not cut cross-ward boundaries or non-slum area. It will thus be possible to compile and tabulate special tables for 'slums'.

4. Electronic Data Processing

A quantum leap was made on the technology front while processing the Census 2001 data both for Houselisting and Population Enumeration. The schedules for both the phases were scanned through high speed scanners in fifteen data centres across the country and hand-written data from the schedules were converted into digitised form through Intelligent Character Reading (ICR) software for creation of ASCII records for furthers processing. So as to ensure uniformity, which was an essential prerequisite for scanning. The selection of appropriate state-of-art technology in data processing has made it possible to produce all the Houselisting as well as Population Enumeration tables on full count basis for the first time in the history of Census. For Census 2001 about 202 million schedules consisting of about 1028 million records were scanned and processed within a span of only ten months starting October, 2002.

There has been a major departure in Census 2001 from the past in respect of the procedure followed for finalisation of the Scheduled Castes and the Scheduled Tribes population. In the earlier census, the total Scheduled Castes and Scheduled Tribes populations were finalised at the time of the manual compilation of the Primary Census Abstracts (PCA) at the Regional Tabulation Offices which were specially set up for this purpose. The individual Scheduled Castes and the Scheduled Tribes population for each states was finalised much later based on manual coding done by coders. In 2001 Census, each Individual Scheduled Caste and Scheduled Tribe have been coded directly on the computers by the Data Entry Operators through a process known as Computer Assisted Coding (CAC) and taken up along with the processing of PCA data. The CAC process involves pulling down, from the relevant dictionary of the Scheduled Castes and the Scheduled Tribes, on the computer screen and coding from the dictionary by referring to the image of the specific individual entry in the Household Schedule appearing on the screen. The CAC of the response on Religion wherever required, was also undertaken along with the processing of PCA. This is because the Scheduled Castes status had to be determined in relation to the religion of an individual.

5. Dissemination of Census Data

At an impressive National Seminar on "Census Data Dissemination" organised by the Registrar General and Census Commissioner (New Delhi, 10 July 2004) and inaugurated by the Union Home Minister (Shivraj V. Patil), the final population totals of 2001 Census were released. (Census of India, 2001, Series 1). There were two sets of figures for India's population because of legal complications in the small state of Manipur. To quote the report:

"It is important to note that the census results for Mao Maram, Paomata and Purul sub-divisions of Senapati district of Manipur were cancelled due to administrative and technical reasons although a population census was carried out in these sub-divisions also as per schedule. However the population by sex and residence only for these three sub-divisions has been estimated."

The total population of India was 1,028,737,436 (on 1st March, 2001) including the population estimates of the sub-divisions of Manipur. The total population of India **excluding** these areas was 1,028,610,328. In Appendix Table 1 we give the final population figures for the states (as arranged by us and not by geographical divisions as in the census):

A new feature of Census of India, 2001 is the use of modern technology to disseminate census data. In 1998, a website was created on the internet to provide census data and metadata. The site was also used to generate awareness about 2001 Census and the census questionnaire. For thematic maps Census GIS India, website was also created for the first time (http://www.censusindiamaps.net) in addition to the Census of India website(http://www.censusindia.net).

The GIS website allows the user to prepare maps up to *taluk* or any sub-district level and the software available on the website is user-friendly. The Census organisation claims that "no other census website in the world provides such a tool" (Registrar General, India, 2004).

6. The Future

The Census website is gaining popularity. In 2003, the website recorded 463,165 visits and 9,018,113 hits. The worldwide census website has an immense potential for reaching out to people. It is estimated that currently there are ten million internet users in India. The figure is likely to reach 46 million mark in 2005. The census organisation has to take steps to meet the vastly increased demand for census data. Now that a beginning has been made to provide consultancy services by the Census organisation and make available tailored data as per the users' demand at a minimal price, the Census organisation will have to set up new structures for the management of the massive census data. The enormity of India's population and the striking diversity make the task daunting. The inevitable conclusion is that we must modernise the Census of India in a big way. According to United Nations projections, India's population will overtake China's population by 2035 or so. As we are heading towards getting in the world's largest population slot, the Census Organisation has the added responsibility of meeting the challenge of conducting the world's largest census operation. As it is, our census is more comprehensive than the Chinese census, in terms of the census questionnaire, scope, coverage and content of the Census. If we want to retain this lead, we have to think in terms of a new organisation in tune with modern technology and not get hamstrung by the Ministry of Home affairs, which is a legacy of the past. The 2001 Census has demonstrated that it is almost impossible to cut down the time gap between census enumeration and the availability of census data to the users in the present setup which is totally inadequate. As of July 2004, we are still awaiting the 2001 Census data on age distribution, industrial classification, religion *etc.* which are priority items for planners, policymakers, researchers and the general data users. All this has happened inspite of a competent demographer–administrator as the Census Commissioner of 2001. Technology snags have been tormenting the Census Organisation. The Home Ministry wakes up only two years prior to the conduct of census enumeration every ten years. The Census Commissioner has a comparatively junior rank (Joint Secretary). I am reminded of what a State Director of Census once told me: "That we have a long history of Census taking running over one hundred years, is both an asset and a liability. The Census Organisation is like a horse with blinkers on its eyes."

Appendix Table 1

Population of India and States, 2001 and Vital Rates (SRS), 2002

	Total Population	Birth Rate			Death Rate			Infant Mortality Rate		
		Total	Rural	Urban	Total	Rural	Urban	Total	Rural	Urban
A. Mega States (10) Population: over 50 million										
Uttar Pradesh	166,197,921	31.6	32.6	26.8	9.7	10.2	7.3	80	83	58
Maharashtra	96,878,627	20.3	20.6	19.8	7.3	8.3	5.6	45	52	34
Bihar	82,998,509	30.9	31.8	23.5	7.9	8.2	6.1	61	62	50
West Bengal	80,176,197	20.5	22.6	14.1	6.7	6.9	6.4	49	52	36
Andhra Pradesh	76,210,007	20.7	21.1	19.3	8.1	8.9	5.5	62	71	35
Tamil Nadu	62,405,679	18.5	19.1	17.5	7.7	8.6	5.9	44	50	32
Madhya Pradesh	60,348,023	30.4	32.3	22.7	9.8	10.5	7.2	85	89	56
Rajasthan	56,507,188	30.6	31.9	24.2	7.7	8.0	6.4	78	81	55
Karnataka	52,850,562	22.1	23.5	18.8	7.2	7.9	5.7	55	65	25
Gujarat	50,671,017	24.7	26.6	20.6	7.7	8.3	6.4	60	68	37
B. Bigger States/UTs(9) Population: over 10 million										
Orissa	36,804,660	23.2	23.7	19.6	9.8	10.3	6.4	87	90	56
Kerala	31,841,374	16.9	17.0	16.4	6.4	6.4	6.2	10	11	8
Jharkhand	26,945,829	26.4	28.5	19.0	7.9	8.6	5.8	51	55	33
Assam	26,655,528	26.6	27.5	18.3	9.2	9.6	6.0	70	73	38
Punjab	24,358,999	20.8	21.7	18.1	7.1	7.4	6.2	51	55	35
Haryana	21,144,564	26.6	27.6	22.6	7.1	7.2	6.4	62	64	51
Chhattisgarh	20,833,803	25.0	26.5	22.6	8.7	9.7	7.2	73	80	59
Delhi NCT	13,850,507	17.2	18.2	17.1	5.1	5.7	5.1	30	31	30
Jammu & Kashmir	10,143,700	19.2	19.9	16.0	5.7	5.7	5.7	45	47	34

Contd..

Contd..

	Total Population	Birth Rate			Death Rate			Infant Mortality Rate		
		Total	Rural	Urban	Total	Rural	Urban	Total	Rural	Urban
C. *Smaller States/UTs(16)Population: less than 10 million*										
Uttaranchal	8,489,349	17.0	18.1	16.2	6.4	9.0	4.4	41	62	21
Himachal Pradesh	6,077,900	20.7	21.1	16.5	7.5	7.7	5.1	52	53	28
Tripura	3,199,203	14.9	15.3	13.3	5.7	5.6	6.2	34	31	30
Manipur*	2,166,788	16.8	17.4	15.3	4.6	4.2	5.8	14	12	21
Meghalaya	2,318,822	25.8	27.8	14.6	7.7	8.4	3.9	61	62	49
Nagaland	1,990,036	NA	NA	11.9	NA	NA	9.4	NA	NA	15
Goa	1,374,668	14.0	14.4	13.5	8.3	9.0	7.2	17	19	14
Arunachal Pradesh	1,097,968	20.2	20.9	12.3	4.8	5.0	2.6	37	38	12
Pondicherry UT	974,345	17.9	18.1	17.7	6.7	8.1	5.7	22	29	17
Chandigarh UT	900,635	14.6	21.5	13.8	3.4	4.1	3.4	21	25	21
Mizoram	888,573	16.9	20.8	12.0	4.8	5.7	3.7	14	14	14
Sikkim	540,851	21.9	22.2	13.4	4.9	5.0	4.1	34	34	25
Andaman & Nicobar Islands UT	356,152	16.8	17.6	14.6	5.5	6.1	3.8	15	17	10
Dadra Nagar Haveli UT	220,490	30.4	31.3	20.4	6.8	7.1	4.0	56	58	21
Daman & Diu UT	158,204	22.4	23.5	21.4	6.6	7.4	5.9	42	42	43
Lakshwadeep	60,650	19.3	20.2	18.3	5.2	5.3	5.1	25	31	18
INDIA										
Total Population	1,028,737,436*	25.0	26.6	20.0	8.1	8.7	6.1	63	69	40

* The total population of Manipur excludes the population of three sub-districts of Senapati district where the census figures were cancelled. The total population of India includes the estimated population of these areas. The total population of India excluding the three sub-districts of Manipur was 1,028,610,328.

Source: Census of India 2001, Series 1: Final Population Totals, Office of Registrar General, New Delhi, 2004 SRS Bulletin, Volume 38 No.1, April 2004, published by Registrar General India.

References

Banthia, J.K. (2004). Papers for the National Seminar on Census Data Dissemination, New Delhi, 10 July. Office of Registrar General and Census Commissioner, India.

————. (2004). Census of India 2001, Series 1: *Final Population Totals: Urban Agglomerations and Towns.*

Bose, Ashish (1973). "The Census of India: A Historical Perspective", *Demography India*, Vol. II, No. 1.

————. (1991 and several reprints). *Population of India: 1991 Census Results and Methodology* (Delhi: B. R. Publishing Corporation).

————. (1993). *India and The Asian Population Perspective* (Delhi: B.R. Publishing Corporation). This book contains my articles published in *The Financial Express* (Chief Editor: Professor A.M. Khusro) during 1992–93.

————. (2000). "Beyond a Headcount: Preparing for Census of 2001", *Economic and Political Weekly*, 22 April.

————. (2001). *India's Billion Plus People : 2001 Census Highlights, Methodology and Media Coverage* (Delhi : B.R. Publishing Corporation). Also abridged edition and paperback edition.

————. (2001). "Census of India 2001 and After", *Economic and Political Weekly,* 19 May.

————. (2003). "Consumer Demographics: People's Assets in Census 2001", *Economic and Political Weekly,* 27 September.

Cohn, Bernard S., (1970). *The Census, Social Structure, and Objectification in South Asia.* Paper for Second European Conference on Modern South Asia, (mimeo.), p. 17.

Government of India (1955). *Report on the States Reorganisation Commission,* New Delhi, pp. 10-11.

Mitra, Asok (1965). Foreword to *Census of India, 1961, Vol. I, Language Monographs Part XI-C (i),* p. iii.

————. (1963). "Introduction to Inter-Documentation Company AG", Index of Microfiche Edition of the *Census of India, 1872-1951,* pp. 6-7.

Srinivas, M.N (1962). *Caste in Modern India and Other Essays.* Bombay, p. 18.

16

Reciprocity between Female Education and Fertility in India[1]

P.N. MARI BHAT

1. Introduction

A relationship that has received much scholarly attention in demography is the one between women's education and fertility. During the last three decades, scores of articles have been published to document, understand and interpret this relationship, and several books have appeared that attempted to synthesise the voluminous research on the subject (Cochrane, 1979; Jejeebhoy, 1995; Jeffrey & Basu, 1996; Bledsoe, Casterline, Johnson-Kuhn & Haaga, 1999). Yet, doubts continue to linger about the nature of this relationship, its significance to fertility decline and about the direction of causality. An attempt is made in this paper to assess the significance of this relationship, and its changing nature in the context of fertility decline in India.

A widely held view among the general public, and researchers with limited exposure to demographic literature is that the association between years of schooling and fertility is uniformly inverse, and unchanging, as shown by the line in the left panel of Figure 16.1. According to this view, the fall in fertility during the course of socio-economic development is due to the change in the composition of population by level of education: fertility is high initially because most people, especially women, are illiterate, and it is low at the completion of the transition because most are well-educated. Such a view is implicit in many econometric analyses of fertility determinants that use aggregated data for countries or other geographical regions.

---

1. This is an abridged version of the paper published in World Development, Vol. 30, No. 10, October 2002. I am grateful to the National Council of Applied Economic Research, New Delhi, for permitting me to analyse the data from the Human Development Profile Survey, 1994 and to Francis Zavier for able research assistance.

Figure 16.1

Two Alternate Conceptions of the Relationship between Women's Education and Fertility

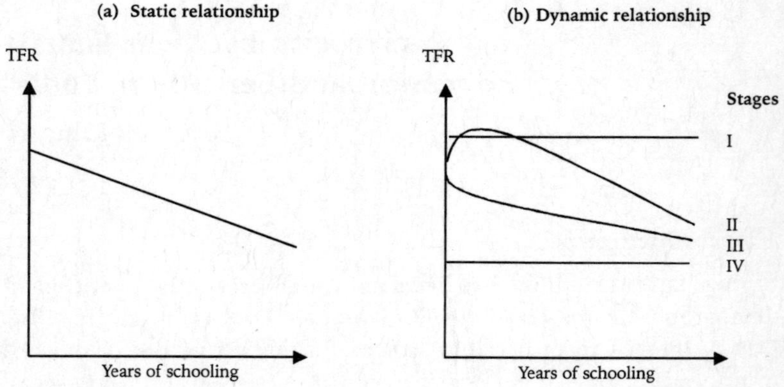

However, survey data on individual women do not always show a uniformly inverse relationship between fertility and level of female education (Cochrane, 1979; Jejeebhoy, 1995). The micro relationship comes with various shapes (for a recent review, see Jejeebhoy, 1995), although some of the diversity in the observed pattern could be attributed to sampling fluctuations and other errors in the data. But until recently, a concave pattern suggesting either an increase or no change in fertility with modest exposure to formal education was the most commonly observed pattern in many developing countries (United Nations, 1989). This naturally raised the question as to whether fertility would decline from a moderate increase in the level of schooling.

In the demographic literature, it is common to attribute the variation in the pattern of the education-fertility relationship to the mediating influence of contextual factors such as social structure, level of development, educational system and family planning programme effort (e.g., Jejeebhoy, 1995; Diamond, Newby & Varle, 1999). Such views typically emerge out of cross-national comparisons. They miss the dynamic aspect of the whole change. As briefly observed in a UN study (United Nations, 1987), even within the same social setting, education differentials in fertility could undergo a characteristic form of change if social diffusion is at the heart of fertility transition. This view is intrinsically different from the more common view because it holds that, the relationship between education and fertility is not causal, but arise out of the mediating role of education in the diffusion process. That is, fertility differentials are the result of lags in the adoption of a new form of reproduction behaviour.

The right panel of Figure 16.1 shows the characteristic forms the education-fertility relationship could take under different stages of diffusion. Initially, as few would have adopted the small family norm, the curve would be virtually flat (stage I). As well-educated elites in the community are typically the first innovators, the relationship would begin to take a curvilinear form as fertility declines (stage II). The curve would be concave downward because there would hardly be any reduction in fertility levels of either illiterates or moderately educated. In fact, the health transition, that usually precedes fertility transition, could make fertility levels to be somewhat higher among the modest levels of education than illiterate women.

But as the ideational change spreads to lower strata, fertility levels would fall among the semi- and moderately-educated class, and the fertility-education relationship would become uniformly inverse (stage III). The curve may even suggest upward concavity (i.e., convex to the origin), as by this time, fertility decline among the well-educated could cease. But when fertility begins to fall significantly among the illiterate women too, the fertility-education curve would regain its original flat shape (stage IV).

There is of course an element of over simplification in this generalisation. The innovation-diffusion framework, while accounting for the major changes during the transition, would be hard put to explain the presence of some minor differentials before the transition, or the emergence of some demand-driven differences after the transition. Also, contrary to what is assumed, it may not be possible to observe (thus test) the entire range of the curve at the beginning and the end of the transition owing to the paucity of women in some specific educational categories.

One significant implication of this dynamic view of education-fertility relationship is that fertility is expected to fall over time, not only from the improvements in levels of education. Besides the independent decline of fertility among illiterate women, fertility is expected to fall also because of the change in the reproductive behaviour of educated women. The analysis of aggregated data for geographical entities would attribute this effect to education (as it will be shown up as a change in the coefficient or elasticity of education variable), at the expense of factors that caused the relationship to change.

Most writers on the subject assume that the observed inverse relationship between education and fertility is almost wholly due to the effect of parental schooling on their fertility choices. Even Caldwell (1980), who was one of the first to underscore the importance of mass education to the timing of fertility transition, spoke primarily about the effect of parental schooling on their fertility. A reverse form of causation, resulting from the possibility that children from large families may receive less schooling owing to resource constraint, was largely ignored. However, in recent years, there has been a growing interest in the relationship between family size and child schooling (Knodel, Havanon & Sittitrai, 1990; Lloyd & Blanc, 1996; Montgomery & Lloyd, 1999), largely arising from the possibility that fertility decline is associated with child quality-quantity trade-off. Economists have always maintained that couples make decisions regarding their family size taking into consideration both direct and indirect costs involved in raising children. As child schooling entails both direct and indirect costs to parents, those wishing to educate their children would choose to have fewer of them. Such a trade-off between child quality and quantity could cause family sizes to be inversely related to child schooling.

The limited research in this area shows that generally, wherever fertility has fallen substantially, the relationship between family size and child schooling is found to be negative (*e.g.*, Knodel & Wongsith, 1991; Sudha, 1997), but occasionally non-significant, positive relationships are also observed in areas where fertility levels are high (see Sudha, 1997). This may be because in peasant societies with high levels of child mortality, there would be a strong preference to retain children in traditional occupations because not many of the children are expected to survive to adult ages. An exogenous fall in mortality would cause unanticipated expansion of family sizes, threatening smaller per capita landholding in the next generation. Under such circumstances, parents might begin to send selectively their later born children to school in order to diversify occupation of their offspring. This would make child schooling to be positively related to family size. In a situation where both trends intersect, one may not observe any significant relationship between family size and child schooling.

In this paper, we will first present some time-series data from India to show that the relationship between female education and fertility is indeed dynamic rather than static. In particular, it will be shown that in recent years there has been a substantial fall in fertility among illiterate women in India. By using micro data from a national survey conducted in rural areas in 1994, we will also show that child schooling among illiterate parents is inversely related to the number of children they have, and positively related to contraceptive practice. By connecting these two pieces of evidence, it will be argued that fertility is falling and child schooling is rising in India because illiterate couples have begun to make a quantity-quality trade-off in reproductive matters. However, before presenting the evidence, it is necessary to digress a bit to consider some issues of measurement.

2. Measurement Issues

Although the empirical research has disclosed vast diversity in the education-fertility relationship, demographers have not tried to measure the diversity, or the changing form of this relationship. This is surprising because demography is one of the more quantitative fields in social sciences. To fill the lacuna, we propose here an index to measure the concavity of the education-fertility relationship. The nature of the available data on fertility differentials dictates that this measure be proposed in terms of the change in the area rather than as a change in the slope of the education-fertility curve. Accordingly, our measure of concavity is the area between the education-fertility curve and the straight line that joins the fertility rate of illiterate women with the fertility rate of the most educated women. From the data on total fertility rates for discrete categories of educational level, this measure could be computed as

$$CI = \sum_{i=2}^{k-1} n_i F_i - \frac{F_1 + F_k}{2} \sum_{i=2}^{k-1} n_i \qquad i = 1, 2, \ldots, k,$$

where F_i is the total fertility rate of educational category i, n_i is the length (in years) of the educational category i. The index value would be positive when the curve is concave downward, and negative when concave upward (i.e., convex).

When studying the trends in fertility differentials by educational level, it is also useful to quantify the relative contribution of the change in the education composition of population, *vis-à-vis* that of the change in education-specific fertility rates. For this purpose, a method devised by Kitagawa to decompose the difference in overall rates or proportions can suitably be applied (Kitagawa, 1955; Preston, Heuveline & Guillot, 2000). We propose a slight modification to his method to make it even more pertinent to the case at hand. Specifically, we propose a decomposition of the overall change in total fertility rate between two points in time as due to (i) change in fertility among illiterate women, (ii) change in fertility among educated women and (iii) change in fertility from the change in the distribution of women by educational attainment. Mathematically, the decomposition formula is written as

$$F_b - F_a = \sum_{i=1}^{k} F_{b,i} C_{b,i} - \sum_{i=1}^{k} F_{a,i} C_{a,i}$$

$$= (F_{b,1} - F_{a,1})(C_{b,1} + C_{a,1})/2 + \sum_{i=2}^{k} (F_{b,i} - F_{a,i})(C_{b,i} + C_{a,i})/2$$

$$+ \sum_{i=1}^{k} (C_{b,i} - C_{a,i})(F_{b,i} + F_{a,i})/2$$

where $C_{a,i}$ and $C_{b,i}$ refer to proportion of women of educational class i at time a and time b, respectively. The three additive terms on the right-hand side of the equation give, respectively, the contributions of the above mentioned three components of overall change in total fertility (with $i = 1$ denoting the category of illiterate women). It may be noted that by using the average values of the two points of time as weights to the category-specific differences, the above decomposition formula neatly distributes the overall change into three components, without leaving anything for the residual category of 'interaction' effects.[2]

3. Trends in Fertility Differentials by Education

Data on fertility levels by educational attainment of women for India from several sources are presented in Table 16.1. The estimates from the 1981 and 1991 censuses are derived from the information on birth order and age of mother for births that occurred during the year

2. Since TFR is computed from age-specific fertility rates, it is affected by educational composition of population by age. Therefore, in the case of TFR, the left- and right-hand sides of the decomposition formula may not exactly tally when educational composition of total population is used. In the applications reported in this paper, the sum of the three components on the right-hand side has been used to compute the percentages.

preceding the census, as the direct estimates are grossly deficient (Bhat & Zavier 2004). The survey-based estimates of total fertility are directly taken from the sources, and refer to periods three-years preceding the date of the respective surveys. The Table shows that total fertility rate (TFR) in India has fallen from a level near five births per woman at the beginning of 1980s to about three births per woman in the late-1990s.

Table 16.1

Estimates of Total Fertility Rate by Educational Level of Women for India from Various Sources

Educational Level of Women	*Approximate Years of Schooling*	*1981 Census*	*1984 SRS Survey*	*1991 Census*	*NFHS-1 1992-93*	*NFHS-2 1998-99*
Illiterate	0	4.8	5.1	4.3	4.0	3.5
Below primary level	1-4		4.2			
Below middle level	1-6	4.3		3.3	3.0	2.6
Primary complete	5-9		3.3			
Middle complete	7-9	3.6		2.8	2.5	2.3
Matriculate & above	10+	2.4	2.4	2.1	2.2	2.0
All women		4.7	4.5	3.9	3.4	2.9
Concavity index		4.6	–0.5	0.3	–1.8	–1.6

Source: India, Registrar General (1989); Bhat & Zavier (2004); International Institute for Population Sciences (1995); International Institute for Population Sciences & ORC Macro (2000).

At any given point of time, the data do indicate an inverse relationship between female education and fertility. Total fertility is highest among illiterates and lowest among women educated up to matriculation or beyond. But it does not show that the relationship has been static. Fertility levels have fallen among women belonging to every educational level. The decline has been impressive even among illiterate women, among whom TFR has fallen by nearly 1.5 births per woman between the early-1980s and late-1990s.

As indicated by the concavity index computed from these data, the shape of the education-fertility curve has been undergoing significant transformation. At the beginning of the 1980s, the education-fertility curve was concave downward as suggested by the index value of 4.3. The downward concavity in 1981 is clearly attributable to the attainment of near replacement level fertility by well-educated women by this date. But owing to the sharper fall in fertility among moderately educated women, concavity of the curve disappeared during the 1980s. This is indicated by the index values of near zero from the two subsequent sources of data after 1981. Continuing this trend, the education-fertility curve has assumed a convex shape in the 1990s as indicated by the index values of -1.8 and -1.6 derived from the fertility estimates of the two National Family Health Surveys. There is thus a clear indication that the education-fertility relationship has undergone a change consistent with the innovation-diffusion model.

But what has been the contribution of improvements in female education to the reduction in fertility? Table 16.2 shows the application of the decomposition technique to the change in TFR as estimated from the 1981 and 1991 census data for all-India. The TFR has been estimated to have fallen from 4.7 in 1980 to 3.9 in 1990, or by 0.8 births per woman in ten years. In the meanwhile, illiteracy among married women had declined from 75 to 67 per cent, and the percentage who were educated at least up to the middle school had increased from 10 to 18 per cent. The decomposition analysis shows that the entire change in the educational composition of women cannot explain more than 20 per cent of the overall change in fertility during the ten-year period. On the other hand, nearly half of the

Table 16.2

Decomposition of Change in Total Fertility Rate between 1981 and 1991 by Educational Level of Women, India

Educational	*1981 Census**		*1991 Census**		*Within Class Decline in TFR*	
Level of Women	*TFR*	*% Women*	*TFR*	*% Women*	*Amount*	*% of Total*
Illiterate	4.8	75.1	4.3	67.3	0.5	48.9
Below Middle	4.3	14.4	3.3	15.5	0.9	20.0
Middle school	3.6	5.0	2.8	7.8	0.8	7.4
Matriculate	2.6	4.3	2.2	7.1	0.4	3.5
Graduate and above	1.8	1.1	1.7	2.4	0.1	0.2
All women	4.7	100.0	3.9	100.0	0.8	80.0

Contribution of fertility change among illiterate women = 49%

Contribution of fertility change among educated women = 20.0+7.4+3.5+0.2 = 31%

Contribution of change in educational composition of women = 100.0-80.0 = 20%

* TFRs refer to the one-year period preceding the census.

Source: Bhat & Zavier (2004).

decline in TFR (49 per cent) was due to its fall among illiterate women. Among this group, TFR declined by half a birth during the 1980s. The remaining 30 per cent of the decline was due to the change in fertility behaviour of educated women during the 1980s, that caused the concavity of the relationship to disappear.

The decomposition technique can also be applied to assess the contribution of educational changes to the rise in contraceptive practice. For this purpose, we have analysed the data on contraceptive practice by educational level of married women from a national survey conducted in 1970 by the Operations Research Group (1971), and from the two rounds of the NFHS in the 1990s. The results of the analysis for all-India are presented in Table 16.3. The survey data show that contraceptive practice among married women has increased from 14 per cent in 1970 to 41 per cent in 1992-93, and to 48 per cent in 1998-99. In the meanwhile, illiteracy among married women has declined from 79 per cent in 1970 to 63 per cent in 1992-93, and further to 57 per cent in 1998-99. The decomposition analysis shows that the change in educational composition of women could account for only 16 per cent of the increase in contraceptive practice between 1970 and 1992-93, and 11 per cent of the rise in contraceptive practice between 1992-93 and 1998-99. On the other hand, the rise in contraceptive practice among illiterate women explains 63 per cent of the increase in overall use between 1970 and 1992-93, and 71 per cent of the rise in use between 1992-93 and 1998-99. Thus the contribution of the change in educational composistion women to the overall increase in contraceptive practice is even smaller than its contibution to the decline in fertility. This could be because fertility rate is also affected by the changes in age at marrige, on which perhaps education has a greater effect.

These results unambiguously show that fertility has begun to fall among illiterate women, and it accounts for the major portion of the overall decline in recent years. In comparison to this effect, the direct contribution of the improvement in female education has been marginal. Perhaps even more significantly, its contribution to fertility decline has been found to decline with time. However, the fall in fertility among females with moderate level of schooling, and the consequent change in the concavity of the fertility-education curve, did contribute significantly to the fertility decline in the 1980s. However, this decline cannot wholly be attributed to female education *per se*. One ought to know what factors favoured this group. Also,

Table 16.3

Contraceptive Use by Educational Level of Women, Educational Composition of Women and Decomposition of the Increase in Contraceptive Practice Recorded by three National Surveys, India 1970 to 1999

Educational Level of Women	*Per cent using Contraception*			*Per cent of Women in the Class*			*Per cent Contribution of within Class Increase*	
	*ORG survey**	*NFHS-1*	*NFHS-2*	*ORG survey**	*NFHS-1*	*NFHS-2*		
	1970	1992-93	1998-99	1970	1992-93	1998-99	1970-93	1993-99
Illiterate	10.0	33.9	42.9	79.3	62.6	57.4	62.9	71.0
Below Middle	20.7	50.4	55.5	10.9	18.3	19.4	16.1	12.6
Middle school	33.5	50.8	52.2	9.0	7.4	8.5	5.2	1.5
Matriculate and above	56.2	54.7	57.0	0.8	11.7	14.7	-0.3	4.0
All women	13.6	40.6	48.2	100.0	100.0	100.0	83.9	89.0

	1970-93	1993-99
Contribution of change in contraceptive use among illiterate women =	63	71
Contribution of change in contraceptive use among educated women =	21	18
Contribution of change in educational composition of women =	16	11

* As this survey used slightly different educational categories, the comparisons shown with the NFHS are only approximate.

Source: Operations Research Group (1971); International Institute for Population Sciences (1995); International Institute for Population Sciences & ORC Macro (2000).

since the concavity of the fertility-education curve has now disappeared, this factor is not expected to play a major role in future fertility declines.

It is of course possible to argue that through demonstration effect, female education is indirectly contributing to the decline of fertility among illiterate women. But in our judgement, this effect could only be assumed to be strong at the early stages of the transition. After a sizeable pool of innovators are formed among the poor and illiterate communities, further diffusion is likely to occur from the interaction of members of similar socio-economic background. Also, in hierarchical societies such as the one in India, the scope for vertical social interaction is limited, and the change depends largely on horizontal, spatial transmission of ideas. It is thus no exaggeration to say that the future pace of fertility transition in India would depend primarily on the speed of ideational change among illiterate women.

4. Effect of Family Size on Child Schooling

It is beyond the scope of this paper to analyse all the possible factors for the substantial fall in fertility among illiterate women. But for a rounded discussion of the education-fertility relationship, it is of interest to know whether fertility decline among illiterate couples was associated with a quantity-quality trade-off, and if so, has this affected the schooling of their children.

The determinants of child schooling have been analysed using data from the Human Development Profile Survey conducted by the National Council of Applied Economic Research in 1994. This survey covered about 35,000 households spread over 1,765 villages in 16 major states of India (Shariff, 1999). As family size, contraceptive use and birth order of children are critical to our analysis, data used here pertain to children aged 6-14 years of mothers aged 20-49 years, and whose sex-specific birth order can be ascertained from the data set.

First, it is useful to remind ourselves of the self-generating principle in educational attainment - namely, educated parents beget educated children. The chance of a child going to school rises significantly even if only one of the parents is literate. Table 16.4 shows the school attendance rate of children aged 6-14 years by literacy status of the parents. Only 49 per cent of the children attend to school when both parents are illiterate. But it increases to 73 per cent when only the father is literate, and 92 per cent when both parents are literate. With respect to female children, it is found that only 40 per cent go to school when both parents are illiterate but it jumps to 64 per cent if the father is literate, and to 90 per cent when both parents are literate. Interestingly, more children go to school when the mother alone is literate than when the father alone is literate. But as cases of the former are few compared to the latter, it can be said that the growth in female literacy occurs primarily as the second-generation effect of the growth in male literacy.

Table 16.4

Percentage of Children Age 6-14 Years Attending School by Parents Literacy Status, Rural India, 1994

Sex of Child	*Both Parents Illiterate*	*Father only Literate*	*Mother only Literate*	*Both Parents Literate*	*All Children*
Total	49.0	72.9	79.5	91.8	68.2
Male	57.1	80.8	84.1	93.2	74.3
Female	39.5	64.0	74.9	90.2	61.2
Sex difference	17.6	16.8	9.2	3.0	13.0
No. of children	13728	11184	599	8645	34157

Source: Micro data from Human Development Profile Survey, 1994 (Shariff, 1999).

Since most of the literate parents send their children to school, there is not much insight to be gained by including these children in our analysis. What is crucial is to know the characteristics of illiterate parents who are sending their children to school. As fertility has begun to fall in this group, it would be rewarding to know what effect it has in raising school attendance. Hence only the children of illiterate parents have been retained for further analysis.

The analysis described below is focused on current school attendance among children aged 6-14 years. As we expect the determinants of schooling to be different for male and female children, and also for first- and later-born children, the analysis has been carried out separately by order of the child by sex. Table 16.5 shows the definitions, means and standard deviations of the variables included in the analysis. The means and standard deviations refer to the all-India sample of 7,498 male and 6,531 female children aged 6-14 years whose mothers were aged 20-49 years at the time of the survey. It has been assumed that demand for schooling is determined by characteristics of children, their parents, and also the household and community they are part off. The child attributes included in the

Table 16.5

Variable Definitions, Sample Means and Standard Deviations

Variable	*Definition*	*Mean*		*Standard Deviation*	
		Males	*Females*	*Male*	*Female*
School attendance	Dummy=1 if child is studying in school	0.57	0.39	0.50	0.49
Age of child	Age of child in completed years	9.72	9.60	2.57	2.52
Age of child square	Square of age of child	101.15	98.55	51.11	49.72
Mother's age	Logarithm of mother's age	3.53	3.53	0.17	0.18
Order of child	Order of child by sex	1.82	1.72	0.97	0.97
Siblings	Surviving children of mother	4.01	4.19	1.55	1.57
Contraceptive use	Dummy = 1 if parents are using contraception	0.48	0.45	0.50	0.50
Scheduled caste	Dummy = 1 for schedule castes	0.29	0.29	0.46	0.45
Scheduled tribe	Dummy = 1 for schedule tribes	0.14	0.14	0.35	0.35
Muslim	Dummy = 1 for Muslims	0.13	0.12	0.33	0.33
Other religion	Dummy = 1 for religion other than Hindus or Muslims	0.03	0.04	0.18	0.20
Mother's work status					
Wage earner	Dummy =1 if mother is agricultural or non-agricultural labourer	0.21	0.23	0.41	0.42
Other work	Dummy = 1 if mother is engaged in any other work, except household work	0.37	0.36	0.48	0.48

Contd...

...Contd...

Variable	*Definition*	*Mean*		*Standard Deviation*	
		Males	*Females*	*Male*	*Female*
Landholding	Land owned by the household in acre	2.53	2.44	6.83	6.71
Landholding square	Square of land owned	53.06	50.96	1823.68	1960.79
Irrigated land	Proportion of irrigated land in gross cropped area of household	0.31	0.29	0.43	0.42
Bus stop	Dummy = 1 if village has a bus stop	0.35	0.37	0.48	0.48
Middle school	Dummy = 1 if village has a middle school	0.35	0.37	0.48	0.48
Village size	Logarithm of village population	7.45	7.40	0.94	0.95
Village development	Index based on village infrastructure				
Medium	Dummy =1 if moderately developed	0.40	0.38	0.49	0.49
High	Dummy =1 if well developed	0.21	0.23	0.41	0.42
Regions					
North	Dummy = 1 for Uttar Pradesh, Bihar, Madhya Pradesh and Rajasthan	0.54	0.50	0.50	0.50
South	Dummy = 1 for Kerala, Tamil Nadu, Andhra Pradesh and Karnataka	0.18	0.21	0.39	0.40
	Number of sample children*	7498	6531		

* Children age 6-14 years of illiterate parents having mothers of age 20-49 in rural areas.

analysis are age and order of the child by sex. The parental characteristics included are mother's age, her work-status, number of living children and current use of contraception. Mother's age has been included in the analysis to control for changes in preferences with age, and also to guard against any censoring error resulting from the inclusion of women who have not completed their reproductive span.

The household-level variables included in the analysis are caste and religion, size of land owned, and proportion of irrigated land in the gross-cropped area of the household. The community-level variables used in the analysis are village population, the presence of bus stop and middle school in the village and a composite index measuring amenities and infrastructure in the village (see Shariff, 1999). Although the village development index is likely to be strongly correlated with the other three community-level variables, it has been included in the analysis to see whether opportunities for off-farm employment induce parents to send children to school.

As the dependant variables of the analysis are binary, logistic regression has been used for analysing the determinants of child schooling. The results of current attendance regressions using the all-India data are shown in Table 16.6. The results have been presented separately for the first son, later-born sons, first daughter and later-born daughters. For the purpose of this study, coefficients of number of siblings and contraceptive use are of particular interest. It can be seen that family size (i.e., number of siblings) has a strong negative effect on school attendance of children, except in the case of higher-order sons. It is interesting to note that detrimental effect of family size on child schooling is larger for daughters, and those who are first-born. This result supports the hypothesis that in a large family, first-born children are either not enrolled in the school, or withdrawn early, either to supplement the family income, or to attend to younger siblings when parents go to work. It also shows that the resource dilution in a large family affects the schooling of girls more than boys, perhaps because more girls are 'unwanted' than boys.

The results also show that contraceptive use has a strong positive effect on child schooling, independent of its effect through family size. That is, in the case of parents having the same number of children, it is the contraceptive users who are enrolling more of their children school. This effect is seen among both boys and girls, and first and

Table 16.6

Logistic Regressions of School Attendance of Children Age 6-14 Years of Illiterate Parents

Explanatory variable	*First Son*	*Higher-order Sons*	*First Daughter*	*Higher-order Daughters*
Age of child	1.483***	1.109***	1.165***	1.073***
Age of child square	–0.072***	–0.055***	–0.060***	–0.055***
Mother's age	0.232	0.413	–0.211	–0.057
Siblings	–0.098**	–0.020	–0.191***	–0.102**
Contraceptive use	0.401***	0.397***	0.436***	0.273**
Scheduled caste	–0.316***	–0.445***	–0.198*	0.034
Scheduled tribe	–0.494***	–0.562***	–0.392**	–0.184
Muslim	–0.709**	–0.680***	–0.314*	–0.301*
Other religion	0.543*	0.108	0.398*	0.400*
Mother's Work Status				
Wage earner	–0.116	–0.218*	–0.323**	–0.194
Other work	0.209*	–0.042	–0.108	0.038
Landholding	0.038***	0.027**	0.029*	0.031**
Landholding square	0.000	0.000	0.000	0.000
Irrigated land	0.098	0.303***	0.245*	0.525***
Bus stop	0.321**	0.309***	0.341***	0.531***
Middle school	–0.107	0.039	–0.159	–0.068
Village size	–0.071	–0.087*	–0.017	–0.117*
Village Development				
Medium	0.464***	0.213*	0.294**	0.224*
High	0.314*	0.029	0.586***	0.326*
Regions				
North	–0.232*	–0.392***	–0.525***	–0.909***
South	0.116	0.280*	0.100	–0.024
Constant	–7.008***	–5.815***	–4.364***	–3.989**
-2 Log likelihood	4264	4999	4080	3491
Goodness of fit χ^2	3443	3950	3406	2896
No. of children	3525	3963	3444	3087

* $p < 0.05$; ** $p < 0.01$; *** $p < 0.001$.

later-born children. This is a strong confirmation of the possibility that illiterate parents have begun to make a trade-off for a better quality of the next generation by controlling their family size. In terms of the magnitude, the odds of school attendance of children for women using contraception is 50 per cent higher than those who are not using contraception. In relative terms, the effect of contraceptive use on schooling of male children is about the same as the difference in schooling between scheduled castes and caste Hindus. In the case of females, the effect is even larger.

We shall only briefly comment on the findings regarding other determinants. There is a strong negative effect of mother's work status on schooling of first daughters. But the effect is present only if mother is engaged as a wage labourer. This could be because such women cannot afford to heir someone else to attend to household chores. Muslims, scheduled tribes, and scheduled castes send fewer of their children to school than caste Hindus, but the differences are larger for boys than girls. This indicates greater sex-discrimination in child schooling among caste Hindus.

The results also disclose that landholding has a strong positive effect on schooling of both boys and girls. If more of the land is irrigate, there is an additional effect on child schooling, but interestingly, it is stronger for later-born children than for the first-born. Among the community-level variables used in the analysis, the presence of a middle school or the village size does not show significant positive influence on child schooling of either sex. However, the presence of a bus stop and the developmental level of the village do show strong positive effect on child schooling. The significance of these variables suggests that beyond the educational facilities, better transportation and opportunities for non-farm employment contribute to child schooling. It is however found that even after controlling these factors, illiterate parents in northern India send fewer of their children to school compared to their counter parts in rest of India. This suggests the operation of some undetermined taste factors, shaped perhaps by the size of illiterate population in the community.

A similar analysis of the determinants of completing primary-level schooling among children aged 10-14 years also showed that children of parents who used contraception were more likely to complete primary education than those whose parents were not regulating their fertility (see Bhat 2002). There is thus strong evidence to suggest that the decline in fertility levels has begun to contribute significantly towards the improvement in education, especially of females. Seen in this light, the connection between mass education and fertility decline seems misinterpreted in the past; rather than suggesting the effect of parental literacy on fertility – which takes at least a generation to materialise – fertility decline during a period of rising levels of schooling signals the beginning of substitution of quality for quantity in reproductive concerns.

But there is an issue of whether the occurrence of quality-quantity trade-off implies a causal connection between fertility and child schooling. Most economists are of the view that both are jointly determined, and it is not correct to speak off fertility as the causal determinant of child schooling (e.g., Montgomery, Kouame & Oliver, 1995). This may appear so when fertility and child schooling decisions are assumed as being taken well in advance, even before marriage, with full information on the net lifetime returns from competing options. It is doubtful that couples, especially in developing countries, make decisions in this manner, nor is it necessary for them to decide once for all, as assumed under the micro-economic framework. It is to be recognised that couples do not have complete control over their fertility, or on their children's survival. Under such circumstances, it pays to take decisions about child schooling depending on one's family size, household composition (especially the presence of elder members in the household) and economic circumstances at the time the child becomes old enough to go to school. If the household happens to have several children by the time the eldest child attains the school-going age, he/she may be withheld from school, either to supplement family income, or to take care of younger siblings. When the youngest child attains the age of schooling, already decisions about family size would have been taken. As a matter of fact, the child may be an 'unwanted' one, which could have a bearing on her/his chance of schooling (surveys in India report about one-tenth the births as unwanted). Therefore, under the sequential model of decision-making, it would seem correct to assume a causal link between fertility and child schooling. Indeed, even those who strongly favour the economic framework seem to have come round to such a thinking (see Montgomery & Lloyd, 1999).

Perhaps more importantly, the rising aspirations for child schooling, could force parents to make greater effort to reduce their fertility. Thus, if fertility decline is not the ultimate *cause*, it could at least be regarded as a *means* for achieving higher levels of child schooling. In demographic parlance, fertility can be interpreted as a 'proximate determinant' of child schooling.

5. Conclusion

The evidence presented in this paper shows that in recent years there has been a substantial fall in fertility among illiterate women in India, and more and more illiterate parents have begun to send their children to school. We postulate a connection between these two trends. Couples have begun to reduce their family size in order to invest more on child schooling. The occurrence of such a trade-off between quality and quantity is evidenced by the higher school attendance and completion of primary education among children of parents who are using contraception to regulate their fertility. Although both fertility levels and child schooling may have been changing because of rising aspirations for better quality of life, to the extent the former is reduced to achieve the latter, fertility can be regarded as a proximate determinant of child schooling. We also find the detrimental effect of family size on child schooling to be more severe on female children, and on the first-born of either sex. When family size is large, these children are either not sent to school at all, or withdrawn early, to supplement the family income and to look after the young ones. Consequently, the first female child would particularly stand to gain from fertility transition.

References

Bhat, P.N.M. (2002). "Returning a Favour: Reciprocity Between Female Education and Fertility in India", *World Development*. 30(10): pp. 1791-03.

Bhat, P.N.M. and A.V.F. Zavier (2004). *Some Indirect Methods for the Estimation of Fertility and Contraceptive Use at District Level*, Delhi: Institute of Economic Growth (unpublished).

Bledsoe, C.H., J. Casterline, J.A. Johnson-Kuhn and J.G. Haaga (eds.) (1999). *Critical Perspectives on Schooling and Fertility in the Developing World*, Washington D.C. National Academy Press.

Caldwell, J.C. (1980). "Mass Education as a Determinant of the Timing of Fertility Decline", *Population and Development Review*. 6(2): pp. 225-255.

Cochrane, S.H. (1979). *Education and Fertility: What Do We Really Know?* Baltimore: Johns Hopkins University Press.

Diamond, I., M. Newby and Varle, S. (1999). "Female Education and Fertility: Examining the Links", in Bledsoe, C.H., Casterline, J.B., Johnson-Kuhn J.A., and Haaga, J.G. (eds.) *Critical Perspectives on Schooling and Fertility in the Developing World*, Washington D.C. National Academy Press.

India, Registrar General. (1989) *Fertility Differentials in India, 1984*. New Delhi: Office of the Registrar General.

International Institute for Population Sciences. (1995). *National Family Health Survey, 1992-93 (MCH and Family Planning)* Mumbai: IIPS.

International Institute for Population Sciences and ORC Macro (2000). *National Family Health Survey (NFHS-2), 1998-99: India*. Mumbai: IIPS.

Jeffery, R. and Basu, A. (1996). *Girls' Schooling, Women's Autonomy and Fertility Change in South Asia*, New Delhi: Sage Publications.

Jejeebhoy, S.J. (1995). *Women's Education, Autonomy and Reproductive Behaviour: Experience from Developing Countries*, Oxford: Clarendon Press.

Kitagawa, E.M. (1955). "Components of a Difference Between Two Rates", *Journal of the American Statistical Association*, 50:168.

Knodel, J., Havanon, N. and Sittitrai, W. (1990). "Family Size and Children's Education in Thailand", *Population and Development Review* 16(1): pp. 31-62.

Knodel, J. and Wongsith, M. (1991). "Family Size and Children's Education in Thailand: Evidence from a National Sample", *Demography* 28(1): pp. 119-132.

Lloyd, C.B. and Blanc, A.K. (1996). "Children's Schooling in Sub-Saharan Africa: The Role of Fathers, Mothers and Others", *Population and Development Review* 22(2): pp. 265-298.

Montgomery, M., Kouame, A., and Oliver, R. (1995). "The Trade-off Between the Number of Children and their Schooling: Evidence from Cote d'Ivoire and Ghana", Population Research Division Working Papers, No. 82, New York: Population Council.

Montgomery, M. and Lloyd C.B. (1999). "Excess Fertility, Unintended Births and Children's Schooling", in Bledsoe, C.H., Casterline, J.B., Johnson-Kuhn J.A., & Haaga, J.G. (eds.) *Critical Perspectives on Schooling and Fertility in the Developing World*, Washington D.C. National Academy Press.

Operations Research Group (1971). *Family Planning Practices in India*, Baroda: ORG.

Preston, S.H., Heuveline, P., and Guillot, M. (2000). *Demography: Measuring and Modelling Population Processes*, Oxford: Blackwell.

Shariff, A. (1999). *India: Human Development Report*, New Delhi: Oxford University Press.

Sudha, S. (1997). "Family Size, Sex Composition and Children's Education: Ethnic Differentials over Development in Peninsular Malaysia", *Population Studies* 51 (2): pp. 139-151.

United Nations, Department of International and Social Affairs. (1987). "Fertility Behaviour in the Context of Development: Evidence from the World Fertility Survey", Population Studies No. 100. New York: United Nations.

17

RCH-care Utilisation and Fertility in India: An Integrated Recursive Model

S.C. GULATI

1. Introduction

Strong linkages between fertility, mortality, contraception, reproductive and child health (RCH) care utilisation, socioeconomic and cultural parameters have often been of interest to researchers, policy formulators and implementers. A comprehensive population policy for cost-effective achievement of short, medium and long run policy objectives of provision of quality health-care, informed choice of contraception, fertility reduction and population stabilisation ought to have such linkages in sight.

Hitherto theoretical considerations and empirical evidences suggest that marriage age patterns, contraception usage, RCH care utilisation and fertility are interdependent. It has often been argued socioeconomic and cultural factors operate on fertility through the conventional proximate determinants *viz.* marriage-age, contraception, abortions and lactation patterns. Several empirical studies have brought forth that higher infant and child mortality have pro-natalistic effects in the form of replacement and insurance effects as well as a reduced *post-partum* ammenohrea effect. Lowered infant and child mortality can lead to lower demand for children through a reduced need for replacement of births to achieve a given targeted family size. Furthermore, couples generally overshoot their targeted family size while insuring against future uncertainties in a high mortality regime (Gulati, 1987). Utilisation of mother and child health care - namely, antenatal, delivery and post-partum and children's immunisation - facilitates a reduction in maternal, infant and child mortality and thus can enable a significant reduction in fertility (Gulati, 2003). All these processes seem to be highly interdependent and intertwined.

2. Objectives

This study intends to formulate a recursive model to highlight the structural linkages between key demographic parameters like marriage age patterns, contraception usage, mother and child health care utilisation - namely antenatal, delivery care and children's immunisation - and fertility. The parametric estimates of the structural linkages are based on the district level data on relevant parameters from alternate sources like DLHS-RCH (IIPS, 1999), CMIE (2000), Census (2001), and Population Commission (2001). These estimates would be utilised to elicit the direct, indirect and total effects of exogenous or predetermined socioeconomic, health and education infrastructure variables and cultural factors in the structural system. The structural estimates and the effects would facilitate a prioritisation of the alternate RCH components and demographic factors to be focused upon towards a cost effective achievement of the population policy objectives.

3. Methodology

This study formulates a recursive model in which its structural equations are ordered in such a way that the first endogenous variable has only predetermined or exogenous variables on the right hand side; the second equation contains predetermined variables and the first endogenous variable in the right-hand side; and so on. The special feature of the recursive system facilitates an estimation of equations one at a time by OLS without simultaneous-equation bias. Furthermore, the OLS estimates of the structural coefficients are unbiased and consistent. The structural relations in the recursive system can be formulated as follows:

$$Y_1 = f(X_1, X_2, X_3, \dots X_k; u_1)$$
$$Y_2 = f(X_1, X_2, X_3, \dots X_k; Y_1; u_2)$$
$$Y_3 = f(X_1, X_2, X_3, \dots X_k; Y_1, Y_2; u_3)$$

and so on.

The random variables are assumed to be independent.

The special features of a recursive model are that its equations may be estimated one at a time by OLS estimation technique obviating the simultaneous-equations bias. Assuming that there are G-endogenous variables and k-exogenous variables in the model the structural form of the recursive model would be as follows:

Recursive Structural Model

$$Y_1 = \gamma_{11} X_1 + \gamma_{12} X_2 + ..+ \gamma_{1k} X_k + u_1$$

$$Y_2 = \gamma_{21} X_1 + \gamma_{22} X_2 + ..+ \gamma_{2k} X_k + \beta_{21} Y_1 + u_2$$

$$Y_3 = \gamma_{31} X_1 + \gamma_{32} X_2 + ..+ \gamma_{3k} X_k + \beta_{31} Y_1 + \beta_{32} Y_2 + u_3$$

$$Y_G = \gamma_{G1} X_1 + \gamma_{G2} X_2 + ... + \gamma_{Gk} X_k + \beta_{G1} Y_1 + \beta_{G2} Y_2 + ... \beta_{G-1} Y_{G-1} + u_{G.}$$

The recursive system being triangular in the sense that coefficients of the endogenous variables (the β's) form a triangular array; the main diagonal of the array of β's contains units, and no coefficients appear above the main diagonal. The array of structural parameters can be rewritten in matrix form as follows:

Matrix Form of the Recursive System

$$\beta_{GxG} Y_{Gx1} = \Gamma_{Gxk} X_{kx1} + U_{Gx1}$$

The estimated structural parameters can be elicited by application of OLS to each equation yielding unbiased and consistent estimates of the structural parameters β and Γ.

The reduced form parameters $\breve{N}$ can be elicited using the estimated structural parameters of the recursive system as follows:

Reduced Form Parameters

$$\breve{N} = \beta^{-1}{}_{GxG} \cdot \Gamma_{Gxk.}$$

The reduced-form parameters measure the total effect, direct plus indirect of a change in the predetermined variable on the endogenous variable, after taking account of the interdependence among the jointly dependent endogenous variables, while a structural coefficient indicates only the direct effect (Koutsoyiannis, 1977).

4. Structural Formulation of the Model

The functional forms of the six structural relations become clear from the following Figure 17.1 as well as Table 17.1, which provide parametric estimates of the recursive system in the Figure.

The first structural relation depicts that marriage age patterns namely, per cent girls married below the age of 18 years (PGMB18) providing extent of girls getting married at younger ages i.e. below 18, the legal age at marriage, is predicted by the eleven socioeconomic and cultural factors under the purview of the present study. The marriage age patterns are presumed to be influenced by women's empowerment enabling factors like women's education and employment *viz.* female literacy rate (FLR) and female work participation rate (FWPR); per cent villages electrified (PVE) and per cent villages not connected by *pucca* road (PVNCPR). Other predictors of marriage age patterns are presumed to be infrastructure variables like village electrification (PVE), road connectivity of villages (PVNCPR), health infrastructure variables like number of ANMs and hospital and dispensary beds per lakh population (HADBEDS), number of primary schools per lakh population (PRMSCHL). Other factors presumed to affect marriage age patterns are overall economic development (DDIO),[1] extent of industrialisation characterised by industrial workers as per cent of main workers (IWPMW). Overall economic development index is also presumed to affect the marriage age patterns. Furthermore, other predictors in the relation are infrastructure variables like number of primary schools per lakh population (PRMSCL), per cent villages electrified (PVE), marriage age patterns. Lastly, proportionate Muslim population (PMUS) has also been inducted as a predictor of marriage age patterns.

The second structural relation depicts that usage of contraception characterised by per cent couples using family planning methods (PCUFP) is determined by all the eleven socioeconomic and cultural factors under the purview of the present study alongwith the first endogenous variable namely, PGMB18.

The third structural relation depicts the extent of utilisation of antenatal care characterised by per cent pregnancies in which the antenatal care was utilised (PPANC) is determined by all the eleven socioeconomic and cultural variables alongwith marriage age patterns (PGMB18) and usage of contraception (PCUFPM).

The fourth structural relation that depicts the extent of institutional deliveries characterised by per cent deliveries in health institutions (PDHI) being determined by all the predetermined

1. The districtwise overall economic development index (DDIO) based on twelve sectoral developmental indices, was elicited by the author for an earlier study published in Journal of Quantitative Economics and used in the World Bank study jointly with Prof. K. Srinivasan. The details on methodology etc. are available in Gulati (1996), Srinivasan (1998), Harman (1970). Some details of the methodology are also made available in Annex 2.

variables alongwith marriage age patterns, contraception usage and extent of utilisation of antenatal care.

The fifth structural relation depicts the extent of children's immunisation characterised by per cent children over age one with complete immunisation (PCWCI) as being determined by all the predetermined variables alongwith the four of the endogenous variables *viz.* PGMB18, PCUFPM, PPANC, and PDHI.

The sixth structural relation depicts that fertility characterised by per cent births of order 3+ (PBO3P) as being a function of all the five endogenous variables *viz.* PGMB18, PCUFPM, PPANC, PDHI, and PCWCI; in the system and all the eleven predetermined variables.

The following figure clearly depicts the linkages and structural formulation of the recursive system under study.

Figure 17.1

Flow Diagram for the Integrated RCH and Fertility Model

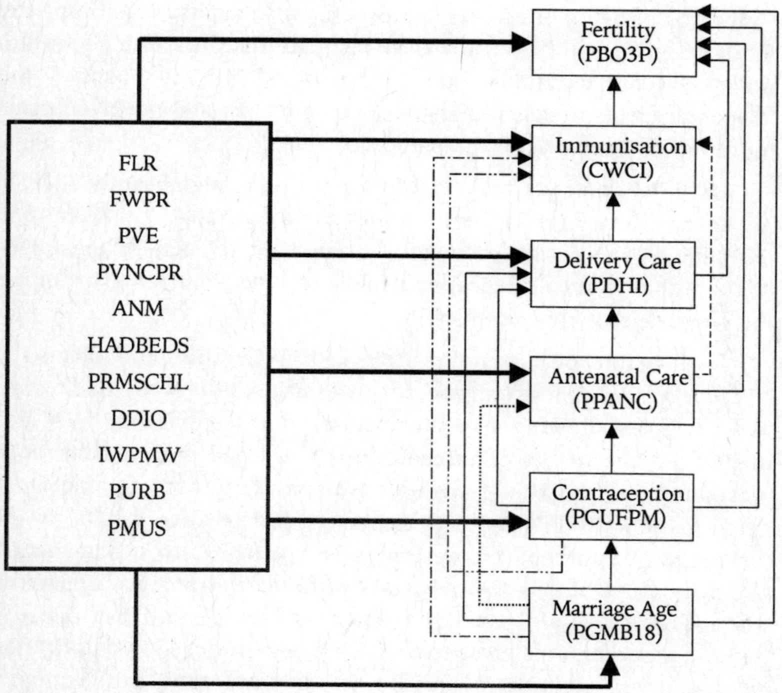

The figure clearly reflects that fertility (PBO3P0) has five endogenous predictors (five arrows from the five smaller rectangular boxes) and all the eleven exogenous variables (arrow from bigger rectangular box). Furthermore, immunisation of children (PCWCI) has four endogenous variables and eleven exogenous variables as predictors. Likewise lowermost small rectangular box depicts that marriage age (PGMB18) has only all the eleven exogenous and none of the endogenous variables as predictors.

5. Parametric Estimates of the Model

Parametric estimates of the structural model are presented in Table 17.1. Perusal of the Table reveals that women's empowerment enabling factors like female education (FLR) and work participation (FWPR) depict significant by inhibiting effect on lowered marriage age patterns. Alternatively, districts with higher female literacy and work participation depict higher marriage age patterns. Furthermore, infrastructure variables like road connectivity of villages (PVNCPR) and overall economic development (DDIO) characterising higher standards of living or economic prosperity also depicts significant and positive impact on higher marriage age patterns. Interestingly, health infrastructure variables like number of ANMs and hospital and dispensary beds in districts also depict significant and positive impact on increase in marriage age patterns.

Usage of contraception (PCUFPM) seems to significantly affected by female literacy (FLR), health infrastructure variables *viz.* ANMs and HADBEDS; and overall economic development (DDIO). Interestingly, we find that women's education depicts relatively much higher impact on the usage of contraception.

Utilisation of antenatal care (PPANC) and contraception (PCUFPM) depict a strong and positive linkage. Alternatively, districts with couples showing a greater use of contraceptive methods also depict a higher usage of antenatal care. Amongst the predetermined variables we find that female education (FLR) and female work participation (FWPR) depict a significant and positive impact on the utilisation of antenatal care. Improvement in health infrastructure facilities (HADBEDS) also depicts significant and positive impact on the utilisation of antenatal care. Furthermore, we find that districts with higher economic prosperity (DDIO) also depict higher utilisation of antenatal care. It is of interest to note that the women's empowerment enabling factors depict relatively stronger impact on antenatal care utilisation.

Table 17.1

Parametric Estimates of the Recursive System's Structural Relations

Predictor Variable	*Dependent Variable*					
	PGMB18	*PCUFPM*	*PPANC*	*PDHI*	*PCWCI*	*PBO3P*
PGMB18		.057	.037	–.011	–.181*	.065**
PCUFPM			.580	.010	.283*	–.394*
PPANC				.406*	.306*	–.080**
PDHI					.127*	–.464*
PCWCI						–.113*
FLR	–.441*	.527*	.153*	.220*	.083**	–.050
FWPR	–.090**	.004	.237*	.024	.094*	–.038
PVE	.015	.177*	–.030	.016	.005	.010
PVNCPR	.111*	–.055	–.112*	–.221*	–.027	.070*
ANMNEW	–.131*	.094**	.033	.128*	.046	–.014
HADBEDS	–.096**	.123*	.061**	.081*	.045	.030
PRMSCHL	–.085**	.063	.066**	–.001	.041	–.030
DDIO	–.291*	.112**	.104**	–.056	.027	.009
IWPMW	–.009	.050	–.005	.018	.011	.019
PURB	–.199*	.001	.043	.163*	.029	–.073*
PMUS	.014	-.037	–.003	–.056**	–.028	.052*
R-Square	.517	.435	.616	.725	.669	.834

* & ** Denote Significance at 1 per cent and 5 per cent, respectively.

Per cent deliveries in health institutions (PDHI) seem to be significantly associated with the extent of utilisation of antenatal care (PPANC). Alternatively, districts with higher utilisation of antenatal care also depict higher utilisation of delivery care especially from health institutions. Also we find that creation of health infrastructure like number of hospital and dispensary beds and number of ANMs also depict promotive impact on the utilisation of delivery care from health institutions. Overall we find that extent of urbanisation also depict promotive impact on deliveries in health institutions. Surprisingly, we find that districts with predominantly higher proportions of Muslim population depict significantly lower utilisation of health institutions for delivery care.

Extent of children's immunisation (PCWCI) seems to be significantly associated with marriage age patterns, usage of contraception, and utilisation of antenatal and delivery care. Directions of linkages or effects turn out to be consistent with general expectations. Alternatively, districts with higher usage of contraception, higher utilisation of antenatal and delivery care also depict higher extent of children's immunisation. Furthermore, we find that women's empowerment factors like female education (FLR) and female employment (FWPR) also depict significant and positive impact on the extent of children's immunisation.

Coming to the fertility (PBO3P) equation we find that all the five endogenous variables *viz*. PGMB18, PCUFPM, PPANC, PDHI and PCWCI; depict significant and expected impact on fertility. Alternatively, districts with higher usage of contraception, antenatal and delivery care and children's immunisation depict lower levels of fertility and districts with higher per cent of girls marrying below 18 years of age depict higher fertility. Interestingly, we find that the impact of utilisation of antenatal and institutional delivery care, which is supposed to affect the maternal and neo-natal component of infant mortality depict significant and relatively higher direct impact on fertility. Interestingly, we find that the impact of utilisation of antenatal and institutional delivery care, which is supposed to affect the maternal and neo-natal component of infant mortality depict significant and relatively higher direct impact on fertility. Furthermore, usage of contraception also depicts relatively much higher and significant and inhibitive impact on fertility. Amongst the predetermined variables we find only extent of urbanisation and road connectivity of villages depict significant impact on fertility. Surprisingly and interestingly, we find that districts with predominance of Muslim population, despite controlling of all the relevant socio-economic and infrastructure variables, depict significantly higher fertility compared with other districts.

6. Partial and Total Effects of Predetermined Variables on Endogenous Variables

The direct or partial effects of the predetermined variables have been highlighted earlier while discussing the parametric estimate in the earlier section. Furthermore, the total effects of the predetermined variables elicited through estimated reduced form parameters are presented in the following Table 17.2.

Table 17.2

Direct and Total Effects of the Predetermined Variables on the Endogenous Variables in the Recursive System Model

Predictor Variable		*Direct and Total Effects on*					
		PGMB18	*PCUFPM*	*PPANC*	*PDHI*	*PCWCI*	*PBO3P*
FLR	Direct	–0.441	0.527	0.153	0.220	0.083	–0.050
	Total	–0.441	0.501	0.427	0.403	0.486	–0.550
FWPR	Direct	–0.090	0.004	0.237	0.024	0.094	–0.038
	Total	–0.090	–0.001	0.233	0.119	0.196	–0.139
PVE	Direct	0.015	0.177	–0.030	0.016	0.005	0.010
	Total	0.015	0.177	0.073	0.047	0.081	–0.096
PVNCPR	Direct	0.111	–0.055	–0.112	–0.221	–0.027	0.070
	Total	0.111	–0.048	–0.136	–0.277	–0.137	0.251
ANM	Direct	–0.131	0.094	0.033	0.128	0.046	–0.014
	Total	–0.131	0.101	–0.030	0.115	0.046	–0.039
HADBEDS	Direct	–0.096	0.123	0.061	0.081	0.045	0.030
	Total	–0.096	0.117	0.125	0.134	0.151	–0.111
PRMSCHL	Direct	–0.085	0.063	0.066	–0.001	0.041	–0.030
	Total	–0.085	0.058	0.096	0.039	0.107	–0.096
DDIO	Direct	–0.291	0.112	0.104	–0.056	0.027	0.009
	Total	–0.291	0.095	0.148	0.008	0.153	–0.080
IWPMW	Direct	–0.009	0.050	–0.005	0.018	0.011	0.019
	Total	–0.009	0.049	0.023	0.028	0.037	–0.020
PURB	Direct	–0.199	0.001	0.043	0.163	0.029	–0.073
	Total	–0.199	–0.010	0.029	0.177	0.093	–0.176
PMUS	Direct	0.014	–0.037	–0.003	–0.056	–0.028	0.052
	Total	0.014	–0.036	–0.023	–0.066	–0.056	0.106

Marriage age patterns (PGMB18) being the first structural relation in the recursive model, would obviously depict direct and total effects being exactly same. Coming to total effects of predetermined variables on usage of contraception we find that most of the significant direct effects get compounded because of indirect effects routed through marriage age patterns. However, the changes are not substantial as marriage age patterns was found to bear insignificant impact on the usage of contraception (see Table 17.1).

Total effect of female literacy on utilisation of antenatal care (PPANC) gets compounded and becomes significant higher (0.427) than its direct effect (0.153) because of its indirect effect routed through age at marriage and contraception usage. Similarly we find that total impacts of female work participation (FWPR), road connectivity of villages (PVNCPR), hospital and dispensary beds (HADBEDS), and overall economic development (DDIO) turn out to much higher compared to their direct effects because of substantial indirect effects routed through marriage age patterns contraception usage.

Coming to total effects on institutional delivery we find that total impact of female literacy (FLR) turns out to be almost double (0.403) compared with its direct effect (0.220). Furthermore significant direct effects of road connectivity, number of ANMs and hospital beds (HADBEDS) and extent of urbanisation (PURB) also get compounded because of the indirect effects routed through other endogenous variables. Furthermore, we find that total effects of Muslim predominance in districts also get compounded and thus the total inhibited effect on institutional delivery (-0.066) is higher than the direct effect (–0.056).

Childcare characterised by per cent children with complete immunisation (PCWCI) gets affected significantly by female empowerment characteristics like female education (FLR) and female work participation rate (FWPR). Furthermore, we find that total effects of these variables are much higher compared with their direct effects of utilisation of child immunisation. For female literacy (FLR) we find that total effect turns out to be much higher (0.486) compared with its direct effect (0.083). Thus, the indirect effects of female literacy on child care routed through other endogenous variables like marriage age patterns, contraception usage, antenatal and delivery care turns out to substantial resulting into much higher total effect of female education on children's immunisation.

Coming to fertility (PBO3P) we find that total inhibitive effect of female education (-0.550) is substantially higher than its direct effect on fertility (-0.050). Similarly we find that extent of urbanisation (PURB) depicts much higher total effect (-0.176) compared with its direct effect (-0.073) on fertility. Interestingly, we find that districts with higher Muslim proportionate populations depict much higher promotive total impact (0.106) on fertility compared with their direct effect (0.052) on fertility. Alternatively, the indirect effects of lower marriage age patterns and contraception usage, lower utilisation of antenatal and delivery care, and children's immunisation amongst the Muslim population also seem to generate a substantial promotive impact on their fertility.

7. Summary and Concluding Remarks

The recursive model comprising six structural linkages integrating the RCH components and fertility as endogenous variables was formulated in the study. The endogenous variables in the recursive structural model comprise marriage age patterns (PGMB18), contraceptive methods usage (PCUFPM), per cent pregnancies in which antenatal care was utilised (PPANC), per cent deliveries in the health institutions (PDHI), per cent children aged one and above who got completely immunised (PCWCI) and per cent births of order three and higher (PBO3P). The structural system comprised twelve predetermined variables like women's empowerment enabling factors like female education (FLR) and employment (FWPR), health and educational infrastructure variables like number of hospital and dispensary beds (HADBEDS) and schools (PRMSCL) per *lakh* population, extent of village electrification (PVE) and road connectivity (PVNCPR), overall extent of urbanisation (PURB), extent of industrialisation (IWPMW), overall economic development (DDIO), and cultural variable like per cent Muslim population (PMUS) in the district. The detailed description and descriptive statistics of the district-wise indicators is furnished in the Appendices.

Perusal of the estimated structural coefficients depicting the partial effects of the predictor variables in the recursive model suggest the following:

1. Fertility gets significantly affected by marriage age patterns, contraception usage, and utilisation of antenatal and delivery care and extent of children's immunisation. Relative impact of contraception and institutional deliveries on fertility seems to substantially higher compared with the other RCH parameters under study.
2. Children's immunisation is significantly higher amongst women who use contraception and RCH care *viz.* antenatal and delivery care. Also we find marriage age patterns also significantly affect the extent of children's immunisation.

Women's empowerment enabling factors like female education and work participation depict significant and positive impact on the extent of children' immunisation.

3. Institutional deliveries are significantly higher amongst educated women. Health infrastructure and personnel depict significant and positive impact institutional deliveries. Muslim dominated districts depict significantly lower level of utilisation of institutional deliveries.
4. Antenatal care is significantly higher amongst women who are using any form of contraception. Furthermore, the women's empowerment factors depict significant and positive impact on the utilisation of antenatal care. Once again we find that the health infrastructure variables also depict significant and positive impact on the utilisation of antenatal care. Interestingly, districts with higher overall economic development also depict significantly higher levels of utilisation of the antenatal care.
5. Usage of contraception gets significantly affected by women's education, health personnel and health infrastructure facilities like hospital and dispensary beds, and overall economic development and standards of living.
6. Marriage age is significantly higher in districts with higher educated women, prosperous villages with road connectivity, better health and education infrastructure facilities, and higher overall economic development.

Reduced form parameters, elicited out of the estimated structural coefficients of the recursive model, depicting the total effects of the predetermined variables in the model suggest the following:

1. On fertility we find that the total inhibitive effects of female literacy and work participation are substantially higher compared with their direct effects. Alternatively, the indirect effects of women's empowerment factors transmitted through higher marriage age patterns, higher usage of contraception, higher utilisation of antenatal and delivery care and children's immunisation are substantial and thus the total effects of these factors turn out to be substantially higher compared with their direct effects on fertility.
2. Total inhibitive effect of health infrastructure, especially hospital and dispensary beds, on fertility also seems to be substantially higher compared with their direct effects on fertility.

3. Predominance of Muslim population in districts also depicts substantial higher positive total effect compared with the direct effect on fertility.
4. Total effects of female literacy on marriage age patterns, contraception usage, antenatal and delivery care and children's immunisation are relatively much higher compared with their effects on the corresponding RCH parameters.
5. Total effects of the health infrastructure, especially hospital and dispensary beds, on fertility, contraception and other RCH parameters are substantially higher compared with its direct effect on the corresponding parameters.
6. Road connectivity of villages is also found to play a significant role towards promotion of utilisation of RCH care and curtailment of fertility.
7. Total effects of overall economic development on different RCH utilisation factors turn out to substantially higher compared with its direct effects on all the corresponding variables.
8. Muslim dominated districts depict significantly lower marriage age patterns, lower utilisation of delivery care and children's immunisation and thus substantially higher total effect on levels of fertility compared with the direct effect.
9. Role of auxiliary nursing midwives and trained birth attendants can be extremely important in the promotion of safe deliveries in far flung and hilly areas with difficult terrains which in turn would reduce fertility and incidence of reproductive tract infections amongst women, and promote children's immunisation.

7.1. Policy Imperatives

Strong inter-linkages between fertility, usage of contraception, marriage age patterns, utilisation of RCH care *viz.* antenatal and delivery care, and children's immunisation are discerned in the study. Relative significance of usage of contraception, institutional deliveries and children's immunisation towards fertility reduction are much higher compared with other endogenous variables like antenatal care and marriage age patterns. Thus, with twin objectives of improvement in the quality of life and fertility reduction we need simultaneous concerted efforts to promote usage of quality contraceptives, institutional deliveries and children's immunisation.

Women's empowerment enabling factors, especially female education and employment, are discerned to play important role towards utilisation of RCH quality care package in India as depicted through their all pervasive effects on promotion of higher marriage age patterns, usage of contraception, utilisation of antenatal and delivery care. Women's empowerment was also placed in the centre stage in the International Conference on Population and Development held in Cairo in 1994, after which paradigm shifts in India's population policy also got documented in the National Population Policy. Thus, women's empowerment can facilitate wider usage of RCH quality care and also fertility reduction.

However, Muslim dominated regions or districts depict significantly lower utilisation of institutional deliveries compared with other districts. Also we find a tendency of lower age at marriage, lower utilisation of contraceptives, lower utilisation of antenatal care and children's immunisation services in the Muslim dominated districts. Thus, Muslim dominated areas require focused attention towards promotion of RCH quality care for improvement in the quality of life of Muslim women in particular in India and thus quicker achievement of fertility reduction goals.

References

Census of India (2001). "Provisional Population Totals", Paper 1 of 2001 Supplement, District Totals, Registrar General & Census Commissioner, India, New Delhi.

Centre for Monitoring Indian Economy (CMIE). (2000). *Profiles of Districts*, Mumbai.

Gulati, S.C. (1988). *Fertility in India: An Econometric Analysis of a Metropolis*, Sage Publications, New Delhi/Newburry Park/London.

————. (1992). "Developmental Determinants of Demographic Variables in India: A District Level Analysis", *Journal of Quantitative Economics*, (January) 8(1): pp. 157-72, Delhi School of Economics, Delhi.

————. (1996). "District Level Development Indices: A Factor Analytical Approach", *Indian Journal of Regional Science*, XXVIII (1), Kolkata.

————. (2003). "RCH-Care Utilisation and Fertility in Uttar Pradesh and Uttaranchal", Working Paper Series No E/239/2003, Institute of Economic Growth, Delhi.

Harman, Harry (1970). *Modern Factor Analysis*, Chicago, Chicago University Press.

International Institute of Population Sciences (IIPS) (1994). *National Family Health Survey*, 1992-93, IIPS. Mumbai.

————. (1999). *India: National Family Health Survey* (NFHS-2): 1998-99. Mumbai.

————. (1999). *Reproductive and Child Health Project: Rapid Household Survey* (Phase I & II). Mumbai.

Khan, M.E. and Bella Patel (1997). "Reproductive Behaviour of Muslims in Uttar Pradesh", *Journal of Family Welfare*, (March) 43(1): pp 13-29.

Koutsoyiannis, A. (1977). *Theory of Econometrics*, Oxford University Press, Macmillan Education Ltd. Hampshire.

Operations Research Group (ORG) (1989). *Third All India Family Planning Survey*, Monograph, ORG, Baroda.

Population Commission (2001). "District-wise Social Economic Demographic Indicators", *National Commission on Population*, Government of India, New Delhi.

Ranjna, P.N., Ajay Kumar Mishra and S. Krishnamurthy (1998). "Impact of Maternal Education and Health Services on Child Mortality in Uttar Pradesh, India", *Asia Pacific Population Journal*, 13(2).

Srinivasan, K., S.C. Gulati *et al.* (1998). "World Bank Projects in Population and Health in India in the Eighties: A Study of Demographic Impact at the District Level", *Population Foundation of India*, New Delhi.

APPENDICES

ANNEX 1

Table A-1

Description of Variables, Sources of Data and Descriptive Statistics

Abbreviated Name	*Description of the Variable and Source of Data*
PGMB18	Per cent Girls Married Before 18 Yrs. of Age (RCH)
PCUFPM	Per cent Couples Using Family Planning Methods (RCH)
PPANC	Per cent Pregnancies in which Antenatal Care was Used (RCH)
PDHI	Per cent Deliveries in Health Institutions (RCH)
PCWCI	Per cent Children 12-36 Months Old with Complete Immunisation (RCH)
PBO3P	Per cent Births During Last 3 Yrs. of Order 3+ (RCH)
FLR	Female Literacy Rate (Census 2001)
FWPR	Female Work Participation Rate (CMIE)
PVE	Per cent Villages Electrified (CMIE)
PVNCPR	Per cent Villages Not Connected by Pucca Road (PC, 2001)
ANM	Auxiliary Nurse Midwives Per Lakh Population (CMIE)
HADBEDS	Hospital and Dispensary Beds Per Lakh Population (CMIE)
PRMSCL	Primary Schools Per Lakh Population (CMIE, 2000)
DDIO	District's Development Index (Gulati, 1996))
IWPMW	Industrial Workers As Per cent of Main Workers (CMIE, 2000)
PURB	Per cent Urban (Census)
PMUS	Per cent Muslim Population (Census)

Descriptive Statistics

	N	*Minimum*	*Maximum*	*Mean*	*Std. Deviation*
PGMB18	504	0	84	34.80	21.67
PCUAM	504	1.7	83.7	45.666	17.458
PPANC	504	.0	100.0	66.663	25.177
PDHI	504	.0	100.0	33.947	24.170
PCWCI	504	1.6	99.5	56.391	24.509
PBO3P	504	1.9	73.7	43.933	14.043
FLR	504	18.49	96.06	53.3378	15.3783
FWPR	451	1.75	60.07	24.9148	13.3210
PVE	360	0	157	87.35	18.40
PVNCPR	488	.00	89.62	36.6441	28.0063
ANMNEW	451	3.38	456.54	101.7282	72.3511
HADBEDS	357	7.66	366.98	73.3371	65.0768
PRNSC	309	11.28	293.69	79.3269	44.1999
DDIO	387	−1.11	3.98	2.062E-02	.7567
IWPMW	409	0	1330	6.58	65.67
PURB	451	.0	100.0	21.726	17.508
PMUS	451	.04	94.31	10.5503	11.9731

ANNEX 2

Methodology for Eliciting District-wise Economic Development Indices (DDIO)

Development being a multi-dimensional phenomenon is difficult to capture by any single development indicator. Most often, per capita income is suggested as an overall measure of economic development. This measure of development has often been subjected to lot of criticism for its inherent limitations and accounting problems in the Indian context (Gopalaswamy, 1983). Nevertheless, the non-availability of even such a limited measure of development at the district level constrains us in investigating the linkages between development and demographic patterns. Furthermore, sectoral aspects of economic development may depict varied linkages with the demography parameters. For the purpose, this study has elicited district level economic developmental indicators highlighting sectoral aspects of economic development.

A vector of 14 developmental indicators for all the districts is selected to highlight the aggregate and sectoral aspects of development. Basic indictors are selected to reflect the sectoral aspects of development, *viz*. agricultural, manufacturing and tertiary, at the district level.

Factor scores are elicited for all the districts depicting underlying sectoral dimensions of development and thereby the factor scores for overall economic development are also elicited by a weighted average of the sectoral aspects of development. A brief description of the varimax rotated factor structure of the 14 underlying development indicators is presented as follows:

Varimax-Rotated Factor Structure for Development Variables

The factorial approach starts with the correlation matrix of the original set of 14 development variables and elicits factors, which account for the inter-district variations among the variables in descending order of magnitude. The number of factors retained in the factor structure is subjected to the Kaiser's criterion of Eigen value greater than unity. It may be noted that the contribution of the rotated factor structure to be variance explained may not necessarily be in the descending order of magnitude as in the case of principal factor solution. The rotated factor structure is presented in Table A2.1.

Table A 2.1

Varimax Rotated Factor Structure of District level Development Indicators

Var. No	*Abridged Name*	*Factor Loadings*			*Communality*
		I (AGR)	*II (IND)*	*III (TER)*	
1	PNASGA	.52(.19)	.36(.20)	–.26(.06)	.46
2	PGIAGCA	.73(.27)	–.18(.09)	.02(.00)	.56
3	PHFC	.85(.32)	.24(.13)	.10(.02)	.79
4	ACFP	.83(.31	–.00(.00)	–.09(.02)	.70
5	ANR	–.54(.20)	.31(.18)	–.00(.00)	.39
6	PVE	.40(.15)	.62(.35)	.34(.08)	.66
7	EHHIPLP	–.05(.02)	.52(.29)	–.12(.03)	.28
8	ADEFPLP	–.10(.04)	.60(.34)	.38(.09)	.51
9	PCBCAI	–.01(.00)	.21(.12)	.72(.18)	.56
10	BOPLP	.02(.01)	.07(.04)	.79(.20)	.63
11	PCBD	.01(.00)	–.07(.04)	.94(.23)	.88
12	PCBASS	–.04(.01)	–.18(.10)	.77(.19)	.63
13	LITPTP	–.16((.06)	.56(.31)	.61(.15)	.71
14	PURBP	–.00(.00)	.22(.12)	.81(.20)	.71
	Eigen-Value	2.71	1.77	4.00	

Notes: 1. Figures in brackets are the factor score coefficients
2. Factor I: Extent of Agricultural Development
3. Factor II: Extent of Industrial Development
4. Factor III: Extent of Tertiary Sector Development.

A perusal of the varimax rotated factor solution reveals that the First Factor (F-1) represents extent of 'Agricultural Activity' as it is basically constituted by per hectare fertiliser consumption (PHFC), per capita food production (PCFP), per cent gross irrigated area to gross cropped area (PGIAGCA) per cent net sown area to geographical area (PNSAGA), *etc.* The factor loading of these variables are much higher on the factor compared to other industrial or tertiary sectoral developmental indicators.

The Second Factor (F-II) is identified as 'Industrial Development' because its predominant constituent variables are extent of employment in factories (ADEFPLA), employment in household industry per lakh population (EHHIPLP), extent of electrification (PVE), and extent of overall literacy (LITPTP).

The Third Factor (F-III) is identified as 'Tertiary Sector Development' because of its relatively much higher factor loading on bank advances to the service sector (PCBASS), per capita bank deposits (PCBD), literacy (LITPTP), and extent of urbanisation (URBTPT).

District Level Development Factor Scores (DDIO)

The three factor scores (m=3) for all the districts representing three sectoral aspects of economic development are estimated. It may be of interest to mention that the three factor scores can be combined to obtain a weighted aggregate index reflecting overall economic development. The composite district's development index (DDIO) was calculated by assigning weights, to the sectoral aspects of development captured by the three factor scores in proportion to the Eigen values of the three factors. The pattern of weights is in close correspondence with the conventional approach of assigning weights to different sectors in proportion to their percentage contribution towards the gross domestic product (GDP), namely, agricultural (0.32), industrial (0.21), and services (0.47).

Section VI

Secularism and Religion

18

Whither Indian Secularism?

Some Reflections[1]

P.C. JOSHI

"When we consider what religion is for mankind, and what science is, it is no exaggeration to say that the future course of history depends upon the decision of this generation as to the relations between them. We have here the two strongest general forces which influence men, and they seem to be set one against the other — the force of our religious instuitions, and the force of our impulse to accurate observation and logical deduction....

"The clash is a sign that there are finer truths and wider perspectives within which a reconciliation of a deeper religion and a more subtle science will be found".

A.N. Whitehead, Science in the Modern World, Penguin Books Ltd., 1938, pp. 210-212.

Indian secularism—its thought and practice as it has evolved with the coming of independence—has evoked a wide-ranging public discourse in recent years. The discourse is not yet concluded and is being pursued with renewed vigour and increasing participation from politicians and public workers, intellectuals and scholars, media experts and art specialists. The ongoing discourse provides abundant proof of the fact that the secular idea is not yet dead and it still evokes vigorous defence from its votaries and fierce criticism from its adversaries.

It must be admitted that to-day the terms and agenda of public discourse are being set not by the committed secularists but largely by the skeptics or the hardened anti-secularists. The committed

1. Initially I thought of presenting a paper on "Agrarian Problem Revisited: Some Reflections" for the A.M. Khusro Memorial Volume as Khusro and I had the longest engagement with the agrarian problem since the beginning of independence. I changed my mind and opted for the theme of future of Indian secularism after my attention was drawn to Khusro's foreword to Mukul Dube's book on the Great Gujarat Killings, perhaps his last writing which showed how deeply concerned Khusro was before his passing away about the grave threat to Indian secularism from belligerent Hindu fundamentalism. The present paper first appeared as an Introduction to a collection of essays on secularism (P.C. Joshi 1995). A revised and enlarged version of the same has been prepared for the Khusro Memorial volume.

secularists have been taken by surprise by the sudden outburst of opposition to the secular idea from the constitutional as well as extra-constitutional forums, from the political as well as semi-political and non-political platforms. The nation's Parliament itself which was so far regarded as the strong bulwark of secular ideology had been suddenly converted into a forum of confrontation and a trial of strength between the secular and the anti-secular forces. In certain major States of India the State Governments became active instruments in the "holy war" against secularism. Most disquieting was the sudden conversion of religious shrines into centres of religious crusade against the secular state. It was as if we had been suddenly transported back to the pre-independence period and that we were seeing the same drama being reenacted with the same slogans, same rhetoric, same banners, and the same battle cry. It is as if the 'two-nation theory' had returned once again with a vengeance. Only the main actors in the drama had changed. The so-called spokesmen of the Hindu majority now took the place of the representatives of the erstwhile Muslim League to assert that religion was the basis of nationhood and that the Hindus constituted a separate nation and that India should be declared a Hindu state. Even when the ideology was not so nakedly presented, its essence was the same for the discerning eye.

It was obvious that the threat to secularism was not just political; it was supported by a major ideological and cultural offensive. It was also obvious that this threat could be met effectively by asking all the inconvenient questions and formulating all the awkward issues which secular intellectuals or intellectuals sympathetic to the secular ideal had been evading so far. To cope with the challenge from the anti-secular forces, it was necessary to understand from what source they had acquired their present influence and hold on the minds of the people and why the secularists were facing a massive setback. In other words, it was necessary that the issues which called for fresh answers should be courgeously confronted and also clearly formulated for a searching enquiry and examination.

A large number of issues have been thrown up into prominence by the emerging situation. Some of the issues on which the ongoing discourse on secularism has been focussed are as follows:

What is the true meaning of secularism? How does one identify any individual, group or party as secular or anti-secular? How does one deal with the threat to secularism at the level of the state and that of the civil society? Under what conditions is the use of force justified against the anti-secular elements? Has the meaning of secularism in India been distorted due to opportunistic considerations? What have been the consequences of such distortions?

What are the fundamental principles of secularism having universal significance? What are the variations arising out of its application to different countries or cultures? Is secularism a concept unique to Western societies and has no basis in the Indian ethos? Or is it an idea which in its fundamentals is a natural growth from within and which has been struggling for fuller expression all through the ages?

Are the sacred and the secular to be treated as antagonistic to each other and are they in constant war against each other? Or was this antagonism a uniquely Western experience? Is it true that in India within the realms of both the sacred and the secular there had been constant creative tension between the outmoded and the living elements, leading to constant reinterpretation and revision of both? Is it not true then that creative forces within both these realms had been the allies rather than the foes of each other?

Why has the secular State, instead of emerging as a force for reconciliation and conflict-resolution, itself become the prime target of attack by religious communities? Why have the non-coercive mechanisms of conflict resolution by the state given way more and more to coercive and repressive methods as exemplified by Operation Bluestar? Is it not one of the major factors responsible for discrediting the secular State?

I must admit that studying no other subject in my research career of forty years or more has meant such emotional involvement, indeed emotional stress and distress, as the subject of secularism. Such an enquiry is not just an intellectual exercise. As a social scientist, I have felt deeply troubled by the fact that we as social scientists have failed to note the scale or depth of sufferings caused to the people by the religious dogmas or, to a lesser extent, the dogmas of the secularists. I have also felt troubled by the fact that, as stated by M.N. Srinivas, "a fundamentalist view of Indian society has made its appearance" in social science studies. It has been embraced by many Euro-American scholars and also by a few gifted and productive young scholars in India" (M.N. Srinivas, 1989: p.6). This 'fundamentalist view' has done much to provide intellectual support to the upsurge of religious fundamentalism in public life.

I have also felt troubled all through as an ardent believer in the secular idea from my younger days as I saw the secular project run into deeper and deeper crisis over the years and as I discovered to my dismay that what was left of secularism was its outward shell or label only and not its animating spirit or inner essence. As admitted by the then President himself, "any duplicity of attitude—any divergence in precept and practice—is causing untold harm" (S.D. Sharma 1989: 28). I could also see that the drift from the secular principle had caused untold suffering and distress to the common people. The wounds inflicted on the common people were sometimes much deeper on the spiritual and moral plane than on the physical plane. The cost of moral betrayal of ideals, of allowing the gap between ideal and practice to widen beyond a point, is incalculable. Any drift from the secular ideal in a multi-religious country results in total loss of moorings for people of all communities. Left without any anchorage and any orienting principle, people are trapped in the unending vicious circle of increasing mutual suspicion and bitterness, conflict and strife.

I felt troubled also as an Indian who had cherished the hope that, freed from the machinations of the colonial masters, independent, secular India would blaze a new trail and create conditions in which different communities would be able to live in harmony and work together for a better future. This hope also proved to be illusory. India on the eve and aftermath of freedom witnessed communal hatred and violence on a scale which had shocked and grieved beyond words all sane persons in the country and all well-wishers of India abroad. Not even the worst cynic could have expected the fruits of freedom to be so bitter and so sour. Not even the worst pessimist could ever have anticipated such naked dance of death and destruction in a country which had produced the greatest apostle of non-violence and which had also been the laboratory of the greatest experiment in non-violent *Satyagraha* in human history. What lesson would the very young in India might have learnt who had the misfortune to grow and come to consciousness in the era of unbridled brutality and violence accompanying the Partition of the country and later of the Punjab and Kashmir killings, the 'Operation Blue Star', the Delhi Riots, the Ayodhya Episode, the Bombay Riots and the other convulsions within and outside in the aftermath of this Episode!

The greatest tragedy was the poisoning of the minds and souls of men, women and children of all communities who were totally alienated from the age-old credo of 'live and let live', 'forget and forgive' and of compassion, kindness and tolerance.

Certain questions are the logical outcome of these traumatic events. Were these possibilities of violence and dehumanisation inherent in the very idea of secularism and implementing the secular project in a deeply religious country? Or did they arise from a merely formal acceptance of the secular idea and not all the obligations which the sincere acceptance of this idea involved? In other words, did they arise from the imperfections of the instruments entrusted with putting this idea into practice or from certain basic imperfections and deficiencies of the secular idea itself? These are questions which cannot be evaded and must not be evaded. But, in actual practice, they are being evaded at all levels.

Critics of the secular idea have argued that the idea itself is to blame for the trail of tragedy that has followed its acceptance as the dominant idea of the modern age and its unimaginative and mindless execution by the secular state. Secularism by its very definition was equated with an aggressive this-worldliness or concentration on earthly life on the one hand and on a break with a religious outlook and values on the other. There is, according to these critics, an inherent compulsion in secularism for effecting a total disjunction of the secular idea from the moral concerns and spiritual orientations that inhered in the religious tradition and that had imposed a certain restraint on man's uncontrolled lust for wealth and power. Religion had introduced mankind to basic moral and spiritual values. As a result man learnt to distinguish between *what is right* and *what is wrong*, between *what is* and *what ought to be*. He also learnt to rise above the 'self' and to relate himself to 'others' in the community. This importance of the moral and ethical element in human life distinguished men from animals.

Secularism grew as a social force through its critique of the religious outlook and of religious institutions. As this critique developed into confrontation with religion, the distinction between religious bigotry and obscurantism which had to be fought and the finer moral values which had to be assimilated, preserved and transmitted through generations was forgotten. Growth of a secular outlook, perhaps unintendedly, resulted in destroying those spiritual and moral values which were nurtured and sustained by religion through the ages. Anti-religious secularism was thus responsible for creating a spiritual and moral void which it could not fill up with secular values.

Discerning analysts of modernity had noted this void arising from the inexorable logic of secularisation (Max Weber 1930). But a keener perception of the consequences of religion-negating varieties of secularism is available from literary classics.

In Tolstoy's classic, *Anna Karenina*, Levin, who is the personification of Tolstoy himself, suffered great spiritual anguish as he could not find answers to the question "what he was" and "what he was living for". Failing to find an adequate answer from all the great modern philosophical treatises, he found himself in great torment and confusion. It is finally his servant, Fyodor, a peasant, who set him on the road of self-realisation by a chance observation:

> "One man lives for his own wants and nothing else, like Mituh; he only thinks of filling his belly, but Forkanitch, is a righteous man. He lives for his soul. He does not forget God" (Leo Tolstoy 1930:923).

How could a poor, illiterate peasant have access to this "great truth", asked Levin, that was denied to him, despite his great knowledge and learning and his faith in reason? And then Levin realised that "these great spiritual truths he had sucked in with his mother's milk" and that they had come to him from the same source as they had come to Fyodor and "to millions of men who lived ages ago and men living now - peasants, the poor in spirit and learned" (Leo Tolstoy 1930: 925).

Only he had begun "living and thinking without recognition of these truths but studiously ignoring them" in the vain belief in the supremacy of reason. The illiterate peasant, Fyodor, made him see the limits of reason. Levin asks himself:

> "By reason could I have arrived at knowing that I must love my neighbour and not oppress him? Reason discovered the struggle for existence, and the law that requires us to oppress all who hinder the satisfaction of our desires. That is the deduction of reason. But loving one's neighbour reason could never discover because it is irrational" (Leo Tolstoy 1950:927).

Levin also realised in a flash that "he had been quite wrong in supposing from the recollections of the circle of his young days at college that *religion had outlived its day and that it was now practically non-existent"*. He saw that "all the people nearest to him who were good in their lives were believers. They believed simply as he had believed in his earliest childhood and ninety-nine hundredths of the Russian people, all the working people for whose life he felt the deepest respect, believed" (Leo Tolstoy 1930: 915).

It may be asked whether radical secular thinkers, both liberals and Marxists, were not guilty of oversimplifying the complexity of religion; and whether they were not guilty of comprehending only the negative side of religion and not its positive side. They rightly understood and dramatised its role, specially the role of religion organised as the church and enforced by the clergy, in mystifying social reality, keeping the masses in fear and ignorance, preaching passivity and fatalism and defending exploitation, oppression and tyranny. But they ignored the finer side of religion as a source of moral and spiritual values. These values lifted up man from the status of a self-seeking animal and taught him to tap the higher side of human nature and not remain just a slave of his lower impulses and passions.

Marx's dictum - "Religion is the opium of the people"— which Lenin accepted "as the cornerstone of the whole Marxist outlook on religion" (Lenin 1977: 402-403) was certainly a bold, profound and insightful statement. It acted as a powerful corrective to the dominant view of religion which was characterised by falsehood, hypocrisy and opportunism. But torn out of its historical context and treated as a complete view and understanding of religion, this half-truth blown up into a total truth did incalculable harm when accepted uncritically by Marxists and revolutionaries in all parts of the world. It did the greatest harm when it was mechanically transferred to non-western countries like India which were still predominantly agrarian, pre-industrial and, as it were, pre-scientific and where religion interpreted in the widest sense of the term constituted the dominant world-view of the major part of the people. One of the major consequences of dismissing religion as "the opium of the people" was to rule it out as a serious subject deserving intensive study and research. As a result of this subject being almost a forbidden area of enquiry, there existed no possibility of reliable knowledge acting as a corrective to the biased view of the unimaginative and over enthusiastic secularists and, indeed, to their ignorance of the "religious factor".

Rejecting religion "as the opium of the people" in countries like India amounted to rejecting the entire civilisational and cultural heritage of the common people. To reject religion as the "opium of the people" was to reject the religious-cum-cultural works of all religions; it was to reject religious epics like *Ramayana* and *Mahabharata,* the teachings of Buddha, Kabir, Guru Nanak and the whole galaxy of *Sufi* saints and sages of all religions who were the greatest social reformers and revolutionaries of their times. It was to reject the great cultural heritage of the people at the grassroots and their oral traditions which were shaped over the centuries and gave meaning, purpose and orientation to their lives. These traditions represented a reconciliation and synthesis of the *sacred* and *the secular* in the finest sense of the term.

It must be admitted that great creative writers like Tolstoy had a better and deeper insight into certain aspects of religion and of its role in agrarian societies than great revolutionaries like Lenin who were engaged in the immediate task of overthrowing the systems of economic, social and political tyranny including religious tyranny in Czarist Russia. Tolstoy had also a better view of religion at its best embodying the fruits of man's spiritual and moral quest than Lenin who was confronted with religion at its worst, that is with religion as a reactionary force, and therefore, with the immediate task of overthrowing the combined power of religious bigots, political tyrants and economic exploiters. In his much quoted essay on "Leo Tolstoy as the Mirror of the Russian Revolution", Lenin rightly extols Tolstoy for his deep and original insight into the contradictions of the Russian peasantry in the nineteenth century and into the peasant's quest for emancipation through semi-religious categories. But in attacking the reactionary role of religion Lenin missed completely the qualitative difference between the religious dogmas and hypocrisy of the exploiting classes and the earth-bound, activist, rebellious "religiosity" of the oppressed peasant masses which had all the seeds of flowering into a resilient, authentic and humane secularity. Revolutionaries had rightly understood that the peasant masses needed emancipation from the Church and the clergy as they needed emancipation from the landlord and the usurer. But getting rid of the Church and the clergy was not the same thing as being able to do without a view of life, a set of norms and the concept of a moral order which were derived from religion and which were not static but subject to change through constant revision and reinterpretation. Many commentators like Maurice Hindus, writing on religion in post-revolutionary Russia had remarked how Marxist dictums had turned into something worse than religious dogmas; and pendulum might swing again in future towards a recovery of religion (Maurice Hindus 1946:216). The present writer had the first hand and, indeed, traumatic experience of the resurgence of religious fervour in Russia following the great upheaval of de-stalinisations during the field visit to Zagor city, the seat of authority of the Russian Church.

Again, we have a better perception sometimes of this religious factor in peasant life from literary classics than from modern social scientific writings. In the Indian context Tarashankar Bandopadhyaya, the great Bengali writer, in the Preface to his well-known novel, *Gana Devata,* makes a very penetrating and perspective comment on the "moral factor" in peasant life in the following words:

> "The traditions on which rural life based on agriculture rests are every where the same in all preindustrial societies. But in the pattern of India's rural life another principle was interwoven which can be called 'discipline' which was derived from the concept of the moral order....
>
> "The sense of right and wrong, just and unjust, emanating from it permeated every sphere of life and was the animating and binding force of all aspects of social existence. Inspite of outward diversity and heterogeneity, this concept of the moral order provided an astonishing inner unity and cohesion to Indian rural life in all parts of rural India. What happens to this concept under the stress of the new forces of a mechanical and commercial civilization is the subject of this story (Tarashankar Bandyopadhyaya 1970: 70; translation by the author from Hindi to English).

Without understanding the significance of what Tarashankar calls the "moral factor" in rural life, we cannot fully understand the emergence of Gandhi and his success as a mobiliser of the vast rural masses on a grand scale. Gandhi used quasi-religious language and idiom which to the 'secular' educated elite from urban India appeared as surrender to medievalism and religious revivalism but which appealed to the rural masses as an affirmation of the moral principle and the moral order.

Even in the contemporary context social radicals have discovered that religion at the level of the people is not just a support for the *status quo*; but it can also act as a moral force in the combat against injustice and oppression. As Gabrile Dietrich has remarked:

> "We do not know how much of people's religion and culture will survive and how much is bound to die. Yet whatever truth is there in their worship, their myths, their legends, will be transformed. To understand people's religion is not just an intellectual exercise. It is a matter of living with people and sharing with their deepest feelings. This is where many theologians and political leaders have fallen short" (Gabriele Dietrich 1977: 168).

In my view the Hindu fundamentalist offensive that has swept the urban areas and that has also spread to the rural areas in most parts of Northern India has been tremendously facilitated by the fact that the spiritual and moral element seemed to have virtually no place in the secular project which was wholly centred on the pursuit of material interests and on the pursuit of power. The fundamentalists have been allowed to appropriate the issue of concern for the disintegration of the moral order which, it appeared, had no place in the secular agenda. Can we meet the challenge posed by the fundamentalists by putting development once again on the high pedestal with new momentum provided to it by the force of the market and by globalisation?

Obviously not, as the new policy would further deepen the moral crisis by making the pursuit of wealth and the pursuit of power more efficient and, therefore, more relentless and the concern for moral and spiritual well-being more and more peripheral to the secular project.

And yet the fundamentalists are not so strong as we imagine them to be. They are more skilful operators of the power game and exploiters of religion for political gain. They have captured only the shell of the moral problem and not its basic essence. Herein lies their fatal weakness and the scope for overcoming them on the basis of a genuine awakening and involvement of the masses from below on the moral question as well as the developmental (i.e. political-economic) problems. Indeed, at the level of the masses the sacred and the secular, the moral and the political economic, are inseparable.

The agenda for mass involvement has, therefore, to be reformulated at two levels: at the level of reconstruction of the moral order and at the level of reconstruction of the political-economic order. In the first place, one must begin grappling with the question of the reconstruction of the moral outlook and the moral order. This can only be done by tapping the vast resources of moral energy inherent in the traditions of Buddha, Kabir, Guru Nanak, the *Sufis* at the macro level and the numberless saints and sages thrown up by the regional and local societies in their long history at the micro levels. Apart from the great tradition of Sanskritic or Brahmanical Hinduism or the great Buddhist, Islamic, Christian and Sikh Traditions of the dominant elites, there have existed heretic, rebellious and dissident, people-oriented traditions within the Great Traditions from above which have represented the great meeting points of man-affirming religious humanism and value-affirming secular humanism. There also existed vast diversity of oral traditions of people's religion and culture from below at the level of local societies in which the sacred and the secular, the pursuit of material and the spiritual well-being, were not dissociated but integrated with each other, continuously enriching and revitalising the process of community living.

The Gandhi Episode in Indian history captured only a fraction of the vast spiritual energy and moral ferment and force latent in these critical tendencies within the Great Traditions and the creative potential within the regional and local Little Traditions. The fundamentalist backlash within all religions that we witness today and that has led to the Great Regression and to counter-reforms can be effectively neutralised not by a half-hearted secularity of the urban, English educated and much publicised "new middle classes". These classes are aping the Euro-American style of life and offering a vast market for the cultural and economic goods and services of the affluent countries that are themselves caught in a deep moral crisis. It can be effectively neutralised only by the Great Awakening from below, by the great creative energy latent in the dissident tendencies of the Great Traditions and the moral forces of the Little Traditions of local and regional communities. These traditions seek not confrontation but reconciliation, not dissociation but integration, between the realms of the sacred and the secular. They alone have the potential to fight the forces of counter-reforms and moral decadence by reconciling the pursuit of material well-being with the quest for spiritual well-being. The secular project which destroys the local and regional communities as viable economies and as resilient cultures degrades the secular and marginalises the spiritual.

The greatest weakness of the secular project under all varieties of secularism is that the pursuit of material interests (tapping the lower-side of human nature) is central to it and the pursuit of spiritual well-being (the tapping of the higher side of human nature) has become more and more formal and has thus become only peripheral. This has been a world-wide phenomenon. Jawaharlal Nehru, the architect of India's secular project, admitted this during his last years in the following words:

> "In our efforts to ensure the material prosperity of the country, we have not paid any attention to the spiritual element in human nature. Therefore, in order to give the individual and the nation a sense of purpose and something to live for and, if necessary to die for, we have to devise some philosophy of life and give, in the wider sense of the world, a spiritual background to our thinking" (Jawaharlal Nehru 1989: 85).

The question is: was the "spiritual element" missing from the original secular vision? Or, was its erosion or marginalisation, a later development, one of its unintended consequences? Secular thinkers have argued that secularism had unintended consequences because the humanist vision (the primary values and ends underlying secularism) receded into the background and instrumental side of secularism was pushed into the foreground. In the words of Bertrand Russell, science as technique overshadowed science as philosophy or science as value system (Bertrand Russell 1962: 21). In the words of Whitehead, "the materialistic basis of science had directed attention to things as opposed to values" (A.N. Whitehead 1938: 235). In the definition of a good life the material side of life became the main concern, while the very means of improving the material side with great efficiency belittled the concerns for moral and spiritual well-being. Thus the pursuit of the material and of spiritual well-being pulled in opposite directions. It may be recalled that the promoters of the secular vision were themselves uneasy on this score. As Raymond Aron remarks:

> "Both Comte and Marx.... wondered about the destiny of a humanity bereft of religion, in the traditional meaning of the word. For a century and a half philosophers and sociologists have continued to ask this question: What will fill the gap left by the death of God? Will Gods' death upset the social (i.e. moral) order?" (Raymond Aron 1968: 198-199).

Did the role performed by God in the traditional religious conception get transferred to the State in the secular conception of the ideal society? If it did, what were the implications arising from the elevation of the State into the pedestal earlier occupied by God? The Marx-Bakunin dialogue touched the heart of this basic issue of putting the State into the high pedestal. Bakunin, according to E.H. Carr, regarded the State "as the most flagrant and the most complete denial of humanity" on the ground that "every State, like every theology, assumes man to be fundamentally bad, and wicked". In Bakunin's view Marx's State-led society "would be like a herd of animals driven together by force, pursuing exclusively material things and knowing nothing of the spiritual side of life" (E.H. Carr 1937: 453).

How perceptive and prophetic these statements appear now in the light of later developments!

It should be recalled that Soviet Socialist experiment in Russia had received the moral support of radical economists like John Maynard Keynes (1979) and many others on the ground of its moral superiority over capitalism. Here was a new economic philosophy and a new economic system which put non-material motivations in the centre and thus tried to correct the disharmony between material progress and spiritual well-being created by capitalism.

In this context what Keynes said in his "A Short View of Russia" written after his trip to the Soviet Union in 1925 was highly illuminating and also extremely relevant. Commenting on the larger significance of the Soviet experiment for the entire mankind, Keynes had remarked:

> "At any rate it seems to me clearer every day that the moral problem of our age is concerned with the love of money, with the habitual appeal to the money motive in nine-tenths of the activities of life, with the universal striving after individual economic security as the prime object of endeavour, with the social approbation of money as the measure of constructive success and with the social appeal to the hoarding instinct as the foundation of the necessary provision for the family and for the future. The decaying religions around us, which have less and less interest for most people unless it be as an aggreable form of magical, ceremonial, or of social observance, have lost their moral significance just because - unlike some of their earlier versions - they do not touch in the least degree on their essential matters. A revolution in our ways of thinking and feeling about money matters may become the growing purpose of contemporary embodiments of the ideal. Perhaps, therefore, Russian communism does represent the first confused stirrings of a great religion" (J.M. Keynes, 1979).

It is this hope of solution of the economic and the moral problem at the same time through the Russian socialist system which made Keynes and others overlook the undemocratic character of this system and support it. That hope did not entirely materialise; the promise of socialism as a viable moral alternative to capitalism was not fully realised. The economic as well as the moral collapse of the socialist project of the Russian as well as the non-Russian varieties has done much to discredit the secular vision itself — the concept of a science-directed world as the realisation of the moral Utopia.

With the collapse of the secular project of the socialist variety and with growing knowledge of the grave moral weakness of the other project of the various alternatives to market-oriented capitalism, has the secular vision itself died, leaving the room open for the 'return of God as the Saviour' (M.N. Srinivas 1993: 8)! Indeed, much before the Indian sociologist, M.N. Srinivas had declared secular humanism to be dead and gone in the context of the Indian experiment with secularism, Raymond Aron, the famous French sociological thinker and philosopher, had articulated very sharply the Western Man's disillusion with Godless modernity and his keenness to put God again on the high pedestal as the presiding deity of the Universe (Raymond Aron 1968). In my view, abandoning secular rationalism and humanism and thereby regressing into unreason and despair would, however, amount to devaluing man himself and losing faith in him and his future. As a maker of his own destiny man must seek the corrective to the distortions and imperfections of secularism not from outside but from the creative tension and ferment within secularism itself. Such a corrective can come from a more honest pursuit of the secular ideals, a more serious and knowledge-seeking discourse among different varieties of secular thought and practice and a more earnest encounter between creative and self-critical secular humanists and radical and forward-looking religious activists. The recovery of hope would turn into a hopeful search if it is addressed towards fresh understanding of the earthly roots of the resurgence of religiosity specially among the oppressed and the more authentic secularity inherent in it.

Postscript

More than a decade has elapsed since this paper was written articulating deep concerns and anxieties about the viability and sustainability of the Indian experiment in secularism. The immediate factor activating these concerns and anxieties at that time was the tragic Ayodhya Episode - the barbaric assault on the *Babri Masjid* and its demolition by the *Hindutva* fundamentalists and fanatics.

The concerns and anxieties expressed here were further resurrected and reactivated and, indeed assumed grave proportions, by the recent Great Gujarat Killings which caused a trauma worldwide. Within the Indian nation it caused a deep churning among all - the intelligentsia as well as the common people. It precipitated a search for the deeper roots of this malady resulting in the monumental tragedy of Gujarat killings. Mass churning occurred among all thinking sections of Indian society barring only the hard core of anti-secularists. Among the committed secularists the Ayodhya Episode and the Gujarat Tragedy initiated a process of serious rethinking on the basic premises of the theory and practice of Indian secularism. Certain basic questions emerged from this churning for rethinking and re-examination.

What explains the crisis of the "secular project" and the resilience and, indeed, the belligerence of the anti-secular political and cultural formations after their total retreat, moral isolation and lack of political support and credibility in the India of Gandhi and Nehru and their successors? What has enabled them to resurrect themselves, gain strength, influence and credibility and to rise almost to the position of hegemony over institutions of the civil society and the nation - state in recent decades? What explains the success of the anti-secular

Hindutva to emerge as a formidable rival of the secular ideology almost setting the terms and agenda for public discourse and claiming the support and allegiance of significant sections of the new middle classes in rural and urban India? What explains the aggressive self-confidence, tremendous energy and intimidating clout of the forces of anti-secularism as embodied in the ideology of *Hindutva* and as articulated and pursued by its major political and cultural formations below and above the socio-political surface? Above all, it is still a mystery as to how this obscurantist and semi-mediaeval and semi-modern political and cultural formation which in essence is "the enemy of reason" acquired legitimacy and influence among a significant section of the Indian intelligentsia. It is also a mystery how this formation without any roots either in the larger process of Indian Renaissance nor in the anti-imperialist freedom struggle had a meteoric rise within a decade or two and acquired such confidence and capability as to challenge the hegemony of the secularists over the nation and to ridicule the very concept of secularism itself. Indeed, they seemed to succeed in creating self-doubt and ideological disarrgry among a large section of committed secularists and to spread confusion and disorientation among the intelligentsia having broadly a secular outlook and orientation. The question remains how this formation acquired the guts to challenge the entire heritage of the freedom struggle and the Indian renaissance associated with the name of Gandhi, Nehru and Tagore and countless others and to pose themselves as the true representatives of Indian "cultural nationalism"?

It seems that every generation has to fight afresh its own battle—the battle between reason and unreason; progress and retrogression; freedom of mind and the slavery of mind. And therefore the questions posed by the emerging situation and the grave threat to Indian secularism has created a favourable context for the new encounter between secularism and anti-secularism. It has also set in motion a process of self-clarification and self-introspection, of dialogue and discourse among the theorists and practitioners of secularism themselves as is clear from the sources cited in the Reference. There is a new release of creative energy in the very recent period after a temporary loss of initiative as expressed in the attempt by the secularists to reexamine the basic issues of secularism in the Indian context both in philosophical and praxiological terms. There is a fresh endeavour to reset the secular agenda in terms of experiences of "building a secular State in a religions" country (Jawaharlal Nehru) and in terms of implementing the secular project in a country of diverse religions faiths and strong religions orientation and deeply rooted religious values, belief and traditions.

There is a fresh realisation among both secular intellectuals and secular activists that religion is much too serious a matter to be left to the sectarian, bigoted and dogmatic ideologues of *Hindutva* and its counterpart in other religions or to self-serving politicians adept in exploiting religious-minded people as "vote banks". Religions need to be studied and explored in depth to reveal the ongoing process of inner change and reforms within all religions and also the dynamic interaction and creative dialogue between religion and reason which at one end humanises reason and at another end reforms religion to suit the needs of changing times.

This implies a break from the over-simplified understanding of the relation of religion and secularism. It makes a break from the established habit of thought which equated the advance of secularism with a retreat and decline of religion itself. It implied the emergence of a new approach which treats religion and secularism not as mutually exclusive categories and processes. The new approach also explores Religions Reformation and Secular Enlightenment as mutually reinforcing, interrelated and interdependent processes. This new conception thus helps to recharge secularism with new meanings and values and to reset the secular goals and agenda according to the new moral vision. It also helps to open up new horizons for religion in the modern age as a sequel to its liberation from fundamentalist aberrations and distortions. It also hopes to reactivate it as a vast source of creative moral energy and as a powerful corrective to the grave danger of reckless wealth-massing, power-seeking and sensual gratification created by modernity which is spurred and buttressed by unchained technological progress.

References

Ahmad, Akbar S. (1993). *Post-Modernism and Islam*, Penguin Books Ltd.

Aron, Raymond (1968). *Progress and Disillusion*, The Dialectics of Modern Society, Pall Mall Press, London.

Bandyopadhyaya, Tarashanker, (1970). *Gana Devata*, Bhartiya Gyanpeeth Prakashan.

Barthwal, P.D. (1936). *The Nirgun School of Hindi Poetry*, Indian Book Shop, Benaras.

Carr, E.H. (1961). *Michael Bakunin*, Vintage Books, New York.

Das, Gurcharan (2004). "Privatise Secularism" *Outlook*, April 12.

Dasgupta, Partha (1993). *An Enquiry into Well-being and Destitution*, Clarenden Press: Oxford.

Dietrich, Gabriele (1977). *Religion and People's Organisation*, The Christian Institute of Religion and Society, Bangalore.

Ganguli, Amulya (2004). "Hindutva Helpline", *Hindustan Times*, New Delhi, July 5.

Gransberg, Donald and Gian Swarup (ed.), (1991). *Essays in Honour of Muzafer Sherif*, Springer-veslag, London.

Hasan, Mnohirul (ed.), (2004). *Will Secular India Survive*? Imprint One, Gurgaon.

Hindus, Maurice (1993). *Mother Russia*, Collins, London, 1947.

Iyer, Raghavan *The Essential Writings of Mahatma Gandhi*, Oxford University Press, Delhi.

Joshi, P.C. (1995). *Secularism and Indian Development: The Indian Experiment*, Vikas Publishing House Pvt. Ltd., New Delhi.

Keynes, J.M. (1979). "A Short View of Russia", *Collected Works*, Vol.XXVIII, The Royal Economic Society.

Khusro, A.M. (2004). "Foreword", in Mukul Dube, *The Path of the Parivar: Articles on Gujarat and Hindutva*, The Essays Collective, New Delhi.

Lenin, V.I. (1977). *Collected Works*, Vol.15, Progress Publishers, Moscow.

Nandy, Ashish (2004). "A Billion Gandhis", *Outlook*, 21 June.

Nehru, Jawaharlal (1989). *Letters to Chief Ministers 1958-64*, Vol.5 Oxford University Press, Delhi.

Pande, G.C. (1991). "Ethics and Economics: A Comment", *Unmeelan*, Jaipur, January (Hindi).

Panikkar, K.N. (1997). *Communal Threat and Secular Challenge*, Earthworm Book Pvt. Ltd., Madras.

————. (2004). "Future of Secularism", Book Review, *The Hindu*, April 20.

————. (2004). "Secularism Under Siege", *The Hindu*, March 31.

Russell, Bertrand (1962). *Unpopular Essays*, Sumon And Schuster, New York.

Sharma, Shankar Dayal (1989). *In the Indian Ethos*, Zakir Hussain Memorial Lecture, Vishva Bharati Shantiniketan, April 29.

Shahabuddin, Syed (2004). "A Counterpoint to Dr. Swamy", *The Hindu*, March 26.

Sen, Amartya (1993). "The Threats to Secular India", *Social Scientist*, 238-239, New Delhi, March-April.

————. (1988). *Ethics and Economics*, Basil Blackwill.

Srinivas, M.N. (1989). *The Cohesive Role of Sanskritisation and Other Essays*, Oxford University Press.

————. (1993). "Wanted A New Philosophy", *The Times of India*, July 9.

Subrahmanyam, Sanjay (2004). "Our Only Colonial Thinker", *Outlook*, 5 July.

Swamy, Subramaniam (2004). "Redefining Secularism", *The Hindu*, March 18.

Tolstoy, Leo (1950). *Anna Karenina*, The Modern Library, New York.

Weber, Max (1930). *The Protestant Ethic and the Spirit of Capitalism*, Allen Unwin, London.

Whitehead, A.N. (1938). *Science in the Modern World*, Penguin Books Ltd.

19

Freedom of Religion

T.N. MADAN

In times that are marked by an overweening accent on mutually exclusive socio-cultural identities, the scope and significance of choosing to live in shared interstitial spaces between cultural traditions unfortunately gets lost and even denigrated. History and sociology are witnesses to the fact that composite cultures are richer than the monolithic ones. Professor A.M. Khusro was a product of such a hybrid milieu; nourished by it in his own and his family's life. His was a 'many splendoured' personality – equally at home in traditional Indian and modern western ways of living as also in Muslim (*Shia, Sunni, Sufy*) and Hindu lifestyles. His pluralist values and inclusivist attitudes were not a posture but the essence of his being.

I offer the following essay on the freedom of religion (written previously[1]) to honour his memory. It is my fond hope that he would have approved of the viewpoint presented here.

As a formal concept, freedom of religion is a modern idea, not more than three centuries old, and western in origin. And it is a contemporary concern everywhere in our human rights conscious days. The major religious traditions of the world cannot truly be considered supportive of it. As we know them today, if these traditions entertain the idea of religious pluralism it is more a concession to empirical reality rather than a matter of orthodoxy. In other words, toleration in the context of the diversity of religious faiths is a historical development in some traditions; and has scriptural sanction in others. Scriptures do not, however, always speak unambiguously; besides, whatever is in the scripture, or in the cultural tradition generally, may not also be for good or bad a matter of social practice.

---

1. Abridged from *Economic and Political Weekly*, March 15, 2003.

One of the countries that voted in favour of the Universal Declaration of Human Rights adopted by the UN General Assembly in 1948 was India, which had become a member of the United Nations soon after the attainment of independence in 1947. The Constituent Assembly was already at work under the shadow of the partition of the subcontinent on the basis of religious difference and the accompanying widespread communal riots and mass migrations. The country had seen the ugly face of religious identity, but it was not at all ready to turn its back on religion. The framers of the Constitution did not write the word secular or secularism into it despite the efforts of one member (K.T. Shah) to have this done. But it also did not accept the suggestion of another member (H.V. Kamath) to open the document with an invocation to God. Words apart, the spirit of the Constitution breathed the ideal of freedom of religion. It was only in 1976, during the 'Emergency' regime of Prime Minister Indira Gandhi, that the word 'secular' was introduced into the Preamble of the Constitution by the 42nd Amendment. It was thus that India came to be characterised as a 'Sovereign, Socialist, Secular, Democratic Republic'. The precise sense in which the word secular is used is clarified by the corresponding term *pantha nirpeksha* (denominationally neutral) in the Hindi version of the document.

Article 15 of the Indian Constitution prohibits discrimination on grounds of religion, caste, sex, or place of birth; Article 16 guarantees equality of opportunity in matters of public employment irrespective of one's religious identity; and Article 17 abolished the practice of untouchability. Articles 25 to 30 deal specifically with the freedom of religion. Leaving aside for the moment the explanatory notes and qualifications, which are important, these Articles guarantee the following fundamental (unalterable) rights: 'Freedom of conscience and free profession, practice and propagation of religion' (Art. 25); 'Freedom to manage religious affairs', which includes the right 'to establish and maintain institutions for religious and charitable purposes' (Art. 26); 'Freedom as to payment of taxes for promotion of any particular religion' (Art. 27); 'Freedom as to attendance at religious instruction or religious worship in certain educational institutions', with the clarification that 'No religious instruction shall be provided in any educational institution wholly maintained out of State funds' (Art. 28); 'Protection of interests of minorities' (Art. 29); and the 'Right of minorities to establish and administer educational institutions' (Art. 30).

It seems to me that Article 25 focuses on the most basic of the various rights defined in the full set and merits further comment. But before I do so, three clarifications need to be made. First, Article 13 declared 'void' any existing laws that might be judged to be 'inconsistent with or in derogation of the fundamental rights listed in Part III of the constitution (Arts. 12-35).

Secondly, all the freedoms and rights conferred by Arts 25-30 were made 'subject to public order, morality and health'. Not only that: they are to be exercised in a manner that is progressive in spirit. Clause 2(b) of Article 25 provides for state intervention within the framework of the said Article to promote 'social welfare and reform', and to throw open 'Hindu religious institutions of a public charter to all classes and sections of Hindus'. (Explanation II attached to sub-clause (b) clarifies that the category Hindu shall for purposes of this clause include Sikhs, Jains and Buddhists. I will not go here into the tricky question whether such categorisation limits in any way the freedom of religion of these latter communities.) Read together, Articles 25 and 26 place public interest above the claims of freedom of religion. In this respect, 'the Constitution is', in Marc Gallanter's words, 'a charter for the reform of *Hinduism*' (1989: 247).

Moreover, since all the fundamental rights must be read together, nothing may be claimed in terms of freedom of religion that would deny or abridge any other fundamental right. Thus, human sacrifice cannot be claimed as essential to any community's religious practice since Article 21 guarantees 'protection of life and personal liberty'. Similarly, the dedication of any girl or woman to a temple deity (as a *devadasi*, for example), who is then compelled to engage in sexual intercourse with specified men, can not be claimed as a religious right as it would violate Article 23, which prohibits 'traffic in human beings'.

Thirdly, although there is no specific prohibition of the establishment of a religion by the state, the spirit of the Constitution, and, after the 42nd Amendment, the Preamble also entail the prohibition.

Thus understood, Article 25 focuses on the entitlements within defined limits. There never has been any doubt or controversy about the connotation of either the phrase 'freedom of conscience', or of the rights to profess and practice a religion of one's choice. It is the right to propagate one's religion that has become a bone of contention. This right was written into the Constitution on the insistence of the Christian members of the Constituent Assembly. Under the Government of India Act of 1935, the right of representation of religious minorities (Muslims, Sikhs, Indian Christians) had been secured through separate electorates and the reservation of seats in the provincial and central legislatures. Such measures had come to be seen by the leadership and the mass following of the Indian National Congress as the imperial stratagem of 'divide and rule' and, therefore, highly mischievous. It had paved the way for the enunciation of 'the two nation theory' by the Indian Muslim League, which eventually became the basis of the partition of the country on the basis of religious identity.

Understandably, the framers of the Constitution wanted to completely do away with what they generally regarded as divisive statutory measures. Separate electorates were discarded forthwith, but reservation survived, notwithstanding the doubts of forward looking leaders like Jawaharlal Nehru. The Christian members of the Constituent Assembly not only wanted quotas for their representation to be retained, they also insisted on the right of conversion as an essential element of their faith, which they therefore wanted to be included under fundamental rights. From the Christian point of view the right to change one's religion was the litmus test of the freedom of religion.

Let me go back in time to sketch a background to this contention. It is well known that conversion has been the principal means by which the Christian faith was established in India two thousand years ago. Those who arrived from abroad and made converts, and those who came specifically to make converts, never came in hordes, and they did not have the support of the state. Indeed, the chaplains of the East India Company were, from the mid-eighteenth century onwards, primarily required to meet the religious and spiritual needs of the British, but the objective of spreading the Christian faith was not wholly ignored. After somewhat uncertain beginnings, reflecting conflicting aims, a policy of non-interference was firmly put in place in 1862 through an order made at Bombay. According to it there was to be 'no compulsory conversion, no interference with native habits, and no cow killing in Hindu quarters' (Smith 1963: 66). Pressures at home to permit missionary work in India continued, however, and eventually bore fruit in 1813, at the time of the renewal of the charter of the East India Company, when the British Parliament allowed the same.

Second generation problems, notably the loss of rights of inheritance following conversion, now made their appearance. A regulation in the Bengal Code of 1832 attended to this problem. Further clarifications were made as and when the need arose. In 1840, responding to a memorial from Hindus and Parsis, asking for restraints on missionaries and for the imposition of disabilities of the kind that the 1832 regulation had removed, the Government pleaded its inability to do so in the name of its policy of 'strict neutrality', in protection of 'the rights of civil and personal liberty', and in compliance with the principles laid down by the British Parliament'. All these steps led to the enactment of the Caste Disabilities Removal Act of 1850, applicable to all of British India, which prevented any disadvantages or disabilities resulting from the change of religion. Orthodox Hindu opinion unsuccessfully protested that this was indeed interference in their religious usages, delinking religious obligations and property rights that had traditionally gone together (see Smith 1963: 70). As far as I have been able to find out, this was the first use of the notion of 'freedom of religion' in the legislative discourse of modern India. And the Christian leadership has held firmly to it.

Just a year before the deliberations of the Constituent Assembly commenced late in 1946, a joint committee of the Catholic Union of India and the All India Council of Indian Christians formally asked that 'the free profession, practice and propagation of religion' should be guaranteed in free India (see Kim 2002: chap. 3). Other Christian bodies also put forward the same demand. Needless to say, many others including sections of the Hindu leadership were opposed to such demands: there had been much disquiet in its ranks regarding the activities of missionaries, particularly among the poorer lower castes and tribal peoples. It was strongly felt, among other leaders by Gandhi, that missionaries were taking undue advantage of the poverty and illiteracy of the masses. The resentment caused by covert and overt official support to the missionaries in the Punjab had led to the emergence of a powerful counter movement from the newly formed *Arya Samaj* in the late-nineteenth century.

This then was the historical background to the debates in the Constituent Assembly. One may add that the Karachi session of the Indian National Congress (1931) also had affirmed the principles of religious liberty and the secular state. Limitations of space preclude further details, but let me highlight a couple of points. Two sub-committees, set up in January 1947, stated their views on conversion and, expectedly, they were not of the same opinion. While the Sub-Committee on Fundamental Rights recommended that 'conversions from one religion to another brought about by coercion or undue influence' should not be recognised by law, the Minorities Sub-Committee, which had a number of Christians as members, insisted on legal sanction for the propagation of faith and conversion. The first Sub-Committee asked that persons under the age of eighteen must not be made to profess a religion other than that in which they were born. The second clarified that, in the interests of family solidarity, if the parents change religion, their minor children too must be converted. And so it went on and on until February 1948, when the revised draft Constitution, prepared by a committee under Ambedkar's chairmanship, was submitted. In it the right to propagate as well as to profess and practice the religion of one's choice was recognised. There was no caveat about minors.

The controversy did not however, die down. Eventually, some highly respected and articulate Hindu members of the Constituent Assembly put their weight behind the acceptance of the wording in the draft. The right to convert, it was pointed out, would surely not be employed in a divisive manner by the Indian Christians who had generally been with the mainstream during the national movement. Moreover, the right would be available to every community that believes in propagation, such as the *Arya Samaj*. And so Article 25, as we know it today, became part of the fundamental rights chapter of the Constitution of India.

Rajeev Dhavan, a jurist, has written about 'the seamy side' of constitution making in India inasmuch as bargains and compromises were made continuously (Dhavan 2001: 309). Thus it has been suggested by a number of commentators that it was in anticipation of the Christian members giving up the reservation of seats in legislative bodies that the Hindu members eventually came round to supporting the notion of propagation as an element of the freedom of religion.

Deep seated and old doubts do not disappear suddenly, and constitutions are not sealed books; they are open to amendment and interpretation. As already stated, the fundamental rights enshrined in the Indian Constitution cannot be amended, but their interpretation is and will remain an on-going process. It is thus that the question whether the right to propagate one's religion, in fulfillment of the constitutional endorsement of the freedom of religion, entails the right to convert without any limitation, continues to arouse controversy even today.

In the years following independence, the work of Christian missionaries, who included foreigners, continued to be the target of suspicion, particularly in areas such as Madhya Pradesh and Orissa, which had large tribal populations, and where strict anti-conversion laws of some of the erstwhile 'native' states had lapsed following the integration of these states into the Indian Union. The Government of Madhya Pradesh took the lead and set up a committee (one of its members was a Christian) to inquire into the activities of missionaries in the state. Its work was opposed by various Christian bodies, and not in Madhya Pradesh alone.

The committee's report focused on, among other things, the inflow of money from abroad, which raised in many minds concerns about foreign interference in Indian affairs. The social service and charitable activities of the missionaries in the areas of education and health came under a cloud insofar as these were seen linked to the objective of conversion. The findings and recommendations of the committee caused widespread anger among Christians. Nevertheless, they became the basis of new legislation on the issue of freedom of religion in Orissa (1967) and Madhya Pradesh (1968). The latter state modelled its legislation on the farmer's. Ten years later (in 1978), the Arunachal Pradesh Legislature also placed on the state statute book a Freedom of Religion Act to prohibit conversions from 'indigenous faiths' to 'any other faith or religion by use of force or inducement or by fraudulent means'. Since 'nature worshipers' as well as Buddhists and *Vaishnavas* were identified as followers of indigenous faiths, the prohibition affected the proselytising activities of the Christian missionaries alone.

The basic premise of the Orissa Freedom of Religion Act (1967) is that: 'Conversion in its very process involves an act of undermining another faith. This process becomes all the more objectionable when this is brought about by recourse to methods like force, fraud, material inducement and exploitation of one's poverty, simplicity and ignorance.' Pursuantly, these acts, while accepting that 'propagation' was allowed by the Constitution, placed various restrictions on the same in the very specific context of conversion. Both acts were challenged: while the Orissa High Court ruled that the Orissa Act was *ultra vires* of the Constitution, the Madhya Pradesh High Court upheld similar legislation of that state. Eventually, the matter was taken to the Supreme Court, which gave its verdict in January 1977, agreeing with the Madhya Pradesh High Court. Chief Justice A.N. Ray ruled that 'what is freedom for one, is freedom for the other, in equal measure, and there can, therefore, be no such thing as a fundamental right to convert another person to one's own religion', because doing so 'would impinge on the "freedom of conscience" guaranteed to all the citizens of the country alike (AIR, Supreme Court, 1977: 908-12).

The foregoing crucial and much quoted opinion is unfortunately not clearly worded, and is too literalist in its reading of the Constitution. It took away, according to its critics, the right to propagate one's religion. The right of propagation without the right of carrying it to its logical conclusion of the right to convert was considered empty. According to H.M. Seervai, 'To propagate is not to impart knowledge and to spread it more widely, but to produce intellectual and moral conviction leading to action, namely to adopt that religion' (1978: 1287). The propagation for 'edification' argument of Justice B.K. Mukherjee of the Supreme Court (AIR, Supreme Court 1954: 391) sounds rather simple minded today. Seervai's appears to be the more practicable interpretation, but it does not invalidate the implication of Justice Ray's argument that freedom of religion is exercised in the act of conversion only when it is the voluntary decision of an individual without the intervention of another person, notwithstanding the latter's goodwill and good faith (no pun is intended here).

An intractable problem that persists in this context is how to determine with absolute certainty that a particular act of conversion is voluntary or not, that it is fair and not fraudulent, sincere and not contrived. As Gandhi used to say, none but God knows a man's heart. The criteria laid down in the various pieces of legislation are not wholly feasible. The latest attempt in this direction, the Tamilnad Prevention of Forcible Conversion of Religion Act (2002), goes well beyond the Madhya Pradesh and Orissa Acts to render conversions, particularly of or by the Dalits, virtually impossible. This is so because of the stringent reporting obligations imposed upon the converts and the converted, the discretionary powers conferred upon law enforcement officers, and the provision of fines and imprisonment for those who may be judged to have violated the law.

It seems that the time is now opportune to argue forcefully that the best guardian of freedom of religion, and the most effective guarantor that unfair conversions, particularly on a collective basis, shall not take place, will not be the state but civil society, or, better still, the two in association. Vigilant public opinion expressed in institutionalised ways, acting as a monitor rather than a substitute, should be preferable to executive authority, particularly if this is to be exercised by the lower rungs of the bureaucracy and magistracy. (One is here reminded of John Locke's recommendation that religious belief should be beyond the reach of civil government). This is at the moment only an idea: it will need serious effort to work it out, particularly if communal dissensions are acute as they are now. Also to be kept in mind is the issue of the role of the secular state in other contexts.

Secularism, understood as the attitude of mutual toleration among the religious communities comprising the nation, and of neutrality or non-discrimination on the part of the state in its dealings with the citizens, irrespective of their religious identity, apparently protects freedom of religion. Two problems must be addressed, however. First, is the secular state neutral through engagement, that is by being respectful towards all religions (*sarva dharma samabhav*), or through disengagement, that is by erecting a wall, as it were, between itself and the religious life of the citizens? Secondly, what is involved in a community's conception of the profession and practice of its religion.

On the basis of the Constitution itself, the Indian state has remained engaged from the very beginning with the religious life of its citizens and, what is more, in disparate ways. What I have in mind is, first, clause 2 of Article 25, which empowers the state to regulate or restrict various kinds of secular activities (economic, political, *etc.*) that may be associated with religious practice. Article 31A also provides for the acquisition of estates and their management in public interest. One of the best known instances of this is the Dargah Khwajah Saheb Act of 1955 of the Indian Parliament that empowered the state to oversee the management of the famous Muslim *Sufi* shrine at Ajmer. A recent example was the takeover of the management of the Vaishnav Devi temple complex in the state of Jammu and Kashmir (while the state was under President's rule) on the ground of mismanagement by the trust that had the responsibility for running its affairs. The same principle was involved to bring the affairs of Vishvanath Temple at Varanasi under the control of a board (see Dhavan 2991: 315). Besides, there is provision in the Constitution for state support to religious activity. Article 290A provides for annual payments to certain Devaswom Funds for the use of Hindu temples in Kerala and Tamilnadu, on the ground that these temples and shrines were the beneficiaries of state patronage before the integration of the states of Travancore and Cochin into the Indian Union.

Further, since the all-important Article 25 holds the state responsible for ensuring the maintenance of 'public order, mortality and health', while granting citizens the freedom of religion, it is arguable that the resources of the state should be drawn upon in a big way for the foregoing purposes on such occasions as the periodic, multitudinous Hindu *Kumbh* melas at Haridwar and elsewhere. Similar administrative back-up (including deployment of law and order and public health personnel) is provided on an appropriate scale whenever and wherever people gather in large numbers for religious performances. Even financial support may be provided as is done, for instance, in the case of *Haj* pilgrims whose travel to Saudi Arabia by sea or air is subsidised by the state, costing the government currently several hundred crore of rupees annually. Government largess has enabled some major places of worship, such as the Jagannath temple complex at Puri, to undertake repairs, restoration or reconstruction. On the very day on which the Babari mosque was demolished by Hindu hooligans in 1992, Prime Minister P.V. Narsimha Rao announced that it would be rebuilt, presumably by the government. That this did not happen is another matter. Limitations of time preclude further examples, but I trust it is clear that the practice of the Indian state in relation to the religious life of the people has not been exactly what would be expected from a secular state if the French or the American state is regarded as the model. Or if Gandhi's conception of the secular state had been adhered to. He emphatically denied any role whatsoever to the state in the religious affairs of the people.

Apart from the involvement of the legislative and executive branches of the government in religious affairs, the judiciary too has entered into such controversial areas – veritable minefields – as the definition of the essentials of religious identity, belief and practice. This has happened on many occasions. As, for instance, when P.B. Gajendragadkar, Chief Justice of the Supreme Court, ordered in 1966 that temples of the *Satsangi* community be thrown open to the Untouchables (so-called). Or when Justice Y.V. Chandrachud, again the chief of the same court, pronounced in 1985 in favour of respondent Shah Bano, a divorced Muslim woman, granting her the enhanced monthly maintenance that the Madhya Pradesh High Court had ordered her husband, the complainant in the Supreme Court, to pay her, rejecting his interpretation of the issues involved, which had been supported by the All-India Muslim Personal Law Board. In both cases the reformist justices could well be said to have been motivated by considerations of fair play and justice, but their pronouncements were seen by those affected — the small sect of *Satsangis*, who unsuccessfully asserted that they were not Hindus and therefore not obliged to allow Hindus of any caste whatsoever into their temples, in the one case, and by millions of Muslims, in the other — as grave interference in the practice of their rights as religious minorities. Given Article 17 of the Constitution, which forbids the practice of untouchability in any form, their small numbers and character as a local community, the *Satsangis* did not have a chance of having things their own way.

The case of the Muslims was significantly different and so not because of numbers alone. Muslim public opinion was widely and rapidly aroused on the ground that the interpretation of *Shariat*-based Muslim personal law was outside the jurisdiction of secular courts. Further, any alteration or abridgement of the provisions of this law was regarded as unwarranted interference that amounted to restriction of the freedom of religion. Keen to calm down the angered Muslim public opinion, the Union government, which was in 1986 in the hands of the Congress, a Muslim-vote dependent political party, enacted through the Parliament the Muslim Women (Protection of Rights on Divorce) Act, which excluded divorced Muslim women from the purview of the relevant provisions (section 125) of the Criminal Procedure Code, that would have been helpful to them, and limited the liability of the husband in respect of his former spouse. The protection of the rights of such women was to be in terms of traditional Muslim personal law. (Incidentally, not all the Muslim communities of India had in past followed the *Shariat* in respect of personal law; in fact, some of them had even followed Hindu personal laws. All this changed in 1937 when the *Shariat* Act made *Shariat*-based personal laws applicable to all Muslims of the subcontinent).

This brings me to the second problem mentioned above, namely the possibility of conflict between the obligation of the secular state to ensure freedom of religion and a community's own definition of the essence of religious belief and practice. The constitutional background to it is provided by the tension between the freedom of religion as a fundamental right (Article 25) and the directive principle of state policy vide Article 44, which requires the state to 'endeavour to secure for the citizens a uniform civil code' throughout India. On this issue, Chief Justice Chandrachud had observed (in the Shah Bano case judgement) that, regrettably, this Article had remained 'a dead letter' (AIR, Supreme Court 1985: 954). Under the belief that it was for the Muslim community to take the initiative in this matter. This is what many leaders of public opinion and scholars of law believe even today, sixteen years after the justices' *obiter dicta*.

At this point we need to turn briefly to Hindu personal law based on the *dharmashastra*, which the Hindus, like the Muslims, have considered a part of their religious tradition. Nevertheless, the Government of India under the leadership of Jawaharlal Nehru went ahead within a year of independence, although not as speedily and comprehensively as it wanted, to enact a number of progressive laws in respect of marriage and divorce (1955), adoption and maintenance (1956), minority and guardianship (1956), succession and inheritance (1956), *etc.* (see Derrett 1978). These broke away from the shastric tradition and represented the initial steps in the direction of, first, the liberalisation and secularisation of Hindu personal law and, second, the formulation of a uniform civil code. Articles 25(2b) and 44 are relevant in this context.

As is well known, there was much opposition to the proposed legislation from conservative Hindu leaders, including the first President of India himself (Rajendra Prasad), but the progressive elements prevailed ultimately. Since the mid-1950s, however, there has been no further progress towards the secularisation of personal laws. In fact, Muslim leadership has come to consider it as an attempt to impose amended Hindu personal laws on the non-Muslims. Another viewpoint holds that the burden of the movement towards a uniform civil code will fall less heavily on the Hindus, in respect of whom a beginning was made in the 1950s, than on the other communities who have remained static. In the event, the feeling has grown that the Hindu right wing exploits the issue of the common civil code to embarrass Muslims. A way out of the impasse, it has been suggested by a Harvard law professor, might be to begin with less controversial issues than personal laws, such as religious and charitable endowments (see Mansfield 2001: 93). It is also high time that reformist Muslim opinions are expressed openly and with conviction.

The foregoing discussion of the implications of the right to propagate one's religion, and of the framing of a uniform civil code, highlights, I trust, the intricacies of securing the freedom of religion in a vast country such as India, marked by religious pluralism, the intertwinning of the religious and the social, and the politicisation of religious identities. The road ahead is long and hazardous.

To conclude, let me return to where I began. I said that the concept of freedom of religion is a modern idea. It is so both chronologically and normatively. It is a gift of the modern state that is not necessarily itself formally secular, but operates in the social setting of widespread secularisation. (The case of the United Kingdom readily comes to mind.) The radical break with traditional ideas about the place of religion in social life in the West went hand in hand with the secularisation of institutions (as well as of attitudes) throughout the nineteenth century. Religion 'retreated from public life', as Max Weber put it, into the transcendental realm of mystic life or into the brotherliness of direct and personal relations'. This was what Weber called the 'disenchantment of the world' (1948: 155). Freedom of religion is an aspect of the liberal ideology of individualism, which, following the collapse of the communist alternative, is in today's world an ideal to strive for everywhere. Understandably, although somewhat paradoxically, freedom of religion is conceived broadly enough to include the freedom to profess no religion at all.

Needless to emphasise, the notion of freedom of religion could not be reasonably expected to spring from within a religious tradition. As I indicated earlier, the most that may be expected from such traditions is the idea of toleration between religions and, perhaps, some degree of freedom of choice within the confines of a particular tradition. The latter possibility is best illustrated by the denominational splits that came in Europe in the wake of the Protestant Reformation, dividing Christians into Lutherans, Calvinists, Presbytarians, Anglicans, Puritans, and others. Within the amorphous Hindu religious tradition, which is a congeries rather than a single tradition, a plurality of belief and practice has long been recognised, as I said earlier, as the cultural dimension of the caste system.

The freedom to move from one religion to another is altogether a different matter. No spokesperson for a religious tradition would sound credible if he or she were to say that, not only are its followers free to embrace another religion, which they of course are, but also that doing so is right or commendable. They could only be called apostates and regarded as misguided if not morally degenerate. Within the value framework of a proselytising religion, such an attitude of toleration would be irrational and self-defeating.

As for non-proselytising religions, notably Hinduism, its most vocal modern exponent, Vivekananda, was emphatic in holding the view that anyone who went 'out of the Hindu pale [was] not only a man less, but an enemy more' (see Punj 2002: 25). Indeed, Vivekananda considered it his mission to 'awaken' India so that it could conquer (not merely convert) the world spiritually. In his own eye his message was of universal scope: it was unfortunate that the Hindus should have at some point of time acquired the notion of the *mlechchha*, the uncultured outsider. Moreover, he considered it absurd that Christian missionaries should want to preach to the Hindus, since Hinduism acknowledged reverence for all religions and was therefore the superior faith. Using their own idiom, he called *Vedanta* 'the wonderful voice of God' (see Basu 2002: 56).

While seeking to unite Hindus as one national community (or nation), and thereby eroding internal pluralism, Vivekananda relocated toleration in the domain of interreligious relations. At the same time, he hierarchised plurality in a manner that placed *Vedanta* at the very apex of the religious heritage of humankinds its highest expression and future possibility.

Dayananda found the 'freedom' of a Hindu to convert to Christianity or Islam to be only serfdom, and set out to define the procedure (purification, *shuddhi*) to reclaim the trapped individuals. And Gandhi argued with absolute conviction that, while the idea of free choice of religion by the individual should be an inalienable right, the effort to convert or reclaim him or her could only come from someone who is an alien to the true essence of religion. 'If conversion is the work of God', he asked with characteristic directness, 'why should that work be taken away from him?' (see Sudhir Chandra 2002: 284). For himself, he was content to be called a *sanatani* Hindu and, at the same time, a multireligious person: it apparently did not require any radical transformation of the tradition to believe (and behave) thus.

If Hinduism too, in its own manner, does not entertain the idea of freedom of religion, what is the record of the premodern state in this regard in the long history of India? The illustrious name of Ashoka readily comes to one's mind, but what we know from his edicts is his exhortation of toleration, mutual respect, and concord, rather than of state support for freedom of choice of religion (Rock Edict XII, see Thapar 1961: 225). Nor did he call upon people to embrace any particular religion. Allowing for the much greater complexity in matters of religion in Akbar's time, we have to say that the emperor's personal catholicity of mind and search for religious syncretism was unique in the annals of world history (see Sharma 1962). Moreover, he did go further than Ashoka in terms of action by the state to protect the rights of citizens (it was the non-Muslims who were the relevant category) to pursue their religions freely. By his own actions he provided symbolic support for religious pluralism at the cost of the charge of apostacy levelled against him by the *ulema*. What is more, he did not impose the syncretic *din-i-Ilahi* on his subjects, and it had few takers. It is noteworthy here that throughout the centuries of Muslim rule, non-Muslims could choose to remain outside the Islamic fold, although at a certain cost. And most of them chose to do so.

Under British colonial rule, as noted above, the policy of non-interference of its earlier period was abandoned early in the nineteenth century, ironically in the name of religious liberty. Thereafter, the association between the government and the Church was close, more openly so in some places, and at certain points of time, than at others. The alleged religious 'causes' of the 1857 uprising did, however, result in an emphatic restatement of the official policy of the neutrality of the state. The royal proclamation of 1858, on the occasion of the assumption of the responsibility of the governance of British India by the British sovereign, declared that 'none be any wise favoured, none molested or disquieted, by reason of their religious faith or observances'; 'all interference with the religious belief or worship' of any 'subjects' was strictly prohibited. But the same proclamation also affirmed at the outset 'the Truth of Christianity' (see Smith 1963: 71-2). By implication whatever was in conflict with it was not true.

In short, freedom of religion as a fundamental right as we find it in the Indian Constitution owes more to modern Western models, particularly the American, and to the Universal Declaration of Human Rights, than to India's religious traditions or the practices of pre-modern Indian states (Hindu or Muslim). The 'doublespeak' policies of the colonial regime may, however, be credited with holding forth the principle of the religious neutrality of the state. The absence of firm cultural and historical roots of the idea of freedom of religion, as it is understood today, is perhaps made good by the fact that some Hindu religious reformers of the nineteenth and twentieth centuries, notably Vivekananda and Gandhi, have been powerful voices in support of religious toleration.

Freedom of religion is, however, threatened today by the ideology of cultural nationalism (*Hindutva*) espoused by Hindu right-wing political and cultural bodies, which would like to require non-Hindus to acknowledge the primacy of various upper caste religious beliefs, symbols and practices as central to a national culture of India. It is also given narrow or excessively combative interpretations by various minority communities, which are more likely to hurt everyone in the long run rather than promote the common good. 'In this situation, 'writes the distinguished journalist B.G. Verghese, 'Muslim Indians must not shrink back into the ghetto or opt out after Gujarat. The community must stir itself to modernise, reform, compete and change. Christians too must reject the carryover of caste that disfigures the Church and admonish revivalist and so-called charismatic preachers who revile other faiths while propagating their own' (2002: 55).

Resistances to the freedom of religion are not peculiar to India: they occur in one form or another elsewhere too. For example, in the USA, where interpretations of the First Amendment continue to be made, notably by the Supreme Court, which is divided between conservatives and progressives among the justices; in China, where Marxist perspectives on religion still influence state policy; in Israel with its unique Zionist tradition that privileges Judaism; or among the Muslim nations that, inter-country variations notwithstanding, are committed to Islam as the most perfect, straight, path to salvation. Freedom of religion may, therefore, be said to be an ideal that is complex (given the wide variety of historical backgrounds), controversial (given not only the prevailing religious discords but also serious and unsettled philosophical doubts: does freedom of religion imply that all religions are of equal merit?), and contemporary or relatively recent. From the *longue durée* perspective of world history, freedom of religion is a young idea with a somewhat uncertain future. It is an idea on trial, as it were, and should be examined carefully so that it may be strengthened. It is an idea worthy of all the intellectual vigour and moral courage that we can muster.

References

Bainton, Ronald H. (1956). *The Reformation of the Sixteenth Century*, Boston: Beacon Press.

Basu, Shamita (2002). *Religious Revivalism as Nationalist Discourse*, New Delhi: Oxford University Press.

Cassirer, Ernest (1968). *The Philosophy of the Enlightenment*, Princeton, N.J.: Princeton University Press.

Derrett, J.D.M. (1978). *The Death of a Marriage Law*, New Delhi: Vikas.

Dhavan, Rajeev (2001). "The Road to Xanadu: India's Quest for Secularism", in Gerald J. Larson, ed., *Religion and Personal Law in Secular India*, New Delhi: Social Science Press.

Dunn, Richard S. (1979). *The Age of Religious Wars 1559-1715*, New York: Norton.

Gallanter, Marc (1989). *Law and Society in India*, New Delhi: Oxford University Press.

Greene, Everts B. (1941). *Religion and the State: The Making and Testing of an American Tradition*, New York: New York University Press.

Huntington, Samuel (1996). *The Clash of Civilizations and the Remaking of World Order*, New York: Touchstone.

Jones, Kenneth W. (1976). *Arya Dharm: Hindu Consciousness in 19th Century Punjab*, New Delhi: Manohar.

Kim, Sebastin C.H. (2003). *In Search of Identity: Debates on Religious Conversion in India*, New Delhi: Oxford University Press.

Mabbott, J.D. (1973). *John Locke*, London: Macmillan.

Mansfield, John H. (2001). "Religious and Charitable Endowments and a Uniform Civil Code", in Gerald J. Larson, ed., *Religion and Personal Law in Secular India*, New Delhi: Social Science Press.

Punj, Balbir K. (2002). "The Hindu Soul in Search of its Body", *Outlook*, Sept. 30.

Seervai, H.M. (1978). *Constitutional Law of India, 4th ed.* Bombay: N.M. Tripathi.

Sharma, Sri Ram (1962). *The Religious Policy of the Mughal Emperors*, Bombay: Asia

Smith, Donald E. (1963). *India as a Secular State*, Bombay: Oxford University Press.

Sudhir Chandra (2002). "An Unresolved Dilemma: Gandhi on Religious Conversion", in Sudhir Chandra, *Continuing Dilemmas : Understanding Social Consciousness*, New Delhi: Tulika.

Thapar, Romila (1961). *Asoka and the Decline of the Mauryas*, London: Oxford University Press.

Troellsch, Ernst (1981). *The Social Teaching of the Christian Churches*, Vol.2. Chicago: University of Chicago Press.

Verghese, B.G. (2002). "India's Forgotten Gospel of Fraternity", *Outlook*, Nov. 18.

Weber, Max (1948). *Essays in Sociology*, London: Routledge and Kegan Paul.

Index

A

B

C

J